p19. chart showing to Evalu...

p38   F, T&L reference
p38   "Productivity Paradox"
p39   Strategic grid
p41   Traditional investment appraisal
        — Techniques
        — Drawbacks

        Other techniques
        (45) — info economics
            — sesame
            — RoM
            — Kobler unit framework
        (48) — AFT approach
Computerised Evaluation tools
            model
            — based on Kobler Unit framework
        (p51) — six steps
        (p54) — risk

C000011255

Investing in Information Systems

Investing in Information Systems

Evaluation and Management

Leslie Willcocks

Fellow in Information Management, Templeton College, Oxford, UK

CHAPMAN & HALL
University and Professional Division
London · Glasgow · Weinheim · New York · Tokyo · Melbourne · Madras

Published by Chapman & Hall, 2–6 Boundary Row, London SE1 8HN, UK

Chapman & Hall, 2–6 Boundary Row, London SE1 8HN, UK

Blackie Academic & Professional, Wester Cleddens Road, Bishopbriggs, Glasgow G64 2NZ, UK

Chapman & Hall GmbH, Pappelallee 3, 69469 Weinheim, Germany

Chapman & Hall USA, 115 Fifth Avenue, New York, NY 10003, USA

Chapman & Hall Japan, ITP-Japan, Kyowa Building, 3F, 2-2-1 Hirakawacho, Chiyoda-ku, Tokyo 102, Japan

Chapman & Hall Australia, 102 Dodds Street, South Melbourne, Victoria 3205, Australia

Chapman & Hall India, R. Seshadri, 32 Second Main Road, CIT East, Madras 600 035, India

First edition 1996

© 1996 Leslie Willcocks

Typeset in 9.5/11.5pt Meridien by Best-set Typesetter Ltd., Hong Kong
Printed in Great Britain at Clays Ltd, St Ives PLC

ISBN 0 412 72670 X

A catalogue record for this book is available from the British Library

Library of Congress Catalog Card Number: 95-74638

∞ Printed on permanent acid-free text paper, manufactured in accordance with ANSI/NISO Z39.48-1992 and ANSI/NISO Z39.48-1984 (Permanence of Paper).

Contents

PART FOUR   ROUTINE OPERATIONS AND IT SOURCING ISSUES

Contributors

C. James Bacon is senior lecturer in information systems at the University of Canterbury in Christchurch, New Zealand. Previously he was for many years a systems consultant in New York and London. Recent publications in major journals cover decision criteria in project selection, principles of systems decentralization, and business benefits of the object-oriented paradigm. His current research is into developing a valid and useful paradigm for the management of information systems/technology.

David G. W. Birch, after graduating from University of Southampton, worked for Logica as a consultant specializing in communications. He helped to found the specialist consultancy Hyperion in 1986. He has extensive consulting experience with clients as diverse as SWIFT, The International Stock Exchange, The Ministry of Defence and the Indonesian PTT. He is visiting lecturer at City University Business School and author of numerous papers.

Virginia Bryant is a lecturer in the department of Business Computing at City University. She has worked in several service industries and the accountancy profession, and has been chairman of the UK CMG DP Accounting Group. Research interests include modelling for quantified analysis of the interface and impacts between the business and information systems domains within organizations. She is founding editor of the *Journal of the Computer Audit Specialist Group* for the British Computer Society.

John Davies holds an MSc, and a PhD in artificial intelligence. He joined British Telecom in 1990 where he has led several projects applying decision support technology to financial analysis and appraisal. His research interests include IT investment and the IT impact on organizations. He is a member of the British Computer Society and a Chartered Engineer.

Jenny Dugmore, after gaining a PhD, worked in service management for over twelve years, in both the private and public sectors. She is a principal consultant specializing in service management, and is the manager of the Hoskyns Desktop Consultancy group. She has spoken on service management at many conferences, in the UK and other European countries, has contributed to specialist service management publications, and has been involved in developing BSI standards for service management.

David Feeny is Director of the Oxford Institute of Information Management at Templeton College, University of Oxford. He holds an MA from Oxford and an MBA from Harvard. He was for many years a senior marketing manager with IBM. His research and extensive writing centres on the connections between strategy, organization and information management. His research on CEO/CIO relationships, achieving competitive advantage, and organizational arrangements for IS has received international recognition, including the best paper award at the 1992 International Conference in Information Systems, and papers in *MIS Quarterly*, and *Sloan Management Review*. He is retained as consultant and adviser to a number of industrial, commercial and public sector organizations.

Guy Fitzgerald is Cable and Wireless Professor of Business Information Systems at Birkbeck College, University of London. He is also co-editor of the *Information Systems Journal* and the Blackwell Information Systems series. Previously he has been university lecturer at Warwick and Oxford Universities. His numerous publications reflect his research interests and include *Information Systems Development* (Alfred Waller, 1995) and *A Business Guide to Outsourcing IT* (Business Intelligence, 1994).

Rudy Hirschheim is Director of the Information Systems Research Center and Professor of IS at the University of Houston in Texas, USA. Previously he was at London School of Economics. He is one of the most published authors in the information systems field, with papers in major journals such as *MIS Quarterly*, *Sloan Management Review*, and *Information Systems Research*. He has published numerous books including *Office Automation: A Social and Organizational Perspective* (Wiley, 1987) and two titles on outsourcing with Mary Lacity. He is also editor of the Wiley Information Systems series.

Phumchai Kambhato holds a BSc and an MPhil in Management Studies from the University of Oxford. He has carried out extensive research on make/buy decisions in several industrial and commercial sectors. After graduating from Keble College in 1992 he has held analyst and management roles in two companies, first in Schroders, then in Flemings.

Mike Knul holds an MSc in knowledge-based systems. He has been working in knowledge-based applications, natural language processing, distributed AI and decision support systems. After working for two years with STC he has been working in several systems development areas for British Telecom.

Mary Lacity holds a PhD in IS from University of Houston. She is Assistant Professor in MIS at University of Missouri, St Louis, USA and an Associate Fellow of Templeton College, Oxford. Previous work was with Exxon as a systems analyst, and as an outsourcing consultant with Technology Partners. Co-authored publications include *Information Systems Outsourcing* (1993) and *Beyond the Outsourcing Bandwagon* (1995). She has published widely in journals including *Harvard Business Review* (with Leslie Willcocks and David Feeny) and *Sloan Management Review* (with Rudi Hirschheim).

Albert L. Lederer is Professor of MIS and Ashland Oil Research Fellow in the College of Business and Economics at the University of Kentucky. He has a BA in pyschology, an MSc in computer and information sciences and a PhD in industrial and systems engineering from the Ohio State University. He previously taught at Ohio State, the

University of Pittsburgh and Oakland University. His major research interest is information systems planning, in which field he has published numerous papers and has international academic recognition.

Stephanie Lester is Technology Change Manager at Cellnet, the UK based communications company. She holds an MSc from City University Business School, and has extensively researched and published on evaluation issues. Her previous management posts over ten years were with the Department of Social Security in audit and with Hoskyns, the computer service company, in customer service and support. Clients included Esso, BP Exploration and Royal Bank of Scotland.

Neil A. McEvoy graduated from Oxford University then worked for Logica in developing their image processing product range, subsequently specializing in security and networking. He is a co-founder of Hyperion and has worked on a wide range of projects including some for the European Space Agency, APACS and The Ministry of Defence. He has sat on a number of BSI Technical Committees and has represented the UK interest at ISO level.

Graeme D. Norris holds a PhD and has specialized for over 20 years in evaluating the benefits and risks of investments in information technology. He has worked for OECD. In 1976 he joined BP where he conducted a variety of assignments to identify more effective business processes and information systems requirements. Since 1986 he has worked as a management consultant specializing in business process re-engineering, IT investment appraisal and the specification of information systems that deliver value for money, and organizational development and the management of change.

Subhash V Parulekar is a Quality Management consultant. His many years' experience include management positions within the London Stock Exchange, Phillips Petroleum, 3M UK, Tube Investments and AEI. His work has spanned IS development, quality management and assurance, project management and support and TQM training. He has higher degrees in electrical engineering and quantitative management, has been a speaker at BCS Software Quality Management specialist group, an active committee member of the IS Quality Association, and a past chairman of the ISQA methods working party.

Glen Peters holds a PhD from Henley Management College, England. He is a partner at Price Waterhouse responsible for consultancy activities in the energy and petrochemicals sector. He is a Chartered Engineer specializing in developing IT investment strategies for companies in the petrochemicals, engineering and defence industries. IT investment mapping was the subject of his PhD thesis.

Jayesh Prasad is Assistant Professor of MIS at the School of Business Administration, University of Dayton, USA. He holds an MBA from the Indian Institute of Management, Calcutta, and a PhD from the Katz Graduate School of Business at the University of Pittsburgh. Besides information systems cost estimating, his research interests include implementation of information technology and management of MIS personnel. He has published widely in major journals on these themes.

Tony Rands is a Fellow in Information Systems and Management Science at Templeton College, Oxford. He graduated from Cambridge in 1962, and was a systems analyst until 1966, when he joined Oxford Centre for Management Studies, later Templeton College. His research interests include developments in the software industry and their implications for managing the implementation of IT strategies. He has published and consulted widely on these themes.

Dan Remenyi is Professor of Information Systems at the University of Witwatersrand in South Africa, and an associate member of faculty at Henley Management College, England. He has spent more than 20 years working in corporate computing as IS professional, business consultant and end-user. In recent years he has specialized in the area of formulation and implementation of strategic information systems and how to evaluate the performance of such systems. His many books include *A Guide to Measuring and Managing IT Benefits* (NCC Blackwell, 1991).

Chris Smart is a Lecturer in the Department of Business Computing, City University, London. He holds a BSc and a Master's degree. He has worked variously in systems design, computer management, database management consultancy and IT applied research. Publications include a number of papers in the database area, while current research is on the integration of IS within the total business system.

Robert Whiting has held senior posts in service industries, including controlling multi-funded operational and strategic budgets. Latterly in British Telecom he led the strategic appoach to cost–benefit analysis for IT within the IT directorate. His main research interests are in the evaluation, risk assessment and strategic impact of IT. He is a member of the Institute of Management and a Chartered Secretary.

Louise Whittaker is Lecturer in the Department of Information Systems at the University of Witwatersrand in South Africa. Awards include the South African Association of University Women Prize for the best woman graduate at Wits in 1991. Her research interests include business process re-engineering, benefits measurement and information systems management.

Leslie Willcocks is a Fellow and University Lecturer in the Oxford Institute of Information Management at Templeton College Oxford, and Editor of the *Journal of Information Technology*. Previously he worked in accountancy and management consultancy for ten years, for Touche Ross and several smaller firms, and as a director of a research centre at City University Business School. Co-authored publications include *Computerising Work* (Paradigm, 1987), two books on systems analysis and design, *Information Management* (Chapman & Hall, 1994) and *A Business Guide to IT Outsourcing* (Business Intelligence, 1994). Research interests are in information systems – human, organizational and evaluation issues.

Introduction: beyond the IT productivity paradox

Leslie Willcocks

The evaluation and management of information systems investments is shot through with difficulties. That fact was responsible for the earlier, complementary volume *Information Management: Evaluation of Information Systems Investments* (Willcocks, 1994a). The focus of that work was very much on evaluation at the early phases of systems appraisal and adoption, and covered the strategic dimension, techniques, processes and perspectives. The present volume takes the discussion further, and investigates evaluation and management issues across systems portfolios and lifecycles.

Throughout this book information technology (IT) is taken to refer to the convergence of computers, telecommunications and electronics and the resulting technologies. As such the term IT focuses attention on equipment and technique. Information systems (IS) is a related term referring to how designed information flows attempt to meet the information needs of the organization. IS may be more, or less, IT based, though the obvious developing pattern in the industrialized and industrializing economies is towards the former. Increasingly, as IT expenditure has risen and as the use of IT has penetrated to the core of organizations, the search has been directed towards not just improving evaluation techniques and processes, and searching for new ones, but also towards the management and 'flushing out' of benefits. But these evaluation and management efforts regularly run into difficulties of three generic types. First, many organizations find themselves in a catch 22 (Willcocks, 1992). For competitive reasons they cannot afford not to invest in IT, but

"The catch 22"

Investing in Information Systems: Evaluation and Management. Edited by
Leslie Willcocks. Published in 1996 by Chapman & Hall. ISBN 0 412 72670 X.

economically they cannot find sufficient justification, and evaluation practice cannot provide enough underpinning, for making the investment. Second, for many of the more advanced and intensive users of IT, as the IS infrastructure becomes an inextricable part of the organization's processes and structures, it becomes increasingly difficult to separate out the impact of IT from that of other assets and activities. Third, and despite the high levels of expenditure, there is widespread lack of understanding of IS/IT as a major capital asset. While senior managers regularly give detailed attention to the annual expenditure on IT, there is little awareness of the size of the capital asset that has been bought over the years (Keen, 1991; Willcocks, 1994a). Failure to appreciate the size of this investment leads to IS/IT being undermanaged, a lack of serious attention being given to IS evaluation and control, and also a lack of concern for discovering ways of utilizing this IS asset base to its full potential.

Solutions to these difficulties have most often been sought through variants on the mantra: 'what gets measured gets managed'. In the present volume Lacity and Hirschheim provide an interesting insight into how measurement, in this case benchmarking IS performance against external comparators, can be used to influence senior management judgement. Throughout this volume contributors put forward suggestions for how measurement can be improved, but they also point to the limitations of measurement, and areas where sets of measures may be needed because of the lack of a single reliable measure. They also point to the key role of stakeholder judgement throughout any IS/IT evaluation process. All too often measurement is advanced as a panacea to evaluation difficulties with little consideration for the difficulties of measurement, the fact that measurement systems are prone to decay, the goal displacement effects, the downside that only that which is measured gets managed, the behavioural implications of measurement and related reward systems, and the politics inherent in any organizational evaluation activity. Such difficulties need to be borne in mind throughout this volume (for a detailed discussion see Currie, 1995; Willcocks, Currie and Mason, 1996). Slowly in the practitioner community the problems with overfocusing on measurement are being recognized, with moves toward emphasizing the demonstration of the value of IS/IT, not merely its measurement (see Banker, Kauffman and Mahmood, 1993; Gillin, 1994; LaPlante, 1994; LaPlante and Alter, 1994 for examples).

The contributors to this volume look to re-emphasize and develop many aspects of IS/IT evaluation that tend to be neglected in practice. They also seek to advance thinking on how evaluation can be conducted across the systems lifecycle. A further contribution is to provide new thinking on emerging areas of some importance, such as IT-enabled business process re-engineering (Chapters 7 and 8) and the use of the external market for IS/IT services. (Chapters 4 and 16). By way of introduction, we will first address critically the overall sense that many have that despite huge investments in IS/IT so far these have been producing disappointing returns. The focus then moves to the organizational and intra-organizational levels, and the structure of the book around the notion of an IS/IT evaluation cycle is introduced. Some brief comment on each chapter and its contribution to the evaluation framework is then provided.

The IT productivity paradox revisited

Alongside the seemingly inexorable rise of IS/IT investment in the last 15 years, there has been considerable uncertainty and concern about the productivity impact of IT being experienced in work organizations. This has been reinforced by several high profile studies at the levels of both the national economy and industrial sector suggesting in fact that if there has been an IS/IT pay-off it has been minimal, and hardly justifies the vast financial outlays incurred. A key, overarching point immediately needs to be made. It is clear from reviews of the many research studies conducted at national, sectoral and organization-specific levels that the failure to identify IS/IT benefits and productivity says as much about the deficiencies in assessment methods and measurement, and the rigour with which they are applied, as about mismanagement of the development and use of information-based technologies (Brynjolfsson, 1993; Glazer, 1993; Willcocks, 1994a). It is useful to chase this hare of 'the IT productivity paradox' further, because the issue goes to the heart of the subject of this book.

Interestingly, the IT productivity paradox is rarely related in the literature to manufacturing sectors for which, in fact, there are a number of studies from the early 1980s on showing rising IT expenditure correlating with sectoral and firm-specific productivity rises (see for example Brynjolfsson and Hitt, 1993; Loveman, 1988; Weill, 1990). The high profile studies raising concern also tend to base their work mainly on statistics gathered in the US context. Their major focus, in fact, tends to be limited to the service sector in the USA (see Hackett, 1990; Roach, 1988, 1991). Recently a number of studies question the data on which such studies were based, suggesting that the data are sufficiently flawed to make simple conclusions misleading. (Brynjolfsson, 1993; Quinn and Baily, 1994). Still others argue that the productivity pay-off may have been delayed but, by the mid-1990s, recession and global competition have forced companies to finally use the technologies they put in place over the last decade, with corresponding productivity leaps (Gillin, 1994; Roach, 1994; Sager and Gleckman, 1994). Moreover, productivity figures always failed to measure the cost avoidance and savings on opportunity costs that IS/IT can help to achieve (Gillin, 1994). Others also argue that the real pay-offs occur when IS/IT development and use is linked with the business re-engineering (BPR) efforts coming onstream in the 1990s (for example, Davenport, 1993; Hammer and Champy, 1993). Chapter 9 of the present volume develops this debate with a review of the results organizations are actually getting through IT-enabled BPR. Finally, Bakos and Jager (1995) provide interesting further insight. They argue that computers are not boosting productivity, but the fault lies not with the technology but with its management and how computer use is overseen. Along with Quinn and Baily (1994), Bakos questions the reliability of the productivity studies and, supporting the positive IT productivity findings in the study by Brynjolfsson and Hitt (1993), posits a new productivity paradox: how can computers be so productive?

In the face of such disputation Brynjolfsson (1993) makes salutary reading. He suggests four explanations for the seeming IT productivity paradox. The first is measurement error. In practice the measurement problems appear particularly acute in the service sector and with white-collar worker productivity – the main areas investigated by those pointing to a minimal productivity impact from IT use in the 1980s and early 1990s. Brynjolfsson concludes from a close examination of the data behind the studies of IT performance at national and sectoral levels that mismeasurement is at the core of the IT productivity paradox. A second explanation is timing lags due to learning and adjustment. Benefits from IT can take several years to show through in significant financial terms, a point also made by Keen (1991) and Strassmann (1990) in arguing for newer ways of evaluating IS/IT performance at the organizational level. While Brynjolfsson largely discounts this explanation, there is evidence to suggest he is somewhat overoptimistic about the ability of managers to rationally account for such

(handwritten margin note: ③ redistribute)

lags and include them in their IS/IT evaluation system (Willcocks, 1994a). A third possible explanation is that of redistribution. IT may be beneficial to individual firms but unproductive from the standpoint of the industry, or the economy, as a whole. IT rearranges the share of the pie, with the bigger share going to those heavily investing in IT, without making the pie bigger. Brynjolfsson suggests, however, that the redistribution hypothesis would not explain any shortfall in IT productivity at the firm level. To add to his analysis we can note that in several sectors, such as banking and financial services, firms seemingly compete by larger spending on IT-based systems that are, in practice, increasingly becoming minimum entry requirements for the sector, and commodities rather than differentiators of competitive performance. As a result in some sectors, for example the oil industry, organizations are increasingly seeking to reduce such IS/IT costs by accepting that some systems are industry standard and can be developed together.

(handwritten margin note: ④ may not really be productive)

A fourth explanation is that IS/IT is not really productive at the firm level. Brynjolfsson (1993) posits that despite the neo-classical view of the firm as a profit maximizer, it may well be that decision-makers are, for whatever reason, often not acting in the interests of the firm: 'instead they are increasing their slack, building inefficient systems, or simply using outdated criteria for decision-making' (p. 75). The implication of Brynjolfsson's argument is that political interests and/or poor evaluation practice may contribute to failure to make real, observable gains from IS/IT investments. There is, of course, considerable evidence for this together with frequent study findings showing patchy strategizing and implementation practice where IS is concerned (see Currie, 1995; Robson, 1994, and Chapter 5 for reviews). However, Brynjolfsson appears to discount these possibilities citing a lack of evidence either way, though here he seems to be restricting himself to the economics literature.

In practice, organizations seem to vary greatly in their ability to harness IS/IT for organizational purposes. In an early study Cron and Sobol (1983) pointed to what has since been called the 'amplifier' effect of IT. Its use reinforces existing management approaches dividing firms into very high or very low performers. This analysis has been supported by later work by the Kobler Unit (1987) and Strassmann (1990), who also found no correlation between size of IT spend and firms' return on investment. Subsequently, a 1994 analysis of the information productivity of 782 US companies found that the top 10 spent a smaller percentage (1.3% compared to 3% for the bottom 100) of their revenue on IS, increasing their IS budget more slowly (4.3% in 1993–94 – the comparator was the bottom 110 averaging 10.2%), thus leaving a greater amount of finance available for non-IS spending (Gillin, 1994). Not only did the top performers seem to spend less proportionately on their IT; they also tended to keep certain new investments as high as business conditions permitted while holding back on infrastructure growth. Thus, on average, hardware investments were only 15% of the IS budget while new development took more than 50%, with 41% of systems development spending incurred on client/server investment (Sullivan-Trainor, 1994). Clearly the implication of this analysis is that top performers spend

(handwritten margin note: Spending focused on areas of maximum business value (Gillin 94))

relatively less money on IS/IT, but focus their spending on areas where it will make more difference in terms of business value. An important aspect of the ability to do this must lie with their evaluation techniques and processes.

Following on from this, it is clear that significant aspects of the IT productivity paradox, as perceived and experienced at organizational level, can be addressed through developments in evaluation and management practice. In particular the distorting effects of poor evaluation methods and processes need close examination and profiling; alternative methods, and an assessment of their appropriateness for specific purposes and conditions need to be advanced; and how these methods can be integrated together and into management practice needs to be addressed. We now turn to look at how this book is structured to deliver on these aims.

Investing in information systems

Evaluation within work organisation,

In this book the authors focus not on assessing IS/IT performance at national or industry levels, but on the conduct of IS/IT evaluation within work organizations. We take a cross-sector approach, dealing with firms and public sector organizations of varying sizes operating in a variety of manufacturing and service settings. As already suggested, IS/IT expenditure in such organizations is high and rising. The United States leads the way, with government statistics suggesting that, by 1994, computers and other information technology made up nearly half of all business spending on equipment – not including the billions spent on software and programmers each year (Sager and Gleckman, 1994). Globally, computer and telecommunications investments now amount to a half or more of most large firms' annual capital expenditures. In an advanced industrialized economy like the United Kingdom IS/IT expenditure by business and public sector organizations was estimated at £33.6 billion for 1995, and expected to rise by 8.2%, 7% and 6.5% in subsequent years, representing an average of over 2% of turnover, or in local and central government an average IT spend of £3546 per employee (Keen, 1991; Kew Associates, 1995; Willcocks, 1994a). If organizational IS/IT expenditure in developing economies is noticeably lower, nevertheless those economies may well leapfrog several stages of technology with China, Russia, India and Brazil, for example, set to invest into telecommunications an estimated 53.3, 23.3, 13.7, and 10.2 billion dollars (US) respectively in the 1993–2000 period (Engardio, 1994).

There were many indications by 1995, of managerial concern to slow the growth in organizational IS/IT expenditure. Estimates of future expenditure based on respondent surveys in several countries tended to indicate this pattern (see for example Kew Associates, 1995; Moad, 1994; Price Waterhouse, 1995). The emphasis seemed to fall on running the organization leaner, wringing more productivity out of IS/IT use, and attempting to reap the benefits from changes in price/performance ratios, while at the same time recognizing the seemingly inexorable rise in information and IT intensity implied by the need to remain operational and competitive. In particular, there is wide recognition of the additional challenge of bringing new technologies into productive use. The main areas being targeted for new corporate investment seemed to be client–server computing, document image processing and groupware, together with 'here-and-now' technologies such as advanced telecom services available from 'intelligent networks', mobile voice and digital cellular systems (Price Waterhouse, 1994; Taylor, 1995). It is in the context of these many concerns and technical developments that the chapters in this volume are positioned.

At the heart of the book's structure is the notion of an IS/IT evaluation and management cycle. A simplified diagrammatic representation of this is provided in Figure 1. The evaluation cycle attempts to bring together a rich and diverse set of ideas, methods, and practices that are to be found in the evaluation literature to date, and point them in the direction of an integrated approach across systems lifetime. Such an approach would consist of several interrelated activities:

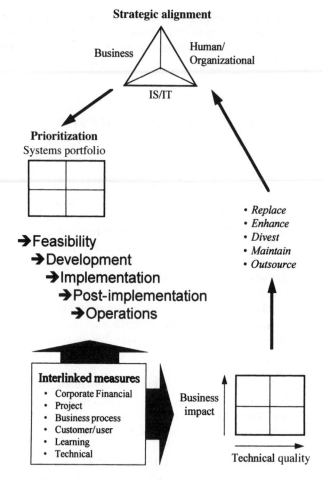

Figure 1 IS/IT evaluation and the management cycle.

1. Identifying net benefits through strategic alignment and prioritization.
2. Identifying types of generic benefit, and matching these to assessment techniques.
3. Developing a family of measures based on financial, service, delivery, learning and technical criteria.
4. Linking these measures to particular measures needed for development, implementation and post-implementation phases.
4. Ensuring each set of measures run from the strategic to the operational level.
6. Establishing responsibility for tracking these measures, and regularly reviewing results.
7. Regularly reviewing the existing portfolio, and relating this to business direction and performance objectives.

Let us look in more detail at the rationale for, and shape of such an approach. In a review of front-end evaluation Willcocks (1994b) pointed out how lack of **alignment** between business, information systems and human resource/organizational strategies inevitably compromised the value of all subsequent IS/IT evaluation effort, to the point of rendering it of marginal utility and, in some cases, even counterproductive. In this respect he reflected the concerns of many authors on the subject (see for example Earl, 1989; Hares and Royle, 1994; Peters, 1994). A range of already available techniques were pointed to for establishing strategic alignment, and linking strategy with assessing the feasibility of any IS/IT investment. At the same time the importance of recognizing evaluation as a process imbued with inherent political characteristics and ramifications was emphasized, reflecting a common finding amongst empirical studies (see for example Currie, 1995; Symons, 1994).

The notion of a systems portfolio implies that IS/IT investment can have a variety of objectives. The practical problem becomes one of **prioritization** – of resource allocation among the many objectives and projects that are put forward. Several classificatory schemes for achieving this appear in the extant literature of which the McFarlan and McKenney IT strategic grid is still the most widely quoted, despite now showing its age. Willcocks (1994a) and others (Butler Cox Foundation; Farbey, Land and Targett, 1992; Hochstrasser, 1994) have suggested classificatory schemes that match business objectives with types of IS/IT project. Thus, on one schema, projects could be divided into six types – efficiency, effectiveness, must-do, architecture, competitive edge, and research and development. The type of project could then be matched to one of the more appropriate evaluation methods available, a critical factor being the degree of tangibility of the costs and benefits being assessed (see Willcocks, 1994b, for a detailed discussion).

After alignment and prioritization assessment, the **feasibility** of each IS/IT investment then needs to be examined. Following this, Figure 1 suggests that evaluation needs to be conducted in a linked manner across systems development and into systems implementation and operational use. The evaluation cycle posits the development of a series of **interlinked measures** that reflect various aspects of IS/IT performance, and that are applied across systems' lifetime. These are tied to processes and people responsible for monitoring performance, improving the evaluation system and also helping to 'flush out' and manage the benefits from the investment. Figure 1 suggests, in line with prevailing academic and practitioner thinking by the mid-1990s, that evaluation cannot be based solely or even mainly on technical efficiency criteria.

Kaplan and Norton (1992) were highly useful for popularizing the need for a number of perspectives on evaluation of business performance. Willcocks (1994a) showed how the Kaplan and Norton balanced scorecard approach could be adapted fairly easily for the case of assessing IS investments. To add to that picture, most recent research suggests the need for six sets of measures. These would cover the **corporate financial perspective** (e.g. profit per employee); the **systems project** (e.g. time, quality, cost); **business process** (e.g. purchase invoices per employee); the **customer/user** perspective (e.g. on-time delivery rate); an **innovation/learning** perspective (e.g. rate of cost reduction for IT services); and a **technical** perspective (e.g. development efficiency, capacity utilization). Each set of measures would run from strategic to operational levels, each measure being broken down into increasing detail as it is applied to actual organizational performance. For each set of measures the business objectives for IS would be set. Each objective would then be broken down into more detailed measurable components, with a financial value assigned where practicable. Responsibility for tracking these measures, together with regular reviews that relate performance to objectives and targets are highly important elements in delivering benefits from the various IS investments. (See Glen Peters' work, in

Chapter 10, for a more detailed exposition.) It should be noted that such measures are seen as helping to inform stakeholder judgements, and not as a substitute for such judgements in the evaluation process.

One all too often routinized phase of review is that of **post-implementation.** Our own research suggests that this is one of the most neglected, yet one of the more important areas as far as IS evaluation is concerned (see Chapters 1 and 9). There remains the matter of **assessing the on-going systems portfolio** on a regular basis. Notoriously, when it comes to evaluating the existing IS investment, organizations are not good at drop decisions. There may be several related ramifications. The IS inheritance of 'legacy systems' can deter investment in new systems – it can, for example, be all too difficult to take on new work when IS staff are awash in a rising tide of IS maintenance arising from the existing investment. Existing IS-related activity can also devour the majority of the financial resources available for IS investment (Robson, 1994; Strassmann, 1990; Swanson and Beath, 1988). All too often such failures derive from not having in place, or not operationalizing, a robust assessment approach that enables timely decisions on systems and service divestment, outsourcing, replacement, enhancement, and/or maintenance. Such decisions need to be based on at least two criteria – the technical quality of the system/service, and its business contribution – as well as being related back to the overall strategic direction and objectives of the organization (see Figure 1).

This book

The chapters in this book serve to put some flesh around this notion of an evaluation cycle. Chapter 1, by Leslie Willcocks and Stephanie Lester, provides a useful overview, based on a United Kingdom study, of how far organizations may be from actually operationalizing what has been widely recognized as better practice on evaluation across systems lifecycles. The authors found feasibility evaluation dominated by limited, finance-based cost–benefit criteria. Few organizations actually took the lessons learned from one stage of evaluation to the next, or from project to project. Most stated they were not learning from their mistakes and, relatedly, recognized the importance of post-implementation evaluation but did little to promote its operationalization. There seemed little recognition for the need to develop evaluation as a social and organizational process and the deeper organizational learning on IS that would entail.

If the first chapter provides an overview of many of the limitations found in actual IS evaluation practice, the subsequent chapters provide detailed insight into how these limitations can be addressed. In the first section there are two chapters that add to the work published in our complementary volume, *Information Management* (Willcocks, 1994a). Robert Whiting, John Davies and Mike Knul offer a critique of traditional methods of IS investment appraisal, and critically review the more recent approaches. In the light of this review, they then derive an integrated IS/IT investment appraisal approach that can itself be computer supported. Virginia Bryant and Chris Smart take the debate on techniques further by developing a transaction value analysis approach. Their contribution is to bring together previous studies of value chain analysis, information economics and cost behaviour, and focus attention on the troublesome concept of value.

The second part of the book deals with systems development, including software development and the evaluation and management of development projects. Tony Rands and Phumchai Kambhato look in detail at make or buy decisions. They utilize detailed research in the UK food and drinks sector, and the limitations in practice this revealed, in order to derive a model for formulating software make or buy policies. The authors provide a challenge to practitioners to make their make or buy policies more strategic. Their work on software make or buy evaluation and policy links closely with that detailed in Chapter 16, where we examine the broader question of how and how far the external market for IS equipment, personnel and services can be utilized. The focus on software evaluation is continued by Albert Lederer and Jayesh Prasad who have studied software cost estimating practices in a variety of US organizations. They point to the recurrent problem of regular underestimation of software development costs, and detail the implications of their findings for both researchers and practitioners. Subhash Parulekar provides an additional dimension to the debate by looking at software development in the context of project management and a quality approach. He details current problems with software productivity and in the management of related IS/IT projects. He then shows how a product lifecycle control framework and a quality management system can be brought to bear on the common problems encountered. Dan Remenyi and Louise Whittaker broaden the project management focus by looking at the evaluation of business process re-engineering projects. Commonly among practitioners it is said that there is no such thing as an IS/IT project; there are only business projects. From the early 1990s this view has been reinforced by the increasing number of IT-supported business process re-engineering (BPR) projects being sponsored, with surveys regularly finding anything between 50 and 70% of respondent organizations undertaking or planning such projects (see Chapter 8). The authors here provide a framework for assessing costs and benefits, and risk and progress in such BPR projects.

The third part looks at the critical area of implementation and how benefits can be assessed and managed. It is quite noticeable how much of the literature in part follows actual organizational practice in focusing inordinately on the early stages of evaluation – those reflected in the first two parts of this book, in fact – while spending altogether less effort and time on the areas covered by Chapters 8, 9 and 10 of the present volume. Leslie Willcocks helps to address the question whether the transformational capacity of IT-enabled BPR is actually being delivered upon, and uncovers from detailed research a much more complex picture than straightforward 'success' or 'failure'. He details the relative costs of BPR projects, and the results organizations have been getting from completed BPR projects. While few can claim 'breakthrough' results, it is clear that most organizations were 'aiming low and hitting low', that is taking a low risk approach to the IS and BPR investment, and achieving, on the whole, some positive business benefits from that investment.

Graeme Norris provides a vital, integrating chapter in focusing on post-investment appraisal. He brings together a range of techniques and evaluation processes, several discussed in earlier chapters, and shows how these can be utilized for post-implementation assessments. Glen Peters provides a carefully thought through approach to delivering on important aspects of the evaluation lifecycle detailed above. Based on research into evaluation practice in 30 projects, the author developed an approach to evaluation which was subsequently piloted successfully in three organizations. The key techniques Peters put forward are IS/IT investment mapping (for linking the IS investment with business strategy), and a cost–benefit hierarchy based on financial and quantitative measures wherever possible, with each measurable objective broken down into more detailed component objectives and measures. He also points to the importance of the process of evaluation – including the assignment of responsibility for monitoring the metrics and ensuring that benefits arise.

The final part of the book deals with an area relatively neglected in the literature. We have therefore chosen to devote six chapters to the important themes. James Bacon sets the scene with a detailed argument supporting the need for improved evaluation of the existing IS investment. He provides an overview of what needs to be evaluated, and also offers techniques and frameworks to further the evaluation process. David Birch and Neil McEvoy provide an insight into the risks faced by operational systems. They then develop an approach to classifying and managing those risks. Both Dan Remenyi and Jenny Dugmore, in their separate chapters, help to give more detail on how the existing IS investment may be assessed. Both are concerned with the quality of service offered by IS professionals to internal users/ customers. Thus Remenyi develops an assessment approach based on the service quality work originated by Parasuraman, Zeithami and Berry (1985). Dugmore focuses on codifying her considerable practical experience in developing and operating service level agreements as an internal IS department or as an external supplier. Mary Lacity and Rudy Hirschheim provide insight into the use, and usefulness, of external benchmarking services for assessing and justifying the performance of the in-house IS function. A particular issue they focus on is whether benchmarking is an effective strategy for selling IS to senior management. Based on in-depth case studies with 19 US companies the answer depends on the source, type, purpose and quality of the benchmarks.

Leslie Willcocks, Guy Fitzgerald and David Feeny conclude the book with a chapter on how IS/IT sourcing can be made. Increasingly senior and IS managers have been questioning whether aspects of IS/IT supply can be delivered more effectively and cheaply by external contractors. In some ways asking such a question provides an ultimate assessment of the business value being provided by an in-house IS function. Based on detailed survey and case work, the authors suggest that, in practice, against an ever-maturing external IS service market, there are many ways in which IS assets and activities can be sourced. In particular their work resists an all-or-nothing approach. Despite high profile cases where organizations have outsourced more than 80% of their IS/IT activity, and much talk in the literature of the need to develop 'strategic alliances' with suppliers, the authors' research, together with that of Lacity and Hirschheim, questions the efficacy of a total outsourcing response to disappointments with internal IS performance (Lacity, Willcocks and Feeny, 1995). The authors proceed to develop a set of criteria and frameworks by which effective sourcing decisions can be made, and show that outsourcing can only be an effective option when arrived at as part of an overall strategic perspective and review of existing and future IS relevance and performance. As such the chapter provides a fitting conclusion to a book on the evaluation and management of IS investments.

References

Bakos, Y. and Jager, P. de. (1995) Are computers boosting productivity? *Computerworld*, 27 March, 128–30.

Banker, R., Kauffman, R. and Mahmood, M. (eds.) (1993) *Strategic Information Technology Management: Perspectives On Organizational Growth and Competitive Advantage*, Idea Publishing, Harrisburg.

Brynjolfsson, E. (1993) The productivity paradox of information technology. *Communications of the ACM*, **36** (12), 67–77.

Brynjolfsson, E. and Hitt, L. (1993) Is information systems spending productive? *Proceedings of the International Conference in Information Systems*, Orlando, December.

Butler Cox Foundation (1990) *Getting Value from Information Technology*. Research Report 75, Butler Cox Foundation, London.

Cron, W. and Sobol, M. (1983) The relationship between computerization and performance: a strategy for maximizing the economic benefits of computerization. *Journal of Information Management*, **6**, 171–81.

Currie, W. (1995) *Management Strategy For IT: An International Perspective*, Pitman, London.

Davenport, H. (1993) *Process Innovation: Reengineering Work Through Information Technology*, Harvard Business School Press, Boston, MA.

Earl, M. (1989) *Management Strategies for Information Technology*, Prentice Hall, London.

Engardio, P. (1994) Third world leapfrog. *Business Week*, 13 June, 46–7.

Farbey, B., Land, F. and Targett, D. (1992) Evaluating investments in IT. *Journal of Information Technology*, **7** (2), 100–12.

Gillin, P. (1994) Is IS making us more productive? *Computerworld Premier 100 Special Issue*, 19 September, 10–12.

Gillin, P. (ed.) (1994) The productivity payoff: the 100 most effective users of information technology. Special Report in *Computerworld*, 19 September, Section 2, 4–55.

Glazer, R. (1993) Measuring the value of information: the information-intensive organization. *IBM Systems Journal*, **32** (1), 99–110.

Hackett, G. (1990) Investment in technology: the service sector sinkhole? *Sloan Management Review*, Winter, 97–103.

Hammer, M. and Champy, J. (1993) *Reengineering The Corporation: A Manifesto For Business Revolution*, Nicholas Brearley, London.

Hares, J. and Royle, D. (1994) *Measuring The Value Of Information Technology*, John Wiley, Chichester.

Hochstrasser, B. (1994) Justifying IT investments. In *Information Management: Evaluation of Information Systems Investments* (ed. L. Willcocks), Chapman & Hall, London.

Kaplan, R. and Norton, D. (1992) The balanced scorecard: measures that drive performance. *Harvard Business Review*, January–February, 71–9.

Keen, P. (1991) *Shaping the Future: Business Design Through Information Technology*, Harvard Business Press, Boston, MA.

Kew Associates (1995) *User IT Expenditure Survey 1995*, Computer Weekly/Kew Associates, London.

Kobler Unit (1987) *Is Information Technology Slowing You Down?* Kobler Unit Report, Imperial College, London.

Lacity, M. Willcocks, L. and Feeny, D. (1995) IT outsourcing: maximize flexibility and control. *Harvard Business Review*, May–June, 84–93.

LaPlante, A. (1994) No doubt about IT. *Computerworld*, 15 August, 79–86.

Laplante, A. and Alter, A. (1994) IT all adds up. *Computerworld*, 31 October, 76–84.

Loveman, G. (1988). *An Assessment of the Productivity Impact of Information Technologies*. MIT Management in the Nineties Working Paper 88-054, Massachusetts Institute of Technology, Cambridge, MA.

Moad, J. (1994) IS rises to the competitiveness challenge. *Datamation*, 7 January, 16–22.

Parasuram, A., Zeithami, A. and Berry, L. (1985) A conceptual model of service quality and its implications for future research. *Journal of Marketing*, Fall.

Peters, G. (1994) Evaluating your computer investment strategy. In *Information Management: Evaluation of Information Systems Investments* (ed. L. Willcocks), Chapman & Hall, London.

Price Waterhouse (1994) *Information Technology Review 1994/5*, Price Waterhouse, London.

Quinn, J. and Baily, M. (1994) Information technology: increasing productivity in services. *Academy of Management Executive*, **8** (3), 28–47.

Roach, S. (1988) Technology and the services sector: the hidden competitive challenge. *Technological Forecasting and Social Change*, **34**, 387–403.

Roach, S. (1991) Services under siege: the restructuring imperative. *Harvard Business Review*, September–October, 82–92.

Roach, S. (1994) Lessons of the productivity paradox. In *The Productivity Payoff: The 100 Most Effective Users of Information Technology* (ed. P. Gillin). Special Report in *Computerworld*, 19 September, Section 2, 55.

Robson, W. (1994) *Strategic Management and Information Systems,* Pitman, London.

Sager, I. and Gleckman, H. (1994) The information revolution. *Business Week*, 13 June, 35–9.

Strassmann, P. (1990) *The Business Value of Computers*, Information Economics Press, New Canaan.

Sullivan-Trainor, M. (1994) Best of breed. In *The Productivity Payoff: The 100 Most Effective Users of Information Technology* (ed. P. Gillin), Special Report in *Computerworld*, 19 September, Section 2, 8–9.

Swanson, E. and Beath, C. (1988) *Maintaining Information Systems in Organizations*, John Wiley, Chichester.

Symons, V. (1994) Evaluation of information systems investments: towards multiple perspectives. In *Information Management: Evaluation of Information Systems Investments* (ed. L. Willcocks), Chapman & Hall, London.

Taylor, P. (1995) Business solutions on every side. *Financial Times Review: Information Technology*, 1 March, 1.

Weill, P. (1990) *Do Computers Pay Off?*, ICIT Press, Washington.

Willcocks, L. (1992) IT evaluation: managing the catch-22. *European Management Journal*, **10** (2), 220–9.

Willcocks, L. (ed.) (1994a) *Information Management: Evaluation of Information Systems Investments*, Chapman & Hall, London.

Willcocks, L. (1994b) Managing information technology evaluation: techniques and processes. In *Strategic Information Management: Challenges and Strategies in Managing Information Systems* (eds. R. Galliers and B. Baker), Butterworth Heinemann, London.

Willcocks, L., Currie, W. and Mason, D. (1996) *Information Systems at Work: people, politics and technology*. Mcgraw-Hill, London.

Part One

Overview and the feasibility phase

1

The evaluation and management of information systems investments: from feasibility to routine operations

Leslie Willcocks and Stephanie Lester

Introduction

By 1996 United Kingdom company expenditure on information technology (IT) was estimated as exceeding £33 billion per year, equivalent to an average of over 2% of annual turnover. The estimates for 1996 public sector IT spend, excluding Ministry of Defence operational equipment, exceed £2 billion per year, or 1% of total public expenditure (Computer Weekly/Kew 1995; Price Waterhouse, 1994; Willcocks, 1994a). The size and continuing growth in investment in IT-based systems has bred an increasing concern in organizations, in the face of the 1989–94 period of recession and

Investing in Information Systems: Evaluation and Management. Edited by
Leslie Willcocks. Published in 1996 by Chapman & Hall. ISBN 0 412 72670 X.

also intensive and rising competition in most sectors, to demonstrate that investments in time, effort and money are, and will be, worthwhile. In practice investment in IT-based systems has frequently been the subject of disappointed expectations (Audit Commission, 1994; CSC Index/DTI, 1992; Banker, Kauffman and Mahmood, 1993; AT Kearney, 1990; PA Consulting Group, 1990; Willcocks, 1992). Major weaknesses occur in how investment in IT is evaluated and controlled (AT Kearney, 1990; Keen, 1991; National Audit Office, 1987, 1989; Touche Ross/IAM, 1991; Willcocks, 1994b; Wilson, 1991). Other commentators point to indifferent IT/IS evaluation practice as a major problem area (see Butler Cox, 1990; Farbey, Targett and Land, 1995; Hochstrasser and Griffiths, 1991; Strassmann, 1990).

Given these developments, the authors decided to carry out detailed research into how evaluation and management of information systems (IS) investment is carried out in public and private sector organizations. In reviewing previous studies in both Europe and the USA we identified a shortage of material on a number of issues in this field, and this guided the construction, content and process of our own investigation. The major objective was to collect data on criteria used for evaluation, methods used, who was involved in the evaluation process, how the process was organized, who was responsible, at what stages in the lifetime of systems evaluation was performed, and how frequently, and the degree of success achieved with the evaluation processes and techniques adopted. A further objective was to identify from the evidence limitations in how information systems investments were being evaluated and managed, with a view to suggesting ways forward. The chapter is therefore empirical, but also seeks to develop prescriptions from the accumulated findings. Later chapters add to these prescriptions by providing more detailed suggestions for taking evaluation practice further. The continuing widespread concerns in the developed economies, into 1995–96, about IS evaluation suggest that the issues identified in these chapters are perennial problems rather than temporary features of economic recession.

It is useful to be clear what is meant by evaluation in the context of information systems and organizations. Taking a management perspective, evaluation is about establishing by quantitative and/or qualitative means the worth of IS to the organization. Evaluation brings into play notions of costs, benefits, risk and value. It also implies an organizational process by which these factors are assessed, whether formally or informally. Information technology (IT) is taken to refer to the hardware, software and communications technologies – essentially equipment – and attendant techniques. Information systems (IS) is a wider concept referring to how designed information flows attempt to meet the information needs of the organization. IS may be more, or less, IT based. In the respondent organizations the systems under review were highly IT based. Therefore the term IS is used throughout this chapter, except where referring to the 'IT industry'. We should also add that respondents in interviews revealed a marked tendency to refer to IT rather than IS evaluation.

The study: background

The research programme has been divided into several phases. Phase 1 was a limited survey, based on questionnaires and interviews, of selected managers within 2 small (fewer than 200 employees and less than £5 million annual sales) and 48 medium and large, private and public sector, manufacturing and service organizations. Initially, 50 questionnaires were issued as a pilot study to complete a final check on clarity and logical format and to assess the quality of replies. On completion of final amendments a further 200 questionnaires were issued. The 200 sample organizations were selected on a random basis from the Institute of Internal Auditors' membership mailing list. This source was chosen as representing a wide spectrum of UK organizations in manufacturing and services in private and public sectors. From this mailing 50 completed questionnaires were received. Phase 1 was completed in December 1990. The second phase of the study, from April 1991 to February 1992, sought to track evaluation practice over time in these respondent organizations. This was achieved with follow-up questionnaires and interviews, and by focusing in more detail on post-feasibility evaluation practice, including that surrounding systems that passed feasibility evaluation in phase 1 of the study.

A cross-sector sample was produced, enabling us to discover whether indicative commonalities were experienced. The individuals who were selected for and completed the phase 1 and 2 survey questionnaires were all of manager status or above. They were identified as organizationally responsible for and/or knowledgeable about IS evaluation methods and outcomes. In practice 90% were IS professionals, and the other 10% were from a more general management background, but responsible for IS in their business unit. There are well-documented limitations to the type of evidence supplied by such questionnaires. Possibly those replying were more likely to carry out evaluation and be satisfied with their evaluation processes than the average non-respondent. Other surveys, for example Farbey, Land and Targett (1992), found a smaller proportion of organizations carrying out formal evaluations than we did. However, we did have a relatively high response rate (25%) for this sort of survey; furthermore respondents' expressions of satisfaction must be set against the limitations in evaluation practice discovered in the detailed questionnaire and interview responses. We attempted to ask questions that would elicit mainly factual replies rather than opinion. Additionally, in both phases 1 and 2, in the case of 32 respondents further in-depth information was gained from follow-up structured interviews of up to two hours. In phase 2, some triangulation of senior, IS and user department managers was achieved by extending the interview programme to half-hour structured discussions with two other managers in each of the 32 organizations.

The sample organizations represented a wide spectrum, as can be seen from Figure 1.1. Some intra-sectoral analysis can be carried out using the survey data in the areas of financial services, information technology and manufacturing. Sectorally the other organizations are spread too thinly to merit any such attention. 'Others' in Figure 1.1 includes organizations in oil, telecommunications, postal services, broadcasting, education and betting and a government executive agency.

There are various proposals in the literature as to the stages into which to divide an information systems project for the purposes of analysis (see for example Cressey, 1985; McLoughlin and Clark, 1993; Preece, 1989; Rothwell, 1984). The present study used a five-stage cycle to guide research and organize its results. The evaluation stages, as communicated to respondents, are described below:

1. **Proposal/feasibility** – evaluating the financial and non-financial acceptability of a project against defined organizational requirements, and assessing the priorities between proposed projects. 'Acceptability' may be in terms of cost, benefit, value or socio-technical considerations.
2. **Development** – monitoring of the project in terms of cost, time and performance measures during systems build. Stages of evaluation such as systems testing and

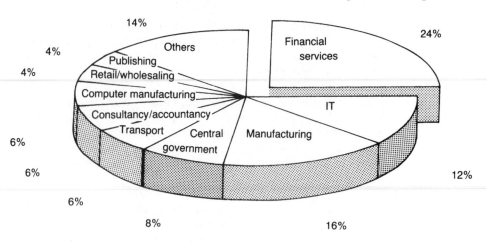

Figure 1.1 Organizations in the research base.

acceptance may be included in the development methodology. The use of different development tools and techniques, e.g. prototyping, database plus 4GL, CASE, may imply less clear boundaries between stages and so require different evaluation techniques.

3. **Implementation** – evaluation of the degree to which a usable system is made operable within time, budget and performance requirements. Evaluation may include comparing the actual implementation against proposed time schedules, assessing how easily the user department is accepting and adapting to the new system, and alleviating foreseen problems. Two methods which may be used are pilot testing and parallel simulation.

4. **Post-implementation** – this may include assessing the completion of the project and comparing it with the expected/calculated outcome, e.g. examining over-spends, productivity, improvements in data quality, and unanticipated benefits.

5. **Routine operation** – evaluation of operations as an everyday activity, e.g. assess-ing how often the system is inoperable, maintenance time and costs, degree of performance degradation, systems efficiency, error rates.

Our major concern, unlike that in the other studies cited, was to analyse how evaluation, not the IS project itself, is managed. A pilot study suggested that evalu-ation practice in the majority of organizations tended to fall into five analytically distinct stages. This finding was subsequently endorsed in the main phase 1 study. All organizations carried out evaluation at the feasibility stage; between 82 and 88% did so at each of the other stages; only 10% carried out evaluation at one unspecified, additional point (Willcocks and Lester, 1991). Second, the literature indicates the need to carry out evaluation throughout the course of an IS project, together with the critical requirement that organizations should learn from their past evaluation ex-perience when it comes to making IS investments (Eason, 1988; Hochstrasser and Griffiths, 1991; Leonard-Barton, 1988; Parker, Benson and Trainor, 1988; Willcocks, 1991). We decided therefore to develop a framework that could be used first as an analytical tool, but also included some elements of prescription, derived from, and assessing evaluation practice against, the literature.

Some general findings

This section looks at where IS issues were considered in organizations, at what stages evaluation of IS investment was carried out, and the degree of satisfaction/dissatisfaction with evaluation procedures recorded by respondents.

Of the organizations surveyed 46 had separate IS departments, and 11 organizations gave consideration to IS within individual departments (7 of these also had separate IS departments). In this context the consideration of IS involves all aspects and not just evaluation. The detailed results (see below) make it clear who was actually involved for the purposes of evaluation.

All the organizations completed evaluation of IS at the feasibility stage (see Figure 1.2). Between 82 and 88% of the organizations completed evaluation at the other

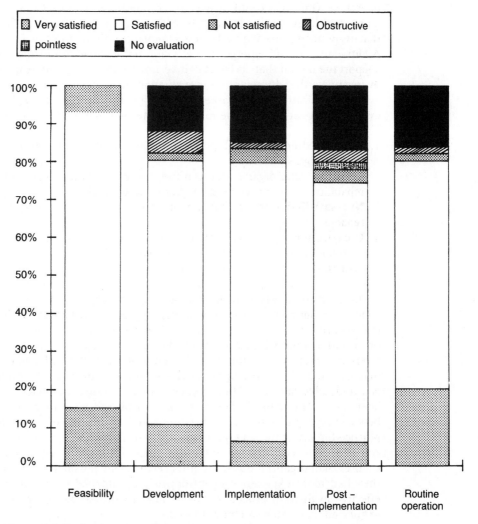

Figure 1.2 Evaluation across five stages.

stages. However, only 66% completed evaluation at all five stages. Thus considerable weight in the evaluation process seemed to fall on getting the feasibility evaluation right. Five of the seven organizations carrying out evaluation at different stages from the stages posited in the questionnaire stated that this was additional to, and not instead of, those five stages. To a large extent this endorses our initial conceptualization of the evaluation process.

The main measure for assessing the success or otherwise of evaluation procedures was respondent perceptions of 'levels of satisfaction'. There are considerable limitations with this measure, not least the subjectivity and personal bias that can creep into the assessment provided by respondents. A further measure sought to compare the effectiveness of IS investment in terms of return on investment (ROI). We asked questions designed to elicit the size of the ROI – whether it was higher, comparable to or lower than ROI on non-IS investments – and the type of evaluation procedures designed to measure the financial return on IS investments once a system was operating. Only 8% could answer these questions. The vast majority, in questionnaires and interviews, admitted to making no such evaluation. This would suggest that respondents needed to be less complacent about their evaluation procedures. Additionally, as will emerge, there is internal evidence from the present survey to support the notion that, as far as IS investments are concerned, respondents tended to overestimate the efficacy of their evaluation procedures.

The organizations were asked to indicate the degree of satisfaction with their evaluation at each stage. The range, together with an 'other' option, was as follows:

1. **Very satisfied** – although perfection is impossible, the results from the evaluation reach a high standard.
2. **Satisfied** – the organization can use the results with a degree of satisfaction and reliability, but improvements would be welcomed.
3. **Not satisfied** – the evaluation process is not satisfactory and is therefore not reliable.
4. **Obstructive** – the evaluation is considered to have a negative effect and is therefore a hindrance rather than a help.
5. **Pointless** – the evaluation is of no benefit to the organization.

The levels of satisfaction on evaluation procedures registered by respondents are codified in Figure 1.2. This shows a high degree of satisfaction (as defined above) by the majority of organizations across all stages at which evaluation takes place. No organization found its feasibility evaluation obstructive or pointless. In follow-up interviews there was a tendency (in 18 out of the 32 cases) for both user and senior managers to be less satisfied with evaluation procedures than IS professionals. There is a noticeable fall off in the number of organizations completing evaluation at the later stages. The main finding was that that by and large there was no relationship between type and sector of organization and the perceived effectiveness of evaluation practice for any of the stages investigated. The exception here is that IT, financial and consultancy services tended to register higher satisfaction with their evaluation procedures than organizations from other sectors. One possibility here is that historically they had more experience of introducing IS and had been able to develop more effective evaluation procedures over time. In this scenario, organizations in other sectors still had some catching up to do.

Most organizations seemed to carry out evaluation at all stages (but with a noticeable fall off after the feasibility stage), with a large majority also registering satisfaction with evaluation procedures, though room for improvement was recognized in many cases. Given a probable respondent tendency to register satisfaction, it is interesting to note how few suggested they were 'very satisfied'. In the light of later findings it may well be that the degree of satisfaction registered needs to be treated with some caution.

Evaluating feasibility: findings

This section summarizes our main preliminary findings already published elsewhere (Willcocks and Lester, 1994), and here updated by analysis of interview material.

Evaluation methods and criteria

Organizations revealed a variety of practice on evaluation at the feasibility stage of projects. The common element, however, could be characterized as cost–benefit assessment described in monetary terms, allied with managerial judgement. Over half (56%) of the organizations used the same evaluation method for all projects, regardless of the different objectives and different types of benefit that might be expected from the investment. Less than 10% reviewed the method on a regular basis in 1990, though just over half the respondents reported for the 1991–92 period a marked trend toward using hurdle rates cost-justification and shorter time scales for investment payback, and more traditional finance-based approaches. Supporting the findings of other researchers (for example Coleman and Jamieson, 1991; Farbey, Land and Targett, 1992), most organizations surveyed used cost–benefit at the core of their evaluation, often of a traditional, finance-based type. Chapters 4 and 5 and an earlier, large literature suggest that such approaches are not always the most appropriate, and are rarely a sufficient, way to evaluate IS projects (see for example Goodwin, 1984; Malitoris, 1990; Parker, Benson and Trainor, 1988; Ward, 1994). In our sample 62% used cost–benefit as their predominant criterion in the evaluation process, 96% used cost–benefit together with one out of (1) competitive advantage, (2) service to the public, (3) quality of product and (4) job enhancement.

Other criteria each used by three or fewer organizations included improved management information; user requirements and time scale; legal requirements; strategic importance; and organizational requirements and necessity. A major finding here is that only 16% of organizations use over four criteria as a basis of their evaluation. The survey evidence here suggests that organizations may be missing IS opportunities, but also taking on large risks, utilizing narrow evaluation approaches that do not clarify and assess less tangible inputs and benefits. In interviews the unanimous view was that all costs needed to be tracked down, however difficult to assess, though some 65% suggested that they were probably failing to identify full costs through the formal evaluation process. In 24 organizations one or more interviewees suggested that in the post-1990 climate the organization could not take the risk of including many types of intangible benefit in feasibility calculations. More generally there was little evidence in interviews of a concern to assess risk in any formal manner.

Involvement and consultation

Some 44% of organizations did not include the user department in the evaluation process at the feasibility stage. Not doing so cuts off a vital source of information and critique on the degree to which an IS proposal is organizationally feasible and will deliver on user requirements. Only a small minority of organizations accepted IS proposals from a wide variety of groups and individuals. Despite the large literature emphasizing consultation with the workforce as a source of ideas and know-how and as part of the process of reducing resistance to change, only 36% of organizations consulted users about evaluation at the feasibility stage, while only 18% consulted trade unions. While the majority of organizations (80%) evaluated IS investments against organizational objectives, only 22% acted strategically in considering objectives from the bottom to the top, that is by evaluating the value of IS projects against all organization, departmental, individual management and end-user objectives. This again could have consequences for the effectiveness and usability of the resulting systems, and the levels of resistance experienced.

Finally, most organizations endorsed the need to assess the competitive edge implied by an IS project. However, somewhat inconsistently, only 4% considered customer objectives in the evaluation process at the feasibility stage. The two organizations in question also involved customers in the evaluation process. This finding is interesting in relation to interview evidence that the majority of IS investments in the respondent organizations were directed at achieving internal efficiencies. Hochstrasser and Griffiths (1991) suggest that this focus results from the type of evaluation techniques used. Our own evidence suggests that the evaluation *processes* adopted may also influence such an outcome.

Evaluating systems development

The major questions investigated here concerned the evaluation methods used, the degree to which projects were dropped or continued during the development stage, who carried out evaluation and to whom reports were made.

Methods used

Martin (1989, 1991) found that, for many organizations, measuring the productivity of applications development was an issue only just beginning to be tackled. To some extent this comment is reinforced by our own findings. The present survey found a variety of methods being used. Table 1.1 indicates the extent to which many organizations were inclined to develop their own methods, perhaps through dissatisfaction with more standardized methods, or their inappropriateness to specific organizational needs. Twenty-one organizations stated that they did not always use the same method(s) for evaluation at the development stage. Table 1.2 shows the criteria by which methods were chosen in these organizations. As can be seen, the size of IS project emerges as the major determinant of the evaluation method used in these organizations.

Table 1.1 Evaluation methods at development stage[a]

	Organizations
SSADM	7
Phased review	1
Common sense	1
BIS Modus	1
Prototyping	1
Organization's own method	17
No method mentioned	1
SSADM and organization's own method	5
Risk assessment	1
SDM	1
Cost-benefit	1
PRISM	1
AA method	1
No standard method	3
SSADM, PRINCE and PROMPT	1
Varies	1

[a] SSADM, BIS Modus, PRISM, PRINCE and PROMPT are standardized methodologies available on the market

Table 1.2 Criteria by which evaluation methods were selected in 21 organizations

	Organizations
Discretion of local director/manager	3
4th Generation language uses own method	1
Size	11
Executive management decision	2
IT committee	1
Varies	1
Finger in the air	1
No answer	1

The survey showed up some confusion on methodologies and tools in a minority of cases; one organization used 'common sense', others used cost–benefit and risk assessment, and one company used the 'finger in the air' as an evaluation method. A third (34%) of organizations had also developed their own methodology; this would indicate that organizations were looking for solutions better than standardized methods but, from our evidence, were not necessarily finding them.

Abandoned projects

In the present survey 80% of organizations had to abandon projects at some time during this stage as a result of negative evaluation. The major reasons given related to changing organizational or user needs and/or projects gone over budget (see Table 1.3). Given the high percentage of organizations abandoning projects at the development stage as a result of changing organizational and/or user needs, we reanalysed the

Table 1.3 Reasons for abandonment

Organizations giving one reason	
Over budget	4
User requirements change	3
Organization needs change	7.
Cost/risks change	1
Organizations giving more than one reason	
Over budget	13
Organization needs change	16
User requirements change	19
Newer technology available	2
Higher priority elsewhere	1

Table 1.4 Evaluators at development stage

Organizations using one group	
IT dept	6
Internal audit	1
Sponsoring user department	1
Project team	10
Board/executive	1
Organizations using several groups	
IT dept	23
Internal audit	8
Sponsoring user department	3
Quality assurance	1
Project team	18
Board/executive	1
Consultants	8

data. Subsequently we found very few organizations actually considering these objectives in the feasibility stage. All the organizations which had to abandon projects going over budget had used cost–benefit only in their earlier feasibility evaluations, thus in all probability understating development and second-order costs. Some methods of minimizing this risk are discussed in Chapters 6 and 8.

Who completes the evaluation

The survey findings on this issue are summarized in Table 1.4. The most significant issue here is that sponsoring user departments were minority participants in carrying out evaluation in the development stage of IS projects.

The stark picture in Table 1.4 is qualified to some degree when project team membership is taken into account. Thus Table 1.5 shows user management and users quite well represented, though it should be borne in mind that not all organizations surveyed used project teams, and two (not shown in Table 1.5) only had the IS department represented on the project teams. A considerable case can also be made for the importance of including not just user management but lower-level users in the evaluation process; the findings show that such users were very often excluded from participation in evaluation.

Reports on evaluation

In 30 cases evaluation reports were carried out at several development stages, in 7 cases when there was something to report, in 3 cases at several stages and also when there was something to report, in 2 cases when development was complete, in 1 case at completion of development or when there was something to report, in 1 case monthly. There would thus seem to be a quite high level of reportage, although in practice there was wide variation in those to whom the reports were made (see Table 1.6).

Comment

The research reveals little evidence of a learning process in operation. Despite the high level of project abandonment at the development stage, in follow-up interviews respondents (two or more in each of 26 organizations) informed us that there had rarely been subsequent changes in evaluation procedures and techniques at the feasibility stage. Again we must question the levels of satisfaction with evaluation procedures and results expressed by the organizations surveyed. With the results highlighted so far it is clear that changes in the evaluation process are required by a

Table 1.5 Representation on project evaluation teams for organizations using several groups

Users	11
Internal audit	3
Board/executive	2
Other managers	7
IT department	23
Planning department	1
User management	16
Specialist	3

Table 1.6 Reporting on evaluation

Report to one group	
Project policy committee	1
User management/liaison	1
Project board/executive	11
IT strategy committee	3
Steering group	2
Department heads	1
Internal audit	3
Report to several groups	
User management/liaison	9
IT strategy committee	1
Department heads	3
Project board/executive	9
Steering group	4
Internal audit	8

[a] Three organizations did not complete this question.

majority of the organizations surveyed. This undoubtedly means improvements in both feasibility and development evaluation and the relationship between them. It is possible that certain conditions for learning were not present, for example the same individuals undertaking the same evaluation process on a frequent basis. We could argue that the high levels of project abandonment are in fact endorsement of the way in which evaluation is conducted at the development stage. A less optimistic view is that if projects were being abandoned after they had started this must be considered a failure, at least of feasibility evaluation. Organizations that had never had to abandon projects used cost–benefit analysis combined with service to the customer or user as their criteria, and none of them used their own methodology in the feasibility evaluation process.

The issue of including lower-level users in the evaluation process is stressed by many sources (see for example Eason, 1988; Land, 1985; Schott and Olson, 1988). However, only 5 organizations included the sponsoring user department in the evaluation. This figure was much lower than we expected, but was supported in the evidence from our interviews, though informal involvement of sponsoring user departments was mentioned in 10 additional organizations. Finally, the findings here endorse the concept of the evaluation cycle discussed earlier. Eason (1988), Hoskyns (1989) and Land (1985) have stated that one of the main reasons for evaluation is to learn from successes and mistakes. In cases where systems development had been abandoned it would surely have been of some use to carry out a detailed investigation as to why this had happened and how the evaluation process could be improved. There was little indication of such learning and improvements taking place in the organizations surveyed. If project abandonment or completion is seen as a sunk cost, about which little can be done, and if the pressure is to manage the next project, as interviewees in 11 organizations mentioned, then this result is understandable; but it does little to maximize the effectiveness of evaluation of IS investment.

The implementation stage

Peccei and Guest (1984) see evaluation as providing valuable feedback while the introduction of IS is actually in progress. It may become clear during what may be quite a lengthy programme of change that progress is falling behind. Benjamin (1988) used a first time user to illustrate the need to learn for future projects and for the current project in hand. While endorsing their concerns, we have found surprisingly little written about the evaluation process during the implementation stage of IS projects. The main issues investigated in the present survey focused on areas that have tended not to receive detailed attention in other studies: objectives of evaluation, criteria, methods used, who conducted the evaluation, who was consulted and reportage.

Objectives of Evaluation

Of organizations carrying out evaluation at this stage 36% stated that they used the evaluation only to learn about any changes required during the implementation; an additional 33% learned for the current project but also wanted to learn for future projects; 5% of organizations used evaluation to determine acceptability of the end system or to correct design or performance; 21% used a combination of these criteria. Additionally, two organizations also used evaluation to release payment. Only one organization used evaluation to make a go/no go decision on the project at this late stage. The objectives of the evaluation did not relate in any way to the type of business the organizations in the sample were involved in.

Evaluation criteria

User acceptance criteria were employed by 78% of the organizations; 36% looked at user requirements and 31% time scale. Most used a combination of these, except for 33% which only used user acceptance criteria. The other criteria were cost/business needs, systems performance, IS department acceptance, effectiveness of training and applications support acceptance.

The IT industry companies utilized user acceptance criteria as the main evaluation measure. This is unsurprising as most IT organizations would be developing systems for customers and their acceptance at this stage must be of great importance. The organizations' own evaluation would be in operation at the development stage. The other groups of organizations showed no particular preference for some criteria over others.

Method of evaluation

The large majority (86%) of the organizations included pilot testing among their methods, with a third of these using pilot testing as their only method. Parallel simulation was included by 55%. Other methods were rarely used but included volume testing, prototyping, systems testing, test database and what the respondent called 'sudden death'. On the whole the method selected had no clear relationship to the effectiveness or otherwise of evaluation, except that the two organizations which were not satisfied with the results used both pilot testing and parallel simulation, and the organization finding evaluation 'obstructive' used volume testing.

Who conducts the evaluation

Two-thirds (68%) of organizations included the user department in the evaluation during implementation. Of these 31% included only the user department, 48% included the IS department, and the same proportion included a project team in the evaluation. The other three groups included were audit, IS board and steering committee. Overall 21% used only the user department; 21% included the IS department, user department and a project team; 16% used only the project team and 16% included the IS and user departments in the evaluation.

The significant points emerging from detailed analysis of the data are that 52% did not included the IS department, and 52% did not include project teams in the evaluation process. Furthermore, a rather surprising 31% of organizations surveyed excluded user departments from the evaluation process at this stage; only two organizations were very satisfied with the evaluation process and these used a combination of IS department, user department and project team. This latter finding would seem unsurprising. However, a manufacturing organization in the sample used such a combination but still registered dissatisfaction with its evaluation process, thus showing that this approach in itself is no guarantee of success.

Who is consulted for the evaluation

Most (83%) consulted user departments during evaluation, a further 9% consulted only the user department, 76% consulted the IS departments, and 60% included the project team; 2% consulted only the project team. The other groups consulted, albeit with very few examples, were unions and internal audit. The most popular combination was IS department, user department and project team – 57% used this selection and 24% consulted just the first two.

It was interesting to note that 43% of organizations did not consult any additional groups who were not already involved in evaluation; 50% of these consulted the IS department, user department and project group. It could be than the project group had included all personnel who would need to have any input into the evaluation. However, this does not explain why the other 50% did not need to look elsewhere for information.

Reporting

Few significant findings on reportage emerged from the data. A variety of practice emerged. Thus 73% of organizations reported to executive management (25% of these reported to no other group), 57% to the IS department and 55% to the project team/manager. The other recipients were user department heads and steering committees. The most popular combination had 29% issuing reports to project team/manager, IS department and executive management. The next most popular recipient at 19% was executive management on its own. The recipient of the report depended on the stage at which reports were written. If reporting was at predefined stages, reports mostly went to a project team. If organizations reported when the need arose they were more likely to report to executive management. Finally, if the organization reported at predefined stages and at completion of implementation, reports were sent to project teams, IS departments and executive management.

Comment

Only 7% of the organizations surveyed consulted trade unions. This is even less than the 18% who consulted unions at the feasibility stage. How serious was their consultation at the previous stage? The need for union acceptance of the implementation plan would seem to be as important as the acceptance of the IS project during the initial stages. The lack of consultation would suggest that management consulted unions mainly as a requirement of procedure rather than to gain useful information and enable a usable and acceptable system to be implemented. As illustrated in the British Rail example given by Peccei and Guest (1984), the lack of consultation with workforce representatives by the organizations in our survey could be passing over many benefits to management. It could also be building in hidden costs to the organization's IS investments.

The pattern is one of low levels of consultation. Only 21% of organizations included the user and IS departments and project teams in their evaluation; 43% of the organizations did not consult any extra groups who were not already involved in the evaluation. The 6% who were very satisfied with their evaluation used user, IS and project teams in their evaluation. If organizations consult all who will be affected this may therefore be considered to have a positive effect on the success of the project.

The need for further investigation into evaluation at this stage is evident from the lack of information available in the literature and the limited results which could be produced from the survey.

The post-implementation stage

A fifth of the organizations did not evaluate at the post-implementation stage. In other words, they did not have any evidence to show that the project was a success or otherwise, nor could they use information from this stage to improve their evaluation techniques at feasibility or other stages. The benefits and methods of post-investment appraisal are discussed further in Chapters 9 and 10. Some reasons cited by respondents for not carrying out evaluation included: it is not necessary; it costs too much; it distracts from other work; the results would be used in a negative way; it is too bureaucratic. Some researchers have suggested that organizations may tend to take a 'sunk cost' view of IS investments at this stage, making evaluation seem fairly irrelevant. The Kobler Unit (1990) found that organizations did not use the same standard of calculation for IS investments as they did for other capital investments, most probably because of the lack of tools to make such rigorous calculations. Many organizations in our sample actually budgeted a certain amount of money per annum for IS; the tendency may be to treat money already allocated as not needing subsequent justification. In several public sector organizations in our survey a separate IS department was given responsibility for issuing computers to other sections. Thus in one respondent organization, 'proof of need' was required in order to gain equipment; however no assessment was carried out on whether or how the IS was used once allocated. In some cases respondents cited examples of employees not wanting or needing a computer who were given the equipment because everybody else had it. The lack of pay-off from the investment was unlikely to be highlighted because no post-implementation review took place. Clearly post-implementation review is, or should be, an integral part in the overall evaluation process.

The rest of the research on this stage focused on who carried out the evaluation, evaluation criteria, reporting and follow-up procedures.

Who carries out the evaluation

Of the 40 organizations carrying out evaluation 31% used only the project team, 26% used only the IS department and 12% only the user department. The remaining 31%

Table 1.7 Several evaluators used

	Organizations
IT department	20
Project team	11
External consultants	4
Quality assurance	1
User department	17
Internal audit	14
External audit	1

of organizations used a combination of evaluators, as shown in Table 1.7. It is noticeable that internal audit had a higher profile at this stage than at other stages, though their absence from the evaluation process at any stage could be questioned, unless the organization had no internal audit section. Interestingly, but perhaps reflecting distrust of 'outsiders', the organization that found evaluation 'obstructive' used only internal audit and external consultants. The different industries did not show a preference for any combination of groups.

Evaluation criteria

Two organizations used only direct comparison with the original proposal or feasibility study, while one organization based evaluation on ensuring that business objectives were being met. The other 37 organizations used a combination of criteria. Overall 83% of the 40 organizations use direct comparison with feasibility study; 63% cost effectiveness; 53% quality of product; 48% systems availability; 44% productivity, and 22% job satisfaction. Other criteria used include management of project controls, correct use of techniques, use of code generators, problems experienced, and appropriate hardware.

The most popular combination of criteria, used by 15% of organizations, embraced the top six detailed above. A further 15% used the top six less job satisfaction, and another 10% used the top six less job satisfaction and quality of product. It would appear that organizations found their own path to evaluation at this stage reflecting the realities of their particular circumstances and the unavailability of widely applicable, robust evaluation tools and techniques (but see Chapters 9 and 10). Further comment on evaluation criteria appears below.

Reporting

The reports were made to various individuals and to many combinations within the organizations surveyed. Executive management was included by 61% in their distribution list, 54% included the IT department, and 51% the user department(s). Three organizations also included external auditors or steering committees. The main preferred combinations were: 27.5% executive management only; 27.5% IT department, executive management and user department; 12.5% IT department and executive management.

Comment

Of the organizations who did complete evaluation at the post-implementation stage 83% included a direct comparison of the outcome with the evaluation at the feasibility stage. This is one area where the organizations had actually used the evaluation cycle and the output from one stage as an input into another. There are many different ways of evaluating the success of the project and many organizations used additional criteria at this stage to those they originally employed at the feasibility stage. For example, six organizations used quality of product at the post-implementation, but not at the feasibility, stage. Some of these criteria could have been included at the earlier stage and the later emphasis on these areas suggest that this should have been the case. Problems can arise when a project is accepted using one set of criteria, and its relative success is measured using another.

Meyer and Boone (1988) suggest that all evaluations need to be compared, and that evaluations by users and their managers are essential. In this way additional benefits may become apparent which were unidentifiable at the earlier stages and any additional criteria can then be added to future projects. The use of additional criteria is therefore not detrimental; in fact the pursuit of additional criteria may need to be encouraged. The main point is that this additional knowledge should then be fed back into the evaluation cycle, for instance by extending the feasibility criteria.

Some organizations (44%) stated that they did not learn from their mistakes. One respondent suggested that the question was pointless because nobody would admit to not learning. In fact this proved incorrect. Of the 56% of organizations which either sometimes or always learnt from their mistakes only 36% received the information through their formal system of evaluation. In other words more organizations (64%) used information regularly or exclusively from informal methods to ensure that mistakes were not repeated.

It is somewhat surprising that with so many organizations admitting to not avoiding foreseeable mistakes and the need for further improvements, 80% claim to have been satisfied with their evaluation. Subsequent interviews revealed a mixture of responses to this apparent contradiction. The main explanations may be summarized as admission of a lack of knowledge on the objectives of evaluation in the first place; satisfaction that personal/departmental and/or informal goals could be achieved through the way the evaluation was conducted and the techniques adopted; scepticism or what several respondents referred to as 'realism' as to how much evaluation could achieve; a lack of concern for the importance of post-implementation review.

Routine operations

In reviewing the literature we found all too little research carried out on evaluation processes at the routine operations stage. Part Four in the present volume seeks to counter this omission. The present research looked at the extent of continuous monitoring, the evaluation criteria used, reporting, and the extent to which evaluation led to changes being made in the system being evaluated. Forty-one organizations carried out evaluation at this stage; 83% of these carried out continuous monitoring.

Criteria

One organization used only 'system reliability' as the criteria for evaluation on a continuous basis. The other organizations on the whole used several criteria, as shown in Table 1.8: 17% used system availability alone, while a further 15% used system availability and capabilities as their evaluation criteria. A major finding is that only 20% of the organizations surveyed included the totality of system availability and capability and the needs of the organization and department in their assessment. These would appear to be the most necessary criteria to use and it is surprising to find so many organizations using such a limited number of evaluation criteria. It also needs to be pointed out that the bases for evaluation adopted at this stage differed from other stages, with few indications in the research sample of relationships being established between the methods and outcomes of evaluation at other stages and at the routine operations stage. Swanson and Beath (1989) suggest that evaluation of routine operations should be extensive and that it should be related to the organization's strategic needs. There is little sign of this happening in the organizations surveyed.

Reporting and resultant changes

The most popular recipient of the report was the IS department (61%); the user department and executive management were equal second (49% each). In all, 42% of organizations reported to only one of these bodies. It is surprising to see how many organizations did not report to the IS department (39%) unless this department was being used to write the reports in these organizations, and was not counted as a report recipient. Frequency of reporting is shown in Table 1.9.

The timing of the reports will reflect upon how often maintenance or emergency action can be taken. Overall the combination of timings preferred were monthly (24%); monthly and when a problem occurred (17%); only when a problem occurred (17%); when a problem occurred and yearly (10%). It was interesting to see that 42% of the organizations reported monthly or even less frequently. In such a volatile area, and given the fact that many organizations now require systems to be reliable at all times, this frequency would not appear to be adequate. It was also surprising to see how many organizations in the IT sector only reported when a problem occurred,

Table 1.8 Major evaluation criteria

	Organizations
System availability	26
Organizational needs	16
Response time	3
IS department operational constraint	1
System reliability	1
System capabilities	18
Departmental needs	15
Cost	2
Traffic on communications lines	1
Technical currency	1

Table 1.9 Frequency of reporting

Organizations offering one response	
When problems occur	6
6 monthly	1
No laid down procedures	1
Varies	1
Monthly	9
Yearly	1
Daily	1
Organizations offering several responses	
When problems occur	14
6 monthly	1
Problem areas are reviewed at predefined stages	1
Monthly	8
Yearly	5
1–2 months	1

unless in practice this was so frequently as to render a time-based reporting system unnecessary. The one organization that found monitoring pointless reported only when a problem occurred.

Four-fifths of the organizations found that these reports sometimes led to changes in the system. Only 12% of the organizations always made changes as a result of evaluation, which either means that the systems must be exceptionally good or that maintenance and enhancements needs are being overlooked. It was obvious that the respondents assessed the success of the evaluation by whether changes took place subsequently, because the majority of organizations that always made changes were also very satisfied with the results.

Comment

As indicated above, the research sample throws up a number of unsatisfactory aspects of how routine operations and maintenance are evaluated in practice. Given that most organizations now possess computer-based systems, getting the evaluation of routine operations right would seem to be a major but, on the evidence of this present study, neglected, prerequisite for effective information systems. Some ways forward are suggested in later chapters.

Conclusions

We would suggest that the way organizations evaluate and manage their IS investments can be assessed against the following criteria. At a minimum a method of evaluation needs to be reliable, that is consistent in its measurement over time, able to discriminate between good and indifferent investments, able to measure what it purports to measure, and be administratively/organizationally feasible in its application. A process should also be in place whereby evaluation techniques are applied and which ensures monitoring of the IS investment across the lifetime of systems. It is clear from the research that organizations were experiencing considerable difficulties in meeting such criteria. To some extent this is not a surprising conclusion, given the widespread and continuing difficulties experienced in this area as reported in the literature (for example Banker, Kauffman and Mahmood, 1993; Farbey, Targett and Land, 1995; Keen, 1991; Strassmann, 1990; Willcocks, 1994a).

Although the majority of organizations claimed to be satisfied or very satisfied with their evaluation practice, the survey indicates many limitations in the evaluation techniques and processes adopted. In general terms organizations neither took the lessons learnt from one stage to another nor from project to project. In particular, 80% of organizations claimed that at some time they had needed to abandon projects during development for several reasons. This did not lead the organizations concerned to change their evaluation practice at the previous stage where it was obviously giving erroneous results. All organizations that had abandoned projects because they had gone over budget had evaluated them at the feasibility stage mainly using cost–benefit analysis. The need for improved methods and calculations at the feasibility stage was therefore apparent; yet they were not forthcoming. The criteria used during the feasibility stage also proved to have an influence on whether the projects would be abandoned at the development stage. The organizations which used cost–benefit analysis allied to service to the customer or user criteria seemed to have more chance of success.

It is evident that the people who participated or who were represented in the evaluation process at all stages could easily have been widened to include more or all of the parties affected, including trade unions. This was highlighted in the implementation stage where the 6% who were very satisfied had included all affected parties in the evaluation.

Some organizations claimed to want to learn from the implementation and post-implementation stages for future projects, and yet their lack of flexibility did nothing to promote this idea. The number of organizations which stated that they did not learn from their mistakes was even less encouraging for the future of IS evaluation processes in the organizations sampled. The fact that 83% used direct comparison with the feasibility study at the post-implementation stage to some extent endorsed the view of an evaluation cycle. In contrast these same organizations also used additional criteria in the assessment and failed to update their feasibility evaluation accordingly.

What implications do our findings have for IS evaluation practice generally? It is clear that in practice organizations need to establish their evaluation objectives. Once these have been clarified the road to more effective evaluation would probably be an uphill climb on an experimentally based evaluation cycle. The concept of learning would seem to be central to evaluation, but it tends to be applied in a fragmented way. A learning cycle can be enhanced by linking evaluation across stages and time, thus making 'islands' of evaluation more integrated and mutually informative, increasing the degree to which key stakeholders are participants in evaluation at all stages, and focusing as much on getting the process of evaluation right, as on the techniques and criteria adopted. Techniques can only complement, not substitute for, developing evaluation as a social and organizational process and the deeper organizational learning about IS that that entails. In this respect a range of literature could be usefully influential on organizational evaluation practice (for example the work of Farbey, Land and Targett, 1993; Flood and Jackson, 1991; Gregory and Jackson, 1992; Hirschheim and Smithson, 1988; Lyttinen, Klein and Hirschheim, 1991). However, the present, and later research detailed in other chapters in this book, suggest that this literature and its tenets have not so far been influential.

References

AT Kearney (1990) *Breaking the Barriers: IT Eltectiveness in Great Britain and Ireland*, AT Kearney/ CIMA, London.

Audit Commission, The (1994) *High Risk, High Potential*. A Management Handbook on Information Technology in Local Government, HMSO, London.

Banker, R., Kauffman, R. and Mahmood, M. (1993) *Strategic Information Technology Management: Perspectives on Organizational Growth and Competitive Advantage*, Idea Group Publishing, Harrisburg.

Butler Cox Foundation (1990) *Getting Value from Information Technology*. Research Report 75, Butler Cox Foundation, London.

Benjamin, A. (1988) A study of successful computer installation for a first time user in a commercial office. In ACAS/IMS, *IT: Its Profitable Introduction to Business*, WRU/ACAS, London.

Coleman, T. and Jamieson, M. (1991) *Information Systems: Evaluating Intangible Benefits at the Feasibility Stage of Project Appraisal*. Unpublished MBA thesis, City University Business School, London.

Computer Weekly/Kew (1995) *IT Expenditure Survey*, Computer Weekly/Kew Associates, London.

Cressey, P. (1985) *Consolidated Report: The Role of Parties Concerned in the Introduction of New Technology (Phase 1)*. European Foundation for the Improvement of Living and Working Conditions, Shankill Co., Dublin.

CSC Index/DTI (1992) *Key Issues Affecting Quality in Information Systems*, CSC Index/DTI, London.

Eason, K. (1988) *Information Technology and Organisational Change*, Taylor and Francis, London.

Farbey, B., Land, F. and Targett, D. (1992) Evaluating investments in IT. *Journal of Information Technology*, **7** (2), 109–22.

Farbey, B., Land, F. and Targett, D. (1993) *How To Assess Your IT Investment*, Butterworth & Heinemann, London.

Farbey, B., Targett, D. and Land, F. (eds.) (1995) *Hard Money, Soft Outcomes*, Alfred Waller/ Unicom, Henley.

Flood, R. and Jackson, M. (1991) Total systems thinking: a practical face to critical systems thinking. In *Critical Systems Thinking: Directed Readings* (eds. R. Flood and M. Jackson), John Wiley, Chichester.

Goodwin, C. (1984) How OA can justify itself. *Computing*, 4 October, 6.

Gregory, A. and Jackson, M. (1992) Evaluation methodologies: a system for use. *Journal of the Operational Research Society*, **43** (1), 19–28.

Hawgood, J. and Land, F. (1988) A multivalent approach to information systems assessment. In *Information Systems Assessment: Issues and Challenges* (eds. N. Bjorn-Andersen and G. Davis), Elsevier, Amsterdam.

Hirschheim, R. and Smithson, S. (1988) A critical analysis of information systems evaluation. In *Information Systems Assessment: Issues and Challenges* (eds. N. Bjorn-Andersen and G. Davis), Elsevier, Amsterdam.

Hochstrasser, B. and Griffiths, C. (1991) *Controlling IT Investments: Strategy and Management*, Chapman & Hall, London.

Hoskyns Group (1989) *Effective IS Project Management: The Key Issues, Risks and Solutions*, Hoskyns Group, London.

Keen, P. (1991) *Shaping The Future: Business Design through Information Technology*, Harvard Business School Press, Boston, MA.

Kobler Unit (1990) *Regaining Control of IT Investments: A Handbook for Senior Managers*, Kobler Unit, London.

Land, F. (1985) Criteria for the evaluation and design of effective systems. *London School of Economics Paper No. SM362/LC2*, LSE, London.

Leonard-Barton, D. (1988) Implementation as mutual adaptation of technology and organization. *Research Policy*, **17**, 251–67.

Lyttinen, K., Klein, H. and Hirschheim, R (1991) The effectiveness of office information systems: a social action perspective. *Journal of Information Systems*, **1** (1), 41–60.

Malitoris, J. (1990) IT Measurement: delivering the goods, Paper at the Technology and People Conference, London, 15 June.

Martin, R. (1989) *The utilisation and efficiency of IS: a comparative study*. Oxford Institute of Information Management Research Paper RDP 89/2, Templeton College, Oxford.

Martin, R. (1991) *IS resources and effectiveness 1990: a survey*. Oxford Institute of Information Management Research Paper RDP 91/5, Templeton College, Oxford.

McLoughlin, I. and Clark, J. (1993) *Technological Change at Work*, Open University Press, Milton Keynes.

Meyer, M. and Boone, M. (1988) *The Information Edge*, Holt Rinehart and Winston, Canada.

National Audit Office (1987) *Inland Revenue: Control of Major Developments in use of IT*, HMSO, London.

National Audit Office (1989) *Department of Social Security: Operational Strategy*, January Session 1988–89, HC-111, HMSO, London.

PA Consulting Group (1990) *The Impact of the Current Climate on IT: The Survey Report*, PA Consulting Group, London.

Parker, M., Benson, R. and Trainor, H. (1988) *Information Economics*, Prentice Hall, London.

Peccei, R. and Guest, D. (1984) Evaluating the introduction of new technology: the case of wordprocessors in British Rail. In *Microprocessors, Manpower and Society* (ed. M. Warner), Gower, Aldershot.

Preece, D. (1989) *Managing the Adoption of New Technology*, Routledge, London.

Price Waterhouse (1993) *Information Technology Review 1993/4*, Price Waterhouse, London.

Price Waterhouse (1994) *Information Technology Review 1994/95*, Price Waterhouse, London.

Rothwell, S. (1984) Company employment policies and new technology in manufacturing and service sectors. In *Microprocessors, Manpower and Society* (ed. M. Warner), Gower, Aldershot.

Schott, F. and Olson, M. (1988) Designing usability in systems: driving for normalcy. *Datamation*, May, 68–73.

Strassmann, P. (1990) *The Business Value of Computers*, The Information Economics Press, New Canaan.

Swanson, E. and Beath, C. (1989) *Maintaining Information Systems in Organizations*, John Wiley, Chichester.

Touche Ross/IAM (1991) *Office Automation: The Barriers and Opportunities*, Touche Ross, London.

Ward, J. (1994) A portfolio approach to evaluating information systems investments and setting priorities. In *Information Management: Evaluation of IS Investments* (ed. L. Willcocks), Chapman & Hall, London.

Willcocks, L. (ed.) (1990) *The Evaluation of Information Systems Investments*, Theme Issue, *Journal of Information Technology*, **5** (4).

Willcocks, L. (1991) Information technology and human resource issues in the 1990s: integration through culture, Paper at the Fifth Annual Conference of the British Academy of Management, University of Bath, 22–24 September.

Willcocks, L. (1992) Evaluating information technology investments: research findings and reappraisal. *Journal of Information Systems*, **2** (3), 1–26.

Willcocks, L. (ed.) (1994a) *Information Management: Evaluation of IS Investments*, Chapman & Hall, London.

Willcocks, L. (1994b) Information technology in public administration: trends and possibilities. *Public Administration*, **72** (1), 13–32.

Willcocks, L. (1994c) Managing information technology evaluation: techniques and processes. In *Strategic Information Management* (eds. B. Galliers and B. Baker), Butterworth Heinemann, London.

Willcocks, L. and Lester, S. (1991) Information systems investments: evaluation at the feasibility stage of projects. *Technovation*, **11** (5), 283–302.

Willcocks, L. and Lester, S. (1994) Evaluating the feasibility of information systems investments: recent UK evidence and new approaches. In *Information Management: Evaluation of IS Investments* (ed. L. Willcocks), Chapman & Hall, London.

Wilson, T. (1991) Overcoming the barriers to the implementation of information system strategies. *Journal of Information Technology*, **6** (1), 39–44.

2

Investment appraisal for IT systems

Robert Whiting, John Davies and Mike Knul

Introduction

Control of IT investment to ensure value for money is currently an issue of major concern to most businesses. In today's increasingly competitive business climate, there is a growing requirement for stricter cost control and a demand for higher returns while minimizing risk in all investments. Recognition of the potential impact of IT systems on the strategic position of companies and increasing levels of IT spend have made the control and justification of IT investment a critically important issue. At the same time there has been and still is widespread doubt concerning the suitability of traditional methods of investment appraisal for the evaluation of IT proposals (Lay, 1985; Powell, 1992; Willcocks, 1994). Overreliance on these methods may lead to an excessively conservative IT portfolio and an associated loss of competitiveness. Failure to perform rigorous investment appraisal may result in a highly ineffective use of resources. In response to these concerns there is a large and rapidly developing literature on modern approaches to IT investment appraisal.

This chapter outlines the major concerns and findings of the literature on IT investment appraisal and suggests ways in which these findings may be modified and utilized to drive the design of a computer-based tool for IT investment appraisal. We then describe a prototype of such a system. There is widespread agreement in the literature that IT investment appraisal can only be effective if the appraisal process is embedded in higher-level business processes (Earl, 1989; Remenyi, Money and Twite, 1991).

Investing in Information Systems: Evaluation and Management. Edited by Leslie Willcocks. Published in 1996 by Chapman & Hall. ISBN 0 412 72670 X.

The problem of evaluating investment in IT

Background

Recent surveys (Farbey, Land and Targett, 1993; Unicom, 1992; see also Chapters 1 and 8) have indicated that the issue of appraisal of IT investment is currently an area of concern to senior management of most large organizations. Although it is not straightforward to establish precisely the amount of investment in IT that is taking place, it is clear that very substantial amounts of money are involved. At the same time there is a widespread sense of unease about the value to organizations provided by this investment. In a survey of the literature dealing with the IT 'productivity paradox' (Remenyi, Money and Twite, 1993) various sources are quoted as claiming that no link between IT investment and business success has been established.

The underlying reasons for this apparently disappointing performance are currently unclear. A report from MIT (Brynjolfsson, 1992) on IT and productivity identified a combination of three major factors underlying this characterization of IT performance. The factors are:

1. mismeasurement of inputs and outputs when dealing with IT;
2. lags between costs and benefits which make short-term results look poor; and
3. mismanagement of information and technology.

There is a broad agreement in the literature that traditional methods of investment appraisal which presuppose financial quantification of costs and benefits may be misleading when applied to IT investments. Since there are as yet no clearly established alternatives to the traditional methods, IT investment may often be misplaced, resulting in poor value to the organization. Similarly, misapplication of traditional appraisal methods may result in poor perceptions of investments that are in fact performing well.

It is widely held that improvements in the processes of measuring IT costs and benefits are the key to securing control over IT, thereby improving the effectiveness of IT investment and, in turn, perception of that performance.

In this chapter, the characteristics which make evaluation of investment in IT problematic are discussed. The results of a number of recent surveys concerning IT investment appraisal as currently practised in organizations are reviewed. Traditional approaches to investment appraisal are examined and consideration is given to the appropriateness of these financial methods when applied to IT. Pursuing the themes in Chapters 1 and 3, and modifications to the traditional approaches are suggested in an attempt to overcome some of the criticisms identified.

Problematic aspects of evaluating investment in IT

Classification of IT systems

There is broad agreement in the literature that the difficulties involved in the evaluation of IT investment stem from the indirect or supporting role that IT usually plays in an organization's business processes. The value of an investment in IT is difficult to quantify in financial terms because benefits directly attributable to the functionality of

Strategic	**High potential**
Applications which are critical to sustaining future business strategy	Applications which may be important in achieving future success
Key operational	**Support**
Applications on which the organization now depends for success	Applications which are valuable but not critical to success

Figure 2.1 Strategic grid.

an IT system may be several steps removed from the actual achievement of profits. Different types of IT system contribute more or less directly to an organization's core business and techniques for investment appraisal need to vary in accordance with that directness.

In the investment appraisal literature the terminology used to classify IT systems varies considerably. Ward (1988) suggests that for the purposes of IT investment appraisal, the role a system plays in the business and the contribution it is expected to make should be the key parameters. Based on work by McFarlan (1984), he proceeds to suggest a strategic grid into which IT systems can be classified. Figure 2.1 shows the type of system which is assigned to each quadrant of the grid.

In Griffiths (1990) systems are classed with respect to their contributions to 'internal efficiency', 'external effectiveness' and 'new business'. The categories in Remenyi, Money and Twite (1993) are systems which 'automate', 'informate' and 'transformate' and Parker and Benson (1989) use the terms 'substitutive applications', 'complementary applications' and 'innovative applications'. All classifications express a similar notion of the degree of distance from a direct contribution to current core business. Innovative systems are at the extreme of the spectrum because they capture new markets and actually change the nature of an organization's business. Systems may also be divided into the categories 'infrastructure' and 'non-infrastructure' (Hochstrasser, 1992). Investments in infrastructure systems are considered the most difficult to evaluate because they 'enable the enabling technology' and are thus furthest removed from the direct effect on the core business.

Intangible benefits

It is characteristic of contemporary IT systems that there may be a complex causal chain between some aspect of a system's functionality and actual achievement of financial gain either in the form of reduced costs or increased revenues. The complexity of this chain may make meaningful financial quantification of a system's value to an organization extremely difficult. The system's functionality therefore is said to have intangible benefits for the organization.

In a survey of the top 200 UK companies conducted at the end of 1990 (Unicom, 1992: 124) it is reported that the intangible benefits of IT systems were widely perceived by senior managers as being as important as harder, more traditional, financial benefits. Over 80% of respondents to the survey believed that intangibles contributed at least 30% of IT system value.

The proportion of benefits for a given IT system which are tangible and intangible will vary with the type and purpose of the system. Systems which are developed to address issues of internal efficiency in an organization are likely to have the highest proportion of tangible benefits. IT infrastructure systems and strategic systems will have the largest proportion of intangible benefits. Examples of typical categories of IT system intangible benefits can be found in King and Schrems (1978), Unicom (1992: 141), and Remenyi, Money and Twite (1993). These include benefits such as:

- more timely management information;
- improved product quality;
- improved customer service;
- improved communication within the organization;
- gaining competitive advantage; and
- job enhancement for employees.

Providing meaningful financial estimates for benefits of this type is not a straightforward matter for a number of reasons:

1. The chain of causation from system functionality to the factor which is of value to the company (e.g. competitive advantage) may be complex and uncertain.
2. Attempts to quantify intangible benefits in financial terms may involve making assumptions and medium- to long-term forecasts in an environment which is very volatile. Changes in the business and economic environment may invalidate assumptions made at the time of the investment appraisal.
3. 'Noise' resulting from unpredictable changes in the environment can overwhelm projected financial targets even though accurate assumptions have been made and the benefits to which the targets have been attached are being achieved (Remenyi, Money and Twite, 1993: 80; Unicom, 1992: 125).
4. Even where reliable quantitative data could in principle be obtained the difficulties and costs of doing so could outweigh the benefits.

Current practice in evaluation of IT systems

In a survey reported in Unicom (1992: 122) traditional investment appraisal techniques were found to be in widespread use for evaluation of IT investment. Almost everyone performed a traditional cost–benefit analysis and many also used techniques such as internal rate of return (IRR), net present value (NPV) and payback or hurdle rates. However, there is also evidence that, whether traditional appraisals are widespread or not, the results are often ignored (McGolpin, 1991).

Interviews in Coleman and Jamieson (1994) revealed that current practice for investment appraisal consisted of variations on the following process:

- sum the tangible benefits;
- loosely quantify the less tangible benefits and add to the total return;
- add guesstimates for the intangible benefits and massage the total until the hurdle rate is exceeded.

The only other technique mentioned by a high proportion of respondents was 'strategic fit', but this usually consisted of a number of points scattered throughout a business case.

There was no mention by any of the respondents of the newer methods of investment appraisal (e.g. information economics, SESAME, return on management etc.).

Coleman and Jamieson (1994) conclude from the absence of any mention of the modern approaches that 'this supports the view that these methods lack something in practical application'.

Traditional techniques for investment appraisal
(A further discussion of traditional techniques also appears in Chapter 7.)

Following Lay (1985), we can say that a traditional cost–benefit analysis (CBA) process typically consists of five steps:

1. **Defining the scope of the project** – in the ideal CBA process, all costs and benefits should be evaluated. In practical terms this is not always possible and it is important that any assumptions and limitations are clearly defined and agreed at the start.

2. **Evaluating costs and benefits** – While direct costs are usually relatively straight-forward to quantify, benefits (direct and indirect) and indirect costs are often more problematic. Potential benefits are often identified by using a checklist of potential benefits and can sometimes be estimated only crudely. Even direct costs can be hard to quantify for some applications.
3. **Defining the life of the project** – this is an important definition since the further into the future the CBA analysis reaches, the more uncertain the predictions will be. Furthermore, benefits will continue to accrue over the life of a project, so that the longer it continues, the more favourable the return on investment will tend to appear (assuming no costs are incurred in later years). Hence this is a key problem and often ongoing costs (e.g. maintenance) are ignored.
4. **Discounting the values** – most CBA studies attempt to take into account the time value of money by discounting anticipated income and expenditure. A variety of financial techniques are available to analyse the costs and benefits and these are discussed in more detail below.
5. **Sensitivity analysis** – it is important to examine the consequences of possible over- or under-estimates in the costs, benefits and discounting rate.

The core of a traditional CBA is step (2), since it is implicitly assumed that all costs and benefits are quantifiable. The plausibility of this assumption is discussed elsewhere in this chapter.

There are a number of financial techniques for assessing the value of investment decisions. These techniques require an estimation of all the costs and benefits of a particular investment to be available as financial values. As discussed below, this may not always be straightforward. These techniques are still important as they offer standard, well-understood ways of analysing this numeric information, no matter how uncertain the information used. Use of these techniques should be accompanied by a clear statement of the confidence attached to each piece of uncertain information.

We will not survey traditional investment appraisal techniques here: for a discussion of the alternative techniques and their merits see Whiting, Davies and Knul (1993). In financial terms, the objective of a profit making organization is to create wealth by producing products and services with greater value than the resources consumed. All traditional investment appraisal techniques aim to quantify the wealth created by a given project and are collectively termed return on investment (ROI) techniques. Among the better known techniques are:

- payback period;
- discounted payback period;
- internal rate of return;
- return on capital employed;
- net present value (NPV).

For reasons discussed in Whiting, Davies and Knul (1993), most commentators on balance recommend the use of the NPV approach to investment appraisal.

Inadequacies of traditional methods for appraisal of IT investment

There are a number of problems associated with the traditional cost–benefit analysis (CBA) process. These vary but they are all rooted in the fact that CBA is essentially an approach attempting to find or calculate a monetary value for each element contributing to the costs or benefits of a project.

In practice, these values can be extremely difficult to quantify. This can often mean that recommendations coming from CBA are overturned by decision-makers who do not accept the monetary values assigned by the analysts. Furthermore, and perhaps even more importantly, benefits can also be hard to identify in the first place.

Estimation problems

IT costs are notoriously difficult to quantify. Mohanty (1981) analysed eight different cost models for software development and concluded that 'no model can estimate the cost of software with any degree of certainty'. While we would not necessarily be this pessimistic, and note that in a sense any reasonable cost model if it is applied as a standard across an organization will probably be worthwhile, his remarks do indicate the complexity of software cost estimation.

A further problem is the quantification of intangible benefits. Some systems, such as executive information systems or customer service support systems, may rely entirely on intangible benefits for their justification. Unfortunately, it is only once a system has been deployed that the earlier estimates of future benefits can be assessed for accuracy. This latter point emphasizes the importance of a post-implementation review: investment appraisal should not stop once the investment has been made (see also Chapter 9).

Unquantifiable factors

System performance is one unquantifiable factor. The costs of a system running slower than anticipated or in retuning a system to improve performance are not quantifiable in advance.

Further examples are non-economic factors. One such is system structure: an unstructured, ill-defined system will be much more expensive to develop than a similar system that is well planned and documented. Similarly, user aptitude can have a major impact on the benefits of a system. These factors are difficult to estimate in any realistic way *a priori*.

There are also a large number of qualitative factors to consider when evaluating IT systems. Some key examples are:

- risk;
- visibility;
- image;
- improvement in customer perception.

Another criticism is that, problematic as CBA is for stand-alone systems, the level of difficulty escalates dramatically when attempting a cost–benefit analysis on complex, integrated systems.

The role of IT

A number of publications throughout the 1980s and 1990s have taken the view that many IT systems can be seen as a corporate 'strategic weapon'. Such systems tend to be complex, networked systems often linking organizations and have developed over a long time frame. Some systems are now so complex and interconnected that it is doubtful whether it is possible to reasonably appraise their value.

Reliance solely on traditional CBA can also discourage innovation within an organization and may lead to the adoption of an overly conservative portfolio of IT projects.

Net present value and IT

In this section, we point out some issues in the use of NPV analysis specific to IT systems. In the light of these, we go on to suggest possible extensions to the NPV approach in the next section.

As mentioned above, NPV is regarded as the theoretically most correct approach to investment appraisal. It has two characteristics which are appealing in the context of IT projects. First, NPV allows for benefits which accrue slowly and are typically delayed from the initial investment to be evaluated. Second, it provides a clear structure which can help in overcoming the political and 'hyped' claims which are sometimes attached to IT projects. Examples of such claims (Earl, 1989) are 'we won't survive without it', 'the competition are doing it, so we must', and so on.

There are, however, some difficulties with NPV for IT projects. First there is the problem of the evaluation of alternatives. It is important when appraising IT projects to consider alternatives to the project proposed. Although alternatives can, of course, be investigated, using NPV does not explicitly encourage it and can tend to lead to thinking that a particular project is the only way. At least three sorts of alternative can be identified for consideration:

1. **The 'do nothing' alternative** – what will happen if current practice continues in the face of anticipated changes.

2. **Replacement alternatives** – where an IT system is proposed to replace an existing IT system, other alternatives may be overlooked. For example, a non-IT project might be a better alternative.
3. **Design alternatives** – an NPV analysis is almost always performed with a particular system design in mind. It is important to consider design alternatives at the appraisal stage.

A second potential problem with NPV is the selection of the correct discount rate. Finance theory dictates that this should be the cost of capital adjusted for project risk. However, the correct adjustment of the rate to take risk into account is a somewhat subjective matter, particularly in IT projects.

Modifications to net present value

There are three ways in which we can adapt the use of NPV models to circumvent to some extent the problems with intangible benefits:

1. Alternative estimates of intangible benefits (e.g. minimum and maximum values) can be entered into the NPV model to explore the project's sensitivity to the delivery of the intangibles.
2. Expected values can be used in the NPV model. Expected values are obtained by multiplying the probability of an intangible benefit by its estimated value. The problem here is of course that the expected values can be massaged to obtain the answer you want!
3. The NPV can be calculated only for cash flows of the tangible benefits and the costs. If the NPV is positive, accept the project. If it is negative, calculate the values required from the intangible benefits to make it zero and then assess the probability of achieving these values for the intangible benefits.

Perhaps a more fundamental objection to NPV is that it is an overly economistic numeric approach for IT projects, which are often complex and aim to deliver 'soft', intangible benefits. This suggests that a multi-stage approach to IT projects may be appropriate, where NPV is used with the modifications suggested above, together with a more qualitative analysis of the intangible benefits of the projects.

IT investment appraisal: further approaches

Overview

Over the last decade a considerable number of approaches to IT Investment appraisal have been developed which attempt to address the shortcomings of the traditional financial methods described above. The frameworks reviewed briefly below have been selected because they are presented as general approaches to the problem of IT investment appraisal, as opposed to partial examinations of some individual aspect of the overall problem. The purpose of the section is to provide an overview of the common concerns of the new approaches rather than a systematic assessment of each. More detail on the nature of these approaches can be found in Willcocks (1994).

The field of IT investment appraisal is characterized by a wide variety of different approaches and shows signs of immaturity. Authors tend to advance their own individual systems and develop their own terminologies, classifications and principles. The approaches are described at a high level and lack detail. There appears to be little or no critical work which takes an established approach as the point of departure and refines or extends some aspect of it. Anecdotal evidence for the successful application of approaches is common, but there appear to be few case studies describing systematic attempts to put high-level approaches into practice. Much of this may be attributable to considerations of commercial confidentiality and concern for intellectual property. There is certainly little doubt that the modern frameworks at least force a consideration of the broader issues in IT investment and encourage the viewing of IT in a more strategic way.

Modern IT investment appraisal frameworks

Information economics

Information economics (Parker, Benson and Trainor, 1988; Parker and Benson, 1989; Parker, Benson and Trainor, 1989) is a framework for IT investment appraisal which classifies IT systems into three types: substitutive applications, complementary applications and innovative applications. Value chain analysis (Earl, 1989; Parker, Benson and Trainor, 1988; Remenyi, Money and Twite, 1993) is used to identify the requirement for IT systems and determine the primary purpose of the system (e.g. cost avoidance, product differentiation etc.). Parker and Benson advance the view (now widely accepted) that the benefits of IT systems should be understood as value to the organization rather than financial benefits. It is argued that IT investment should be evaluated with respect to six major categories of value to an organization. A number of different techniques are presented which are used to structure the process of evaluation of investments in the different types of IT system.

The main thesis of information economics, that the benefits of IT should be regarded as value to the organization (rather than considering only financial value), is certainly valid. However, although some useful techniques are suggested, no coherent methodology is offered for an IT investment appraisal strategy. Furthermore, the classification of IT systems used is in our opinion less useful than the strategic grid approach described above.

SESAME

SESAME (Lincoln, 1986, 1988) is an approach to IT investment appraisal which primarily addresses the issue of retrospective appraisal of existing IT systems. The aim of the method is not to accurately measure the financial returns associated with a system (although costs and benefits are represented in financial terms), but to provide an objective evaluation which will satisfy senior executives. This is achieved by comparing the costs and benefits of the IT system to the costs and benefits of 'a reasonable manual alternative'.

It is unclear from the details available how intangible benefits are captured by this approach. It may be that the problem of valuing intangible benefits is avoided because the approach is based on comparison of two methods. Both methods achieve identical end results (and thus the same intangible benefits) so there is no need to factor out intangible benefits for special consideration. However, this would ignore any side-effect benefits of the IT system (or indeed the manual system). Examples of side-effect benefits arising from the introduction of IT could be improved computer literacy among staff, the provision of an IT infrastructure making further IT developments cost-effective, and so on. The suitability of the method for appraisal of IT investment prior to implementation is also unclear, as is its potential for evaluating alternative possible IT investment proposals.

RoM (return on management)

RoM is an approach to IT investment appraisal developed by Paul Strassmann (Strassmann, 1985; Willcocks, 1989). After investigation Strassman identified quality of management, rather than size of capital investment, as the critical factor in superior IT performance. RoM is a measure of the value-added which comes from managerial activity in an organization as compared to the costs incurred by that activity. It is defined as the residual value after deducting from total revenue the cost of, and value added by, each resource (including capital) except for management resources. Strassmann revealed that the organizations with the highest RoM consistently achieved better results with IT while having a lower IT spend.

RoM may be used to evaluate IT investment by calculating the RoM for the company before and after installation of the system. The difference between the two values corresponds to the value of the IT system to the organization. Evaluation of the investment prior to installation of the system requires estimating the increase in revenue generated by the system. Difficulties in obtaining this figure may mean that, like SESAME, RoM is best suited to evaluation of existing systems.

Kobler Unit framework

Recent research at the Kobler Unit (Griffiths, 1990; Hochstrasser, 1992; Willcocks, 1994) has led to the development of a framework for evaluating and prioritizing IT investment.

The proposed framework consists of four modules. Each module corresponds to a stage in the evaluation process. Making the appropriate entries on the worksheets may require performing a range of evaluation and information-gathering activities. For example, an affirmative answer to the question 'Is the proposed system user-friendly?' on worksheet 1 could be based on activities ranging in size and complexity from, at one end of the spectrum, cursory examination of the system design to, at the other end of the spectrum, an elaborate series of user trials with a system prototype.

Activity within the first module consists in evaluating a proposed project against a checklist of previously identified critical success factors. Evaluation of the investment proposal would not begin until all questions on the checklist can be answered affirmatively. The checklist presented contains factors which research at the Kobler Unit has found to be particularly important with regard to the deployment of IT.

The purpose of the activities in module 2 is to ensure that the appraisers have a clear grasp of the true costs of the proposed IT system prior to evaluation of the investment. This is felt to be necessary because research has consistently pointed out that most companies tend to underestimate the total costs of IT projects. Experience at the Kobler Unit suggests that it is not unusual for post-implementation costings to be 50% greater than those undertaken prior to implementation.

Activity in module 3 is concerned with the identification and specification of business performance indicators (i.e. metrics) which can be used to evaluate the performance and benefits of the proposed IT system. Establishing these metrics is important for these reasons:

1. Specification of concrete metrics encourages decision-makers to accurately identify their requirements of the IT system in terms of real business practices and objectives.
2. Specification of metrics and assessment of system performance at a pre-implementation stage lays a foundation for later evaluations of the system.
3. Concentration at the start on the expected changes to be induced by the system encourages the perception of investment appraisal as an ongoing process rather than a one-off cost justification exercise.

Activites in module 4 enable the comparison of the relative merits of alternative IT systems. The decision-makers are required to provide scores for each system across a number of predetermined dimensions. Each dimension also has a weight associated with it reflecting the perceived importance of that dimension within the organization in which the evaluation is taking place. The weight on each dimension is thus the same for every system being evaluated. The overall project priority value of a given system is then calculated by summing the weighted scores for each value dimension.

The Kobler Unit framework is a good one. It is practical and can be implemented readily and it is easy to see how it can be adapted to the specific requirements of a particular organization. One potential problem with it, however, is that it does not take account of the stage in the system development cycle at which an appraisal is performed. Two key points are at the feasibility study stage to decide whether investment may be worthwhile and at the post-design, pre-implementation stage when the decision is whether to implement and which hardware and/or software platforms to use. Clearly, less detail is available at the first stage than the second and any useful framework must deal with both decision points. In fact, we find in the Kobler Unit framework a mixture of higher and lower level factors in each module.

A second criticism of this approach is its overcomplex classification of IT systems into nine (potentially overlapping) areas. The strategic grid classification, for example, would be a more practical technique.

The application transfer team (ATT) approach

The ATT perspective is that cost justification is not only a numerical process. The ATT study (Hogbin, 1984; Hogbin and Thomas, 1994) is a methodology which is intended to help in deciding how to invest successfully in IT. It first evaluates the business need for a proposed investment and proceeds to produce an implementation plan for the recommended IT system.

The study is performed by a team drawn from a wide range of relevant units within an organization. A study is run by an expert familiar both with the methodology and with financial techniques for investment appraisal.

ATT identifies three stages of cost justification:

1. **Concept** – here strategic issues are considered.
2. **Calculations** – at this stage, the high-level justifications are quantified as far as possible.
3. **Control** – concerned with monitoring costs and benefits during project implementation.

The ATT study attempts to take a cost justification exercise from the first stage and move it forward into the second.

The ATT study proceeds by the potential project client setting the terms of reference and selecting the team for the study. The team typically consists of three to eight user managers and two IT managers, as well as the study leader who is familiar with the ATT methodology and any appropriate technical and financial specialists. At the end of the study, the team produce a report and recommendation for the client.

This methodology sounds relatively complex and time consuming and requires a high degree of commitment from a relatively large team of managers. It might be more appropriate for larger projects.

Evaluation

The brief reviews above indicate that there is a considerable diversity of approach to the problem of deciding what should be measured and how that measurement ought to be conducted when appraising IT investment. Despite the apparent difference of approach and terminology, a group of common themes and concerns do emerge from the descriptions of the different approaches.

There is a consensus that traditional investment appraisal methods are only adequate when applied to investment in restricted types of IT systems. These methods are completely inappropriate for evaluation of IT infrastructure systems or systems whose primary value is strategic. Even when applied to investment in systems concerned with organizational efficiency and effectiveness, reliance on traditional methods may lead to an overly conservative IT portfolio with potentially damaging effects on the competitive position of the company. Approximate measurement of relevant factors is to be preferred to the precise measurement of irrelevant factors which are brought into consideration only because it is possible to measure them precisely.

All contributors to the literature stress that the appraisal of IT investment must be embedded within high-level business procedures for strategy formulation and for the monitoring, management and evaluation of costs and benefits throughout the lifetime of the system. Appraisal of investment in IT depends crucially on having available a detailed and relevant set of management objectives for the business and for IT against which to compare the functionality and potential benefits of the proposed systems. These management objectives should preferably be already identified specific business critical success factors on to which the system's functionality can be mapped. Moreover, the benefits of IT systems (not just the costs) need to be reviewed and managed throughout their lifetime. IT investment appraisal will not be effective if it is viewed as a one-shot cost justification exercise.

There is a general acknowledgement that the difficulties regarding quantification of intangible benefits are so severe as to make complex numeric approaches to IT investment appraisal of limited value. The prevailing attitude appears to be that methods of aggregation and comparison used within the investment appraisal framework should be kept as simple as possible. Complex mathematical methods cannot compensate for the unreliable nature of the input values. The actual process of investment appraisal is widely regarded as being more important than the details of the aggregation method or the precise figure eventually attributed to a system. The new approaches to investment appraisal attempt to increase confidence in investment decisions by ensuring that scrutiny of investment proposals is structured and systematic, that assumptions underlying the analysis of the investment are made explicit and that the appraisal is conducted in the light of clearly identified and agreed business needs.

There is widespread agreement that different types of IT system may have different kinds of value for an organization and that different techniques are appropriate in the analysis of the differing values. The dimensions along which authors choose to classify systems vary widely but most classifications have at their core the notion of the degree of directness with which a system's benefits affect core business. Investment in systems which directly affect core business may be evaluated using simple or extended models of traditional cost–benefit analysis. Systems further removed from the actual achievement of bottom-line profits will require different techniques (e.g. various types of risk analysis, value chain analysis, information flow analysis etc.). It should be noted that while there appears to be agreement among authors on these basic issues there is little consistency in terminology, in the selection and organization of the evaluation criteria against which systems are scored, and in the techniques suggested for obtaining scores. Most authors are agreed, for example, that a thorough analysis of risk factors is an essential element of a complete appraisal; but each author will stipulate different categories of risk to be considered and introduce the weighting for risk into the scoring method in a different way.

The organization and structure provided by investment appraisal frameworks is very high level, with little in the way of detailed recommendations or support for the potentially complex analysis and information gathering which could underlie the process of obtaining a score for a specific evaluation criterion. Applying any of the approaches described in the literature would in practice require a considerable degree of refinement and adaptation to meet the specific requirements of the IT system which is being evaluated and the business context in which the evaluation is taking place. This refinement would involve:

1. Modification of high-level evaluation criteria according to the requirements of the organization which is performing the evaluation. For example, criteria relating to competitive advantage may not be relevant to public sector organizations.
2. Refinement of high-level evaluation criteria into finer grained hierarchies of evaluation criteria. In the Kobler Unit framework, for example, one of the top-level evaluation criteria is 'improved external business effectiveness'. One possible subcriterion of this would be 'enhanced customer base' which in turn could be refined to criteria such as 'improved economic profile of customers', 'increased size of customer base' and 'increased market share of some (high quality) product X'.

At this level it may be possible to identify metrics and associated information-gathering techniques for the refined evaluation criteria (e.g. surveys to establish the percentage of customers in socio-economic categories C2 and above etc.). As mentioned above, these criteria should preferably be previously identified critical success factors.

3. Identification, within the context of a particular business, of specific benefits, costs (direct and indirect), disbenefits and risks associated with individual IT systems or types of IT systems.

The modern approaches to IT investment appraisal advance evaluation criteria of a very general nature. The literature dealing with the subject area covered by an individual criterion may be extensive in its own right (e.g. IT and organizational change, social and political implications of IT, impact of IT on job functions etc.). It should be noted therefore that refinement of these criteria down to a useful level could require considerable effort and a high degree of familiarity with the specific subject area.

Computer-based support for IT investment appraisal

Research reported in the literature indicates a widely perceived need to develop and systematize investment appraisal for IT systems. In order to address the issue of intangible benefits, an effective framework for IT investment appraisal must include a broader set of evaluation criteria than those associated with traditional methods of cost–benefit analysis. Where possible, ROI calculations should inform the investment appraisal process but should not be given undue emphasis.

As we have seen, there are a number of approaches to IT investment appraisal which extend evaluation criteria in the required manner. However, the complex role played by IT in the operations of organizations and the relatively underdeveloped state of current work on investment appraisal means that it is not currently feasible to meet the objectives of this project by simple appropriation of a framework off the shelf. The framework proposed by the Kobler Unit is the most thorough and focused that we have so far encountered, and as such promises to make the most effective starting-point, but a considerable degree of adaptation and refinement of the suggested evaluation criteria will be necessary to achieve the coverage required for practical and convincing investment appraisal.

Below we describe a prototype computer-based tool which has been implemented to support IT investment decision-makers and those who formulate IT investment proposals.

Organizational issues

We concur with the findings of the ATT practitioners (Hogbin, 1984) that an organizational culture conducive to producing a cost–benefit analysis is vital if the process is to produce meaningful results. We give here some of the most important factors contributing to the successful implementation of an IT investment appraisal methodology. Without these, the IT investment appraisal methodology lacks the underlying processes for it to succeed:

1. **The right managers** – the monies to be spent, saved or acquired by various facets of a project should be estimated by authorized budget holders who have, or have access to, the necessary skills and information.
2. **Multiple perspectives** – cross-functional views of the problem and proposed solution must be obtained from all relevant units and levels of the organization.
3. **The frameworks** generally assume that a clear and agreed IT strategy and business strategy are in place.
4. **Agreed** methodologies for analysing, evaluating and estimating costs and benefits are vital.
5. **Management** understanding and commitment.

Software support for IT investment appraisal

It is believed that the implementation and adoption of a computer-based tool to support investment appraisal would bring many benefits, including:

- standardization of business cases;
- the ability to more easily compare competing proposals;
- consideration of a broader set of factors in the appraisal process;
- improved visibility of the structure of an organization's IT programme.

The major advantage of the Kobler Unit framework is that it is a practical and simple framework. It is easy to see how the framework could be applied in practice. A key requirement is perceived to be simplicity of use and this makes the Kobler Unit's use of checklists attractive.

However, the main criticism of the Kobler approach is that each of its four modules addresses issues at varying levels of detail. For example, module 1 has as investment factors 'Are there valuable business benefits?' and 'Is data backup planned for?', which should be considered at different stages in the project lifecycle. A second problem was Kobler's overcomplex classification of IT systems into nine categories.

The current proposal attempts to avoid these problems by considering a six-stage investment appraisal framework where relevant factors are considered at the relevant stage in the project lifecycle. Kobler's classification technique is replaced by the strategic grid (described above), which has already been used successfully in the area of project portfolio management. The six stages are:

1. strategic grid analysis;
2. project initiation;
3. feasibility study;
4. post-design;
5. post-implementation;
6. review.

Stage 1 places the proposed project in one quadrant of the strategic grid. This classification is determined on the basis of the user's answers to a checklist of questions about the proposed system. This project classification then influences the checklists provided at each of the following stages.

At stage 2, investment factors are considered at a relatively high level.

In stages 3 and 4, benefits, costs and risks are all considered. The data available at stage 4 will of course be more detailed than those at stage 3. Both of these stages have been implemented via a checklist in the Kobler style. Some of the items on the checklist are hard (e.g. NPV analysis, risk analysis) while others are softer (e.g. social implications, political implications). A project priority value is calculated at stages 3 and 4 using the method of module 4 of the Kobler approach.

Stage 5 involves a reappraisal of the project after the system has been implemented and rolled out. Detailed data concerning the system and its effect should now be available, allowing an accurate comparison between expected and actual costs and benefits. In addition, this stage may highlight some unforeseen types of cost or benefit which can then be used to improve the investment appraisal framework for future projects.

Stage 6 involves benefit management (Price Waterhouse, 1991): the measurement, realization and delivery of the benefits promised at the outset as a system is used. This is a non-trivial task in its own right and one we believe to be an essential complementary process to any form of investment appraisal.

A PC-based prototype system has been designed and implemented supporting stages 1 to 4 of the six-stage investment appraisal procedure defined above, using Microsoft's Visual Basic tool. The system generates a detailed analysis to support the business case and provides an aid to its production. This is based on the information supplied by the user, and provides advice on the strengths and weaknesses of the proposal.

Stage 1

Stage 1 places the proposed project in one quadrant of the strategic grid. It is implemented using a set of questions which the user answers by checking a box using the mouse-driven GUI provided by Visual Basic. On the basis of the answers, the system being appraised is classified into one of the four areas of the strategic grid. This classification then affects the following stages of the process (for instance, a strategic system places less importance on an NPV analysis than an operational system).

The information entered by the user provides the automatic production of a report to support the business case which the system performs at the end of the consultation with the user.

Stage 2

At stage 2, investment factors are considered at a relatively high level. Typical investment factors at this level might be:

- Has the project got a business sponsor?
- Are there valuable business benefits of the investment?
- Does the investment influence any business critical success factors?
- Have other similar projects (if any) been taken into account?

Stage 2 is again implemented as a checklist against which the user can assess the proposed system's match to the business objectives and critical success factors.

A set of business processes supporting the business model are exploited at this stage of the system. The business model is a description of the organization's operations and is the formal repository of its analysis of business activities. It models business activity in terms of processes and the information which is used in and flows between the processes. The high-level activities of the company are broken down in a functional decomposition, which shows how they are composed of their component processes.

The user is invited to identify those areas of the business model which the proposed IT application is intended to address. This ensures there is a good 'business match' between the application and the organization. Hypertext help is available to describe each aspect of the business model in more detail.

The system again uses the information provided by the user when preparing its highlight and detailed reports for use in the production of business cases.

Stages 3 and 4

In stages 3 and 4, benefits, costs and risks are all considered. The data available at stage 4 will of course be more detailed than those at stage 3. At the highest level there is an implementation of the Kobler Unit model, whose purpose is to structure the investment appraisal activity. Simple spreadsheet-type functionality supports the required aggregation of the weighted scores in the different activity modules. From this high-level checklist, access is provided to a suite of modules to support specific activities within the framework, as described below.

The first module available from the checklist provides support for traditional ROI modelling and calculations. This module enables proposed investments to be analysed quickly and easily in a user-friendly Windows-based PC environment. Results are available in tabular, graphical and printed formats. The program will provide discounted real price cash flows, net present value (NPV) and other financial information (internal rate of return, payback and so on) based on input provided by the user and taking into account corporation tax and depreciation of assets. Sensitivity analysis is also provided.

The program can function over any time period starting at any date. The user can set the test discount rate required and the corporation tax rate. RPI and inflation percentages are also set by the user for each year of the study. The following data categories for cash flows are available:

- income for the project;
- working or current expenditure; and
- expenditure on fixed assets.

These categories can be further broken down into subcomponents.

The system can display the following results in tabular format:

- real price cash flows;
- outturn price cash flows;
- net present value analysis, including a year-by-year discounted cash flow; and
- payback and IRR calculations.

It can also display graphically:

- cumulative and year-by-year graphs for all cash flow categories and their subcomponents;
- cumulative and year-by-year income; and

- sensitivity analysis graphs showing the sensitivity of NPV to changes in the test discount rate and the cash flow values.

The second module supports risk analysis. This part of the system is based on work by Ward (1992) in assessing and managing the risks of IT investments. A computer-based questionnaire to assess the relative risk of a particular IT system development is provided. The scoring in the risk analysis is weighted according to the strategic grid classification of the system being appraised. The results of the questionnaire are analysed and seven types of project risk are estimated:

- overall project risk;
- people issues;
- project size;
- project control;
- complexity;
- novelty;
- stability of requirements.

The results of the risk estimation are presented to the user of the system and a report detailing any particular areas of concern and explaining the nature of the risk in more detail is generated.

The third module in the current system is composed of a checklist of soft issues and intangible benefits which the user may wish to consider. The user can specify the weighting he wishes to attach to these issues and can score them.

A project priority value is calculated at stages 3 and 4 using the method of module 4 of the Kobler approach. The priority value gives a comparative measure of a project's benefit to the organization (as opposed to a hard monetary estimate) and takes into account both the scores and weights assigned to the soft issues and the results of the risk analysis and ROI calculations. Some of the weightings are adjusted internally by the system in order to take into account the type of system under consideration as identified by the strategic grid classification.

Business case guidance

The prototype system generates guidance for the preparation of a business case for the IT investment being proposed. This analysis can be used as an appendix to support and accompany the business case. The system instantiates various areas of a standard business case format. Among the main headings are:

- objectives;
- benefits;
- risks;
- financial analysis.

The system also generates a report to the user highlighting any areas of concern and in some instances recommending remedial action. The report mentions strong points and gives an overall assessment of the strength of the investment proposal under consideration.

Further software support for investment appraisal

It is proposed to widen the scope of the tool to include more novel techniques: in the longer term it is possible to envisage the implementation of more complex tools such as a standard model for value chain analysis and a tool to enable classification across different dimensions of IT investment proposals.

The software could act as a focus for internal standards governing investment appraisal and as a repository for knowledge gained from practical experience by providing a browsable library of templates containing the details of investment proposals for different types of IT system. These templates would contain descriptions of detailed factors, e.g. costs (direct and indirect), risks, disbenefits, benefits (tangible and intangible), metrics and techniques for the gathering and analysis of data considered in the course of previous appraisals of specific IT systems. The templates could then be used as a resource for refining the general model to meet the specific requirements of a new investment proposal. The library might initially be seeded with a number of representative cases and would then be incrementally developed through use of the tool.

Conclusion

Control of IT investment to ensure value for money is currently an issue of major concern to most businesses. Recognition of the potential impact of IT systems on the strategic position of companies and increasing levels of IT spend have made the control and justification of IT investment a critically important issue. At the same time there is widespread doubt concerning the suitability of traditional methods of investment appraisal for the evaluation of IT proposals. The major reason for this is the intangibility of many of the benefits to be gained by the deployment of IT systems.

Traditional methods for investment appraisal have been described and some consideration given to the problems associated with the application of these techniques to IT investments. Results of surveys describing current practice in IT investment appraisal were presented and recommendations made as to the most appropriate traditional techniques and how these can be modified to circumvent to some extent the problems of dealing with intangible benefits.

Other approaches to IT investment appraisal have been evaluated with a view to establishing the common concerns of the new approaches and identifying possible limitations to their practical use. This chapter proposes the incorporation of traditional IT investment techniques (modified to deal with the problem of intangible benefits) into a broader framework. The framework takes into account the wider benefits and issues involved in the deployment of IT systems.

A demonstrator system incorporating our proposed investment appraisal process has been developed. The system is a computer-based tool which facilitates the gathering and analysis of data and enables decisions on IT investments to be made. It generates highlight and detailed reports for users to assist in the preparation and production of business cases and forces them to consider wider issues than a simple cost–benefit trade-off, including strategic match, risks and intangible benefits. As such, it represents a considerable advance on traditional CBA techniques.

References

Brynjolfsson, E. (1992) *The Productivity of IT: Review and Assessment.* MIT Industrial Liaison Program Report CCS-TR-125.

Coleman, T. and Jamieson, M. (1994) Beyond return on investment. In *Information Management: Evaluation of Information Systems Investments* (ed. L. Willcocks), Chapman & Hall, London.

Earl, M.J. (1989) *Management Strategies for Information Technology,* Prentice-Hall, London.

Farbey, B., Land, F. and Targett, D. (1993) *How To Assess your IT Investment,* Butterworth Heinemann, London.

Griffiths, C. (1990) Justifying the costs of IT. *Update on Computer Audit, Control and Security,* **3** (2).

Hochstrasser, B. (1990) Evaluating IT investment: matching techniques to projects. *Journal of Information Technology,* **5** (4).

Hochstrasser, B. (1992) Justifying IT Investments, Proceedings of the Advanced Information Systems Conference, 17–19 March, London, UK.

Hochstrasser, B. and Griffiths, C. (1990) *Regaining Control of IT Investments,* Kobler Unit, Imperial College, London.

Hogbin, G. (1984) *The Decision to Invest.* IBM Internal Report, London.

Hogbin, G. (1994) *Investing in Information Technology,* McGraw Hill, London.

King, J.L. and Schrems, E.L. (1978) Cost benefit analysis in information systems development and operation. *Computer Surveys,* **10** (1).

Klammer, T.D. (1973) The association of capital budgeting techniques with firm performance. *Accounting Review,* April.

Lay, P.M.Q. (1985) Beware the cost/benefit model for IS project evaluation. *Journal of Systems Management,* **36** (6).

Lincoln, T. (1986) Do computer systems really pay off? *Information and Management,* **11** (1).

Lincoln, T. (1988) Retrospective appraisal of IT using SESAME. In *Information Systems Assessment: Issues and Challenges* (eds. N. Bjorn-Andersen and G. Davis), North-Holland, Amsterdam.

McFarlan, F.W. (1984) IT changes the way you compete. *Harvard Business Review,* May–June.

McGolpin, P. (1991) *Investment Management of IS Strategies.* Cranfield Institute of Technology, PhD Review Paper.

Mohanty, S.N. (1981) Software cost estimation: present and future. *Software: Practice and Experience,* **11**, 103–21.

Parker, M. and Benson, R. (1989) Enterprise-wide information economics: latest concepts. *Journal of Information Systems Management,* **6**.

Parker, M., Benson, R. and Trainor, H. (1988) *Information Economics: Linking Business Performance to Information Technology,* Prentice-Hall, London.

Parker, M., Benson, R. and Trainor, H. (1989) *Information Strategy and Economics,* Prentice-Hall, London.

Pike, R. (1983) A review of recent trends in formal capital budgeting processes. *Accounting and Business Research,* Summer.

Powell, P. (1992) Information technology evaluation: is it different? *Journal of Operational Research Society,* **43** (1).

Price Waterhouse (1991) *IT Review 1991/2,* Price Waterhouse, London.

Remenyi, D., Money, A. and Twite, A. (1993) *A Guide to Measuring and Managing IT Investments,* NCC Blackwell, Oxford.

Strassmann, P. (1985) *Information Payoff: The Transformation of Work in the Microelectronic Age,* The Free Press, New York.

Unicom (1992) *Evaluating and Managing the IT Investment.* Workshop 28–29 January 1992, Unicom Seminars, London.

Ward, J.W. (1988) Information systems and technology application portfolio management: an assessment of matrix-based approaches. *Journal of Information Technology,* **3** (3).

Ward, J.W. (1992) *Assessing and Managing the Risks of IT Investments.* Cranfield School of Management Report SWP 24/92, Cranfield.

Whiting, R.E., Davies N.J. and Knul, M. (1993) Investment appraisal for IT systems. *BT Technology Journal,* **11** (2).

Willcocks, L. (1989) Conference report: measuring the value of IT investments. *Journal of Information Technology,* **4** (4).

Willcocks, L. (1994) *Information Management: Evaluation of Information Systems Investments,* Chapman & Hall, London.

3

A transaction value analysis approach for evaluating the IS investment

Virginia Bryant and Chris Smart

Introduction

IS investments are made to acquire IS support for business activities. The key to evaluating and managing the IS investment is to determine the contribution IS makes to business performance. This contribution is widely considered to be substantial, yet unquantifiable. This problem is not new; many other business inputs have these characteristics. However, the pervasive nature of IS support to an organization's activities, and the relative size of the IS spend, both serve to keep the question over IS evaluation on the management agenda.

A recurring problem in managing the IS investment arises from the remoteness of the IS domain, in which the investment is being made, from the business domain, in which the benefit from the investment will be realized. An evaluation approach is needed which relates to the underlying business reason why the investment is made. Uncertainty regarding the value obtained from IS investments has often been cited as a major factor holding back further investments in IS (Hares and Royle, 1994; Price

Investing in Information Systems: Evaluation and Management. Edited by
Leslie Willcocks. Published in 1996 by Chapman & Hall. ISBN 0 412 72670 X.

Waterhouse, 1989). There are multiple perspectives on the contribution of IS to business (Symons, 1990), but an analysis approach is needed which will aid the reconciliation of the views across the two domains by building an organization-wide model using a consistent analysis schema.

Much attention has been directed at developing IS strategy (e.g. Earl, 1989), the integration of IS strategy and business strategy (McFarlan, McKenny and Pyburn, 1983; Ward, 1990), and to the identification of opportunities for competitive advantage through the use of IS (Porter and Miller, 1985). The benefits of such strategy studies are those of better understanding of the issues, rather than in terms of solutions. The usefulness of any approach, in terms of the value of the solutions it provides, requires prediction of the impact on the business of the proposed solution, followed by analysis of the actual outcome. Such IS impact predictions and analysis require some means of assessment.

Strategy considerations require analysis at the logical level, whereas evaluation of the impact of strategy decisions requires analysis of the actual IS support provided to actual business activities. Instantiations are only possible at the physical level. Figure 3.1 shows the interface between the two domains of interest, viewed from Anthony's (1965) managerial-focus-type hierarchy, and logical and physical levels.

There is a gap between the high-level strategic view at which policy questions can be addressed, and the lower operational level at which the transactions in the two domains interact and can be analysed. Analysis at both levels is useful, and will lead to better understanding of the complex relationship, which can be characterized as shown in Figure 3.2.

The transaction value model proposed here provides analysis of the interface between the domains at the level of the IS support provided for business transactions, i.e. by alignment of IS with business requirements. Analysis of the business opportunities created by IS is more difficult because of the potential for novelty involved

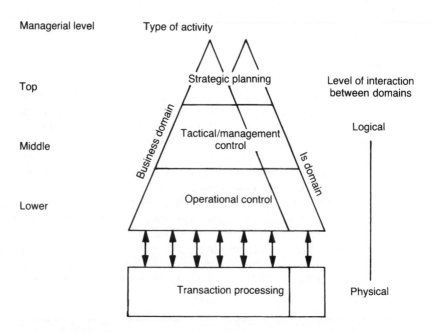

Figure 3.1 View of the IS domain and business domain showing interactions.

Business domain   Technology domain

Proposed change here   ---->   Expected impact/implications here
                                      Alignment
                                      and

Expected impact/implications here   <----   Proposed change here
                                      Opportunity

Figure 3.2 Dual-relationship model.

and will not be considered here, although enhancement of the model to analyse the opportunity aspect of the relationship is also envisaged. The opportunity relationship between the two domains requires analysis of alternative instantiations of all possible relationships determined from the logical view with an open boundary.

The importance of information, and hence information systems, is explicitly recognized in adding value to activities and optimizing the links between them (Porter and Miller, 1985). By analysing the support provided by IS to the business at a transaction level it is possible to evaluate the contribution made by IS to business activities. A transaction value approach requires analysis at a detailed level where transactions have identifiable inputs and outputs. The approach outlined here demonstrates an allocation to the IS transactions of part of the value created by the business products they support.

The transaction value analysis proposed here is derived from models using activities, their contribution to the product cost and their relationships. The basic accounting ideas of cost allocation based on cost behaviour, contribution and value-added are used in developing this transaction value model. The model is described and illustrated here by the use of a simple business product supported by a simple IS product and the business transaction that links them across the domain interface.

The use of transaction value analysis in meeting control and decision support objectives for the evaluation of investments in IS is also outlined later in this chapter.

Model and analysis requirements

A model is required which links information system domain concepts with some commonly accepted concepts of activity in the business domain. Predictions are required about the impact in one of these domains of changes in the other. To do this, we need to identify a suitable organization-wide representation, a single common framework representative of the main goals and constraints in each area, and of the relationships between the areas.

Figure 3.3 models the relationship between the business domain and the IS domain. The interface between them is considered to be at the physical level of abstraction, since we are interested here in the actual support for real-world business activities provided by the actual IS implementation, rather than their logical counterparts. Physical activities have duration, costs and constraints capable of analysis by reference to their instantiation. Logical activities are less useful in this since they state 'what' rather than 'how', and are capable of many different instantiations.

The modelling terms adopted here are for illustrative purposes. They are not meant to represent any other extant modelling schema.

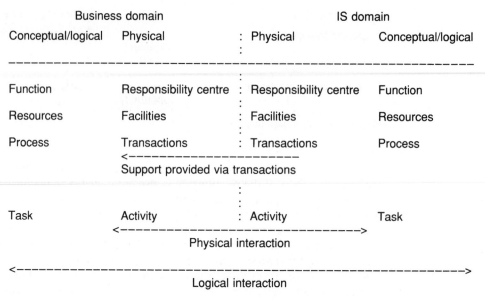

Figure 3.3 Two-domain model showing support relationship in the form of transactions at the physical level.

The characterization of the two domains in Figure 3.3 shows how they are linked by IS transactions which provide support for business activities. Activities are the prime unit of effort in producing valuable output. Activities have resource inputs, which in turn have direct costs. Indirect costs may be allocated to activities by reference to their demand on resource inputs. Activities together comprise transactions which create value for the business, but activities themselves have only a potential, not an actual value. Actual value is created by assembling a chain of activities which deliver a product to an external entity. From the business domain, these external entities are customers: from the IS domain the external entity is the business domain.

Goodhue (1986) stated that 'systems and functionality have no value in themselves, but only in relation to the tasks'. The same can also be said for business domain tasks. It is only by reference to exchanges with external entities that transactions create value from the activities which comprise them. Such an approach, using financial analysis of IS impacts in the business domain, implies a focus on the organizational context for IS, rather than the narrow technical view so often criticized.

For control and decision support purposes, analysis in terms of cost and value is needed. An analysis of the activities in the two domains and the simple alignment relationship between them can provide this if some common metric is applied.

Such a formalization at the activity and transaction level capable of quantification, provides a platform for reasoning about the relationship between the IS domain which supplies IS products and the business domain in which these IS products are used as part of the business transaction that creates value. Analysis can be developed from this for IS process control and costing, for evaluating proposed IS investments, and similar IS management tasks.

Transaction value models can provide a quantitative link between the business domain and information system domain, permitting 'what is' and 'what if' analysis.

While the transaction analysis is illustrated here by the use of financial measures, the formalization of the two domains at an activity and transaction level would support analysis in other terms which are common to the components, e.g. time, volume and other business performance metrics.

Theoretical foundations and developments

This section outlines and discusses other approaches to IS evaluation and their contribution to, or relationship with, the transaction value analysis model described in the next section.

The main theories that have been applied to IS evaluation are those underlying cost–benefit analysis, value chain analysis, value-added analysis and business performance metrics.

Cost–benefit analysis

Investment appraisal techniques can be used to analyse IS impacts in terms of costs and savings over the lifespan of the system, as discounted cash flows. This narrow view of the impact of an IS proposal can be extended to include statements about the intangibles and other factors which are difficult or impossible to quantify. Consideration of riskiness and sensitivity analysis can also be included (ICAEW, 1988). See also Chapter 2.

Value chain analysis

In the analysis of business activities Porter (1985) suggests using the economic idea of 'value'. Organizations are conceptualized as a collection of value chains each serving a different line of business. There are exchanges with external agents at each end of the chain, crystallizing the 'value' at those points. In this there is an assumption, which we do not propose to consider further here, that market price equals value.

Figure 3.4 shows how certainty about value exists only at the beginning and end of any chain of activities when an exchange with an external entity occurs. At interim

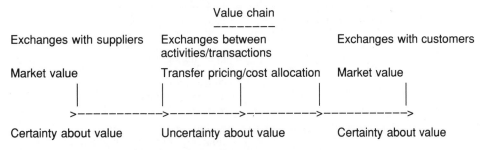

Figure 3.4 An alternative value chain model.

stages of production, products move from a previous production activity to the next without any certainty about the value of the output from one production activity, which in turn becomes the value (or cost) of the input to the next. Ultimately all costs arise from bought-in goods and services, but few costs are directly related to a product. Allocations of the indirect costs to the products allow the amount of profit earned by the product to be determined. Transfer pricing is necessary if that profit is to be allocated to the separate inputs to the production process.

Within the value chain a focus on the activities and the linkages enables analysis of both the business activity and the supporting infrastructure. This is proposed for identifying competitive strategies and for evaluating the application of technology (of all types) to the business activities. However, Porter (1985) does not attempt quantification.

Porter's (1985) value chain consists of two types of activities, as shown in Table 3.1. In order to evaluate the contribution of IS support to the business transactions, further decomposition of these activities is needed to provide a granularity at which mapping is possible between the transactions in the two domains.

Transactions in the transaction value model could be related to the activities at the level described by Porter's (1985) value chain to provide analysis at the strategic level.

An application of the value chain approach is demonstrated for information technology project evaluation by Parker and Benson (1989). The expected impact of an IT project in terms of its benefits is evaluated using a formal quantification and assessment technique. The quantification extends traditional cost–benefit analysis by including consideration of the IS proposal's impact in terms of changes to access to information (linking), the timing of cash flows (acceleration), workload modelling (restructuring) and the extra revenue and costs from innovation. Quantification of this extended impact is by discounted cash flow analysis. To bring in all the intangible factors, management consensus is sought on the proposal's characteristics (e.g. its riskiness) and its impact on the business. The need for a single measure of a project's worth for ranking purposes implies converting all the method's output to scores under various headings and then weighting them. This weighted score-based assessment results in relative values rather than absolute values, and confines its usefulness to project ranking.

The emphasis on activities in value chain analysis has been developed into activity-based costing by Kaplan (1988) and Cooper (1990). Conventionally, indirect costs are charged to output (i.e. products) using a measure of input volume as the absorption basis. Labour time and machine time are commonly used for this. This volume-based approach has been criticized for its limitations in reflecting the relationship between

Table 3.1 Porter's value chain activities

Direct (primary) activities	Those activities which acquire, create, market and deliver the product
	Inbound logistics
	Operations
	Outbound logistics
	Marketing and sales
	Service
Support (overhead) activities	Enterprise infrastructure
	Human resource management
	Technology development
	Procurement

the activities which create costs and the products produced by these activities, resulting in the under-costing of complex products and the over-costing of simple products. The use of activity-based costing which does reflect the direct relationship between activities and products provides a better basis for the allocation of indirect costs to units of production (Innes and Mitchell, 1990).

Value-added analysis

As used in the accounting context, value-added is the difference between an organization's revenue from products sold and the cost of bought in goods and services incorporated into the products sold. Generally, the amount of value-added tax (VAT) payable by a business is calculated by reference to this. For value-added analysis, the value-added figure is divided to show how it was applied to the various groups and interests with the business. The usual categories are to employees (wages and pensions), to the providers of capital (loan interest and dividends), to the government (tax), and for the maintenance and replacement of fixed assets (depreciation and retained profits). Some company annual reports contain an analysis of value-added along these lines as an alternative way of viewing the profit and loss account information.

A form of value-added analysis is suggested by Strassmann (1990) as the basis for calculating a return on management metric. This requires deducting taxes and dividends from the value-added figure described above, then dividing the remaining figure (amounts paid to employees, interest and depreciation) between operations costs and management costs.

The return on management metric is the retained profit (management value-added) divided by the management costs. Strassmann claims that 'measuring managerial productivity is the key to knowing how to invest in information technologies' and that RoM is a measurement of management productivity. By analysing the profit and loss accounts of almost 300 companies, Strassmann was able to develop characterizations of 'under-achievers, below average, average, above average, and over-achievers' in RoM terms, by their relative spending on IT between operations and management, and their percentage IT spend to business value-added. This approach is based on an organization-wide, large-grain resolution, and it does not currently provide any empirical evidence of the value of the analysis at lower levels of aggregate. Theoretically the business value of IT could be determined by calculating this metric both with and without the IT investment and its effects.

Strassmann (1989) stated that 'the value of today's information technology investments is the risk-adjusted present cash value of committed future productivity gains'. Analysis of the transaction value model could be used to identify such 'future productivity gains' and their implications in cash flow terms. This approach is described in the section on exploiting the transaction value model.

Business performance metrics

Rockart (1979) describes the 'critical success factor' approach to help executives to define their significant information needs. This is based on identifying, from the business goals, the metrics that are needed to track performance. Peters in Chapter 10 describes a cost–benefit hierarchy which quantifies the impact of a proposed IS project in terms of changes in key business performance variables, the financial benefit derived from these changes, and the effect on profit. This idea of linking changes in physical performance variables (e.g. 50% increase in the numbers of suppliers' invoices processed per person day, results in staff cost saving of £0.5 million per year), is not new, but the fact that it is still being regarded as valuable is significant, and suggests that methods for quantified evaluation are still relevant, despite the changing nature of the relationship between IS and the business.

Many current evaluation techniques are converging on activity analysis via performance indicators and the measurement of operating variables.

What can cost behaviour models add to IS evaluation?

Useful descriptive and analytic business models which have a practical utility in managing business organizations often use responsibility, resource inputs and product output as their main constructs. The revenue/cost behaviour relationship is modelled by organizations to determine product costs. Financial responsibility (e.g. cost, budget, profit, investment) centres are widely used for management planning and control purposes (Bhaskar and Housden, 1985). 'What if' analysis based on these budgetary control and costing models is often used in decision support. The adoption of the concepts of revenue, cost, contribution and volume for a transaction value model will permit analysis in terms already used widely.

Marginal costing and contribution

The relationship between costs, contribution and value is shown in Figure 3.5.

1. **Contribution** – the difference between output value (revenue) and direct costs.
2. **Cost (direct)** – costs which vary directly with production volume.
3. **Cost (indirect)** – costs which do not vary directly with production volume.
4. **Cost (total)** – direct plus indirect costs.
5. **Product** – output, in the form of goods or services provided to an entity external to the business.
6. **Profit** – the difference between revenue and total cost.

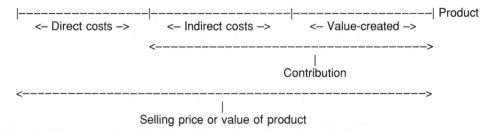

Figure 3.5 Model of costs, contribution and value.

7. **Value-created** – the difference between the total costs and the selling price of the product.

The objective of costing is to determine the true cost of producing the product, given that the total cost of producing all products must be equal to the total costs of the enterprise. Products will differ in terms of the activities and resources required to produce them.

To determine the cost of any particular product it is necessary to identify and cost its production characteristics. Costing involves identifying the costs which apply to a particular product by examining its inputs. The cost of some inputs change directly with changes in the volume of outputs produced, e.g. paper costs would increase with the number of pages of report produced, while other input costs do not vary directly with product volume, e.g. accommodation costs.

Conventionally, the relationship between costs and production volumes, i.e. cost behaviour, has been used to divide costs into direct and indirect costs. Direct costs are directly attributable to a unit of output. If a unit is produced the costs are incurred; if that unit were not produced then the cost would not be incurred. Direct costs are also called variable costs since they vary with the volume of output.

Indirect costs are sometimes called fixed costs, because they do not vary directly with product volume (and sometimes do not vary at all). Sometimes they are called overheads or burden.

For product costing purposes, all direct costs are identified and aggregated; then an amount is added to represent the product's share of the indirect costs. Where there is no direct cost, the total cost is the share of indirect costs based on absorption. As the proportion of direct cost decreases, the focus on indirect cost absorption increases.

The value-created as identified in Figure 3.5 differs from value-added. Value-added is the difference between the revenue and the bought-in inputs. Value-added, as widely understood, includes the amounts paid to employees, the providers of capital and taxes. For the purpose of value-created these internal costs are deducted. Value-created is only the surplus after all costs, both internal and external, have been deducted from revenue.

Since the true amount of indirect costs used up by producing the product cannot be measured, a share of the indirect costs is 'absorbed' by the product according to an 'absorption rate' based on the amount of other measurable inputs to the product. This many be volume- or activity-based, but the more complex the product is to produce the greater the costs incurred in producing it. It is product complexity that determines cost, rather than the volume of physical inputs required to produce it. This can be reflected by using activity-based costing for determining indirect cost allocation.

While total costs are necessary for product pricing, for planning and decision-making purposes the direct costs are compared with the potential income to determine the contribution made by a product to the indirect costs and profits. This marginal costing approach is accepted as useful for decision-making because it uses only directly attributable costs in product costing, and does not add amounts by allocation which may not represent true costs.

Proposal for a transaction value model

The decomposition of organizational functions into transactions as sequences of activities provides the basis for analysis of the impact of IS support on the business. The contribution of the IS support to the business domain transaction can be determined by reference to the value created by the business transaction. The value created by the IS transaction can be determined by taking a proportion of that value. The proportion can be determined by reference to the characteristics of the inputs and activities comprising the related transactions, in the same way that indirect costs are allocated to production. For IS decision-making, the value of IS support can be determined by considering the cost and value of the business domain transaction with, and without, IS support.

Proposed modelling schema

The simplified characterization of the main components of the two domains in Figure 3.6 shows how it is the transactions which produce products rather than resources or production facilities *per se*. In this model, a responsibility centre is a physical group of facilities for which an identified human is responsible, and facilities are constrained resources. Transactions comprise a chain of activities which deliver the product to an external entity. A product is identified by the chain of activities (the transaction) which produce it, and the cost of the product is the sum of the cost of those activities. Super-products are possible, as aggregations of one or more products, presented together as a single product to a customer.

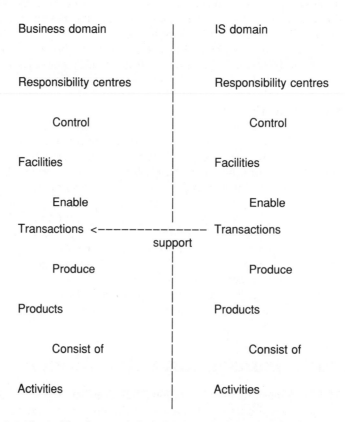

Figure 3.6 Physical level expanded model showing relationships.

The model considers IS products as the output from an IS transaction which supports a business transaction. Where the IS product is exchanged with an entity (customer) external to the business, this will occur through the business domain interface with the outside world.

Two domains related by transactions

For the purpose of illustration the simple model in Figure 3.7 shows how the concepts of cost, contribution and value can be related to the transactions in the two domains. The interface between the domains is described by the relationship between the

Transaction 1 (Respond To Simple Customer Query)
- - - - - - - - -

	Activity 3	Activity 2	Activity 3
	Trivial Conversation with Customer	Make Simple Enquiry of IS	Trivial Conversation with Customer
Inputs	F1	F1 P2 WIP1	F1 WIP2
Outputs	WIP1	WIP2	P1

Facility 1 (F1) is small amount of clerical time (e.g. <2 mins) in × environment during period y.

Work-in-Progress (WIP) 1 is customer enquiry with type determined.
2 is WIP1 + IS process

Product 1 (P1) is a response to a simple customer query.

Transaction 2
- - - - - - - - -

	Activity 1	Activity 4	Activity 1
	Receive/Send Record Data	Access Record	Receive/Send Record Data
Inputs	F2	WIP5 F3 F4	F2 WIP6
Outputs	WIP5	WIP6	P2

Facility (F2) – Data Comms
(F3) – Storage
(F4) – Processing

WIP5 – Message received and stored
WIP6 – WIP5 + Response Identified

P2 – Provide Access to Customer Record

(Inputs are described here in terms of the physical resources required to carry out the activity, not the data flows.)

Figure 3.7 Showing transactions as production processes

business transactions and the IS transactions, i.e. here transaction 2 produces P2 which is an input to activity 2 in P1. Only one business transaction and one IS transaction are shown for simplification. It is possible to have business transactions which require a number of supporting IS transactions. In reality the number and nature of these relationships makes the modelling a complex task. Work-in-progress, as passed from one stage of the production process to the next, is also defined.

Value created by delivering one unit of product to customer

If we consider the inputs and outputs shown in Figure 3.8, we can identify direct cost of inputs, allocate indirect costs on a transaction basis, and identify the surplus of revenue as value-created. The value-created has been determined by deducting the costs from the price, or total value of the product. Value-created can have a negative value, but we would expect this to be balanced against a positive value created for some other product which is dependent on the loss making product for part of its value. Further analysis of this may suggest the aggregation of transactions into a line-of-business (Porter, 1985) grouping to reflect this.

Splitting the value-created between the business activities and the IS support

Figure 3.9 shows how much of the value-created, as identified in Figure 3.8, is attributable to the IS transaction. Here we are faced with the same problems as those which characterize the allocation of indirect costs to products. The relationship between transaction and value-created is not discernible, but some other existing relationship can be used in substitution. In this example we could allocate the value created by product 1 between the business domain transaction and the IS domain transaction the basis of the proportion of each transaction's cost to the total costs. Theoretically this is no better or worse that the indirect cost allocations that occur everywhere in costing; what will make it acceptable or not in practice is the degree to which the allocation is deemed to represent the true but overcomplex relationship.

Direct Costs £	Indirect costs £	Value-created £	Product 1 Price £
F1 0.25			
F2	0.20		
F3	0.15	0.25	1
F4	0.15		

Figure 3.8 Determining the cost and value created by product 1. Indirect costs are allocated to products for the purpose of costing. In order to reflect the relationship between the product and the activities which create it, activity-based costing can be used. The origin of the figures shown here is not given.

Direct costs £	Indirect costs £	Value-created £	Product 1 Price £
F1 0.25		0.08 ?	1

Direct costs £	Indirect costs £	Value-created £	Product 2 value £
F2	0.20		
F3	0.15	0.17 ?	0.67 ?
F4	0.15		

Figure 3.9 Determining the cost and value created by product 2.

The basis for the indirect costs absorption rate chosen is important where a significant proportion of the total costs are indirect costs, since the absorption basis chosen has a greater influence on the total product cost. The absorption basis chosen should reflect the relationship between the product and the indirect costs.

In conventional volume-based absorption the indirect costs would be allocated according to the volume of some resource input or a combination of inputs, ignoring the other factors such as complexity, frequency or timing. Activity-based costing gives a cost figure for each of the products which appears to reflect the characteristics of the production process more closely than volume-based absorption costing. It is proposed to use an activity-based costing approach to the allocation of indirect costs to the activities, and thus to the transactions.

Allocations, activity-based costing and the need for predictions of volume

Activity-based costing has been suggested as a better way of identifying the links between costs and products because it considers the activities that produce the product, as a basis for product costing. Activity-based costing requires the identification of activity-based cost pools and activity cost-driver-based rates.

Choosing activity-based cost pools

Cost pools are chosen by identifying the major activities which cause indirect costs. Each functional area will be examined to identify the activities that comprise it. This can be done by finding out how all the staff employed in that area spend their time. An activity list will be developed for each function. The labour costs of each activity can be derived from the staff worktime analysis, while managerial estimates can be obtained of how equipment is utilized and how other items are consumed.

The list of activities should be obtained by direct consultation with the departmental manager concerned, who should be encouraged to select the activities for listing. A useful approach is to question the manager on the purpose of each member of staff.

When the worktime of all staff is accounted for, the activity listing will be reasonably comprehensive. In fact there may be too many activities to include. The significance of the cost of each activity listed (to determine whether it warrants its own cost pool), and the possibility of combining costs which have common driver/behaviour types, will be looked at to judge whether rationalization is possible.

The categories chosen in practice should be consistent with categories used for capacity management, service-level management and internal reporting purposes, as far as is possible.

Identifying cost drivers

The cost drivers for each activity are best obtained by the managers and staff directly involved in the activity. Innes and Mitchell (1990) suggest that if identification of cost drivers is difficult, questions such as those given below be used to prompt an assessment of the reasons for committing resources to an activity:

1. Why do you need more than one person on this activity?
2. Under what circumstances would more staff be required on this activity?
3. Under what circumstances could staffing be reduced on this activity?
4. Why is overtime worked on this activity?
5. Why does idle time occur on this activity?

From the above investigation in should be possible to develop an activity cost pool analysis for each function.

Which cost drivers?

A selection of cost drivers has to be made from the candidate cost drivers listed. The choice is guided by the need to obtain a balance between the accuracy and the costs of complexity. (The costs and difficulties of operating a more complex system.) The significance of the various costs identified, and their proportions, related to the candidate cost drivers, will be examined.

To complete the design of the activity-based costing system, data need to be collected on periodic volumes of the chosen cost driver, to determine how this total cost driver volume should be split between the product's inputs.

Limitations inherent in model

The transaction volume approach has utility in a number of areas, and the models built using it can be developed in a number of ways. However, it is subject to all the general limitations inherent in using representations of the real world for predictions and analysis. In addition there are some specific points to consider when using this type of representation:

1. The relative instability of the model over the longer term and for large changes in output volume. Periodic reviews of the cost drivers and their relationship to the activities that make up transaction will be required.
2. A cost driver may not provide a comprehensive basis for controlling the related cost. (There are many other factors to be considered here.)
3. Transaction-based analysis will not solve all the problems associated with the provision of analysis information to management.
4. Actual costs and values are generally historic and tell us more about the past than about the future. Decision-making requires predictions of future costs. However, historic costs, particularly more realistic analyses of historic costs, can provide an important basis for predictions.
5. There is the danger of considering only what is easy to measure, rather than what is important, however, since 'few would disagree that the business case [for investments in IS] should be a sharp and quantified as possible' (Silk, 1990) the quest for useful measures will continue.

How this approach could be used for evaluating and managing IS investments

Models which analyse the business and the IS support at the transaction level provide quantitative and qualitative analysis of how discrete activities can create value for the business. This is useful for management of all activities, but here we will focus on the analysis that will be useful for evaluating and managing IS investment. By exploring the relationship between the products and the transactions in the two domains, the factors that determine the value of IS to the business can be identified and used for evaluating and managing the IS investment.

The semantics of the transaction value model proposed here show considerable conceptual convergence with information system modelling concepts, allowing integration with information system models (e.g. the activity analysis approach proposed by Rock-Evans, 1989) to permit reasoning about business activity and IS support for those activities. Models for decomposing functional requirements into transactions and activities can be adopted from systems analysis methodologies such as MERISE and SSADM.

Conventional evaluation techniques have been criticized for not reflecting the impact of IS on the business adequately. The range of factors and the difficulty in identifying or measuring them is widely recognized by managers as well as by management accountants. Transaction value based analysis providers 'what is' and 'what if' analysis to meet control and decision support requirements.

Justification of IS investments

Proposed investments in IS can be evaluated by reference to the changes in facilities they provide, and their effect on costs. Transaction value analysis can provide information about the likely impact of a proposed information system change. Impact analysis can be in terms of the changes to the sequence and type of activity a transaction comprises in both domains. These changes can be quantified in terms of cost and value-created.

Proposed IS investments can be evaluated by comparing the present value of the change in future cash flows arising from the impact of the change in IS acquired by the investment, with the cost of that investment. Transaction value analysis will provide data about the changes in activity cost and in the value created by the transactions. These can then be evaluated as discounted cash flows by considering their volumes and timing.

It is also possible to carry out 'what if' analyses of trade-offs between the cost of IS resource increases on the one hand and value gains on the other, for example through a reduction in transaction costs or quicker product delivery times.

The impact in terms of value created by predicted changes in other performance metrics, e.g. number of products, stock lines, staff, suppliers or customers, could also be evaluated based on analysis of the proposed transaction value model.

The availability of cost driver rates has an impact on the design of new products and can result in modifications to the design of existing products in both domains. The nature, cost and impacts in the IS domain of the IS support required for a proposed new business product can also be determined from the transaction value model.

Costing and pricing IS services

Virtually all IS production costs are relatively fixed in the short term and much of the cost of providing IS services is not directly related to the volume of service supplied, so some method of allocating the total cost to the various services provided is needed. In costing for IS accounting purposes, it is therefore necessary to use some method of indirect cost absorption. The basis used for charging indirect costs to output will be important where there is a high proportion of indirect costs relative to the amount of direct costs, as in the case of IS services. The activity-based costing approach outlined above can be used to represent the underlying relationships here.

The total cost of providing information services is substantial in most organizations, and attempts are often made to recharge these costs to the users of the IS outputs. The rationale and bases for recharging IS users have been discussed elsewhere (e.g. Price Waterhouse, 1989; Sen, 1988). Here we will examine the question of how a transaction value based approach can be used in determining IS transaction prices.

There are calls for IS costs to be expressed for business units; by aligning the IS activities more closely with the business activities it is possible to provide good operational decision support information. The cost of using a data centre service can be viewed in relation to the value to the business of using that service. The price of the IS transaction can be determined from determining the value created by the business transaction of which it forms part, and taking a proportion of that value-created as attributable to the input of the IS transaction.

From an organizational viewpoint all IS costs are likely to be regarded as indirect (unless the organization is developing information systems for, or selling DP products to, external customers). However, within the IS function some identification of cost classes is often used. e.g. staff, accommodation, equipment (processing, storage and communications), overheads etc. This is not inconsistent; it just represents a view of the costs from a different perspective.

Management control

Transaction value based analysis can be used to determine the extent of slack IS resources, to make predictions about workload modelling useful for capacity planning and service-level management. Transaction timing dependencies between the two domains could be analysed for disaster planning purposes. By evaluating IS activities in terms of their contribution to business transactions and value-created, opportunities for eliminating redundant activities and for combining similar activities may be identified. The IS transaction's internal price (total cost plus an allocation of value-created) can be compared with the cost of outsourcing. The model will support analysis over time to highlight where cost changes are occurring.

Budgetary control

Many budgetary control models use a simple direct/indirect cost classification and responsibility centres as their basis. For control purposes, the responsibility centres are used for the aggregation, and then allocation, of indirect costs to units of production based on predicted volume of output. Differences (variances) are analysed to provide information for management control. General management support of the budgetary control type can be provided by incorporating actual versus budget comparisons for all costs, volumes etc. into the model.

The relationship between product volume and cost behaviour will be modelled allowing identification of how costs change with changes in activity/production volume. The knowledge of cost behaviour for cost driver analysis can be useful in setting and flexing budgets (Innes and Mitchell, 1988).

Conclusion

A transaction value approach can provide analysis of the contribution to the business of IS for evaluating and managing the investment in IS. Activities, dependencies, costs and value-created, volumes and resource usage will need to be modelled to permit this. To provide the useful answers, the business and IS domains will need to be modelled at a simple activity level, with complex relationships and dependencies indicated by sets of typed links. Aggregation of the simple activities into transactions and other types of extraction from the model will be required. The resulting model is likely to be complex and will need to be provided with extensive interaction support, if it is to be useful for IS management.

In choosing the IS/business two-domain model, formalizing the interface in terms of transactions and attempting to split the value-created between the two domains, there is a danger that this approach will be viewed as driving the two domains apart, rather than encouraging integration. Existing problems in this respect may be exacerbated by a third group, the accountants, bringing their own culture and concepts to the analysis of the interface between the two domains. The objective is to develop organizational consensus on the contribution of IS to business activities, not to drive the domains apart by traditional transfer pricing arguments about where the value was created. We believe that fostering greater understanding of the relationship and the dependencies between the two domains will lead to improved exploitation of IS in the service of the business.

References

Anthony, R. (1965) *Planning and Control Systems: A Framework for Analysis*, Harvard University Press, Cambridge, MA.

Bhaskar, K. and Housden, R. (1985) *Accounting Information Systems and Data Processing*. Institute of Cost and Management Accountants, London.

Cooper, R. (1990) ABC: a need, not an option. *Accountancy*, September.

Drury, C. (1990) Product costing in the 1990s. *Accountancy*, May.

Earl, M. (1989) *Management Strategies For Information Technology*. Prentice-Hall, London.

Goodhue, D. (1986) IS attitudes: toward theoretical and definition clarity. In: *Proceedings of the Seventh International Conference on Information Systems*, San Diego, California, p. 191.

Hares, J. and Royle, D. (1994) *Measuring the Value of Information Technology*, John Wiley, Chichester.

ICAEW (1988) IT Statement 4: Cost Benefit Analysis for IT Projects, Institute of Chartered Accountants in England and Wales.

Innes, J. and Mitchell, F. (1990) *Activity-Based Costing: A Review with Case Studies*, CIMA, London.

Johnson, D. and Kaplan, R. (1987) The importance of long term product costs. *The McKinsey Quarterly*, Autumn.

Kaplan, R. (1988) One cost system is not enough. *Harvard Business Review*, January/February, 61–6.

McFarlan, W., McKenny, J. and Pyburn, N. (1983) *The Information Archipelago: Plotting a Course*, Harvard Business School. January–February.

Parker, M. and Benson, R. (1989) Enterprise-wide information economics: latest concepts. *Journal of Information Systems Management*, 6.

Peters, G. (1990) Beyond strategy: benefits identification and management of specific IT investments. *Journal of Information Technology*, **5** (4), 205–14.

Porter, M. (1985) *Competitive Advantage*, Free Press, New York.

Porter, M. and Miller, V. (1985) How information gives you competitive advantage. *Harvard Business Review*, July/August.

Price Waterhouse (1989) *Information Technology Review 1989/90*, Price Waterhouse, London.

Price Waterhouse (1990) *Information Technology Review 1990/91*, Price Waterhouse, London.

Rockart, J. (1979) Chief executives define their own data needs. *Harvard Business Review*, March–April.

Rock-Evans, R. (1989) A simple introduction to data and activity analysis, *Computer Weekly*, London.

Sen, D. (1988) DP accounting: a business within a business. *Accountancy*, Summer.

Silk, D. (1990) Managing IS benefits for the 1990s. *Journal of Information Technology*, **5**, 185–93.

Strassmann, P. (1989) *The Business Value of Computers*, Computer Weekly Seminar Notes, *Computer Weekly*, London.

Strassmann, P. (1990) *The Business Value of Computers*, The Information Economics Press, New Canaan.

Symons, V. (1990) Evaluation of information systems: IS development in the processing company. *Journal of Information Technology*, **5** (4), 194–204.

Ward, J. (1990) A portfolio approach to evaluating information system investments and setting priorities. *Journal of Information Technology*, **5** (4), 222–31.

Part Two

Development: software and projects

4

Software make or buy practices: towards a decision-making framework

Tony Rands and Phumchai Kambhato

Introduction

Despite growth of the applications software sector into an international industry, relatively little research has been undertaken into software make or buy decisions. Although several studies have considered different aspects of software packages, such as problems with their use (Gross and Ginzberg, 1984), surprisingly few papers on software make or buy have appeared in major journals during the last ten years. These papers were reviewed by Rands (1993), and a number of gaps in their collective approach identified. For instance, researchers have tended to concentrate on software make or buy for individual IT projects, rather than develop make or buy strategy models which allow the planning of internal software development resources. Rands argued that the lack of strategic software make or buy models could seriously affect the ability of firms to achieve IT strategies.

Rands also pointed to a lack of primary data on software make or buy practices in firms. For instance, although Lees and Lees (1987) had found that 59% of 400 small

Investing in Information Systems: Evaluation and Management. Edited by
Leslie Willcocks. Published in 1996 by Chapman & Hall. ISBN 0 412 72670 X.

firms used industry-specific software packages, while DeLone (1988) reported that 55 out of 93 small firms were totally dependent on external software, neither paper shed light on the make or buy procedures used in those firms. Hence these papers provided little insight into how the observed patterns of software purchase were derived. Such absence of primary data on software make or buy contrasts with other goods and services. Here surveys have revealed that managers, by and large, take such decisions on a day-to-day basis (Dale and Cunningham, 1983; Ford and Farmer, 1986). This is despite the availability of models, e.g. Harrigan (1984), Walker (1988), which may assist managers to analyse strategic aspects of make or buy.

This chapter seeks to fill some of these gaps in our knowledge. It describes a survey into practices in the UK food and drinks industry. Although the conclusions drawn apply primarily to that sector, they may provide an indication of make or buy practices in other industries. From the research and a review of past models we then develop a framework for software make or buy decision-making. This chapter only focuses on software development issues; the later chapter on IT outsourcing adds to the analysis of make or buy decisions by extending the scope to all IT assets and services, and focuses on the conditions under which the market can be used effectively across the systems lifecycle (see Chapter 16).

The research approach

Given the absence of research into software make or buy practices, with the consequent lack of data, there were no immediate precedents for the survey. Accordingly, we turned to research into other goods and services. In particular, a survey by Ford and Farmer (1986) was felt to provide a useful framework. From their survey, Ford and Farmer drew a number of conclusions. One was that different approaches could be discerned:

1. **Operational approach** – make or buy decisions are taken individually, usually on the basis of cost or operational advantage. A decision to make therefore may be succeeded by a buy decision on the next occasion. However, repeat decisions can be, and frequently are, made.
2. **Business approach** – decisions are based around broad factors, and commit firms one way or the other for a period until conditions change, when the decisions are reviewed. The factors assessed usually relate to long-term business needs, such as concentrating capital investment in key areas.
3. **Policy approach** – this also commits firms for the long term. Make or buy decisions are usually based on a desire to focus internal production only on the core part of a firm's business, purchasing peripheral activities.

While approach (1) views make or buy as a short-term issue, approaches (2) and (3) treat it as strategic, and therefore may provide a framework for capacity and resource planning. However, we believe potential overlaps exist between (2) and (3), possibly making it difficult to categorize individual firms precisely.

A further conclusion was that factors influencing buy or make decisions were efficiency, location of special skills, price and pressure to reduce staff numbers. Meanwhile speed of delivery appeared not to be significant, a conclusion confirmed by Dale and Cunningham (1983), who found it important in only a few cases.

Although a replication of the Ford and Farmer survey was felt to provide a satisfactory core to the survey, we decided a prior limited field study would be advisable. This would provide a basis for the survey, which would have to be based on a postal questionnaire, as resources were insufficient for interviews with many managers.

In choosing which companies to approach for the field study, it was recognized that Rands (1992) had argued that external software market conditions were a major factor influencing make or buy, and that these were likely to vary across different industrial sectors. We therefore confined the survey to one industrial sector, the food and drinks industry (FDI). Although this meant conclusions could not necessarily be drawn for other industries, it allowed software market conditions to be excluded as a variable accounting for different behaviour by firms, as these would be common.

The field study

With these aspects in mind, the interview pattern to develop the field study was developed. As discussed earlier, Ford and Farmer identified several approaches which influenced make or buy decisions in the case of general goods and services. One aim was to ascertain whether these might apply to software. A further was to identify which evaluation criteria (e.g. Bryce and Bryce, 1987; Gershkoff, 1990; Leon and Mikita, 1985; Parker, 1990) should be used in the questionnaire.

There are numerous food and drinks companies in the UK, many owned by holding companies. Three were eventually chosen. Company A was a small subsidiary of a holding company, but run as an autonomous unit with an annual turnover of £200 million. It had a small IT department, headed by a business systems manager, under whom were six business area managers for sales order processing, depots, finance, distribution, stock and service.

The other two companies, B and C, were larger, each comprising a number of strategic business units (SBUs) and a separate IT division. Company B was a UK conglomerate dealing in the agricultural and food sectors, with five decentralized divisions, of which four were operating subsidiaries and the fifth a management services division. Each SBU had freedom to exercise control over its own IT systems, for which it could seek for advice or expertise from a central IT services function. Company C also had a number of SBUs including its own autonomous IT division, which functioned as the central information management core providing group computing and consultancy services. As in Company B, its SBUs were free to make their own IT decisions, or use the central IT division.

Initially, semi-structured interviews were conducted with IT, rather than line, managers, as it was felt that, if line managers were the purchasing agents for software in their areas, IT managers would be aware of this, and interviews would reveal purchases. If line managers appeared to be the main agents, they could be interviewed later. Interviews revealed a number of common issues across the three companies. Some of these were:

1. **Preferences** – there was a strong preference for the buy solution in all three companies. This surprised us, as we felt IT managers may have seen packages as a threat to their software development empires. Instead we discovered packages were felt to be quicker and imposed less demand on resources. In fact, Company A

had a policy of purchasing all its software and IT services, as it was felt this would lead to quicker implementation. In Company C, there was a tendency to seek packages because they were perceived as cheaper than bespoke solutions. Company C regarded its IT department as a scarce resource to be used when there was no viable alternative.

2. **Approaches** – using Ford and Farmer's categories, the previous discussion meant that Company A had adopted a policy approach to software. We felt the approach of the other two companies was operational, as decisions appeared to be made on a project by project basis. Make or buy decisions in these companies were perceived as a means of living within IT budgets, and make or buy appeared to provide no input to planning development resources.

3. **Procedures** – make or buy decisions for IT projects in all three companies began with a business analysis, and requirements specification by an IT steering committee, chaired by the relevant head of department or the managing director. An invitation to tender (ITT) was then issued, and sent to software suppliers. In the case of Companies B and C, potential suppliers included in-house IT departments. Make or buy decisions were then based on their responses.

4. **Decision criteria** – the criteria used for make or buy decisions were similar across the three companies, but each used different weightings. For instance, all three considered speed of delivery, functionality, systems integration, vendor reliability, and technical features, but ranked these differently. No company regarded cost as important. Provided the project did not eventually exceed its budget, cost was only considered when other criteria were equal. In this case, it became the deciding factor.

5. **Purchasing agents** – no clear picture emerged as to the identity of purchasing agents. In Company A, the business systems manager was the main driver and agent, apparently acting alone. In Companies B and C, however, line and IT managers often worked together on make or buy decisions for applications.

6. **Make or buy options** – managers in all three companies recognized that a complex range of options were open. The lack of perfect fit for most packages meant decisions about adapting needed to be considered; in other words managers perceived potentially complex buy plus make options had to be considered.

7. **Implementation difficulties** – all three companies identified problems with software packages. First, as just mentioned, amendments could be necessary. Some firms had tried to change their business to fit purchased software, but found this had adverse effects on culture. Amending packages also posed problems, for instance by overcomplicating them. Company B had tried to solve this by requiring users to acquaint themselves with unaltered packages for about six months, after which essential changes only were made. Difficulties had also been encountered in ensuring systems compatibility, with some packages being written in out-of-date languages. Difficulties described in interviews mirrored several findings by Gross and Ginzberg (1984), and highlight inherent problems in purchasing software.

8. **External agents** – one issue was identified, which had not been anticipated, thereby justifying the field study prior to the survey. It emerged that external parties played a significant role in the make or buy decisions of all three companies, even selecting packages on some occasions. We have called this group external agents. They appear to form an adjacent sector to the software industry, being composed mainly of management consultants and IT consultants and software suppliers as well as hardware manufacturers.

Given the unexpected influence of external agents, we felt it important to identify their motivation, their perception of the software market, and their understanding of their clients' software make or buy processes. Consequently, interviews were conducted with several IT consultants. These led us to conclude that one stimulus for the growth of external agents was the nature of the FDI software market. This was targeted by a wide range of producers, with many overlapping product and service specifications. One consultant recounted producing a short list for a client from over 40 candidate packages, when despite using rigorous rules, 15 packages passed. As he remarked, 'What can one do with a short list of 15?' As a result, the FDI software market is highly fragmented, with the manufacturing systems brand leader, for instance, commanding about 3% market share.

In this climate, the market presents a confusing picture; there is too much product choice, and information channels appear insufficiently clear to allow managers to be confident with make or buy choices. Concerns were also expressed about the vulnerability of suppliers, and difficulties in assessing their reliability. In consequence, managers appear to turn to outsiders with established reputations, asking for help in assessing both products and suppliers.

Developing the survey

The questionnaire was designed around the field study and literature research, and had the main aim of collecting primary data. Following this, the data would be appraised, to ascertain, for example, the extent firms followed the approaches identified by Ford and Farmer. The questionnaire set out to collect data about:

- attitudes;
- decision criteria;
- external agents;
- market information;
- outcomes.

Questions concerning attitudes were included, as we wished to establish if the preference for buying software, expressed in the field study, was widely held. Criteria used in make or buy decision were identified by asking respondents to rank a list of factors, and name others not listed. The list was derived by combining Bryce and Bryce (1987), Gershkoff (1990), Gremillion (1982), Leon and Mikita (1985), Martin and McClure (1983), Parker (1990) and Romberg (1986), a list supported by the field study.

Insights into how respondents obtained market information came mainly from questions about data sources. We also sought to estimate the extent of respondents' understanding of the software market. Finally, outcomes questions concerned the mix of internally developed and purchased applications which resulted from make or buy decisions. In addition, a number of questions were aimed at ascertaining the approach adopted to software make or buy. Several models for determining make or buy strategies have pinpointed the leveraging effect of switching skilled personnel to areas where they may make the maximum impact. Rands (1993) applied Walker's (1988) principle of comparing relative external and internal skills levels, to software, using this as an input for planning IT development resource levels.

Collectively the four sections of the questionnaire covered the five aspects described earlier. Consistency tests were included to ensure validity of the responses. As the field study indicated that IT managers were likely to be involved in many software make or buy decisions, we decided the survey population would be information technology or data processing managers. A list of 165 food and drinks companies was compiled from a data base held at Templeton College. This provided a cross-section of large, medium and small firms in different sectors of the FDI. As the database recorded mainly chairmen, chief executives, managing directors and other non-IT directors, these were mailed, with a request to pass on the questionnaire.

Analysis of findings

Out of the 165 questionnaire mailings, 49 were returned, a response rate of 30%. Over half (57%) came from beverage producers, while 22% were manufacturers of prepared foods and 16% of confectionery, preserves, sauces and soups, and 27% were involved with the manufacture of 'other foods'. Company size ranged from an annual turnover of £0.25 million to £7.3 billion, with a mean of £775 million and mode of £100 million. These figures had a similar distribution to the selected sample, which in turn was chosen to represent the FDI. From this it was concluded that replies were representative of the FDI as a whole.

Of responding firms, 52% had IT departments with fewer than 20 IT staff, 27% between 20 and 50, and 21% had over 50 staff. Typical departments had between one and two staff members at the management level. Average development backlogs were just over 10 months, representing five projects. Nearly two-thirds (63%) of respondents indicated that IT budgets were determined by the IT strategy based on business strategy, the next favoured method basing budgets on fixed increases over the previous year. Analysis of the responses revealed the following.

Attitudes

Make or buy was regarded as an important issue by 88% of respondents: reasons included cost (57%), delivery time (20%), skills requirements (10%), flexibility (10%), integration (6%), and reduced risk (4%). Many who did not consider it important had already decided to purchase all their software. The majority of respondents favoured buying software (65%), against 8% who preferred producing their own, while the remainder (27%) had no preference. This was checked for consistency, for which similar proportions were found (59% preferred to buy, 10% make and 31% had no strong preference). Statistical tests (such as Kolmogorov-Smirnov) showed no significant difference between the two responses.

Decision criteria

ANOVA tests on importances attached to the criteria revealed no significant F-values for differences between beverage and non-beverage firms and none between departments of different sizes, other than for functionality. This produced $F = 3.02$, significant at the 5% level, managers in smaller departments regarding functionality as less important than did those in larger departments. The overall ranking of criteria considered in make or buy choices for individual IT projects is shown in Table 4.1. These were obtained by averaging across all respondents.

The dominance of functionality over other criteria in Table 4.1 suggests that, in general, IT managers are less concerned with seeking easy to use solutions quickly, which may not satisfy all their requirements, than finding solutions which match defined needs. The high ranking for vendor reliability may reflect general worries about software suppliers. Although managers in small departments regarded functionality as less important than did those in large departments, it still dominated, with a 'very important' rating by 76%, with 8% not considering it. One point to note is that the questionnaire did not ask whether importances differed with the criticality of individual applications projects. Hence we are unable to comment on whether IT managers vary make or buy criteria to suit different applications.

External agents

External agents had been used up to five times in the last two years by 70% of respondents; 72% of departments with fewer than 20 staff had used external agents, 57% with between 20 and 50, and 60% with over 50 staff. Agents had been used mainly for collecting market information and providing advice on packages, but 27% of respondents had used them to select packages. Management consultants were the most popular, being used by 35% of firms. Independent IT consultants were next with 29% followed by hardware manufactures (22%), and software producers (15%). We feel this level of use shows that external agents play an identifiable role in software make or buy in the FDI, as first suggested by the field study.

Tests on the above figures revealed no significant differences at the 0.05 level between the use of external agents by IT departments of different sizes. This suggests managers in larger departments seem equally as reliant on external agents as man-

Table 4.1 Criteria influencing make or buy decisions[a]

Rank	Criteria	Most important	Very important	Not considered
1.	Functionality	51	82	4
2.	Systems integration	6	57	8
3.	Vendor reliability	8	53	10
4.	Flexibility of software		45	8
5.	Technical features		33	12
6.	Ease of use		33	29
7.	Cost of project		31	18
8.	Speed of delivery		31	18
9.	Expertise required		27	25
10.	Existing investment		25	27
11.	Availability of IT staff		12	43

[a] Figures represent percentage expressing the view, or considering the criterion, 'most important'.

agers in small departments, and feel no more confident of collecting market information to take make or buy decisions.

Market information

ANOVA tests revealed no difference between departments of various sizes and their frequency of use of the different data sources. However, significant differences were revealed at the 0.05% level between beverage and non-beverage firms in the frequency they used trade associations ($F = 4.7$), and word of mouth ($F = 4.86$). In both cases, beverage firms used the source less.

An overall ranking for the frequency with which respondents used different sources is shown in Table 4.2. In measuring the extent of respondents' market knowledge, we found that about half of respondents (49%) either said they did not know which software suppliers contributed most to the FDI or failed to express any opinion. Just over a third (35%) named three suppliers, 12% named one, with 4% two suppliers. Although we felt this suggested IT managers generally had a low awareness of the FDI software market, those who failed to express an opinion presented some difficulty, as one comment indicated possible wording ambiguity, which prior testing had not revealed. This ambiguity may have led some respondents to believe we were trying to identify their software suppliers, which they were not prepared to divulge.

We attempted to overcome this by looking at respondents who expressed no opinion, to measure the extent they had used outside suppliers or sent out ITTs, suggesting some, rather than no market knowledge. In this test all but one of the respondents who expressed no opinion had used outside suppliers in the past two years. This may have suggested they possessed certain market knowledge; it is possible this was less than with those who were sufficiently confident to express an opinion.

Outcomes

During the previous year only 8% of respondents had installed no new IT applications, with 61% installing more than five. Most firms mixed buying and making,

Table 4.2 Ranking of software market data sources[a]

Rank	Source	Frequently	Seldom/never
1.	Hardware companies	57	12
2.	Advertisements	47	24
3.	Mailshots	35	16
4.	Word of mouth	29	22
5.	IT consultants	22	27
6.	Market research	14	37
7.	Trade associations	18	49
8.	Exhibitions	12	22
9.	Directories	10	41
10.	Databases	10	74

[a] Figures are percentage responding to each frequency. The balance answered 'occasionally'.

only 2% developing all their software and 24% purchasing everything. Of the new applications installed, over 140 (37%) were developed internally, compared with more than 230 (63%) which were purchased; 39% of purchased applications were packages installed unaltered, 23% packages amended internally, 24% amended externally, while 14% were tailor made.

The proportions of purchased (unaltered and amended) and internally produced software for different IT department sizes are shown in Figure 4.1. Tests on these revealed significant differences at the 0.05% level, suggesting smaller departments purchase a higher proportion of their software than larger departments. Over half the firms (51%) used between three and five software suppliers, with 16% dealing with more than five. Three-quarters (76%) of respondents were satisfied with the software products, 8% being dissatisfied. However, only 47% were satisfied with the service they received from suppliers, 14% being dissatisfied. In both cases, the balance had mixed feelings.

Software make or buy approaches

Only 12% of respondents said their firms always bought software and never produced their own, while a further 21% had an explicit make or buy policy. For the majority of the latter, the policy was to purchase applications, if a suitable package could be found, otherwise develop internally. Reasons for this 'buy-if-available' policy included reducing head counts and in-house overheads, faster delivery, ease of upgrade and integration, avoiding reinventing the wheel, reducing backlogs, flexibility, and reliability and quality.

Meanwhile, the remaining respondents (67%) said their firms had no explicit policy. Decisions were generally taken on a project by project basis, depending on the

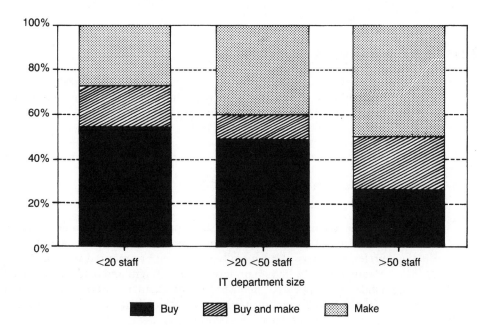

Figure 4.1 Proportion of software make/buy.

availability of packages, project uniqueness, integration and ability to upgrade, as well as the balance between workload and staff availability. In our opinion, there was little difference between the make or buy practices of the firms with 'buy-if-available' policies and those firms with no policies, who purchased if packages were available for individual projects. Thus we concluded that firms with 'buy-if-available' policies were operational in their approach to make or buy, as decisions were taken project by project, rather than in a framework which provided a basis for planning software development resources. As a result, we concluded that, other than the 12% of firms which only purchased software, thereby adopting a policy approach, many of the remaining firms took an operational approach.

We feel our conclusions are corroborated both by the low ranking for expertise required, shown in Table 4.1, and responses to IT staff training questions. The latter suggested that IT managers undertake little skills planning for key functional areas, as a strategic approach to software make or buy would require (Rands, 1993). Indeed, only 26% of firms sent IT staff on external/internal courses in key functional skills, half used on-the-job training, and a quarter provided no training at all. In contrast, there was strong emphasis on technical training, 73% sending IT staff on external/internal courses on CASE, languages, methodologies etc. with 19% using on-the-job training; the balance provided no technical training at all.

Although it would seem that IT managers tend towards an operational, rather than a strategic, approach to software make or buy, we have one qualification in making this judgement. This stems from the observation, described earlier, that smaller IT departments appear to purchase a higher proportion of their software than larger departments. This suggests that broad forces may be shaping the overall size of some IT departments, which, in turn, influence the make/buy mix resulting from what appear, at first sight, to be unrelated project by project make or buy decisions. The survey does not allow us to determine the nature of these forces, however, but one possibility might be the tightness of IT budgets.

Further analysis

In addition to the analysis to provide the data above, a number of other analyses were made, offering several further insights into software make or buy in the FDI.

Matching preferences

A comparison of software acquisition patterns with respondents' preferences revealed a measure of consistency between the two. For instance, about 45% of respondents preferred to buy and generally purchased or preferred to make and generally made. Meanwhile 38% had no preference and bought and made in comparable proportions, while 14% appeared inconsistent, for example, preferring to purchase but mainly making. Possibly circumstances, e.g. lack of suitable packages, forced the latter group to pursue non-preferred courses of action.

The importance of speed of delivery

Gremillion (1982), Martin and McClure (1983) and Romberg (1986) have suggested that development backlogs should determine make or buy decisions on IT projects. Despite this and the claim of several respondents that speed was one reason why software make or buy was important, Table 4.1 shows that speed of delivery was given a low overall ranking. Moreover, a Kolmogorov-Smirnov test indicated no relationship at the 0.05 level between each respondent's development backlog and the importance attached to speed of delivery. This appears to suggest that internal backlogs and delivery times do not significantly influence choices, and may confirm the findings of Ford and Farmer and Dale and Cunningham for general goods/services.

However, before dismissing speed of delivery as an unimportant factor, one possible explanation for the low ranking may need exploring. This is that IT managers generally expect purchased packages to be operational more quickly than internally developed applications, in the same way as the field study revealed that they expect them to be cheaper. As a result, our respondents may have attached low importance to speed of delivery, as they had already discounted it.

We believe that the responses to the survey demonstrate that software make or buy is an important issue for the FDI. As mentioned earlier, a large majority (88%) said it was important, with two-thirds favouring purchasing. More significantly, our estimate that about two-thirds of new applications are based on purchased software indicates that software purchasing is normal across the FDI, irrespective of IT department size. Although the questions did not link purchasing pattern and application size, meaning that we cannot estimate the percentage of total software development effort purchased externally, these figures imply that the issue of which software to develop or purchase is important in the FDI, and should be taken seriously. This predominance of purchased software in the FDI is similar to patterns in UK engineering firms (Marsh, 1988), another major industrial sector. Should these trends be repeated in other major sectors, it would support Rands's (1992) argument that academics' and researchers' approaches to IT planning should be modified to account for acquiring software from external sources.

One noticeable feature of the survey was respondents' low satisfaction with the service received from software suppliers, despite the importance attached to vendor reliability in determining whether to make or buy. Moreover, comments from several respondents suggest that inadequacies in vendors' services could account for some of the dissatisfaction expressed about software products. One example indicated a lack of coordination between a vendor's sales and installation teams, with the result that the installed system did not match expectations raised at the time of purchase. This low ranking for service, and remarks during a field study interview about the nature of market research undertaken for software suppliers, may suggest they focus too heavily on enhancing product features, at the expense of service basics.

A proposed framework for managing make or buy

The above analysis establishes the importance of the software make or buy decision, and weaknesses in actual practice in organizations. In the remainder of this chapter we develop a framework for more strategic decision-making. This combines methods for formulating make/buy policies with those for planning internal and external software sources. The structure of the proposed framework is shown in Figure 4.2. There are a number of points to note about the framework.

Required IT service level

The service level required from IT applications in order to achieve the IS strategy refers to the timing, specification and quality, and cost (Hill, 1991) constraints to which IT applications must conform. The effects of one of these, namely lead times to acquire software, on planning software supply resources has been examined by Rands (1991a).

The applications supply portfolio

For several years, new IT applications required by a firm have been referred to as the application development portfolio (McFarlan, McKenney and Pyburn, 1983).

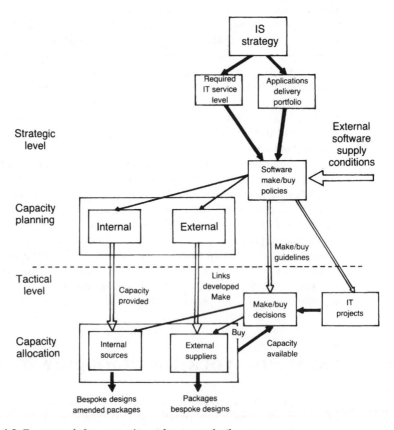

Figure 4.2 Framework for managing software make/buy.

Earl (1988) identifies seven application types within this portfolio, being mandatory, strategic, infrastructure developments, system renewals, maintenance and enhancement, and niche developments (see also Chapters 2, 7 and 9). The applications development portfolio should yield 'a smooth flow of deliverables' (Earl, 1989), being decomposed into a series of IT projects. However, McFarlan coined the term in the early 1980s, when firms usually developed applications, rather than purchased them. As its use today may possibly imply 'deliverables' should come solely from internal sources, another term may now be preferable. It is therefore proposed the term 'applications supply portfolio' is appropriate in today's conditions, when 'deliverables' may be supplied from external, as well as internal, sources. It has therefore been used in Figure 4.2 instead of applications development portfolio.

Software make/buy options

Options for supplying software for 'deliverables' in an applications supply portfolio from internal and external sources are likely to be wide (Rands, 1990). For instance, some applications may be purchased from external sources in turnkey form, using standard software products or bespoke designs. On the other hand, other applications may come from packages, purchased and then installed by the firm itself, either in adapted or unadapted form. Meanwhile further applications may be fully developed by internal sources, while in other instances, existing applications may be changed by internal sources to produce new applications (Parker, 1990).

A number of possible options for supplying applications software are suggested in Figure 4.3. These range from options which mean the firm buys all stages of the software development cycle for the application, to those where the firm makes all the stages. Between these extremes are options where the firm partially makes and buys, undertaking some stages itself, while purchasing others.

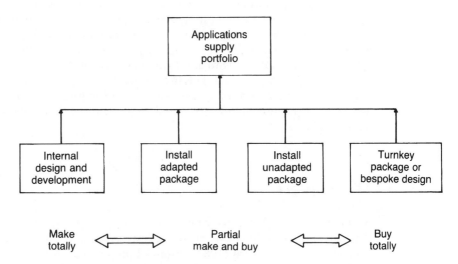

Figure 4.3 Possible make/buy options for applications.

Make/buy policies

In order to manage software make/buy within the framework of Figure 4.2, it is important that software make/buy policies provide guidelines, within which make/buy decisions may be taken. To this end, it is proposed policies should indicate whether the preferred sources of software for different application types or areas are external or internal, as well as the nature of the relationships with those sources. For instance, in the case of external sources, software make/buy policies should determine whether relationships ought to be quasi-integration, for instance through strategic alliances, or the purchasing of products and services on the open market.

Make/buy decisions

In Figure 4.2, make/buy decisions refer to individual IT projects, taken within guidelines provided by make/buy policies. This suggests, for example, if the policy for an application type were to use a particular external source, a make/buy decision for a project of that type should ideally be based on software from that source. Within this guideline, the decision would then determine whether the source supplied software in turnkey form, based on a standard product, or whether the product is installed by the firm itself, in adapted or unadapted form. A few of the possible options for supplying applications, already shown in Figure 4.3 have been included in Figure 4.2.

External software supply conditions

External software supply conditions have been included to allow for the impact of the software market on integration patterns This is consistent with research by Miller (1988), who argued that 'complementarities of strategy with environment . . . appear to lead to good performance'. Information about external software supply conditions includes not only data about the type and availability of individual software packages, but also the number, sizes and history of software suppliers, and the nature, direction and extent of their skills. The latter is consistent with Walker (1988), Dale and Cunningham (1983) and Ford and Farmer (1986), who recognized the importance of relative internal and external skills in formulating make/buy policies. It is also consistent with the emergence of specialized software markets (Rands, 1991b), with the associated acquisition of industry-specific skills by software suppliers (Romberg, 1986; Rands, 1991b).

IT projects

A number of models for determining IT development projects from the applications development portfolio have been suggested, such as McFarlan, McKenney and Pyburn (1983) and Ward (1987). A model proposed by Earl (1989) decomposes the applications development portfolio into a pattern of deliverables using a grid with two axes, pay-off and goalposts. Earl defines goalposts as a composite measure of risk, time-scale and difficulties.

In Figure 4.2, decomposition of the applications supply portfolio takes place after software make/buy policies have been determined. For this Earl's model would appear to provide a useful basis as, at this stage, the nature of the source for the type or areas of applications is known. Hence an assessment of the risks, timescales and difficulties encountered by that source in supplying those application types may be made.

Differences from traditional planning methods

In a number of earlier methods developed for formulating an IT strategy consistent with a firm's IS strategy, the sequence of stages is to proceed from determining the applications development portfolio to identifying the resources required. The likely effect of this, in what may now be regarded as traditional IT planning methods, is that resource planning makes inadequate allowance for external software sources (Rands, 1991b).

It can be seen the framework in Figure 4.2 contains important differences from these methods. One is the inclusion of the formulation of software make/buy policies, between the determination of the applications supply portfolio and resource planning, and was originally proposed by Rands (1991a). It permits resource planning to make allowance for the provision of both internal and external applications sources (Hill, 1991). A further difference is that this inclusion is reflected at the tactical level, by the addition of software make/buy decisions before capacity allocation.

A model for formulating software make/buy policies

Harrigan's (1984) argument, that firms' integration policies may be based around a make/buy mix which frees internal resources to undertake a more profitable range of activities, appears consistent with Porter and Millar's (1985) notion that firms should seek to use strategic investments in software to advantage. It is also consistent with Durbin's view (1986) that software make/buy policies should utilize the leveraging effect of switching scarce and skilled systems analysts to areas where they have the maximum impact.

In deciding to which areas to switch internal software development resources, it would appear (Walker, 1988; Dale and Cunningham, 1983; Ford and Farmer, 1986) that allowances should be made for their skills and competences *relative* to those of external software sources. As scale economies mean skills levels in external sources are likely to be at a lower cost than similar internal skills (Dearden, 1987; Romberg, 1986), it would appear that firms should adopt software make/buy policies which allowed scarce systems analysts to be switched to areas where they could develop and maintain special competencies (Harrigan, 1984), superior to external producers. As the discussion in the previous section suggests, these areas should ideally be of strategic importance to the firm, to maximize the impact of exploiting superior internal skills. By this means, inherent penalties of internal software development (Rands, 1991b) may be counterbalanced by benefits.

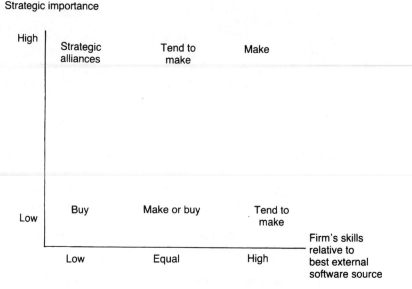

Figure 4.4 Software make/buy policy.

A proposed model for formulating software make/buy policies is shown in Figure 4.4 and was developed from Walker (1988) by Rands (1991a). The horizontal axis is the firm's skills relative to the best external software source in order to allow for the relative competence of internal and external sources. The vertical axis is the strategic importance of applications within the applications development portfolio, making the model consistent with Earl (1989), McFarlan, McKenney and Pyburn (1983) and Ward (1987). It is also consistent with Gremillion and Pyburn (1983), who used impact as a basis for determining whether software should generally be bought or made in an area.

The model may be applied to the applications supply portfolio to determine the software make/buy policy for a firm. This specifies for which areas the firm should provide its own software development resources, or use external suppliers. For instance, if the strategic impact of applications in a particular area were high, possibly because product traits (Rands, 1990) make applications key, the model suggests a firm should produce that software itself, if the firm's skills relative to the best external software source were high. However, the firm must guarantee the absolute skills level of these resources are adequate to produce software with the required performance for this high impact area.

Policies for using external software sources

When a firm's skills relative to the best external software source are low, Figure 4.4 suggests the firm should use those external sources. With applications of high strategic importance, it would appear the firm should create a strategic alliance, or other arrangements, with the best software source, or other high skilled suppliers. External software suppliers normally possess high skills in an area, either because of the commonality (Gremillion and Pyburn, 1983) of applications there, or because of specialization (Rands, 1991b). In this case, suppliers may market specialized software packages for the area concerned, often providing added value services, or undertake bespoke applications projects.

Francis (1987) described several examples of firms in the financial sector using joint ventures with vendors as a means of gaining access to software developments. Meanwhile, Hellebust (1988) has argued that traditional relationships between IT customers and vendors are often unsatisfactory and that, if an alliance is properly managed, a vendor can improve a firm's market position. He cites Citibank which has exploited vendor relationships to advantage. However, Figure 4.4 suggests that strategic alliances with external software sources only provide advantage to firms with fewer skills than these sources, when alliances concern high impact, or strategically important applications. Should it not be possible for a firm to forge special relationships, it may be forced to provide its own resources, and ensure these possess the requisite skills.

In the case when the strategic importance of applications is low, Figure 4.4 suggests the software make or buy policy for the firm's use of external sources would be different. Instead the firm should purchase software from the supplier on the open market, without engaging in special relationships. This may mean buying software packages from the supplier, even though they may not fit the application exactly. However, if packages are not available, the firm may be forced to commission designs from the external producer. Alternatively, it may be decided to delay or cancel IT applications in these areas.

Planning internal software development resources

It has been argued that, in a growing number of industries, the software market is becoming more specialized, and producers are acquiring significant industry and function specific skills (Romberg, 1986; Rands, 1991b). This suggests that the likely effect on a typical firm's internal software development resources of formulating make/buy policies around skills comparisons would be to restrict those resources to selected areas. These areas would be where the firm already possessed, or could easily develop, competencies superior to external software suppliers.

As a result, therefore, the typical firm's internal software development resources would become niche (Rands, 1990). To achieve this, resource planning in Figure 4.2 would involve the switching of scarce and skilled systems analysts (Durbin, 1986) towards areas of high importance, where they could provide the greatest impact. This may mean reinforcing skills and competencies in these areas, while divesting away from others. Thus planning internal software development resources involves deciding areas to invest and divest.

A proposed model which allows resource planning to be undertaken is shown in Figure 4.5. This has been produced by dividing the horizontal axis of Figure 4.4 into the current absolute skills levels for internal and the best external software sources, for the case of applications with high strategic impact. For simplicity, skills in Figure 4.5 have been ranked as either high or low.

Figure 4.5 provides more insight for switching internal software development resources than Figure 4.4. Here, for equal relative skills, it was suggested a firm should tend to make high importance applications. However, in Figure 4.4, equal relative

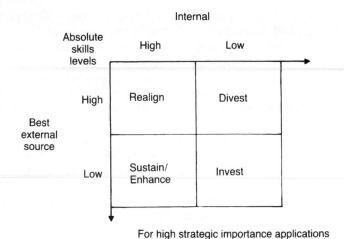

Figure 4.5 Internal software development resource planning.

skills may occur when absolute skills levels are either high or low. It is possible, therefore, that no internal or external source has adequate skills for applications of high importance to the firm.

In Figure 4.5 equal relative skills occur in both the top left and bottom right cells. Using the two figures together it would appear, where current relative skills are equally high (i.e. Figure 4.5, top left cell), the firm should seek a strategic alliance with the best external source, and realign its high skills towards another high importance applications area. This is because, as mentioned earlier, external skills are likely to be available at a lower price (Dearden, 1987), due to scale economies. However, if current relative skills were equally low (i.e. Figure 4.5, bottom right cell), the firm would need to invest in developing resources with sufficiently high skills for the area, so it could produce its own applications.

Figure 4.5 also suggests that, if the skills of a firm's own resources are currently low for an application with high strategic impact, while the skills of the best external source are high, the firm should divest those resources, and switch skilled systems analysts to other areas. However, if the skills of a firm's own resources are currently high for an application with high strategic impact, while the skills of the best external producers are low, the firm should sustain, and possibly enhance, those resources.

By way of summary of the argument in this section, a high-level version of the proposed framework for managing make/buy decisions is shown in Figure 4.6.

Conclusions

This chapter has reported on a survey to explore the nature of an activity which we believe has been taken for granted for many years, namely the taking of software make or buy decisions. Given the early stage of work specifically aimed at software, we feel it was inevitable that the survey element, in particular, would contain weaknesses, limiting its usefulness. Some limitations, such as confining data collection to one industry, have already been discussed. However, despite these, we believe the survey has gathered data which yield useful insights into IT managers' handling of software make/buy. Moreover, we feel the experience gained points to several directions where further research may usefully be conducted.

The survey appeared to confirm the results of the field study that, in general, IT managers in the FDI do not resist the use of software packages, but perceive them as a way of making IT resources stretch further. This finding may run counter to an image of IT managers insisting on developing applications in-house, even though adequate packages exist (the not-invented-here syndrome).

It is possible that our views that software make/buy is not treated as a strategic matter will not be modified by further research in the short term. The conclusions Ford and Farmer drew were based on research across a range of sectors and commodities, and we feel reflected a general management perspective on make/buy. In our opinion, there is nothing to suggest that further surveys into software make or buy in other industrial sectors say will produce different results, at least until general attitudes change.

There seems to be some comfort for traditional hardware manufacturers. For although today's conventional wisdom is that, because software is purchased first with equipment a less important decision, hardware manufacturers are in a weakening position, the survey suggested they can still exercise considerable power. Not only do they act as external agents in many firms' make/buy processes, but they are also the most popular data source about software products and suppliers. This may mean that hardware manufacturers' main competitive weapons may lie in the control of software product and supplier information flows.

The chapter has also proposed a framework for managing software make/buy decisions. This framework is further developed in Chapter 16 for IT activities across a system's lifecycle. In the present framework, one of the main parameters has been skill levels. At this stage, the nature of these skills has not been elaborated or debated. However, it is unlikely that such skills would be limited to possessing IT or computing knowledge. Instead skills are likely to relate to the ability to incorporate company-specific or process competencies within IT. Developing this ability suggests that firms put procedures in place which ensure that company-specific and process competencies are eventually incorporated in internally developed software. Another aspect of software make/buy policies, not discussed in detail here is that the emergence

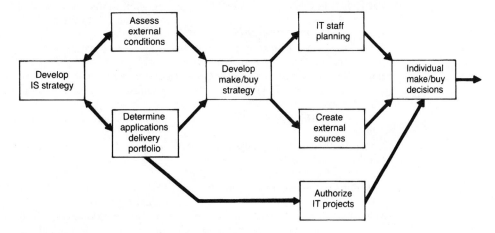

Figure 4.6 Proposed planning procedure.

of specialized skills within a firm's internal software development resources may, in its turn, become a driver of business strategy. Thus, if a firm trading in bonds had special skills in options and swaps, say, it may develop its own software by switching systems analysts to this area. This may result in the firm developing additional skills in the area, which it could incorporate in future business strategies.

References

Bryce, M. and Bryce, T. (1987) Make or buy software. *Journal of Systems Management*, August, 6–11.

Dale, B.G. and Cunningham, M.T. (1983) The importance of factors other than cost considerations in make or buy decisions. *International Journal of Operations and Production Management*, **4** (3), 43–54.

Dearden, J. (1987) The withering away of the IS organisation. *Sloan Management Review*, Summer, 87–91.

DeLone, W.H. (1988) Determinants for success for computer usage in small business, *MIS Quarterly*, March, 51–61.

Durbin, G. (1986) Should I buy applications software or develop it in-house? *Computerworld*, 10 March, 59–65.

Earl, M. (1988) Formulation of information systems strategy: emerging lessons and frameworks. In *Information Management: The Strategic Dimension* (ed. M. Earl), Oxford University Press, Oxford.

Earl, M. (1989) *Management Strategies for Information Technology*, Prentice Hall, Hemel Hempstead.

Ford, D. and Farmer, D. (1986) Make or buy: a key strategic issue. *Long Range Planning*, **19** (5), 54–62.

Francis, R. (1987) Joint development deals lure banks, software vendors. *Datamation*, 1 October, 28, 30.

Gershkoff, I. (1990) The make or buy game. *Datamation*, 15 February, 73–7.

Gremillion, L.L. (1982) Improving productivity with applications software packages. *Business Horizons*, March/April, 51–4.

Gremillion, L. and Pyburn, D. (1983) Breaking the systems development bottleneck. *Harvard Business Review*, March/April, 130–7.

Gross, P. and Ginzberg, M. (1984) Barriers to the adoption of applications software packages. *Systems, Objectives, Solutions*, **4** (4), 211–26.

Harrigan, K.R. (1984) Formulating vertical integration strategies. *Academy of Management Review*, **9** (4), 638–52.

Harrigan, K. (1986) *Managing for Joint Venture Success*, Lexington Books, Lexington.

Hellebust, K. (1988) Creating a strategic alliance with information technology suppliers. *Journal of Information Systems Management*, Winter, 32–7.

Hill, T. (1991) *Production/Operations Management: Text and Cases*, Prentice Hall, Hemel Hempstead.

Lees, D.D. and Lees, J.D. (1987) Realities of small business information systems implementation. *Journal of Systems Management*, January, 6–13.

Leon, G.L. and Mikita, R. (1985) When to soup up standard packages, *Computer Decisions*, May, 90–4.

Marsh, J. (1988) Identified: the top software packages. *Engineering Computers*, September, 15–20.

Martin, J. and McClure, C. (1983) Buying software off the rack. *Harvard Business Review*, November/December, 32–52.

McFarlan, W., McKenney, J. and Pyburn, D. (1983) The information archipelago: plotting a course. *Harvard Business Review*, January/February, 145–56.

Miller, D. (1988) Relating Porter's business strategy to environment and structure: analysis and performance implications. *Academy of Management Review*, **31** (2), 280–308.

Parker, M. (1990) Managing successful applications. In *Managing Information Systems for Profit* (ed. T. Lincoln), Wiley and Sons, Chichester.

Porter, M. and Millar, V. (1985) How information gives you competitive advantage. *Harvard Business Review*, July/August.

Rands, T. (1990) *Software Acquisition and Changes in the Software Sector*, MRP 90/11, Templeton College, Oxford.

Rands, T. (1991a) *The Impact of Software Leadtimes on Implementing IT Strategies*. MRP Templeton College, Oxford.

Rands, T. (1991b) *The Key Role of Software Make/Buy Decisions during the 1990s*. MRP, Templeton College, Oxford.

Rands, T. (1992) The key role of applications software make/buy decisions. *Journal of Strategic Information Systems*, **1** (4), 215–23.

Rands, T. (1993) A framework for managing software make or buy. *European Journal of Information Systems*, **2** (3), 273–82.

Romberg, F.A. (1986) Should I buy applications software or develop it in-house? *Computerworld*, 10 March, 59, 66–74.

Sibley, E.H. (1985) How to select and evaluate a DBMS. *Journal of Information Systems Management*, Spring, 40–9.

Walker, G. (1988) Strategic sourcing, vertical integration and transaction costs. *Interfaces*, **18** (3), 62–73.

Ward, J. (1987) Integrating information systems into business strategies. *Long Range Planning*, **20** (3), 19–29.

5

Reducing the costs of IT development

Subhash V. Parulekar

Introduction

The failure of IT management to establish and maintain a record of strength in the consistent, successful completion of projects is chronic and widespread. Although this problem has received a lot of attention, and although a number of approaches have been developed over the years (e.g. structured methodologies, prototyping, automated programming aids etc.), the record of consistent completion of IT projects within the original project deadlines remains rather bleak in many organizations (Brynjolfsson, 1993; Griffiths and Willcocks, 1995). Concern about the quality of work produced by an organization's IT function is extremely important to the eventual success of the business. The combination of the rapid advances in IT, and the increasing degree to which IT is becoming an integral part of the total organization, demands the development of an environment where a high standard of quality is developed and maintained.

There are a number of factors which inhibit the ability of IT departments to develop and maintain a high level of project completions which are on time and within budget. Partly this is because of the complexity of the system development process, particularly for large application system projects, and partly because of inadequate management and a lack of attention to quality. According to several sources the inability of project managers to manage is one of the main reasons why projects go out of control. In particular, project managers do not give sufficient time to the people-

Investing in Information Systems: Evaluation and Management. Edited by Leslie Willcocks. Published in 1996 by Chapman & Hall. ISBN 0 412 72670 X.

related aspects, such as, for example, recruitment, skills training, management training and performance monitoring (Gibson, 1992; National Audit Office, 1990; Walton, 1989; Willcocks and Margetts, 1994).

In a survey conducted by KPMG Management Consulting (1991), the following reasons were cited for IT projects going out of control:

- unclear business objectives;
- absence of process model;
- absence of adequate project auditing;
- insufficient user involvement;
- absence of user ownership;
- lack of understanding of project versus process;
- lack of change management;
- uncontrolled third parties; and
- resistance to methodologies.

According to this study, the lack of a quality management system framework is the main reason for the above problems. In one study quoted by Charette (1991), 25% of large systems (i.e. those with more than 64 000 lines of source code) are abandoned before completion and never used, while 60% significantly overrun their cost and schedule budgets. Less than 1% finish on time and within budget, and meet all user requirements. Finally, the average large system in completed more than a year late, and the cost is almost twice as much as originally estimated. The recent picture shows some development on this but is hardly encouraging (see Willcocks and Margetts, 1994, for a review).

Software development involves three major areas of expense:

- project-related work;
- code-related work; and
- defect-related work.

When comparing small computer programs with large systems, the relative costs of different elements vary as shown in Figures 5.1 and 5.2. It can be seen that defect removal is a high cost area in both of these types of systems. Prime/key factors towards improving software productivity and building in quality must therefore be those which address defect prevention. By minimizing the defect potential we can improve the software quality and hence the productivity. This would have a significant influence in reducing the costs relating to IT development.

This chapter examines the management of information technology and discusses the current problems associated with the management of IT projects. It addresses how organizations can reduce the overall IT development and maintenance costs by introducing a quality approach throughout the IT development lifecycle. Further suggestions for improving project control also appear in Chapter 9.

Current problems with the management of IT projects

The following list of problem statements is commonly attributed to IT projects (see also the study described in Chapter 6):

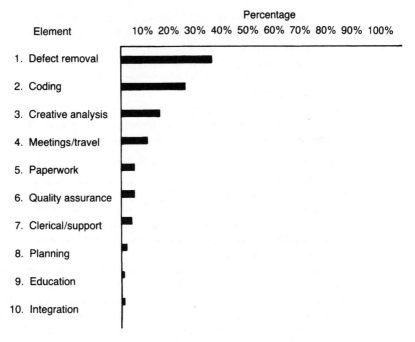

Figure 5.1 Small program software expense elements.

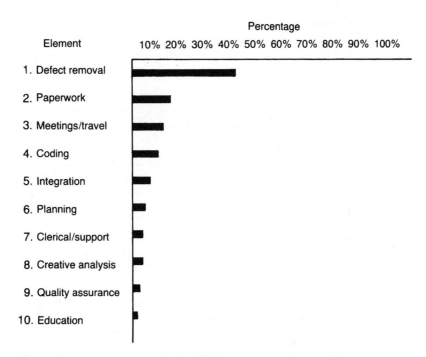

Figure 5.2 Large system software expense elements.

1. The project takes too long to develop, causing the entire system to slip its schedule and thus commensurately raising the development costs.
2. When delivered, the system does not perform as expected.
3. Requirements that were to be implemented in software have had to be scaled down in order to make a reasonable delivery schedule.
4. The number one problem in getting information systems up and running quickly and reliably is poor requirements definition.
5. Rework is usually forgotten in the original time and effort estimates, and is one of the main reasons why schedules and budgets are so often overrun.

A number of project managers consider that technical problems specific to software development are the major cause for IT projects going over budget and schedule estimates. Even though this may be partially true, the emerging software engineering methods and tools are designed to address these software-related technical problems. In spite of the considerable increase in system development methodologies, tools and aids available in the market, the costs of many IT projects still exceed the original estimates. Why should this be?

In a survey conducted by Price Waterhouse (1988) for the DTI, it was estimated that the costs resulting from poor quality software developed by UK suppliers and sold to UK users may be over £500 million a year (see Table 5.1). These estimates relate to marketed software only and do not include in-house development. As seen from Table 5.1, 40% of these costs are incurred by suppliers, although most of the costs incurred by suppliers will be passed on to users in higher prices. Subsequent studies indicate that the problem of poor quality software has hardly gone away since 1988.

In addition to these direct resource costs, there are also likely to be significant indirect costs such as:

• impact on users' business resulting from software which is delivered late, lacks relevant functions or contains errors;
• damage to the reputation of suppliers and consequent loss of business if users are dissatisfied.

A major source of user dissatisfaction arises from a mismatch between user requirements and the functions of the delivered software. Poor quality software has an impact on the following major components of costs:

• the financial costs of overruns;
• the costs of correcting errors before and after delivery of the software; and
• unnecessary expenditure on maintenance.

Table 5.1 Estimated total costs of poor quality software (£ million) (from Price Waterhouse)

Item	Total cost	Cost incurred by	
		Suppliers	Users
Low productivity	50	50	
Overruns on time and budget	50	25	25
Errors	150	130	20
Poor maintainability	270		270
Total	520	205	315

Redmill (1990) concludes in his paper that most of the problems relating to software-based development projects arise from management failings. Among the most common reasons given by project managers for failure to meet budget, timescale and specification, two in particular require a great deal of project manager's time. These are:

- the difficulty in obtaining a complete and correct specification from users; and
- uncertainty in cost and resource estimation.

Other reasons which could be attributed to the failure of IT projects are:

- lack of project management skills;
- lack of quality awareness;
- false pride which results in a belief that on time and within budget means a successful project;
- lack of understanding in meeting the customer requirements during and after development.

According to Murray (1987a,b), a primary concern of any information processing system project should be a clear understanding of the purpose and the scope of the proposed project. A significant contribution to the failure of IT projects, particularly those developed in-house, is the failure to start with an accurate understanding on the part of all involved parties as to what is really required.

This does not mean that the users do not have a reasonable understanding of their needs; it is rather the case that those needs are too often stated in general, rather vague terms. Problems arise because the users assume that everyone else involved in the proposed project shares their understanding. When application systems of any size are developed on the basis of vague requirements, this almost ensures future difficulty. The probability of success of a project is much greater if a well-defined, precise and complete statement of requirements exists. Based on a well-specified statement of requirements, senior management may decide that a project will not produce sufficient payback, or that it will simply be too risky. Although cancellation will be a disappointment to the users who have requested the project, and probably to the development team assigned to the project, in the long term the best interests of the organization will be served by such an approach (Murray, 1987a,b).

The increased use of fourth generation programming languages and their extended use outside the IT department, in conjunction with the increased use of prototyping methods, may reduce the emphasis on the need for a carefully prepared statement of requirements. The ability to move through the preliminary development process more rapidly does not mean that the statement of requirements is less necessary. In fact, it is becoming even more important to have a well-prepared statement. This is because using the rapid development methods discussed above, it is possible to lessen some of the disciplined control associated with sound project management. This will certainly create more difficulty at a later stage in the development lifecycle. So, as some parts of the process become less difficult, the requirement for strong control in other areas increases. At least some of the serious project problems faced by many IT managers could be avoided if more care and attention were devoted to the statement of requirements (Murray, 1987a,b).

Murray (1985) also mentions lack of client commitment as one of the problems encountered in the management of information processing projects. Changes to the project well after it is under way also cause disruption and delay. Misunderstanding and a lack of adequate project documentation create problems during the course of the project which require both extra work and rework, which in turn cause missed project deadlines.

According to Murray, in many installations a situation has been allowed to develop which tends to encourage the late delivery of projects. An analysis of these installations would very probably indicate that IT projects are seldom completed within the original target dates, or within the original budgets. In these installations there is an attitude to treat project completion dates as 'targets' rather than as absolute deadlines. In such cases there is unlikely to be a strong commitment on the part of the project team to meet the project deadline (see also Gibson, 1992; Griffiths and Willcocks, 1995).

There is a belief among some IT managers that because of the inherent complexity, it is almost impossible to manage large IT projects effectively so as to meet the original deadlines. There are, however, sufficient examples of successful implementation of large projects to prove that given the correct environment and attitudes, and sufficient risk analysis and management, projects can be consistently delivered on time, within budget and of desired quality (Griffiths and Willcocks, 1995; see also Chapter 7).

According to Murray, an important factor in the management of IT projects in organizations with good project completion records is that they have developed, and maintained, an appropriate internal discipline. This allows them to build an environment which makes successful project completion a matter of course. In time, a high standard of IT project management is established. Without the appropriate internal discipline among the project team members, even a sound project management system would not help to deliver high quality projects on time and within original budgets. It is not unusual for some projects to fare poorly at the executive review level because those who are leading the project have not exercised sufficient discipline to challenge the assumptions of other members of the project team.

In can be concluded that the main problem with the management of IT products and services is a lack of control. The solution to this problem lies in establishing a control framework which would enable management to address the following questions:

1. Is IT strategy in alignment with business needs and organizational capabilities?
2. Is there a continuous evaluation of feasibility throughout product development, implementation and in-service operation?
3. Is there an on-going assessment of costs and risks?
4. Are we confident to identify where the benefits are; whether these benefits are being achieved and, if not, how this could be remedied?
5. What improvements could be made in managerial arrangements?
6. Could we explore different methodologies for evaluating and managing IT?

The most important element in the management of IT products and services is to be able to re-establish control over IT investment through improved evaluation, monitoring and management techniques and processes. Some organizations are now focusing major management attention on:

- the productivity of software development;
- the cost associated with the development of software; and
- the quality of the delivered product.

Software productivity, or the rate at which software can be delivered, is limited by current development practice. Software scientists generally believe that software productivity will not dramatically improve without major technology breakthroughs creating more automated programming techniques. Many software scientists believe, however, that the rigorous employment of modern disciplined software engineering practice can achieve significant software quality improvement over current practice without a corresponding increase in cost. By concentrating on engineering practices to achieve software quality, concomitant improvements in software productivity will also be obtained (Evans and Marciniak, 1986).

A quality approach to management of IT products and services

From the discussion in the previous sections it was emphasized that a control framework is essential for the development and operation of products and services to enable IT management to monitor and control the costs and quality of products and services. For any organization, repeatable success demands standards and control mechanisms relating to their financial, technical and administrative functions to promote consistent quality levels in all aspects of the business. The achievement of quality requires that the following three objectives are satisfied:

- a clear definition of what is to be achieved and when (specifications and plans);
- a description of the activities and functions that need to be performed (standards and procedures); and
- the control and monitoring of the performance of activities and functions (quality control).

This section describes the principles relating to a quality approach which is based upon a system of controls. The following subsections describe the concepts of controls and their application to the system development process together with the explanation of how quality can be built incrementally using a quality system approach.

This approach has been used by two organizations the author has worked for. In one of these organizations, a limited commitment approach was used within the development lifecycle using some of the control mechanisms discussed below. This involved, for each project, a cost–benefit assessment at the end of each phase of the development lifecycle together with a quality and funding review. Go or no go decisions were taken at the end of each phase based on the outcome of these reviews. They also had project selection criteria based on quantitative risk assessment. In another organization, controls were incorporated within the organizational product lifecycle together with detailed roles and responsibilities associated with these controls. These included activities relating to the production, review and approval of deliverables. Audits were conducted on critical projects to give an independent quality view to senior management regarding the way in which the projects were being managed.

Controls

A typical IT divisional objectives statement could be written as follows:

> To ensure that all work undertaken within the IT division meets the business objectives of the organization by making the most efficient and effective use of money, time, resources while minimizing risk and maximizing quality.

In order to achieve the above IT divisional objectives, we need to apply controls relating to money, progress, resources, quality, sequence, scope and change. The following is a summary of why we need these controls:

1. **Control of money** – to be able to control the financing of all projects; to be able to estimate the costs and benefits; and to be able'to measure the return on investment.
2. **Control of progress** – to be able to meet the objectives within the agreed deadlines; to monitor how we are doing.
3. **Control of resources** – to be able to control costs.
4. **Control of quality** – to minimize the risk of things going wrong; to minimize rework costs.
5. **Control of sequence** – to be able to control quality, progress, costs.
6. **Control of scope** – to be able to stabilize the requirements within projects, across projects and against IT divisional business objectives.
7. **Control of change** – to control the cost of changes, impact and approval of change (i.e. scope).

Applying the controls to IT development projects

Table 5.2 is a controls matrix showing the criteria which need to be considered when applying the above-mentioned controls to the IT development process. Regardless of the requirements and characteristics of any IT development project, the criteria shown in the controls matrix in Table 5.2 need to be incorporated into a product lifecycle control framework for all IT developments. Table 5.3 shows such an example.

Product lifecycle control framework

A product lifecycle control framework offers a sound basis for the management of IT products and services. The extent to which such a framework is applied would determine the overall benefits resulting in lower development costs, improved quality and considerably reduced maintenance costs.

A model product lifecycle should consist of stages, phases, steps and activities required to develop and maintain the products and services. It should also define the entry/exit criteria for each stage/phase/step/activity and the expected inputs/outputs to/from these. In addition, it should also define the roles and responsibilities across all stages of the product development and operation process, including the reviewing and approving roles. Thus a product lifecycle framework should define *who* does *what, when, where, why, how* and in *what sequence*. Using this approach, the product is reviewed in smaller, more easily examined pieces during its development. Because this approach defines the work effort involved, it also aids effective project estimating, scheduling and control. The review process should not only check the quality of the current phase deliverable but also the quality of all previous phase deliverables. Thus the quality is built incrementally throughout the development of the product, hence reducing the cost of unnecessary rework later in the lifecycle.

Table 5.2 The controls matrix[a]

Criteria ↓	Money	Progress	Resources	Quality	Sequence	Scope	Change
At what level?	Budgets For the project Within project Within service Spent versus to complete	IT strategy Milestones Deadlines	Staff Hardware Software Materials Data	Finished system and its strategic components Reviews Standards Procedures	Inter-project Within project Predefined steps	Business Strategy Within project Inter-project	Scope Budgets Quality Service Software and hardware
What is affected as a result of this control?	Development costs Maintenance costs Profitability	Project deadlines Development costs	Development costs Productivity	Progress Development costs Maintenance costs Serviceability	Business Strategy Project deadlines Productivity Quality	Requirements Business objectives Development costs	Documentation Approval procedures Development costs Maintenance costs
Who is responsible for managing this control?	Directors Senior project managers Project managers	Directors Senior project managers Project managers	Senior project managers Project managers	Senior project managers Project managers QA	Directors Senior project managers Project managers	Directors Senior project managers	Senior project managers Project managers CM
What is the frequency of control?	On-going Monthly At the end of each distinct piece of work	On-going	Monthly	At the end of each distinct piece of work	At the end of each distinct piece of work	On-going	On-going

[a] We need to decide what aspects we want to control and when. This will help in determining what goes into the systems development lifecycle.

Table 5.3 Matrix showing controls and systems development process

Controls	Initiation		Scope	Requirements		Construction			Installation
	Idea gets initiated / Business strategy requires it / Service queries are raised	Is the request/ concept feasible from business viewpoint?	What is the scope of the project?	What are the business requirements?	Are these requirements technically feasible?	Design the computer system to meet these requirements	Develop the computer system to meet the computer system design	Test the computer system developed	Install the computer system
Money		▲	▲		▲			▲	→
Progress	On-going								→
Resources Quality Sequence Scope Change	On-going Incremental		▲	▲		▲	▲	▲	→

The pursuit of a high level of quality, in addition to increased effectiveness and customer satisfaction, can also work to reduce costs. The expense associated with the rework effort created by having to clean up poor quality work can be considerable. An analysis of the value of the time expended by management, users, development staff, coupled with hardware expense involved, would produce some large figures (Murray, 1987a,b).

There should be more emphasis on defect prevention in order to build quality early in the development of IT products and services. This could be through documented internal standards and methodologies, education, tools, and quality improvement teams. In addition, anything that helps to prepare programmers or automate error-prone tasks can be considered as defect prevention mechanisms.

Quality management system approach

The DTI *TickIT Guide* (*A Guide to Software QMS Construction and Certification using ISO9001/ EN29001/BS5750 Part1 (1987)*) expresses a general concern that software contains too many errors which become difficult to correct as a project approaches maturity. The *TickIT Guide* recommends a system of controls which make software and development activities visible, and hence manageable, at all stages throughout the development lifecycle and it suggests that such a system of controls may be combined as a quality management system (QMS).

What is a QMS?

A QMS is the enabling mechanism within an organization which coordinates and controls the functions needed to achieve the required quality of product or service as economically as possible. A QMS will involve every organizational function that directly or indirectly affects a delivered product or service. The QMS will normally be documented in an organization's quality manual (cf. DTI *TickIT Guide*, 1990).

A QMS is intended to accomplish the following key objectives:

- to provide the mechanisms for achieving efficient, effective and economical development of product and supply of services;
- to provide both a procedural and engineering base to support the scope of the organization's activities;
- to coordinate business needs by adopting common national (e.g. BS 5750) and international (e.g. ISO 9000 series) QMS standards, leading to marketing advantages.

Figure 5.3 shows an example of a QMS structure emphasizing the importance of a product lifecycle control framework.

The elements described in Table 5.4 are considered to be the optimum effective set for a quality system and as such should be applied in total, with selection decisions being on the type and complexity of the methods within each element, commensurate with the size and function of an organization (cf. DTI *TickIT Guide*, 1990). A project manager is responsible for the extent and control of quality and, therefore, must interact closely with all the quality activities.

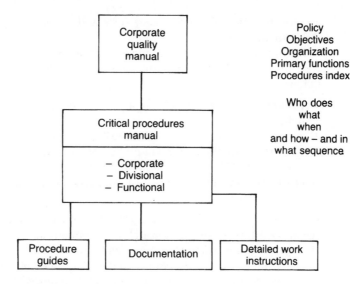

Figure 5.3 Example of a QMS structure.

Table 5.4 Quality system elements

- Implementing and maintaining a quality system
- Managing the organization and its interfaces
- Reviewing
- Documenting projects and products
- Recruitment, training and staff development
- Configuration management
- Backup, security and archiving
- Quality system reviews and audits
- Procurement
- Progress monitoring and reporting
- Non-conforming material
- Corrective action
- Quality information

It is important to ensure that the QMS allows the delivery of a product and service to the user against a mutually understood requirement and business environment. In many cases a quality plan may be produced which is a manifestation of the QMS expressed in project terms. This permits flexibility and prevents quality procedures becoming unnecessarily bureaucratic for any given application (*TickIT News*, 1991).

Quality-related costs

Studies have shown consistently that defects discovered late in the lifecycle cost more to fix by an order of magnitude than defects discovered early (cf. for example, Boehm, 1981; DeMarco, 1982; Price Waterhouse, 1988). Rework and spoilage typically account for 30% of development costs and 50–60% of product lifecycle costs (DTI *TickIT Guide*, 1990).

The importance of Quality Management can only be demonstrated objectively if the costs of non-conformance are made visible. Quality-related costs can be classified as follows:

1. **Prevention cost** – the cost of action to investigate, prevent or reduce defects and failures.
2. **Appraisal cost** – the cost of assessing the quality achieved.
3. **Failure cost** – the cost of failure before and after delivery to the customer, i.e. the cost of not achieving the desired quality.
4. **Opportunity cost** – the cost of lost market opportunity or loss of alternative use of resources.

According to the DTI *TickIT Guide* (1990), a software product where a larger percentage of the effort is used in thorough requirements analysis, in planning its design and in employing prevention techniques will result in lower lifecycle costs. This is because, although more money is spent in the initial stages of product development and in planning and installing QMSs, less money is required to cure problems later in the lifecycle. According to one survey, quality assurance techniques such as reviews, inspections and testing reduce the rework cost by a factor of 2 or 3 to 1. For each dollar spent on quality assurance activities, you can save about two dollars on rework, which equates to about 100% return on investment.

System Development (Murray, 1985) mentions that, according to Leon Ellsworth of IBM, increasing the emphasis on prevention and appraisal yielded a 34% reduction in the failure costs and an increase in the funds available for new development of nearly 140% in one instance.

Benefits of a quality approach

The benefits of a QMS approach are likely to vary depending on the nature of the software product. The larger and more complex the project, the higher the level of reliability required in the final product, and the tighter the schedule, the greater the benefits of using a QMS (Price Waterhouse, 1988).

The main benefit of a QMS is to improve the software quality, which in turn significantly reduces the overall costs relating to the development and operation of IT products and services. According to Price Waterhouse (1988), a quality system has an effect on cost, timeliness, reliability, functionality, maintainability, which are all dimensions of software quality. These are discussed below.

Cost

A quality system can reduce both planned costs and budget overruns as explained below.

As a result of the standardization which takes place using a quality system, the procedures to be followed by development staff become well defined and understood and therefore development staff do not waste time reinventing the wheel. This therefore contributes to a reduction in costs from improved productivity.

Standardization also helps to improve staff utilization, because of uniformity of working practices across projects. The use of formal procedures can also lead to reductions in project management time.

Formal procedures also assist the project manager in resource planning by helping to ensure that all necessary tasks are identified and scheduled in the most cost-effective way. A control mechanism is provided for management by monitoring progress against the plans.

A quality system incorporates various control mechanisms such as configuration management, change control, documentation control etc. These controls enable management to review and approve the changes by analysing the impact of the changes. This has considerable effect on cost by avoiding any unnecessary changes to systems and documentation.

A quality system approach promotes the building of quality throughout the development lifecycle. This contributes towards early identification and correction of errors and thus significantly improves the productivity and avoids expensive maintenance costs.

Timeliness

Overruns against time and budget normally occur because of poor project management and inaccurate estimating. A quality system can affect both of these in the following ways:

1. A quality system requires the preparation of a project resource plan, and monitoring the progress against that plan. This enables potential problems to be identified at an early stage, thus reducing the risk of the project going badly wrong.
2. A quality system provides a framework for controlling changes to user requirements by emphasizing user liaison and change control. Thus all changes are agreed and documented so that their impact can be quantified. Configuration management procedures help to ensure that changes are implemented in a controlled way.
3. The existence of a quality system should help to ensure that time records are accurate, and available for analysis. By adopting standard procedures for development it should be possible to ensure that a consistent definition is applied to work undertaken on previous projects and thus provide a consistent basis for estimating.
4. According to Price Waterhouse (1988), there is no hard evidence that a quality system reduces overruns. However, by improving the accuracy of estimating and increasing control over projects, a quality system should increase the chances that projects are completed on time and within budget.

Reliability

1. A quality system can reduce the number of faults in the software delivered to the users through the procedures specified for project control, development and testing.

2. Configuration management and change control procedures ensure that the user gets the correct version of a system. Configuration management also makes it easier to trace the effect of any detected errors through the system.
3. A QMS can provide information on the effectiveness of development techniques and thus allow management to ensure that the most effective development techniques are applied.
4. A quality system provides the framework for selecting the most appropriate level of testing for a project. In addition, it can give confidence that a given level of quality has been achieved, because the procedures used in error prevention and appraisal will be documented in the project quality plan, and together with test results will be available to management and users.
5. As a quality system improves estimating, it will therefore bring additional benefits in terms of reliability.

Functionality

Functionality is concerned with meeting the user requirements. It is a common problem that a software delivered to the users is difficult to use, lacks the required functions or does not perform as expected. A quality system addresses this problem to a certain extent as explained below:

1. A quality system will include procedures for maintaining control of the user's technical requirement, including agreeing changes. A formal methodology, specified in the quality manual, makes the process of specifying user requirements easier and more reliable.
2. Design reviews at each stage provide a means of assuring that requirements are being implemented. Acceptance testing of the finished system provides the final test of the system against its specification.

Maintainability

According to Lientz and Swanson (1980), at least 50% of total lifecycle effort is spent in maintenance. Many organizations continue to experience similar time investment for maintenance even in the mid-1990s. A quality system can reduce this maintenance effort in the following ways:

1. Using a quality system allows a closer match between user needs and the functions of the system. This should therefore reduce maintenance requirements because the need for changes in the system after delivery will have been reduced.
2. A quality system also permits the development of software that is more easily changed and expanded. Because of the better project control and development techniques used, maintenance becomes easier to handle.
3. Change control and configuration management techniques provide a framework for managing error correction and changes to meet new requirements. Using documentation control allows management to ensure that system documentation specification is reliable and accurate.

Quality assurance

In addition to the above benefits of a quality system, quality assurance related activities can have an impact on software quality, as explained below:

1. Project audits provide a means by which management can be assured that agreed procedures are being followed.
2. Function audits provide a mechanism for monitoring and assessing the effectiveness of procedures. This allows management to monitor the cost-effectiveness of individual tools and techniques.
3. Quality assurance can be regarded as a means available to management to maximize the benefits from their investment in the quality system. The existence of quality assurance enables a more effective management of the technical operations of the company.

Estimates of costs and benefits using QMS

According to Price Waterhouse (1988), it is difficult to determine by how much software failure costs could be reduced by suppliers if they were to adopt better quality management. However, it would be possible to work out what savings would have to be made to justify the expenditure involved, and consider whether such savings are possible. Table 5.5 shows the estimated quality system costs and benefits as reported by Price Waterhouse (1988).

Considering software suppliers and users, it can be seen from Table 5.2 that a 13% reduction in failure costs would be required to cover the costs of implementing quality systems. If suppliers consider an improvement of this magnitude probable, then it can be concluded that there are net benefits of implementing a quality system. In spite of the lack of data relating to software supplied by in-house IT departments, it is clear from the discussion so far regarding the incidence of failure costs, that there is a strong case for implementing a QMS from a company-wide perspective.

Considering software suppliers only, most of the costs of quality management are incurred during the development phase and are borne by the suppliers, while many of the potential benefits appear during maintenance and are enjoyed by users. Figure 5.4 shows that the net benefits of quality system do not appear until the maintenance phase (Price Waterhouse, 1988).

Table 5.5 Quality system costs and benefits (from Price Waterhouse, 1988)

Item	Suppliers and users (245 firms)	Typical supplier
Total costs	550	3
Annual quality system costs	43	0.23
Annual failure costs	340	0.61
Reduction in costs required to justify investment		
Failure costs	13%	38%
Total costs	8%	8%

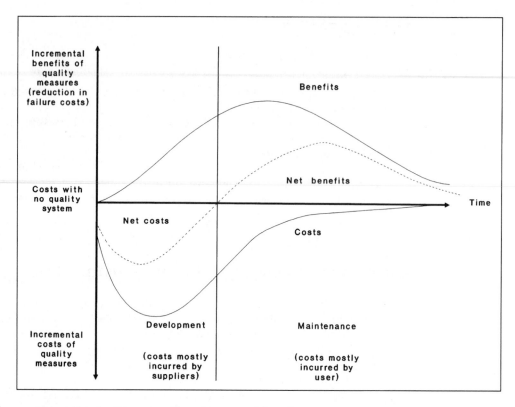

Figure 5.4 Quality system lifecycle costs and benefits.

Case studies

This subsection gives some examples of organizations where a quality management system approach has been used according to the requirements of BS 5750, Part 1 (1987)/ISO 9001, and the benefits obtained from it.

A major organization in the medium/heavy engineering sector claims that as a result of applying the quality system approach to its IT function it achieved the following major benefits:

- reduced error correction costs;
- reduction in project overruns; and
- improved maintainability.

A financial division within a large software house considers the main benefit of a quality system to be the customer satisfaction and repeat business. They claim that by continually improving the quality of their products and services, they are able to optimize their opportunities and provide the means for future growth. According to this organization, the auditing aspect of the quality system approach allows them to keep better control of the following aspects relating to their software projects:

- number of errors;
- budget versus actual cost;
- actual versus planned timescales;

- response in turnaround time in support areas;
- effectiveness of testing; and
- number of complaints from internal and external customers.

A small software house (fewer than 100 people) which implemented a quality system approach mentions the following benefits obtained from it:

- ability to produce what the client wants at an acceptable quality level, more *quickly*;
- better management reporting and review;
- coherence between project phases;
- better definition of authorities and responsibilities; and
- greater confidence in winning competitive bids.

Another small software house (fewer than 100 people), which implemented the quality system about two years ago, considers traceability (e.g. of documentation, procedures etc.) as the immediate benefit. It also claims that increased confidence among staff, greater quality awareness among customers, management, and staff have been the added benefits resulting in extra business.

This organization has been able to eliminate duplication of documentation by nearly 30% by using the audit process, therefore reducing the overall development costs proportionally. It also believes that, in spite of considerable increase in its customer base, the number of errors has gone down. It also has better control over subcontractors. A much greater emphasis is now placed on planning as a result of quality system implementation.

According to one major international management consultancy firm, a quality system gives an organization the following benefits:

- much improved visibility of the process;
- quality culture;
- marketing advantage; and
- conformance to specification.

Move towards total quality

The DTI *TickIT* initiative promoted the QMS within the context of total quality management (TQM). TQM was designed to permeate and improve every process and system within an organization. It encourages companies to measure the price of not conforming to quality, to assess how much quality costs, and then to work out the savings once TQM has been introduced. Woolfson (1989) argues that considerable cost savings can be obtained by companies embarking upon TQM, and he cites cases where such cost savings have been achieved.

TQM is about improvement, and essentially there are three driving components as shown in Figure 5.5:

- management commitment for improvement;
- motivation for improvement; and
- measurements for improvement.

These driving components operate on the QMS. Should any element be missing, the organization's QMS may fail to achieve its objectives. In this context, the term QMS

Figure 5.5 TQM improvement model (from DTI).

includes procedures from the conventional management system where they can affect quality, for example, the recruitment programme (DTI *TickIT News*, 1991).

Conclusions

Continuing problems with the management of IT projects are frequently the result of lack of planning and adequate control. This means late delivery, higher costs, and dissatisfied users. Based on industry surveys (e.g. Price Waterhouse and other examples), it has been shown that many of these management problems can be addressed by implementing a QMS framework. A QMS approach enables an organization to achieve the following benefits:

• early detection of errors;
• lower development and maintenance costs;
• improved overall quality of products and services;
• greater user satisfaction;
• improved return on investment;
• improved quality culture;
• improved marketing advantage.

In addition to the above, organizations can obtain further cost savings through continuous improvement by promoting QMS within the context of total quality. Many of the recommendations made in this chapter help to address the indifferent development evaluation practices identified in Chapter 1. The organizational benefits from moving toward a total quality approach would seem to be considerable. The difficult part may be in convincing senior management that in order to reduce the costs of IT development, it may be necessary to spend to save.

References

Boehm, B. (1981) *Software Engineering Economics*, Prentice Hall, New Jersey.

British Computer Society (1990) *A Guide to Software Quality Management System Construction and Certification using ISO9001/EN29001/BS5750 Part 1 (1987)*, Prepared under contract to the UK Department of Trade and Industry, Issue 1.1.

Brynjolfsson, E. (1993) The productivity paradox of information technology. *Communications of the ACM*, **36** (12), 67–77.

Computing Services Association (1988) *Quality Systems for Software: A Briefing Note*, Computing Services Association, London.

Charette, R. (1991) *Application Strategies for Risk Analysis*, McGraw Hill, New York.

DeMarco, T. (1982) *Controlling Software Projects*, Yourdon Inc, New York.

Department of Trade and Industry (1990) *TickIT Guide*, Department of Trade and Industry, London.

Dorling, A. (1989) *Are you Geared up for Software Quality?* A booklet for the Department of Trade and Industry, Issue 1.1, Department of Trade and Industry, London.

DTI *TickIT News* (1991) Issue 1, Department of Trade and Industry, London.

Evans, M. and Marciniak, J. (1986) *Software Quality Assurance and Management*, John Wiley, New York.

Gibson, R. (1992) *Managing Computer Projects: Avoiding the Pitfalls*, Prentice Hall, Hemel Hempstead.

Griffiths, C. and Willcocks, L. (1995) Managing risks in major IT projects. In *Hard Money, Soft Outcomes* (eds. B. Farbey, D. Targett and F. Land), Alfred Waller/Unicom, Henley.

KPMG (1991) *Runaway Computer Projects*, KPMG, London.

Lientz, B. and Swanson, E. (1980) *Software Maintenance Management*, Addison-Wesley, New York.

Murray, J. (1985) Project leadership begins at the top, *System Development*, **4** (12), 1–4.

Murray, J. (1987a) The issue of quality assurance: can we afford not to do it right the first time? *System Development*, **7** (1), 1–3.

Murray, J. (1987b) Requirements statement. *System Development*, **7** (7), 1–3.

National Audit Office (1990) *Managing Computer Projects* in the National Health Service, HMSO, London.

Price Waterhouse (1988) *Software Quality Standards: The Costs and Benefits*. A Review for the Department of Trade and Industry, Price Waterhouse, London.

Proceedings of Third National Conference (1985) Measuring data processing quality and productivity. *System Development*, **5** (5), 1–3.

Proceedings of System Development Conference (1987) Improving productivity in EDP system development. *System Development*, **7** (4), 1–6.

Proceedings of National Conference (1987) Data processing quality assurance. *System Development*, **7** (9), 3–6.

Public Meeting Notes (1991) *Runaway Computer Systems: A Panel Debate*. Software Quality Management Specialist Group of The British Computer Society, BCS, London.

Redmill, F. (1990) Considering quality in the management of software-based development projects. *Information and Software Technology*, January/February, 18–22.

Walton, R. (1989) *Up and Running*, Harvard Business School Press, Boston, MA.

Willcocks, L. and Margetts, H. (1994) Risk and information systems: developing the analysis. In *Information Management: Evaluation of Information Systems Investment* (ed. L. Willcocks), Chapman & Hall, London.

Woolfson, K. (1989) British companies discover the truth of total quality. *Financial Weekly*, 17–23 November, 20–2.

6

IS cost estimating and the investment justification process

Albert L. Lederer and Jayesh Prasad

Introduction

Accurate software development cost estimating is crucial to the decision to invest in new technology. When IS analysts underestimate costs, management may authorize new systems that later overrun their budgets and fail to achieve their expected return on investment. Extreme overruns are sometimes cancelled before completion and thus waste the precious resources invested in them. Moreover, overruns can reduce the credibility of IS management and thereby discourage future user cooperation.

When IS analysts overestimate costs, management may choose not to develop potentially beneficial systems. When a new system with major benefits is proposed, but estimators predict unrealistically high costs beyond the maximum permitted to cost justify it, management typically declines to approve it and thus loses its potential benefits (Emery, 1971; King and Schrems, 1978). Hence, both underestimates and overestimates can have a significant, deleterious impact (Tate and Verner, 1990). They can both cause lost strategic opportunities (Benjamin *et al.*, 1984).

The impact of inaccurate estimating on business practice has been very significant. *Businessweek* (1988) reported several US information systems development calamities.

Investing in Information Systems: Evaluation and Management. Edited by
Leslie Willcocks. Published in 1996 by Chapman & Hall. ISBN 0 412 72670 X.

An Allstate Insurance system initially estimated at US $8 million was begun and then while still incomplete was re-estimated at US $100 million. A State of Oklahoma project initially estimated at US $500 000 was later completed at US $4 million. The *Businessweek* article also reported a Peat Marwick Mitchell survey that found that 35% of its largest clients admitted major cost overruns.

Despite the prevalence of cost overruns, no previous study has investigated current cost estimating practice in business and industry. This chapter describes a study of the cost estimating practices reported by 112 IS managers and other IS professionals. The study sought to better understand the current degree of success of estimating, the influences on it, its process, the causes of inaccurate estimating, and practices associated with greater accuracy.

A current assessment of a practice can be valuable. By understanding cost estimating practices, researchers may be able to identify methods of improving cost estimating accuracy. As a result, managers may be able to implement new practices to improve estimate accuracy and thus improve the return on their organization's investment in new information systems.

Background

Prior research on IS development cost estimating has largely concentrated on the study of algorithmic techniques. Some of this research has identified factors that are believed to affect IS development and must therefore be considered while estimating development costs (Benbasat and Vessey, 1980; Boehm, 1984; Boehm and Papaccio, 1986; Mohanty, 1981). These diverse factors include system size and complexity, personnel capabilities and experience, hardware constraints, the use of modern software tools and practices, users' understanding of information systems technology, the volatility of their requirements and many others.

Most algorithmic methods are based on one or more such factors (Conte, Dunsmore and Shen, 1986). The estimator quantifies each factor based on historical data about past development projects or on intuition and experience (Aron, 1976; Mohanty, 1981). Different methods, however, may define the same factors in different ways. For example, many methods operationalize system size in terms of the projected number of lines of executable code in the proposed system (Boehm, 1984; Conte, Dunsmore and Shen, 1986; Freiman and Park, 1979; Herd *et al.*, 1977; Jensen, 1983; Nelson, 1966; Putnam, 1978; Walston and Felix, 1977; Wolverton, 1974) whereas relatively fewer methods use the number of functions, modules or program features in the system (Albrecht, 1979; Demarco, 1982; Donelson, 1976; Halstead, 1977; Jones, 1986; McCabe, 1976).

The algorithmic methods utilize these quantified factors to produce an estimate of the proposed system's cost. These methods vary widely in mathematical sophistication. Some use simple arithmetic formulae based on such summary statistics as means and standard deviations (Donelson, 1976), while others employ regression models (Walston and Felix, 1977) and differential equations (Putnam, 1978). Some algorithmic methods are available for use in computer-based software packages. For example, ESTIMACS (Computer Associates, 1987) is based on Albrecht's (1979) function point method (Rubin, 1983). An expert system has even been proposed to calibrate the model used by the estimating process (Cuelenaere *et al.*, 1987).

Objective studies of these methods have been few. Often the developers of a method have described their own technique and reported their own assessment of its accuracy (Donelson, 1976; Jensen, 1983; Putnam, 1978; Walston and Felix, 1977; Wolverton, 1974). Other researchers have tried to predict the cost of projects but only after their completion and hence with full knowledge of their final scope (Banker and Kemerer, 1989; Kemerer, 1987; Kitchenham and Taylor, 1985; Miyazaki and Mori, 1985).

For example, one study evaluated the accuracy of four algorithmic methods by predicting the durations of projects which had already been completed (Kemerer, 1987). However, it found considerable inaccuracy with error rates averaging from 85 to 772%. In a related study, experts estimated these same projects without using formal algorithmic techniques generally and found a better performance than the models in the original study although mean error rates ranged from 32 to 1107% (Vicinanza, Mukhopadhyay and Prietula, 1991). A third study (using different projects) found error rates averaging 166% (Miyazaki and Mori, 1985) and a fourth study (again with different projects) found similarly high error rates (Martin, 1988). These studies are admirable as preliminary efforts; however, the researchers' knowledge of the scope at the time of estimating (knowledge generally available only in laboratory settings) has caused speculation that the techniques would be even more inaccurate when the scope is initially unknown (Kemerer, 1987).

Nevertheless, the elegance of the algorithmic methods is so impressive that it has inspired the view that 'the methods available today are more than adequate to establish an estimation approach. All that is needed is management's willingness to employ the planning and control philosophy used in other functional areas in the information systems department' (Benbasat and Vessey, 1980, p. 42). However, the extent to which organizations use these estimating methods is unknown. Besides a few prescriptive articles (Boehm, 1981; Demarco, 1982), research on the actual practice of cost estimating and its problems is also scanty.

However, a more recent case study did describe the actual practice of cost estimating at the largest division of a *Fortune* 200 organization (Lederer *et al.*, 1990). The research revealed that cost estimates were used for a variety of purposes that included selecting projects for implementation, staffing and scheduling projects, controlling and monitoring their progress, evaluating employee performance, and also marketing proposed systems to users. It also demonstrated how cost estimates were initially prepared and later revised at different stages of the systems development lifecycle. It identified the participants in the preparation and approval of the estimates, described the management of the estimating process, and highlighted reasons why cost estimating is often inaccurate.

The case study also stressed the tight link between the preparation of an estimate and the actual development of the estimated system. That is, the touchstone of an estimating method is the comparison of the final cost of the completed system to its original estimate. However, the proximity of the final cost to the original estimate is governed not only by the quality of the estimate but also by the quality of the management of the development effort. Hence, researchers must consider the entire development process when studying the estimating process. Understanding a process as a whole – or *gestalt* – can explain its parts (Kohler, 1929).

While the case study revealed the actual practice and problems of cost estimating in a single organization, no empirical study of a large sample has described the current state of cost estimating practice in industry until the current one. It extends the case by examining questions it raised but did not answer.

Objectives

The current study sought answers to eight questions about IS cost estimating. The purpose was to enable researchers to understand current cost estimating practice since the literature described above has not yet done so. The answers might thus help researchers identify methods of improving cost estimating accuracy or suggest avenues for research to do so in order to reduce the potential management problems of inaccurate estimates. More accurate cost estimates would then facilitate new IS investment decisions with a higher return on their investment. The rationale for asking each question, and the question, follows.

First, confirmation of the importance of the issue would lend credence to reporting the results. Conversely, if the issue were unimportant (a possible but unexpected finding), then the need to report the results might be much less. Thus the research asked:

• How important is cost estimating to IS managers and professionals?

Second, if the respondents reported being highly successful (again a possible but unexpected finding), the need for further study might be less critical. Thus we asked:

• How successful are IS managers and professionals at cost estimating?

Third, the uses of cost estimates might help researchers understand the rationale for the cost estimating procedure. This understanding, combined with an understanding of actual cost estimating procedure, might identify problems with the procedure and suggest means to improve it. Hence, the research asked:

• For what purposes do IS managers and professionals use cost estimates?

The broad backgrounds for cost estimating and the specific factors influencing it might be flawed. If so, the grounds and factors might suggest efforts for improving cost estimating or for further research to do so. Hence the research asked the following two questions:

• What broad grounds influence cost estimating?
• What specific factors influence cost estimating?

Because the causes themselves of inaccurate cost estimates might likewise suggest further research about their nature or about practices to eliminate them, the research asked:

• What are the causes of inaccurate cost estimates?

Finally, by understanding contemporary cost estimating practices and identifying those associated with greater accuracy, researchers may find inconsistencies and flaws that might cause inaccuracy. With an understanding of the reasons for the association, researchers might also suggest practices to improve accuracy. Thus, we asked these last questions:

• What practices do IS managers and professionals use in cost estimating?
• Which practices are associated with more accurate cost estimating?

Methodology

To study these issues, we developed a questionnaire based on the case study and other software development cost estimation literature just described (with additions noted below). Major sections were:

- **A list of potential uses** (e.g. to staff projects) of cost estimating. Subjects identified the importance of each on a five-point Likert-type scale.
- **A list of cost estimating activities** (e.g. user management sign-off on the cost estimate). Subjects identified the percentage of their organization's large projects that follow each.
- **A list of factors** (e.g. the size of the system in number of programs) typically influencing cost estimating. Subjects identified the influence of each on a five-point Likert-type scale.
- **A list of general bases** (e.g. intuition) of cost estimating. On a five-point Likert-type scale, subjects identified the extensiveness of their use of each.
- **A list of recognized software packages** (e.g. ESTIMACS) for helping estimate development costs (Coursey, 1987; Datapro, 1988a; Datapro 1988b; Kemerer, 1987). Subjects stated if they used each.
- **A list of potential causes** (e.g. overlooked tasks) of inaccurate estimates. Subjects identified on a five-point Likert-type scale the extent to which each was responsible for inaccurate estimates.
- One question asking the **percentage of large project overruns** at their organization and another asking the **percentage of underruns**.
- **Demographic questions**.

Subjects were asked to answer the questions in terms of what their organization defined as 'large projects' (e.g. some companies such as the one in the case study consider large projects to be those estimated to exceed an arbitrary figure such as US $50 000) to prevent them from considering trivial tasks routinely handled without formal estimating. Subjects were permitted to augment the lists. For example, they could add a software estimating tool if it was not identified in the instrument.

After a pilot test with four IS managers and analysts followed by a revision to improve the questionnaire's clarity, we mailed it to 400 randomly selected members of a large, nationwide association of IS managers and analysts. A second mailing to non-respondents yielded an overall total of 116 responses.

Using the respondents' job titles and functions from the demographic items, the researchers eliminated a manager of telecommunications, director of office automation, records manager and EDP auditor since they may have lacked knowledge of estimating in their firms. Because all of the remaining 112 participate in the development of estimates, their approval, or system development based on estimates, they were knowledgeable about the questions in this study and were appropriate participants.[1] However, it should be noted that their responses represent the perceptions of IS managers and analysts and these could differ considerably from those of users.

[1] Of the final 112 respondents, 94% were responsible for systems department management, project management and/or systems estimating; 6% were responsible solely for systems analysis and programming. However, very similar statistical findings resulted both when excluding this 6% and when including the other four dropped subjects.

Table 6.1 Respondents' industries

Industry	Percent of respondents
Manufacturing	33
Insurance	17
Banking and finance	9
Government	5
Utilities	5
Retail	5
Education	4
Systems consulting	8
Other	14

All subjects were North Americans. A well-educated group, 87% possessed at least a four-year college degree and 33% at least a Master's degree. Respondents supervised an average of twelve employees and averaged fourteen years of experience in information systems with eight at their current firm. Thus respondents were responsible, educated and experienced professionals familiar with their current firm.

The firms varied in size and industry. Their annual sales averaged almost US $2 billion. Each averaged 10 797 employees while the mean number of employees in their IS departments was 478. Annual IS department budgets averaged US $28 million. No two subjects came from the same firm. Table 6.1 shows the industries. The sample represents a wide variety of industries and sizes. Thus the results of the study are probably fairly generalizable.[2]

Findings

The findings with respect to each objective are described below.

How important is cost estimating to IS managers and professionals?

The study confirmed that system development cost estimating is an important issue for IS managers and professionals; 43% of the respondents gave it the highest possible rating, indicating it was 'very important', while an additional 41% gave it the second

---

[2] The establishment of an instrument's psychometric properties conventionally requires demonstrating validity and reliability. The literature basis and pilot testing reflect the instrument's content validity. Because the analysis described later exclusively used single-item rather than multi-item measurement scales, the popularly used Cronbach's alpha was not applicable to assess reliability. Single-item scales were used to reduce the length of the instrument and encourage responses while enabling the study to cover the wide variety of issues. The psychometric properties of this instrument are consistent with exploratory as opposed to confirmatory research testing established theory (Straub, 1989). Because this is a first survey of current practice and only the section on the practices associated with accurate estimates had a solid theoretical background, it tested only hypotheses.

highest, 'moderately important'. Only 10% indicated it was 'moderately unimportant' or 'very unimportant'. The overall rating on the one- to five-point scale of importance was 4.17 and was higher than the expected mean of 3.00 at the 0.01 level of statistical significance.[3] Hence, the value of reporting the results is greater than if the subjects said the matter was unimportant.

How successful are IS managers and professionals at cost estimating?

Although IS cost estimating is important, IS professionals are not successful at it. Respondents reported that approximately 63% of all large projects significantly over-run their estimates while approximately 14% of all large projects significantly underrun their estimates (probably a less serious problem). This suggests that only about one of every four projects is completed at a cost either reasonably above or below its estimate. Hence, the importance of cost estimating, along with its inaccuracy, confirms that the study of methods of improving accuracy is worthwhile.

For what purposes do IS managers and professionals use cost estimates?

Since cost estimating is important, its uses are likewise probably important. As seen in Table 6.2, the study revealed that cost estimating is used more for project planning and control than for evaluation. The cost estimate is used to staff projects, control project implementation, select projects, schedule them and quote charges to users. In contrast, it is used, but is significantly less important, for auditing project success, evaluating project developers, and evaluating project estimators. The importance of use rating of each of those three latter uses in Table 6.2 was lower than the former five at the 0.05 level of significance or better. (More specifically, the rating of 3.22 for auditing project success was lower than the 3.51 rating for quoting charges to users at the 0.05 level of significance.) The division of the table into the two parts may suggest

Table 6.2 The uses of the cost estimate

Use of estimate	Importance of use Mean rating (1–5 scale)
To staff projects	3.78
To control or monitor project implementation	3.72
To select proposed projects for implementation	3.69
To schedule projects	3.66
To quote the charges to users for projects	3.51
To audit project success	3.22
To evaluate project developers	3.06
To evaluate project estimators	2.90

[3] This paper used t-tests to compare means (as in this case) and Pearson r correlations to describe relationships.

Table 6.3 Basis of the estimating process

Basis	Extensiveness of use Mean rating (1–5 scale)
Comparison to similar, past projects based on personal memory	**3.77**
Comparison to similar, past projects based on documented facts	3.41
Intuition	3.38
A simple arithmetic formula (such as summing task durations)	3.09
Guessing	2.76
Established standards (such as averages, standard deviations, etc.)	2.33
A software package for estimating	1.80
A complex statistical formula (such as multiple regression, differential equations, etc.)	1.49

that the estimate is used insufficiently for evaluation and, since evaluation may be tied to improved performance (Lawler *et al.*, 1984), if it were so used more extensively, estimates might be met more frequently.

What broad grounds influence cost estimating?

A variety of general grounds for estimating are possible. As seen in Table 6.3, this study found that estimators claim to rely more heavily on their personal memory of past projects than on documented facts, established standards, estimating packages and formulae. The participants' rating of the extensiveness of use in Table 6.3 for the comparison to similar, past projects based on personal memory at 3.77 was higher than the other grounds in the table at least at the 0.01 level of significance. However, the participants also rely more heavily on using intuition (i.e. quick and ready insight) than on guessing (i.e. forming an opinion with little or no evidence), two slightly similar means. The rating of 3.38 for intuition was significantly higher than the rating of 2.76 for guessing at the 0.01 level of significance. The reliance on personal memory rather than documented facts may suggest a flaw in the estimating process: its basis is not very scientific. However, the unimportance of guessing implies that this process was not based on pure conjecture.

In addition, only 17% reported using a software package to help estimate the development costs of large projects. Table 6.4 identifies the packages they reported using and the number of respondents using each.[4]

What specific factors influence cost estimating?

Of the numerous potential factors in Table 6.5, the complexity of the proposed application (with a 4.26 rating) and its required integration with existing systems (with a 4.19 rating) influenced cost estimating most heavily. Both were higher than all of the remaining influences at the 0.05 level of significance or better.

[4] Readers familiar with the literature on estimating software may be surprised to see so few actual users. Still, the authors see no reason to doubt the number of users. However, we question whether all the packages actually produce estimates, and we discuss this later.

Table 6.4 Software packages in use[a]

Software package	Users
*ESTIMACS	6
*SPECTRUM/ESTIMATOR	4
In-house package	2
Project workbench	2
*Nolan/PROMPT	1
Project Manager	1
AGS PAC III	1
DEC/VAX Sofiware Project Manager	1
Microsoft Project	1
*SLIM	0
*SOFTCOST	0
*SPQR/Estimator	0
*Before You Leap	0

[a] Packages with an asterisk appeared by name in the questionnaire. Respondents wrote in those without asterisks. Those with no users appear in the table to show the comprehensiveness of the study.

Table 6.5 Influences on the estimate

Influence	Extent of influence Mean rating (1–5 scale)
The complexity of the proposed application system	**4.26**
The required integration with existing systems	**4.19**
The complexity of the programs in the system	3.92
The size of the system in number of functions	3.77
The capabilities of the project team members	3.63
The size of the system in number of programs	3.60
The project team's experience with the application	3.49
The anticipated frequency or extent of potential changes in requirements	3.44
The project team's experience with the programming language	3.43
The data management system (flat files, database etc.)	3.39
The number of project team members	3.30
The availability of software productivity tools (such as screen generators or code generators)	3.14
The extent of programming or documentation standards	3.13
The development mode (batch or on-line)	3.10
The particular programming language used	3.06
The project team's experience with the hardware	3.05
The availability of testing aids	2.84
The availability of test time on the hardware	2.68
Computer memory and secondary storage constraints	2.65
The size of the system in number of lines of code	**2.23**

Because many estimating methods are based on the number of lines of code in the application, it is striking that this factor (with a 2.23 rating) was the least influential. In fact, it was lower than the second lowest (and thus all other factors) at the 0.01 level of significance. This suggests that information systems professionals may see research on lines of code as unwarranted. The result is consistent with previous

Table 6.6 Causes of inaccurate estimates

Causes	Extent of responsibility Mean rating (1–5 scale)
Frequent requests for changes by users	**3.89**
Users' lack of understanding of their own requirements	3.60
Overlooked tasks	3.59
Insufficient user–analyst communication and understanding	3.34
Poor or imprecise problem definition	3.29
Insufficient analysis when developing estimate	3.21
Lack of an adequate methodology or guidelines for estimating	3.09
Lack of coordination of systems development, technical services, operations, data administration, etc. functions during development	3.06
Changes in IS department personnel	2.95
Insufficient time for testing	2.86
Lack of historical data regarding past estimates and actuals	2.83
Lack of setting and review of standard durations for use in estimating	2.83
Pressures from managers, users or others to increase or reduce the estimate	2.83
Inability to anticipate skills of project team members	2.81
Red tape	2.80
Users' lack of understanding of data processing	2.77
Lack of project control comparing estimates and actuals	2.76
Reduction of project scope or quality to stay within estimate resulting in extra work later	2.73
Inability to tell where past estimates failed	2.71
Lack of careful examination of the estimate by IS department management	2.61
Lack of participation in estimating by the systems analysts and programmers who ultimately develop the system	2.60
Performance reviews don't consider whether estimates were met	2.49
Lack of diligence by systems analysts and programmers	2.34
Removal of padding from the estimate by management	2.30

research showing that the use of lines of code is less effective than other measures of size (Kemerer, 1987; Low and Jeffrey, 1990). Combined with the previous finding, it might suggest that researchers focus more on application complexity and integration.

What are the causes of inaccurate estimates?

Table 6.6 shows several potential causes of inaccurate estimates. The most responsible cause, frequent requests for changes by users, had a 3.89 rating for extent of responsibility, higher than the remaining causes at least at the 0.05 level of significance. That cause, along with the second highest one, users' lack of understanding of their own requirements, suggests that information systems managers and professionals attach considerable user responsibility to their inaccurate estimates. Although user inadequacy may be the main cause of inaccuracy, perhaps by assigning the fault to users, estimators can rationalize their own shortcomings and might even be less diligent in their estimating.[5]

What practices do IS managers and professionals use in cost estimating?

Cost estimating is carried out almost routinely. Respondents indicated that a cost estimate is prepared for 87% of their organizations' large projects. To better understand the process, this study inquired more about specifically how these organizations prepare their estimates.

Who prepares the estimate?

Frequently, the estimator later develops the estimated system. For 61% of all large projects, the same systems analysts and programmers who eventually developed the system had also participated in the preparation of the initial cost estimate. Thus, conversely, for nearly two of every five projects, after the initial estimate, projects are handed over to different analysts and programmers for final development.

Who approves the estimate?

For 58% of an organization's large projects, a cost–benefit analysis is used to justify system development. IS department management carefully studies and approves the cost estimate in 61% of all large projects, while user management signs off on the estimate in 59%. Thus conversely, about two out of five projects can be carried out without a formal cost–benefit analysis, IS department management's approval of the estimate, or user management's approval of it.

Is the estimate monitored?

The estimate can be used as a control standard in system development. For 70% of all large projects, a formal monitoring of the progress of a project compares it to its estimate in its project plan. Hence, about three of ten projects are not monitored in this fashion.

When the estimate is used to monitor a project, it is done so primarily by those involved with the project. That is, for only 8% of an organization's large projects, an

---

[5] Prototyping, computer-aided software engineering (CASE) methods, object-oriented programming (OOP), and other techniques are emerging as possible aids in cost estimating. However, this research did not assess their impact on it.

evaluation of the development process (meaning comparison of the cost estimate to the actual cost) is carried out by independent auditors.

Are variances from the estimate used to evaluate personnel?

As expected, the cost estimate is used much less extensively in the performance reviews of users than of IS personnel. The evaluation of the completion within the estimate is included in user management's performance review for 26% of an organization's large projects and is included in the performance review of user representatives (i.e. liaisons from the application area of the business organization to the information systems department) for 19% of the projects.

In contrast, the evaluation of the completion within the estimate is included in IS department management's performance review in 54% of all large projects, in the performance review of systems analysts and programmers responsible for final project development in 48%, and in the performance review of the IS department's initial estimators in 42%. Responses in all three categories for IS managers and other professionals were higher than those for users at the 0.05 level of significance or better.

When is the estimate prepared?

The cost estimate is prepared at the beginning of a project and is revised during the project as suggested by the case study but with decreasing frequency; for 77% of an organization's large projects, a cost estimate is prepared during an initial project proposal stage. For 63% of its large projects, a cost estimate is prepared (or revised) during a feasibility study. For 51%, a cost estimate is prepared (or revised) during systems analysis. And finally, for 47%, a cost estimate is prepared (or revised) during systems design. Hence, while most organizations prepare at least one estimate, they frequently, but not universally, reconsider and revise the estimate over the course of the project.

In addition, for 63% of an organization's large projects, the cost estimate is revised to accompany changes in user requirements. This implies that for 37% of its large projects, changes in user requirements are not accompanied by changes in the estimate. This may suggest some reluctance to adjust the estimate when warranted.

Which practices are associated with more accurate estimating?

The extensive research and publication about estimating algorithms have suggested that organizations using an established, sophisticated algorithm would have more accurate estimating than other organizations (Benbasat and Vessey, 1980). The use of algorithm-based packages would be responsible for this, suggesting the following hypothesis:[6]

> H1: Organizations that use software packages for estimating large projects have fewer overruns than organizations that do not use such packages.

However in this study, users of established, sophisticated estimating software packages (namely ESTIMACS, SPECTRUM/ESTIMATOR and Nolan/PROMPT – those 11 packages in Table 6.4 that the researchers had *a priori* recognized as accepted)[7] reported that approximately 71% of all large projects significantly overran their estimates while non-users reported that only about 62% overran their estimates. The difference was statistically significant at the 0.10 level and is at first glance surprising. At a minimum, this failure to support H1 suggests that these packages, when used, have not solved the problems of inaccurate estimating. However, this finding is consistent with Kemerer (1987) and Vicinanza, Mukhopadhyay and Prietula (1991).

It also suggests the need for a closer look at the association of the practices described above with more accurate cost estimating.

Identity of the estimator

Job enrichment (combining several related activities into one job) provides the worker with more autonomy and responsibility and thus stimulates improved performance (Ford, 1973). In the estimating procedure, this implies the following hypothesis:

> H2: Organizations that more extensively use the same analysts and programmers to initially prepare large project estimates and later develop the same projects, have fewer overruns than organizations that do so less extensively.

The correlation between the percentage of an organization's large projects that overrun their estimates and the percentage of its large projects for which the same systems analysts and programmers who eventually develop the system had also participated in the preparation of the initial estimate was negative and significant at the 0.05 level. This support for H2 is consistent with the view that developers show stronger commitment to timely project completion when they personally perform the estimate.

---

[6] Because expectations about practices are reasonably founded in the literature, hypotheses about them were tested. The remaining hypotheses are generally modelled around the principles of management control (Mockler, 1972; Newman, 1975) but are augmented by the performance evaluation (Lawler, Mohrman and Rosnick, 1984) and job enrichment (Ford, 1975) literature. Details accompany each hypothesis.

[7] The authors report findings in the text for only the three recognized packages because of their knowledge that at least some of the others were project management rather than estimating tools. However, a test using all 19 packages showed the use of the packages to produce slightly more inaccurate results than no use of them, although not statistically significantly so. This interesting finding may attest to the value of project management software rather than estimating software!

Approval of the estimate

Management control principles state that when management approves standards and performance measures, it gives subordinates realistic targets and thus inspires performance (Newman, 1975):

> H3: Organizations where management more extensively studies and approves large project estimates have fewer overruns than organizations where management does so less extensively.

The correlation of the percentage of an organization's large projects that overrun estimates with the percentage of projects for which IS department management carefully studies and approves the estimate was significant at the 0.01 level (and negative as expected). However, the correlation of the percentage of projects that overrun their estimates with the percentage of projects for which user management also signs off on an estimate was not. This partial support for H3 is consistent with a belief that IS department management approval may reduce overruns but that user management approval may not.

Monitoring of the estimate

Management control principles state that when management compares actual performance to standards, it increases supervisor and subordinate awareness and inspires performance (Newman, 1975):

> H4: Organizations that more extensively monitor large projects against their estimates have fewer overruns than organizations that do so less extensively.

As seen in Table 6.7, the percentage of large projects that overrun their estimates correlated significantly and negatively at the 0.01 level with two items about monitoring. The items were (1) the percentage of large projects where a formal monitoring of their progress compares them to projects plans; and (2) the percentage of those where the evaluation of the development process was done by independent auditors. This support for H4 confirms both the importance of monitoring projects and of using independent auditors to do so to complete them within its estimate.

Use of estimate variances to evaluate personnel

Performance evaluation is often used to improve performance because employees anticipate rewards or sanctions and thus modify their performance (Lawler *et al.*, 1984):

> H5: Organizations that more extensively use large project estimates to evaluate project personnel have fewer overruns than organizations that do so less extensively.

The correlations in Table 6.7 of the percentage of large projects that overrun their estimates with the percentage of large projects for which project personnel are

Table 6.7 Management practices and overruns

	Significance level	Sign of correlation
Identity of the estimator		
Same systems analysts and programmers who eventually develop system also prepared initial cost estimate	0.05	negative
Approval of the estimate		
IS management carefully study and approve of cost estimate	0.01	negative
User management sign-off on a cost estimate	ns	
Monitoring of the estimate		
Evaluation of the development process by independent auditors	0.01	negative
Formal monitoring of the project progress by comparing it to its project plan	0.01	negative
Use of the estimate to evaluate personnel		
Evaluation of completion within estimate in IS management's performance review	0.01	negative
Evaluation of the accuracy of the estimate in the performance review of IS department estimators	0.05	negative
Evaluation of the completion within the estimate included in the performance review of systems developers	0.05	negative
Evaluation of completion within estimate in user management's performance review	ns	
Evaluation of completion within the estimate in user liaisons' performance review	ns	
Timing of the estimate		
Preparation of a cost estimate during an initial project proposal stage	0.05	negative
Preparation or revision of a cost estimate during feasibility study	ns	
Preparation or revision of a cost estimate during systems analysis stage	ns	
Preparation or revision of a cost estimate during systems design stage	ns	
Cost estimate revised to accompany changes in user requirements	ns	

evaluated were statistically significant at the 0.01 and 0.05 levels for IS management, estimators and developers but not for user management and user liaisons. This partial support for H5 confirms the importance of evaluating information systems project personnel in order to complete a project within its estimate.

Timing of the estimate

Management control principles state that when management compares actual performance to predetermined standards and takes action when it finds deviation, it can improve performance (Mockler, 1972). In cost estimating we would expect that the preparation of the initial estimate and its revision (one form of action) during system development would be associated with fewer overruns.

H6: Organizations that more extensively prepare and revise large project estimates have fewer overruns than organizations which do so less extensively.

As seen in Table 6.7, the correlation between the percentage of an organization's large projects that overrun their estimates and the percentage of those for which a cost estimate is prepared during an initial project proposal stage was negative and statistically significant at the 0.05 level. This was not surprising because it merely attests to the importance of preparing an estimate during an initial project proposal.

However, the correlations between the percentage of an organization's large projects that overrun their estimates and the percentage of those for which a cost estimate is prepared (or revised) during a feasibility study stage, during a systems analysis stage, or during a systems design stage were not significant. This was very surprising because it fails to support the belief that the revision of the estimate reduces overruns. Before attempting to explain this, one more analysis will be worthwhile.

As seen in Table 6.7, the correlation of the percentage of an organization's large projects that overrun their estimates with the percentage of those for which the cost estimate is revised to accompany changes in user requirements was not significant. This again is an unusual result because we would strongly expect accuracy to improve when assessed in terms of late revisions to the estimate.

We suggest that the lack of support for H6 stems from the survey's not explicitly asking respondents to identify the percentage of overruns as measured against a specific estimate in a systems development stage. Had this been done (requiring a slightly more complex instrument), we suspect the hypothesis would have been supported. However, the current finding is more interesting.

This is because the current finding implies that respondents were probably answering questions about overruns in terms of earlier estimates rather than later ones. Thus the finding supports the notion that revising to respond to user changes, although it may prevent overruns against late estimates, does not prevent the *perception* of them. In other words, while estimators may prefer to be held unaccountable for their early inaccuracies, they may still recognize that later estimates do not exculpate them. In fact, revising to respond to changes may simply call attention to initial estimation errors.

Implications

The contribution of this study to the literature is a portrayal of how organizations carry out cost estimating. The study is unique in its treatment of cost estimating as coupled with, rather than separate from, other systems development activities. Because it studied cost estimating with a survey of current practice (rather than by reporting the developer of an algorithm's assessment of its accuracy or by predicting completed projects' costs with full knowledge of their scope – the two approaches previously used), it demonstrated an alternative and useful approach to learning about the subject.

In doing so, it has revealed an unsettled state of practice. Estimators appear to select an estimate with a limited factual basis. What separates the more accurate estimators from the less accurate ones appears to be that the organizations of the former use the estimate more extensively to evaluate their IS managers, estimators and developers and that they monitor these individuals more closely during estimation and development.

This study revealed little evidence of the ability to estimate costs accurately. It simply suggested that effective project management rather than accurate estimating may be the key to project completion within an estimate. The major impediment to accurate estimating, namely frequent requests for changes by users, may be very difficult for systems developers to anticipate and control.

Thus the study also reaffirmed the paradox of cost estimating; systems developers may not know the estimated cost of the proposed system until they know its complete user requirements and scope. They may not know its complete user requirements and scope until they have finished developing it, adjusting and readjusting the specifications along the way. However, after they have finished developing it, they may have spent (and perhaps overrun) its estimated cost.

Implications for researchers

This study has affirmed the importance of cost estimating and the deficient state of its current practice. It thus offers several suggestions to researchers to build on its contributions.

First, the investigation of cost estimating represents a major opportunity. Researchers should study it to contribute significantly to practice.

Second, this research has suggested that cost estimating software is used infrequently. This may be because when it is used, it is not very accurate. Researchers should therefore continue to try to improve cost estimating algorithms. The research spearheaded by Banker and Kemerer (1989), Kemerer (1987), Martin (1988), and ·Miyazaki and Mori (1985), using the final, working specifications of completed projects should continue. It may be the best empirical research to date to have assessed the accuracy of the algorithms and shown that it can be improved through better calibration. However, it has done so in a research setting where user requirements remained stable, although the current research suggests that unstable requirements are the most serious cause of inaccurate estimates. It might therefore be improved by using earlier, more uncertain user requirements rather than the final, certain ones.

Thus, third, and in a similar vein, researchers should study the estimating and development processes simultaneously in ongoing organizational activities. A major contribution of the current research is its recognition of the link between estimation and development. Researchers should thus track individual projects by investigating their cost estimating techniques, initial estimates, user requirement changes (the major cause of inaccuracy in this research), re-estimates (an ongoing process recognized in this research), and final costs simultaneously to assess the accuracy of the estimating techniques. Such longitudinal studies may reveal strengths and weaknesses in estimating and development techniques. They may have the greatest likelihood of contributing enduring improvements in estimating accuracy.

Fourth, researchers should independently study information requirements analysis, given its important link to inaccurate estimation.

Fifth, because the current research used broad questions to obtain a general view of current practice, future research should examine many of its individual questions in more detail by asking exactly who does what when. As examples, research should further investigate the combined estimator/developer role, the estimate approval process, the monitoring of the estimate, personnel evaluation using it, and its timing. This could provide a much more precise picture and suggest more definitive methods of improving estimating.

Sixth, although the current research confirmed some relationships between those practices and project completion within an estimate for large projects, other related variables might have great influence. Examples include estimators' and developers' education and experience, the organization's reward systems, management styles and others matters. These variables offer opportunities for research.

Seventh, given the apparent contribution of user changes to cost overruns, researchers should investigate the question of securing systems and supporting them against the instabilities that may result from these changes.

Eighth, replication of this study with a different sample might be valuable. For example, perhaps the estimation and development of engineering systems differ from those of business IS. Perhaps estimating practices vary in different geographical areas. A different sample might teach useful lessons.

Implications for managers

This study offers no immediate key to better cost estimating. However, because current practice in cost estimating is so problematic, we do suggest several possible guidelines to IS managers seeking to increase the accuracy of their estimating and thus the return on their new IS investments. We offer them with the assumption of causal relationships between the practices we studied and cost estimating accuracy but also with the caveat that intervening variables may play a role. The suggested guidelines are as follow:

1. Assign the initial estimating task to the final developers. We suggest that this approach increases the commitment of the developers to meeting their estimates; they are unable to attribute overruns to other estimators because they created the estimate themselves. In addition, the approach probably reduces the chances of estimators putting in an unduly low estimate (something they may do if they personally need not meet the estimate because lower estimates are more likely to result in project approval). Finally, the approach reduces the knowledge of the new system which would be lost if estimators had to explain their work to those who were to develop the new system.
2. Delay finalizing the initial estimate until the end of a thorough study. This guideline tells estimators that if their initial estimate cannot be accurate, they should delay announcing it until it can be as accurate as possible. The popular process of preparing an initial cost estimate at the beginning of a project and then revising it during the project does not necessarily improve its accuracy in the eyes of management. Instead, the revision of an estimate may be seen as an admission of inaccuracy and may merely focus attention on the initial error. Managers and users (computing and otherwise) probably remember the initial estimate best and may continue to judge project success by it.

   To illustrate this, consider a hypothetical system initially estimated at one cost and then, while well under development, re-estimated as substantially higher. If the system were completed at the higher estimate, very few observers would declare the estimate accurate (although the estimator who predicted the higher one might). More would consider it very inaccurate because they would compare the final cost to the initial estimate rather than to the revised estimate.

3. Anticipate and control user changes. The most severe cause of inaccurate estimates was frequent requests for changes by users. Estimators should thoroughly understand the user requirements that motivated the proposed system before they estimate its costs. By doing so, they can probably reduce and thereby control the frequent requests for changes that would have ensued had they failed to understand the requirements sufficiently at the outset. This guideline further emphasizes the importance of techniques for accurately identifying user needs and anticipating changes in them (i.e. prototyping, CASE tools etc.).

   The guideline also suggests that during development, analysts and programmers might discourage unnecessary user changes that will ultimately invalidate their estimates. To discourage unnecessary changes, developers should first carefully define the changes that users have thought absolutely necessary. They should perhaps then try to convince users to incorporate them into subsequent projects. If that fails, developers should be sure that users are charged extra for the changes.

4. Monitor the progress of the proposed project. IS management should monitor the course of a project from the preparation of the estimate through the completion of the development of the project. Formal monitoring may be important to developers because they feel forced to complete their project within its estimate. Moreover, this also provides an advance warning to estimators, indicating management's commitment to meeting the estimate. As such, it may inspire diligence and accuracy in creating the estimate.

5. Evaluate proposed project progress by using independent auditors. The independent evaluation of project progress is again an advance warning to estimators and developers alike that IS management is concerned to create an accurate estimate and meet it. Independent monitoring may dissuade estimators from expecting developers to rely on inaccurate reporting of project progress, on deferring an existing part of the project (this practice is recommended but for users' additions to a project rather than developers' deletions from it), or on crashing the project. These three practices are not uncommon (Lederer *et al.*, 1990).

6. Use the estimate to evaluate project personnel. IS department management can use the cost estimate to evaluate estimators, developers and others involved in the project. During formal performance evaluations, management can reward these personnel with pay increases, bonuses and promotions for making accurate estimates or meeting them. We suggest this because we found greater accuracy when such evaluation was carried out. Moreover, we suggest informing project personnel in advance of this intended use of the estimate. We also advocate favourable recognition for those personnel whose projects meet their estimates.

7. IS management should carefully study and approve the cost estimate. We recommend this because we found that IS management's careful study and approval of the cost estimate was associated with greater estimating accuracy. IS management's interest in estimates will probably inspire estimators to try harder and be more conscientious.

8. Rely on documented facts, standards, and simple arithmetic formulae rather than guessing, intuition, personal memory and complex formulae. Reliance on documented facts, standards and simple arithmetic formulae rather than guessing, intuition, personal memory, and complex formulae were associated with more accurate cost estimating. This is simple and careful analytic practice.

9. Do not rely on cost estimating software for an accurate estimate. We did not find that software packages were associated with a reduction in overruns or with the satisfaction of computing managers and other computing professionals with estimating. We suggest that while IS management may perceive some value in sophisticated cost estimating software packages, the package may probably not have major, favourable effects on the accuracy of an organization's cost estimates. We do not advocate that information management refrain from using them but simply point out that accurate estimating probably requires much more than cost estimating software.

References

Albrecht, A.J. (1979) Measuring application development productivity. *GUIDE/SHARE Application Development Symposium Proceedings*, October, 83–92.

Aron, J.D. (1976) Estimating resources for large programming systems. In *Software Engineering: Concepts and Techniques* (ed. J.M. Buxton *et al.*), Litton Educational Publishing Inc.

Banker, R. and Kemerer, K. (1989) Scale economies in new software development. *IEEE Transactions on Software Engineering*, **15** (10), 1199–1205.

Benbasat, I. and Vessey, I. (1980) Programmer and analyst time/cost estimation. *MIS Quarterly*, June, 30–43.

Benjamin, R.I., Rockart, J.F., Scott Morton, M.S. and Wyman, J. (1984) Information technology: a strategic opportunity. *Sloan Management Review*, **25** (3), 3–10.

Boehm, B.W. (1981) *Software Engineering Economics*, Prentice-Hall, Englewood Cliffs, NJ.

Boehm, B.W. (1984) Software engineering economics. *IEEE Transactions on Software Engineering*, January, 4–21.

Boehm, B.W. and Papaccio, P.N. (1986) Understanding and controlling software costs. *IEEE Transactions on Software Engineering*, **14** (10), 1462–77.

Businessweek. (1988) It's late, costly, incompetent: but try firing a computer system. 7 November, Issue 3078, 164–5.

Computer Associates (1987) *CA-ESTIMACS: An Applications Development Project Estimation Systems*, Computer Associates, Mt Laurel, NJ.

Conte, S.D., Dunsmore, H.E. and Shen, V.Y. (1986) *Software Engineering Metrics and Models*, Benjamin/Cummings Publishing Company Inc., Menlo Park, CA.

Coursey, D. (1987) Level five's new tool figures software cost. *MIS Week*, 20 April.

Cuelenaere, A.M.E., van Genuchten, M.J.I.M. and Heemstra, F.J. (1987) Calibrating a software cost estimation model: why and how. *Information and Software Technology*, **29** (10), 358–67.

Datapro Research Corp (1988a) *Datapro Directory of Microcomputer Software*, Datapro Research Corp., Delran, NJ.

Datapro Research Corp (1988b) *Datapro Directory of Software*, Datapro Research Corp., Delran, NJ.

Demarco, T. (1982) The estimating dilemma in *Controlling Software Projects: Management, Measurement and Estimation*, Yourdon Press, New York.

Demarco, T. (1984) An algorithm for sizing software products. *Performance Evaluation Review*, **12** (2), 13–22.

Donelson, W.S. (1976) Project planning and control. *Datamation*, June, 73–80.

Emery, J.C. (1971) *Cost/Benefit Analysis of Information Systems*, The Society for Information Management, Chicago, IL, 16–46.

Ford, R.N. (1973) Job enrichment lessons from AT&T. *Harvard Business Review*, **51** (1), 96–106.

Freiman, F.R. and Park, R.D. (1979) PRICE software model – version 3; an overview, *Proceedings of IEEE – PINY workshop on Quantitative Software Models*, IEEE Cat. TH0067–9, October, 32–41.

Halstead, M.H. (1977) *Elements of Software Science*, Elsevier North Holland, New York.

Herd, J.R., Postak, J.N., Russell, W.E. and Stuart, K.R. (1977) *Software Cost Estimation Study: Study Results*. Doty Associates, Inc., Rockville, MD, Final Technical Report RADC-TR-77-220, Vol. 1 (of two), June.

Jensen, R.W. (1983) An improved macrolevel software development resource estimation model. *Proceedings of the 5th ISPA Conference*, April, 384–9.

Jones, T.C. (1986) *Programming Productivity*, McGraw Hill, New York.

Kemerer, C. (1987) An empirical validation of software cost estimation models. *Communications of the ACM*, **30** (5), 416–29.

King, J.L. and Schrems, E.L. (1978) Cost-benefit analysis in information system development and operation. *Computing Surveys*, March, 19–34.

Kohler, W. (1929) *Gestalt Psychology*, H. Liveright, New York.

Kitchenham, B. and Taylor, N.R. (1985) Software project development cost estimation. *Journal of Systems and Software*, **5** (4), 267–78.

Lawler, E.E., Mohrman, A.M. and Resnick, S.M. (1984) Performance appraisal revisited. *Organizational Dynamics*, **13** (1), 20–35.

Lederer, A.L., Mirani, R., Neo, B.S., Pollard, C., Prasad, J. and Ramamurthy, K. (1990) Information system cost estimating: a management perspective. *MIS Quarterly*, **14** (2), 159–78.

Low, G.C. and Jeffrey, D.R. (1988) Functions points in the estimation and evaluation of the software process. *IEEE Transactions of Software Engineering*, **16** (1), 64–71.

Martin, R. (1988) Evaluation of current software costing tools. *Software Engineering Notes*, **13** (3), 49–51.

McCabe, T.J. (1976) A complexity measure. *IEEE Transactions on Software Engineering*, Vol. SE-2 308–20.

Miyazaki, Y. and Mori, K. (1985) COCOMO evaluation and tailoring. *Proceedings of the 8th International Conference on Software Engineering of the IEEE*, 292–9.

Mockler, R.J. (1972) *The Management Control Process*, Prentice-Hall, Englewood Clifts, NJ.

Mohanty, S.N. (1981) Software cost estimation: present and future. *Software: Practice and Experience*, **11**, 103–21.

Nelson, E.A. (1966) *Management Handbook for the Estimation of Computer Programming Costs*, System Development Corporation, AD-A648750 31 October.

Newman, W.H. (1975) *Constructive Control*, Prentice-Hall, Englewood Cliffs, NJ.

Putnam, L.H. (1978) A general empirical solution to the macro software sizing and estimating problem. *IEEE Transactions on Software Engineering*, July, 345–61.

Rubin, H.A. (1983) *Macro-estimation of Software Development Parameters: The ESTIMACS System*, published by The Computer Society of the IEEE, document CH1919-0/83/0000/0109.

Straub, D.W. (1989) Validating instruments in MIS research, *MIS Quarterly*, **13** (2), 147–69.

Tate, G. and Verner, J.M. (1990) Software sizing and costing models: a survey of empirical validation and comparison studies, *Journal of Information Technology*, **5**, 12–26.

Vicinanza, S.S., Mukhopadhyay, T. and Prietula, M.J. (1991) Software-effort estimation: an exploratory study of expert performance. *Information Systems Research*, **2** (4), 243–62.

Walston, C.E. and Felix, C.P. (1977) A method of programming measurement and estimation. *IBM Systems Journal*, **16** (1), 54–73.

Wolverton, R.W. (1974) The cost of developing large-scale software. *IEEE Transactions on Computers*, June, 615–36.

7

The evaluation of business process re-engineering projects

Dan Remenyi and Louise Whittaker

Introduction

In the past three decades many management theories have emerged (Nohria and Berkley, 1994) and been embraced by practitioners and theorists alike, in an attempt to achieve greater efficiency and profitability. At the same time, since the 1970s it has become evident that some firms have transformed the way in which they do business by exploiting innovative information technology (IT) (Sutherland, 1994). More recently, in the 1990s, a new approach has emerged which combines the transforming potential of IT with a new managerial approach which challenges the basis on which previous theories were established. This new approach is business process re-engineering (BPR) and it has captured the attention of management, theorists and IS people around the world.

In a recent study conducted in South Africa, in-depth interviews were conducted at 14 large companies which had undertaken BPR or were currently engaged in a BPR project. All the respondents expressed enthusiasm for the ideas underlying BPR and all but one claimed that the project was successful thus far. However, although most of the projects were undertaken with very explicit objectives in mind, many of the respondents indicated that the firm was encountering difficulty in the evaluation of

Investing in Information Systems: Evaluation and Management. Edited by
Leslie Willcocks. Published in 1996 by Chapman & Hall. ISBN 0 412 72670 X.

the project as a whole. Given that BPR can be a very expensive and disruptive exercise, this difficulty is one which needs to be addressed, as some evaluation of the costs and benefits of a BPR project is required for the effective management of the project, and indeed the company itself. This chapter aims to provide an assessment of both the costs and potential benefits of a BPR project, and some suggestions for how these can be measured. Chapter 8 then provides an assessment of the costs and benefits encountered in completed BPR projects.

Business process re-engineering

Hammer and Champy (1993) define re-engineering as 'The fundamental rethinking and radical redesign of business processes to achieve dramatic improvement in critical contemporary measures of performance such as cost, quality, service and speed.' A BPR project therefore, would attempt to redesign a hierarchical company of functional 'silos' into a process-based organization in which activities are organized around a particular outcome, and then implement the resulting changes in company structures, activities, IS and attitudes.

There are at least two different approaches to the implementation of this type of programme. BPR may be implemented in a revolutionary form whereby a function or a process is substantially changed throughout the organization. This requires the re-engineering exercise to have a major impact both in terms of depth and breath on the business area being changed (Hall, Rosenthal and Wade, 1993). This type of change can be referred to as radical BPR. On the other hand, BPR may be applied much more cautiously, perhaps through the vehicle of pilot studies, or through the development of prototype applications. This can be referred to as creeping BPR and at least initially this type of programme will not have either the same depth or breath or impact as a radical BPR.

Radical BPR

The implementation of a radical BPR project implies a major transformation of a substantial portion of the organization. In such circumstances a large number of costs are incurred as well as the opportunity of a wide range of benefits. The cost of a BPR project include but are not limited to management time, consulting fees, hardware and software acquisition, training, reorganizational costs such as redundancy, legal and auditing advice fees, planning costs, systems testing, and commissioning costs which may include hiring new people. Radical BPR projects nearly always address urgent problems which by their very nature are critical to the survival of the business. The result of this is that many such radical projects are not properly cost justified as the attitude of management is that if they are not undertaken the organization may not survive. In this case, provided the cost is not prohibitive the project is undertaken and the benefit is seen as survival.

The cost profile of a BPR project may be assessed by examining each stage of the project and determining the nature and the amount of the expenditure necessary. A detailed assessment of the cost profile of a BPR project is provided below.

Creeping BPR

While radical BPR can produce substantial, even order of magnitude benefits (Davenport, 1993), the risks and costs involved are often correspondingly large. Rather than take on this huge challenge, many companies are starting with smaller BPR projects, dealing with single issues or smaller processes (Cafasso, 1993; see also the findings in Chapter 8). This may be referred to as creeping BPR. Projects such as these are highly controlled, involving more modest funding and staffing than radical BPR projects. Often a pilot study is used to assess the potential of such a project. Alternatively the organization may use prototyping to do this, or a combination of both techniques.

Firms who undertake creeping BPR usually do not have a compelling problem to solve in order to survive. These firms are looking for ways and means of dramatically improving the organization – as opposed to continuous improvement – but they are approaching this improvement in a more conservative manner (Cafasso, 1993). Creeping BPR does ultimately aim to reinvent the company as much as radical BPR, but in a step by step fashion, through a series of BPR projects.

Advantages of creeping BPR

Each of these projects will therefore have the same pattern of costs as a radical BPR project, on a smaller scale. However, as the urgency of implementing the re-engineering has been removed, there will generally be more time for a complete cost–benefit analysis, both at the beginning of the project and after the pilot study. By its very nature, creeping BPR is more conservative and cautious than a radical approach, and so an extensive analysis is more likely to be performed. After the pilot study is complete, a full picture of the costs should be available, as well as an improved view of the benefits likely to be realized from a full implementation of the project.

The orders of magnitude of radical BPR involving whole business change is seen to be so great that it requires a divide and conquer incremental approach (Johansson *et al.*, 1993). The advantages of creeping BPR are thus that the project is much more easily controlled at all stages. It is also easier to focus on the essential aspects of the process being re-engineered, and to ensure that all the detail involved in the project is attended to. In addition, the reduced scope of the project means that problems with training and testing are less likely to be encountered. This further reduces the risks and costs associated with the project, while ensuring that anticipated benefits will be realized.

Disadvantages of creeping BPR

These benefits are however, substantially lower than those typically sought in a radical BPR project. Not only are the amounts of improvement sought smaller, perhaps 10% instead of 50% (Cafasso, 1993), but the scope of the improvements is typically limited to within the process itself. It has been suggested that bottom-line improvements can only be obtained through re-engineering projects which have sufficient breadth and depth to be termed 'radical' (Hall, Rosenthal and Wade, 1993).

At the same time the more conservative approach of creeping BPR requires less commitment from management, both in terms of time staffing and funding. With a mush smaller investment in the project, management is more likely to abandon the project, cut the funding or turn to an alternative solution as a result of a change in priorities (Moad, 1993).

In terms of a cost–benefit profile, we may say that costs in a creeping BPR project are incurred in a similar pattern to those in a radical BPR project, but on a much smaller scale. In addition, costs and benefits are more carefully planned and evaluated. However, the benefits likely to be realized are limited, both in terms of their magnitude and their scope (Thackray, 1993).

A cost profile of a BPR project

The cost profile of a BPR project may be considered under three major headings:

- pre-BPR preparation;
- BPR implementation;
- post-BPR evaluation.

Pre-BPR preparation

During this phase the main activity involves conceptualization of the project, deciding on the metrics to be used, feasibility study, detailed planning, and obtaining authorization for funding. This part of the BPR project will normally consist of about 10% of the entire work, although in some special cases it may grow to as much as 30%.

Conceptualization of the project

Conceptualization of the project involves identifying which function or business area of the organization is to be re-engineered. In some instances this may be a rather trivial matter, while in others a substantial amount of work may be required. Conceptualization involves identifying the functions and activities which should be regarded as a process and this can be a difficult and controversial task. Selecting a process is a critical step in the project, as it is likely to fail if the wrong process is selected (Harrington, 1991).

One technique which is frequently employed in the conceptualization stage of the project is benchmarking (Richman *et al.*, 1993). Benchmarking involves finding out how other firms perform a particular process and attempting to equal or better their performance in this respect. It is regarded by many managers as one of the most important tools available to them in helping to make their organizations perform better in the highly competitive environment which business faces today. According to Plantling (1994) in Rank Xerox UK benchmarking 'has become a way of life in every single thing we do'. Similarly according to Owen (1994) at Rover's Body-in-White plant, 'We benchmark everything'. These firms are just two examples of many organizations which perceive benchmarking as a critically important approach to business (see also Chapter 15). To others benchmarking is just another business tool which may sometimes lead to superior performance but which can also 'soak up resources and fail to deliver value' (Faull, 1994). Benchmarking may certainly consume substantial amounts of both resources and management time. However, if managed correctly this investment may lead to operational improvement which in turn can produce a very significant return on investment.

It is now generally recognized by many managers, consultants and academics that only by establishing operating targets based on best practices in the industry can superior performance and thus competitive advantage be achieved (Bendell, 1994). Benchmarking has become an issue which most organizations cannot afford to ignore.

It is particularly valuable in the context of BPR as it often sparks creative, innovative ideas, especially if companies use as bench marks organizations from outside their own industry (Hammer and Champy, 1993). However, benchmarking is not easy as it is not always possible to obtain information about the performance of a particular process in the type of firms or organization which is similar to that being considered for BPR. Many organizations engage consultants to assist with this, and the cost of such assistance may be considerable.

Identification of metrics

Once the function to be re-engineered has been identified, it is necessary to decide what metrics are to be used in assessing the performance of the BPR project. In many instances the focus of BPR projects is directed towards the client and thus preferred metrics relate to identifying how BPR has improved service to the client. The 'value metrics' which directly affect the customer's perception of the business are product quality and/or service, reduced cycle time and reduced cost to the customer (Johansson et al., 1993). Thus, measures such as speed of order fulfilment, time taken to develop new products, reduction in paper handling and ease of access to service are suitable metrics for the evaluation of BPR.

During this stage of the project it is useful to attempt to define the criteria by which the BPR programme will be judged either a success or a failure. It is important that this exercise is conducted early on in the process as it is still possible to retain a degree of objectivity at this point. In addition, Schaffer and Thomson (1993) note that results-oriented programmes which set measurable short-term improvement goals at the start are more likely to produce bottom line improvements. These authors claim that 'the performance improvement efforts of many companies have as much impact on operational and financial results as a ceremonial rain dance has on the weather'. They believe this is because measures often stress improvement activities instead of actual outcomes. This leads to a lack of any measures of improvement in actual company results. They therefore believe that any improvement programme requires ambitious short-term performance goals, and that these should be set at the start of the programme, so that there is no ambiguity as to what the programme is trying to achieve.

Although financial measures such as ROI and payback are also very important, and are frequently required by the decision-makers before authorization is given for BPR projects, such financial measures are essentially extremely blunt instruments in measuring the real benefits of BPR (see also Chapter 2). The relative merits of financial and non-financial measures are discussed below.

Feasibility study

A feasibility study requires a consideration of technical aspects as well as the financial implications of the project. As far as the technical aspects are concerned, these will usually require a considerable amount of effort, often involving outside specialists to advise on the suitability of the enabling information technology. Some BPR projects may require client evaluation of the appropriateness of the proposed scheme.

Another important part of the feasibility study is the identification of the risks to which the project may be susceptible. In the first instance a list of all the possible problems which might occur in the implementation of the project should be created. Then against each problem a solution or a way of minimizing the chance of the problem occurring should be listed. Subsequently financial values may be associated with each risk category (Remenyi, Money and Twite, 1993). The type and degree of risk to which a BPR project may be subject are discussed further below.

Finally, financial estimates of costs and benefits will have to be prepared. However, as these will only be available as approximations it is important that they be performed quickly and that not too much effort is applied to trying to make them accurate. Such financial feasibility figures should not be given too much credibility. In general, probabilistic or stochastic techniques are much more reliable for BPR feasibility studies than the traditional deterministic approaches. Probabilistic or risk techniques, which are also sometimes referred to as risk analysis, are useful for the quantification of the risk elements mentioned above. These concepts will be discussed in more detail below.

Planning

The next step in this phase of a BPR project is to reduce the project to a series of activities or tasks, which will lend itself to the tools and techniques of project management. If this work is undertaken by staff members the expense level need not be high; however, consultants are again often used in this area, incurring large costs.

Authorization for funding

The authorization for funding may in some instances be simply a matter of informing the board of directors of the proposed plan. This will generally be the case if the BPR project has been undertaken as a matter of urgency in order to rescue the organization from a potentially disastrous set of circumstances, which is often the case for radical BPR projects. However, where the need for BPR is not quite so obvious, it is possible that the authorization of funding may become an extended and reiterative process whereby estimates will be revised as many as a dozen times before they are finally accepted.

Cost implications of pre-BPR work

In some organizations all the above work is undertaken internally, so no additional or marginal cost will be incurred. Where organizations do not have the expertise, or their staff do not have the time to undertake the work involved in the BPR project, outside consultants may be engaged. For a small project it would be possible to anticipate fees in the order of £10 000 while a large project could cost up to and even more than £100 000.

All the cost estimates described above are generally referred to as *ex ante* in that they are established before the project begins. When cost–benefit analysis is performed after the event it is normally referred to as *ex post*.

The BPR implementation process

The major steps in the BPR implementation process are the analysis of the current situation, design of the new processes and job descriptions, selection of appropriate hardware and software, development of programs and databases, training of staff, testing of the new system and commissioning of the new application. This phase will normally consist of about 80% of the entire work, although in some cases it may be less. Most of the costs incurred are expended during the implementation phase. Many of these costs may be absorbed from internal resources, although some organizations use outsourcers extensively for implementation.

Analysis of the current situation

To understand how any business function or process can be improved, the first step must always be to comprehend how the current system performs (Harrington, 1991). In general terms, this is no different for BPR than for any other business change or organizational improvement. However, BPR practitioners caution that if too much time is spent on the analysis of the old approach it is likely that the proposed re-engineering will actually focus more on improvement than on substantial change. The implication of this is that the analysis phase should be tightly controlled and therefore should not represent a major cost for the project. In fact it is sometimes argued that for BPR projects the analysis needs only to be relatively superficial and that the focus should be on the new design (Hammer and Champy, 1993).

During the analysis stage 'quick hits' should be looked for. A quick hit is an opportunity to make a distinctive improvement to the performance of the organization which does not require an inordinate amount of time or effort or investment. Quick hits should deliver almost instant benefits and it is such benefits which many proponents of BPR believe may be used to fund the substantial cost of the whole project (Valentino, 1993). The effect of a quick hit would be as shown in Figure 7.1.

Another deliverable of the analysis stage is a 'breakpoint'. A breakpoint is a new process or new routine which may be used to revolutionize the way the organization conducts its business resulting in a disproportionate and sustained increase in market share (Johansson *et al.*, 1993). Breakpoints are areas where the organization is able to

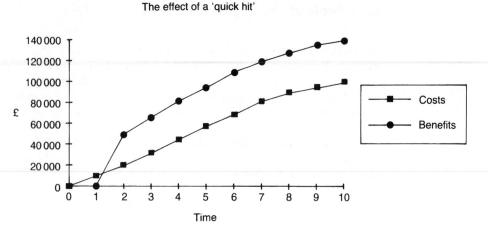

Figure 7.1 Costs versus benefits for a 'quick hit'.

depart from previous practices and undertake its business in innovative ways. They are the key to the major benefits which BPR can deliver. Identifying breakpoints is the major objective of the analysis stage of the BPR project.

Design of the new processes and job descriptions

The key to the successful design of new processes is to approach this activity with a fresh mind set which is not focused on the way things have been done in the past. This will allow for a totally innovative approach. Of course, the focus of the design activity must be the client's requirements, and thus process designers are encouraged to continually ask the questions 'how does the client want to do business with us?' (Hammer and Champy, 1993) and 'would the customer pay for this if he knew about it?' (Davis 1993).

BPR frequently involves the restructuring of jobs which in a large number of instances may lead to redundancy or retrenchment (Strassmann, 1993). This is always a painful and expensive business which in some cases may require considerable payments to be made to employees who no longer have a role to perform in the organization.

It is impossible to lay down general guidelines as to the time or the cost of this step of a BPR project as these will depend entirely on the scope of the application being considered. Individual firms will be able to estimate design times and costs for themselves in the usual way. However with BPR it is important to ensure that the proposed changes will be acceptable to the client base and therefore more time must be spent on external consultation with clients than normally. This can incur considerable expense.

Selection of appropriate hardware and software

Many, if not most, BPR projects result in the acquisition of hardware and software. Guidelines for the purchase of such commodities are well established and include developing an invitation to tender. As this subject is covered extensively in other works it is not considered appropriate to expand on it at this point.

Development of programs and databases

The development of programs and databases is so specific to the area under consideration that it is once again not possible to lay down guidelines as to the time and costs of this step of the BPR project. Note, however, the findings in Chapter 8 where IT costs fell between 22 and 36% of total costs in completed BPR projects. As a general rule, packaged application programs will be less expensive and more reliable, and may be implemented in a much shorter time period, although substantial hidden costs may be associated with the implementation of a package system. However, as BPR is often introduced in order to obtain or to enhance a competitive advantage it is not possible to derive such a benefit from a package which is widely available.

Because BPR can frequently involve the reorganization of functions, the currently used databases may not be appropriate and may require substantial modification, or in some instances, complete restructuring. The cost of this could well be a considerable portion of the cost of the whole project.

Training of staff

It is hard to envisage a BPR situation in which training will not be required. Some projects may only require a nominal amount, whereas others will need training right across the organization, from hourly paid staff to directors. This is especially true in the case of radical BPR. If the training is undertaken internally, the cost will be significantly less than if external agents are used. Chapter 8 found staff retraining as the second largest in BPR, representing typically between 13 and 26% of total anticipated and actual costs across all types of process re-engineering.

It is very important not to leave training to the very end of the project as the staff must know enough about the re-engineered process to be able to perform competent testing.

Testing the new process

Testing BPR projects is a most important part of the programme. Testing is more important for BPR than for many other projects because as most BPR projects directly affect the client base, a failure could be critical. In large BPR projects the cost of testing can be quite substantial and should be clearly budgeted for at the time of the feasibility study. Testing may be begun long before the work is totally finalized, and this has the advantage of enabling errors and problems to be picked up before the very last stages of the project.

Testing should not only include checking if the new process functions as it was designed, but it should also include measuring the outputs and activities of the process against the expected benefits. Most often measurement takes place only in the *ex post* evaluation (Dué, 1989), but it is more valuable to track progress as the project proceeds, both as a means of ongoing evaluation and as a means of motivation (Schaffer and Thomson, 1992). Many practitioners insist that the establishment of a 'war room' (Valentino, 1993) and an obsession with the measurement of progress (Lloyd, 1993) are imperative to success.

Commissioning the new system

When the testing is complete the BPR project may be commissioned. This involves the new application going live, which may or may or may not coincide with the old application being discontinued.

Cost implications of BPR implementation process

In some organizations only the hardware and the communications requirement will be purchased outside. All the other work may be undertaken internally. In such cases it is possible that no additional or marginal cost will be incurred by the organization for the human resource component of the BPR project. However, BPR often requires that valuable staff be assigned full time to the project, while many authors contend that re-engineering can only produce lasting results if senior executives invest their time and energy (Hall, Rosenthal and Wade, 1993). It may therefore be necessary to account for the cost of this in the cost–benefit analysis.

Where organizations do not have the expertise, or their staff do not have the time to undertake the implementation activities, outsourcing may be used for consultants or contractors or for the purchase of packages. The cost involved here is often very large as consultants commonly charge US $3000 a day (Thackray, 1993). In either case the cost of the implementation phase of a BPR will usually be quite substantial. In the completed BPR projects described in Chapter 8, organizations regularly underestimated external consultancy costs and external consultants were being widely used.

Post-BPR evaluation

There is increasing pressure to evaluate all systems to ascertain whether the funds spent on them represent a sound investment. BPR is no exception to this rule. The process of evaluation will entail establishing the benefits provided by the BPR project, which may be done in several different ways, as described below. This may be done as an *ex post* evaluation, or on a continuing basis as the project progresses (Valentino, 1993). If the evaluation is done as an *ex post* exercise it should comprise 10% or less of the entire work. Chapter 8 provides details of post-implementation evaluations of some 67 BPR projects.

Summary of the cost profile

Total expenditure over the course of a BPR project may be expected to occur as shown in Figure 7.2. The total amount expended on the project can vary enormously, from estimates of £100 000 to £1 000 000 and upwards depending on the scope of the project, and the extent to which outside consultants are used, as has been discussed above.

It should be noted that it is not always possible to assess in advance exactly what long-term costs will be involved in a radical BPR exercise. This is because the nature of the change is often such that the project itself creates opportunities and ideas of which the firm may not previously have thought. Chapter 8 gives some analysis of typical costs in ongoing and completed BPR projects.

The conflict between needing to cost justify project activities and the difficulty in predicting what will be needed in the long term may be expressed as the difference between 'tactical' and 'strategic' re-engineering. Tactical re-engineering is the initial project carried out to establish processes and activities for further change, while strategic re-engineering encompasses the 'ideas and opportunities that the firm had not thought of'. With tactical re-engineering a firm would want to see benefits within the lifetime of the project phased in over three years and reaching a maximum in the third. Strategic re-engineering might overlap that phasing at about the second or third year. An *ex ante* analysis of the costs of project thus appears to be appropriate for a tactical re-engineering project, at the start of the project. For a strategic re-engineering project it should be done individually for each initiative.

Assessing the benefits of a BPR project

As mentioned earlier in this chapter, there are two basic approaches to the challenge of assessing BPR benefits: traditional cost–benefit analysis, and alternative time-based measures.

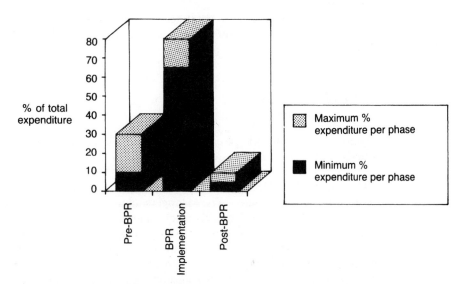

Figure 7.2 Cost profile of a BPR project.

In the first instance standard financial measures such as payback, return on investment, net present value and internal rate of return are used. Although these measures are very commonly used there is considerable agreement that they are not the most suitable measures for the evaluation of IT-based investment (Remenyi, Money and Twite, 1993; see also Chapter 2). At least it is almost universally agreed that these financial measures alone do not adequately offer a means of assessing the benefits of such investments. Where these financial measures are used analysts will seek to find staff reduction, administrative cost decreases, asset utilization improvements and additional sales as the key areas of benefit. These types of benefit, where they exist, lend themselves relatively easily to being expressed in financial terms.

What is more frequently required is a set of operationally based metrics such as those described above. These types of measure, which focus on the work being performed and the organization's ability to deliver value-added to the client, are frequently more appropriate to the BPR environment. Of course these benefits can, at least on occasions, be quantified and monetary values can be associated with them.

The real value to the organization may not be in the money value but rather in the continued client and/or personnel satisfaction which add value to the organization (Menkus, 1989). Such benefits actually cannot be accurately described in financial terms and are thus regarded as intangible. They can, however, be measured to some degree using non-financial time-related measures, which are themselves indicative of expected financial gains. This method is discussed below.

A statement of typical costs and benefits of a BPR

The actual financial measures to be used in a cost–benefits analysis are a function of the organization concerned. In Figure 7.3 an example of a cost–benefit statement for a BPR project is provided. This cost–benefit statement has been initially developed using a deterministic approach and is then subsequently enhanced to incorporate a risk model.

The cost–benefit statement described in Table 7.1 is a very general one which covers a wide range of different types of cost and benefits not all of which would be expected to accrue to one project.

Deterministic analysis

Deterministic analysis is based on the philosophical concept that people and organizations exist in a predetermined world where certainty and confidence may be placed in basic laws being obeyed (Reason and Rowan, 1981). This view permits us to make assumptions which are regarded as being based on repeatable facts which, if they vary at all, vary in predictable ways. Managers taking this approach thus assume that the exact nature and value of the variables under investigation can be identified and fully known. The variables used in deterministic analysis are referred to as single point estimates when the value of the variables are input and, by using a logical, algorithmic path, precise and unique results are calculated. The input variable provides the uniqueness; the algorithm provides the generalizable and repeatable processing pattern. This provides a mechanistic approach to profit planning, evaluation and

Table 7.1 A typical deterministic statement of costs and benefits of a BPR *(ex ante* deterministic evaluation, 000's)[a].

	Year 0	Year 1	Year 2	Year 3	Year 4	Year 5
Investment costs						
Hardware	375					
Software	633					
Development costs	500					
Commissioning	375					
Total	1883					
Ongoing costs						
Maintenance		178	178	178	178	178
Personnel		125	125	125	125	125
Depreciation		450	450	450	450	450
Occupancy		50	50	50	50	50
General expenses		100	100	100	100	100
Total		903	903	903	903	903
Total costs	1883	903	903	903	903	903
Annual Benefits						
Staff reduction		750	750	750	750	750
Cash release		417	417	417	417	417
Additional sales		500	500	500	500	500
Total benefits		1667	1667	1667	1667	1667
Net cash flow	−1883	763	763	763	763	763

Summary data	
Cost of capital	25%
NPV	169
IP	1.09
IRR	29%

[a] This statement was derived from a recent study conducted by the department of a BPR project at a firm in the manufacturing industry.

expenditure budgets as well as capital investments. It is by far the most popular approach to evaluating IT investment portfolios. As Strassmann (1990) points out:

> Information technology permeates every aspect of a business and therefore only financial policies and methods provide the unifying measure of the dollar to cope with the diversity of its effects. Financial planning and budgeting are therefore the choice tools for dealing with the questions that concern costs and benefits.

Risk analysis

Stochastic or risk analysis recognizes the uncertainty with which the business world functions and thus uses a range of values in order to evaluate the potential costs and benefits of IT. This approach attempts to estimate the degree to which variables may fluctuate from an original, base estimate. This method is also called simulation or sometimes Monte Carlo analysis since the risk inherent in an investment is the potential of the input and the output variables to fluctuate from the original estimates (Remenyi, Money and Twite, 1993). Managers need to be able to assess the extent of the risk, including data from areas which might not initially appear to be affected by the investment; in addition the size of the risk should be estimated.

In determining the size of the risk group brainstorming is sometimes used. This involves a group of informed people so that it is possible to identify a wide range of variables which may have an effect on the investment. The group then attempts to quantify the value of each variable, together with making an appraisal of the limits those variables might be expected to reach. Thus the minimum and maximum ranges, or the distribution patterns of the variables, are defined by the group, often after a series of meetings to gather and share information.

Another approach, and potentially the fastest way to measure the risk, might be to employ the advice of an expert. Such a person is expected to provide the variable data, limits and size of the potential risk using his or her own knowledge of the business. Clearly the danger lies in placing great faith in an individual's judgement when that person may well not be employed within the organization.

Finally, assumption analysis takes each assumption which may be made concerning the variables and questions them in detail. The assumptions are modified in order to reveal the worst possible outcome; factors which disadvantage the investment are thus explored in depth. Figures 7.3 to 7.5 indicate the results of risk analysis on the above cost–benefit statement in a graphical format.

In general, risk analysis is superior to deterministic analysis, in part because it allows a realistic evaluation of the input variables to be made, and also because it offers a much more comprehensive picture of the possible outcomes of the investment.

The concept of risk in a BPR project

The risk associated with a BPR project, or for that matter any information systems project, may be defined as the possibility that the actual input requirements and the

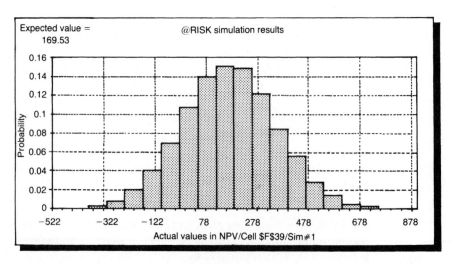

Figure 7.3 Risk analysis of net present value for BPR project.

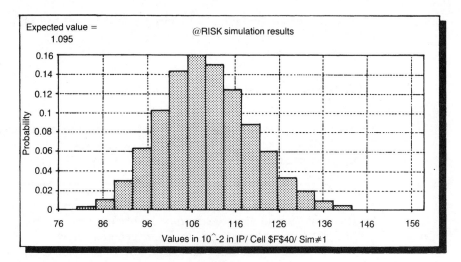

Figure 7.4 Risk analysis of payback for BPR project.

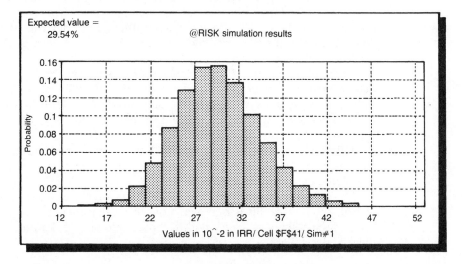

Figure 7.5 Risk analysis of internal rate of return for BPR project.

outcomes may vary from those originally estimated (Remenyi, Money and Twite, 1993). There is always a degree of risk associated with an investment and the management issue is thus whether the risks can be identified and thus managed. Although most managers associate the term risk with negative implications, it may be seen from the above definition that intrinsically risk may be either positive or negative; for example, projects may finish either early or late or be under or over budget.

There are many sources of risk to either a BPR or an information technology investment. McFarlan (1989) argues that there are two main types of failures that beset IT projects. These are failures of execution and failures of conceptualization. Failures of execution are described as failures that occur during the implementation of a project for various reasons, and the risk of these occurring can be relatively successfully managed. Failures of conceptualization are bad ideas. Only failures of execution are addressed here.

Failures of execution

The risk associated with failures of execution can be categorized under three headings. These are the risks related to the structuring of a project, the degree to which a project incorporates company-specific technology, and the size of a project. The structuring of a project refers to the completeness of the definition of its end outputs. Projects with a high degree of structure would incorporate such examples as the automation of existing forms where the original lay-out was to be maintained. Such projects would be, from the point of view of structure, low-risk exercises.

Projects which utilize a high degree of generally new or company-specific new technology entail higher amounts of risk. Such a situation is typical of BPR projects. These increased risks must be weighed against the dramatic benefits that it is hoped the project will realize.

The project's size is the final category of risk. Simply stated, projects which cost £1 000 000 have inherently greater risk than projects which cost £1000.

In general IT-based BPR projects will be rather large. They will often use technology with which the organization will not necessarily be too familiar, such as moving from centralized mainframe computing to client–server architecture, and will sometimes address applications which are relatively unstructured. Thus risk identification and management is certainly an important issue in BPR projects.

It is possible to use a two by two matrix to position the different levels of risk relative to the dimensions of structuredness of the project and novelty of the technology. Table 7.2 shows such a matrix.

In quadrant 1 (Q1) the project has low structure and makes extensive use of technology which is new to the organization. Projects in this category must be considered extremely high risk. Many BPR projects will fall into this category when new processes and new technological architectures are being simultaneously employed, and it is for this reason, amongst others, that there is a very high failure rate. Senior project managers with both technical and people skills are required to make these projects work.

Table 7.2 A matrix showing different degrees of risk (from McFarlan)

High technical inexperience	Q1 Very high risk	Q2 Medium risk
Low technical inexperience	Q3 Lowish risk	Q4 Low risk
	Low structuredness	High structuredness

In quadrant 2 (Q2) the project has both a high degree of structure and uses technology which is new to the organization. These sort of projects are generally not associated with BPR work as they involve computerizing currently established systems and do not engage with a new process view of the organization.

In quadrant 3 (Q3) the project has both a low degree of structure and low use of technology which is new to the organization. Occasional BPR work will fall into this class, for example when an organization tries to use an established mainframe as the platform for new process-orientated applications. These projects are relatively low risk, but have potentially hidden problems. Many projects in this category often fail when they should succeed. To ensure success in projects such as these, it is important that a strong and highly assertive user manager be placed in control, or at the very least that high user involvement be sought both at the outset of the project as well as on a continuous basis for the purposes of verification. The problem or risk with this class of project is the potential midstream change requests. Very strict parameters need to be constructed around the project, otherwise a continuous stream of change-requests from users will arise and the project will in all likelihood flounder and fail.

In quadrant 4 (Q4) the project has highly specified outputs but low use of technology which is new to the organization. It is unlikely that BPR work will include this type of project as these projects usually involve little more than computerizing current functional activities.

From the above it is clear that different types of projects have different types of implementation risk and that different projects need different project management approaches if they are to be successful. However, BPR projects will generally only appear in two of the four classifications.

Risk is an intrinsic part of any investment, especially investment in IT and BPR. Failures of execution have three dimensions – structuredness, company-relative technology and project size. It is very important to understand the causes or drivers of the risk which a project faces in order to be able to assess and put in place a risk management programme which will be able to reduce both the probability and the effect of the adverse circumstance which the risk represents.

The above taxonomy provides a useful and succinct way for viewing these potential risks, and allows managers to plan ahead and avoid these problems in their own environments. In the BPR projects analysed in Chapter 8 there were few indications that such risk techniques were being used. On the other hand, the survey found that most organizations were going for low risk 'aim low, hit low' re-engineering.

Time-based analysis

The basis of a cost–benefit analysis approach, whether deterministic or stochastic, is financial. This assumes that the significant metrics in assessing performance, whether of a BPR project or any other initiative, are those which can be measured in terms of money. Increasingly, however, managers are realizing that financial figures are not the best foundation for performance measurement, and that they should instead be used as part of a broader set of measures (Eccles, 1991; Kaplan and Norton, 1992). Financial reports are those which are required of companies by investors and regulatory bodies, and as such they have become omnipotent. There are, however, many problems with the financial standards in use, including the following (see also Chapter 2):

- Costing assumptions underlying accounting methods very often do not match the situations which they purport to reflect (Cooper and Kaplan, 1991).
- Income-based financial figures measure the effectiveness of past decisions and provide no indicator or future performance.
- The internal nature of financial measures breeds a false sense of security.
- Financial performance measures often fail to support investment in new technologies.
- Quarterly earnings reports create a short-term mindset in management.

Problems such as these have led many managers to realize that existing measurement systems often undercut the company's strategy, Overhead costs can be buried, along with the inefficiencies that breed them, and capital investment opportunities rejected on the basis of erroneous conventions. What is needed is a new means of measuring strategic benefits.

The Importance of time

BPR is essentially a strategic exercise. Typical strategic objectives of a BPR project might be:

- to increase customer satisfaction;
- to reduce manufacturing/sales/development overhead;
- to cut excess inventory;
- to increase product variety.

What all of these objectives have in common is time (Merrills, 1989). This means that time can be used to measure the degree to which the objectives have been achieved. The following discussion describes how the objectives are linked to time, and then goes on to discuss the appropriate measures.

Increasingly customers are no longer willing to sacrifice choice and speed of delivery for price, and are prepared to pay higher prices for faster service or more choice. The time which it takes for a customer to receive goods which he/she has ordered is important to the customer, and delays lead to dissatisfaction. Once a customer has purchased a good or service, the speed at which after sales service can be provided has a direct impact on customer satisfaction. In addition, choice of products is important to customers, and this itself depends on time, as will be demonstrated below. In short, the perceived quality of a product or service is directly related to the time it takes to deliver it to the customer.

The longer a product or service spends in a manufacturing, sales, development or any other cycle, the more overheads it attracts. Organizations which reduce cycle time by organizing tasks in cross-functional teams are able to reduce overhead per the cost of sales to one-third of that of comparable bureaucratic companies (Stalk and Hout, 1990). The layers of management that were previously required to coordinate the individual functions in the extended cycle are no longer required, and overheads are reduced. In addition, shorter throughput time increases the utilization of capacity of fixed capital and hence enables a decrease in fixed asset investment and the associated depreciation overhead (Meyer, 1992).

Time affects the inventory a company must carry in a number of ways. Many companies attempt to reduce their response time to the customer by building buffers of inventory from which customer requests can quickly be fulfilled (Rockhart, 1994). This, however, amounts to robbing Peter to pay Paul in strategic terms as the customer satisfaction strategy is achieved at the expense of carrying large amounts of costly inventory. By reducing the overall throughput time from supplier to customer, companies are able to satisfy customer requirements without raising, and in many cases by substantially reducing, inventory levels.

In most manufacturing facilities, cycle time is inversely proportional to work-in-progress turns. Flexible manufacturing techniques (such as smaller lot sizes) which increase the number of work in progress turns may reduce the lead time by a factor of ten (Stalk and Hout, 1990), significantly reducing the inventory which is held, both in the form of work in progress and raw materials. This is because factories which use larger lot sizes have to carry larger amounts of raw materials to process those lots. In addition, work in progress may spend as much as 66% of the cycle time either waiting for completion of the batch it is part of and the completion of batches ahead of it, or waiting for management to get round to sending it on to the next step. These factors lead to very low work in progress turns, and correspondingly high levels of inventory.

Time factors external to the company also affect inventory levels. Inventory is often held at many points in the supply chain. The amount held is directly related to the time taken for information to filter through the chain. The longer this takes, and the less frequent the information flows are, the more susceptible are the companies at the lower end of the chain to apparently sudden fluctuations in demand. Where large, unpredictable orders 'crash' through the system periodically, distributors and manufacturers hold more and more inventory in an attempt to stave off disaster. In addition, it is very often the case that a supplier and a customer will hold large amounts of the same stock (finished goods for the one, materials for the other), each unaware that the other is doing the same.

Timely information which flows frequently and quickly through the supply chain can eliminate these problems, as unexpected orders no longer occur. Compressing the collective cycle of the supply chain allows for lower inventory levels throughout the chain. For example, by ensuring the rapid transmission of order information to Italy, and organizing cut and sew and dye house to work in fast turnaround, small-lot cycles, Benetton keeps its retail stores around the world stocked with current items, without large amounts of inventory.

Where a vendor falls within a quick-response supply chain, it is likely to encounter request for various types of delivery arrangements from different customers (Kokuryo and Konsynski, 1992). The information systems necessary to meet those requirements cannot always be supported by traditional systems and architectures, and so the re-engineering of both systems and processes is often necessary to take advantage of the benefits provided by compressing time in the supply chain.

Increasing the variety of products which it can provide to its customers requires a company to manage both innovation and production, both of which are time-sensitive activities. Innovation, both in terms of new products, and in terms of new services and ways of doing business, is essentially measured by time. As Stalk and Hout (1990) point out, 'Innovation means change, and change is measured by time, The magnitude of change is measured as innovations per unit of time.' The pace of innovation varies by industry. Nevertheless, within an industry, competitors can innovate at dramatically different rates. Fast innovators can provide a much greater variety of goods and services, while experimenting with their customers, introducing test versions, and quickly adjusting them to reflect consumer reactions. For a fast innovator, time is the key performance variable to be managed, and time benchmarks are set by the faster of competitor performance, or technological possibility.

Fast innovators organize their development structures much along the lines of a fast-response factory. Analogous to lot sizes, fast innovators plan smaller, but more frequent improvements. Development is organized by product rather than by function centre, and scheduling is done locally, by the product team. Applying these techniques allows the amount of time and human resources required to be cut in half, enabling fast innovators to introduce four times more products than other slower innovators (Stalk and Hout, 1990).

In terms of production, product variety can only be achieved in a cost-effective manner by companies which make use of flexible manufacturing, with its small lot sizes and short cycle times. These strategies allow the production of a variety of goods without increases in inventory and variety-driven costs such as materials handling.

Time-based competitive strategy and BPR

Time can be used to create competitive advantage in two ways. The first is to create a price premium for a product which is supplied much more quickly than the market norm in a market where convenience is important, such as airline travel. The time elasticity of price will determine the premium which the customer is prepared to pay. The second strategy is to use time to provide economic advantage to the customer, so that the customer can make more money by buying more product which is available more quickly, even though it is more expensive. This is possible because the customer will experience the turnover advantages of a flexible producer, and save enough on inventory costs to more than compensate for the additional price paid.

Having received a higher price from the customer, the time-based producer will itself also be producing at a lower cost, on the basis of the principles discussed above. The double competitive advantage which time-based strategies can provide is often unassailable.

The time-based advantage is attained by making use of time-based strategies such as those discussed above. These strategies centre around shortening throughput time without raising overhead or inventory levels. As such, these strategies require the organization to be re-engineered to be effective across functions. Thus we see that time-based strategies and BPR are intimately linked, the latter being necessary to implement the former. The survey detailed in Chapter 8 found considerable concern among respondents to develop time-based strategies through BPR.

Measuring performance

BPR as defined by Hammer and Champy (1993) is closely linked to time. It is therefore appropriate to measure the benefits of a BPR project in time-based terms. This means that time is the primary metric, and that physical, throughput oriented measures should be used. There are appropriate time-based performance measures for all types of processes. Some of these are shown in Table 7.3. The most appropriate measures are those which are physical, and as close to the customer as possible.

Table 7.3 Time-based performance measures

New product development	Processing and production
Time from idea to market	Value-added as percent of total elapsed time
New product introduction rate	Uptime* yield
% first competitor to market	Inventory turnover
	Cycle time (per major phase)

Decision making	Customer service
Decision cycle time	Response time
Time lost waiting for decisions	Quoted lead time
	Percent deliveries on time
	Time from customer's recognition of need to delivery

New product development metrics track the rate of innovation in the company, which is important because of the product variety fast innovation brings to customers. These measures are also not difficult to measure, given an existing information base in the organization.

The most important measure here is the elapsed cycle time, particularly the cycle time of major processes. This is an indicator of throughput which has a direct effect on costs, and is a measure of what the customer experiences when dealing with the company. The proportions of value-added time to total elapsed time measure the efficiency of the process. The higher this proportion is, the shorter the elapsed time is likely to be.

Inventory turnover measures how quickly materials or goods move through the plant or company, while uptime* yield measures the actual first time throughput for any multi-stage process. Stalk and Hout (1990) explain this as follows:

> In any processing sequence where work goes from station to station, the actual throughput of work relative to potential is a function of how often each station is operating (that is, uptime percentage) times how often the work coming out of that station is done right the first time (that is, yield percentage). For example, if you have three work stations and each is up 99 percent of the time and does the job correctly 99% of the time, overall throughput is 94% − six times 0.99 – of potential. This measure is useful in operations like claims processing, product lines and so on, where there are several people working in line.

Quick decision-making is critical in compressing time. Not only does time waiting for decisions slow the cycle, but delayed decisions can amplify forecasting errors elsewhere in the systems. The metrics of decision-making essentially measure the flow of information through the organization.

The metrics of customer service are crucial, particularly where the process is close to the customer, as it is in many BPR projects. It is very important to consider these metrics, not only in relation to past performance, but also in relation to competitors. Many measures of competitor performance are available because customers tell you about them.

The benefits of a BPR project can also be measured comparatively using external benchmarking. This is best done against a time-based competitor. Companies which have unusual practices, or do things which seem impossible, are good candidates for benchmarking. The advantage of using time-based measures is that it is possible to obtain time metrics from public sources.

Time-based metrics

Time-based metrics are important measures because they avoid the problems of the financial standards discussed above, and because time itself is such an important source of competitive advantage. Financial measures are generally based on cost which is largely a lagging indicator of symptoms, rather than cause. Time measures, on the other hand, address the reasons why increased/decreased costs or greater/lesser benefits occur.

Cost measures generally also include arbitrary allocations of overheads and deferrals. It is not possible to distinguish which items add value to the end product or service, and which simply add cost – in some cases even decreasing the value to the customer. For example, if an item has to be reworked this will add cost, but the delay in delivery to the customer will reduce its value.

Cost analysis is shaped by conventions and hides what is actually happening in the company. Time, on the other hand, is objectively measurable as it is spent. Time measures are particularly suited to 'making the invisible visible', which is after all, what BPR is about (Brown, 1993).

An additional benefit of these metrics is that they are related to traditional financial measures. A study conducted by Dr Jürgen Meyer (1992), using the data in the PIMS database, showed that shortening innovation and throughput time had an effect on the financial results of the organizations surveyed, as shown in Figure 7.6.

Conclusion

The problem of identifying the cost and the benefits of business process re-engineering projects is, on the cost side for what may be termed a 'tactical' re-engineering project, essentially no different from that of any other investment exercise. In common with other capital investment projects, especially those involving IT platforms, it is important to think carefully and clearly about the implications of the work being undertaken. If this analysis is done professionally then reasonably accurate estimates of cost may be obtained, while much more accurate estimates may be obtained using risk analysis.

Where strategic re-engineering is undertaken and the firm commits itself to radical, but as yet unknown, change, the *ex ante* assessment of costs becomes very difficult for the project as a whole, and must be undertaken for each initiative as it arises. Chapter 8 may help to provide some rough guidelines on costs apportionment.

The question of benefits is more difficult and requires more work than the cost estimates. Benefits can be intangible and thus present difficulties in their estimation. Risk analysis techniques can help to some extent in this respect. None the less, there is a growing belief that financial measures are not particularly relevant in evaluating and understanding the performance of IT and BPR investment. However, Chapter 10 provides a way of linking financial and quantified measures for managing benefits into fruition.

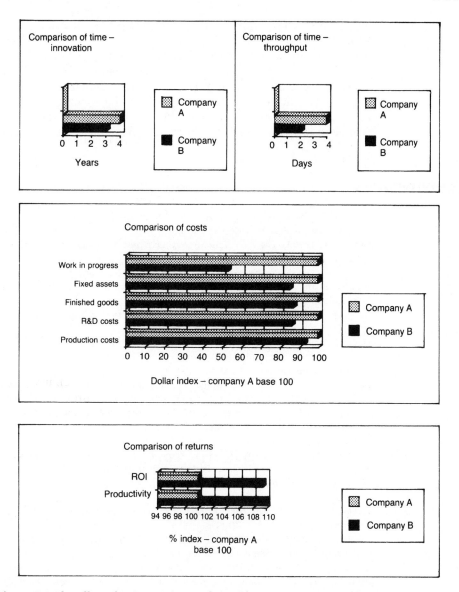

Figure 7.6 The effect of a time saving on financial measures (Meyer, 1992).

An alternative means of benefit evaluation is to use time-based measures. Hammer and Champy (1993) originally defined the expected improvements of re-engineering as being improvements in 'cost, quality, service and speed'. Time-based measures are therefore particularly appropriate to BPR efforts, and a number of organizations will focus on these, rather than on financial metrics, in the future.

The difficulty of attaching precise financial figures, either to costs in advance, or even to benefits once they have been realized, means that it is very difficult for a firm to determine precisely the 'net worth' of a BPR project in financial terms. Firms which have undertaken BPR projects generally assess the success or failure of the project by determining whether or not the project has achieved its initial objectives. These objectives should be quantified for this purpose, but are not necessarily expressed in financial terms.

It should finally be pointed out that the ultimate aim of a BPR exercise is, in many cases, to improve the overall results of the company and the position of the shareholders. The evaluation of a BPR project would then be whether or not there has been an improvement in the 'bottom line'. For this to happen, however, the project needs to have been sufficiently broad, and sufficient time must be given for the effects of the change to filter through to the financial statements of the firm or organization.

References

Bendell, T. (1994) *Benchmarking to Win*, Longmans-Financial Times, Financial Times Business Toolkit, Management Video Series, London.

Brown, A. (1993) *The First Annual Conference and Exhibition on BPR*, Conference Report, City University Business School, London.

Cafasso, R. (1993) Rethinking reengineering. *Computerworld*, 15 March.

Cooper, R. and Kaplan, R.S. (1991) Profit priorities from activity-based costing. *Harvard Business Review*, **69** (3).

Davenport, T.H. (1993) *Process Innovation: Reengineering Work through Information Technology*, Harvard Business School Press, Boston, MA.

Davis, J.E. (1993) A master class in radical change. *Fortune*, December.

Dué, R.T. (1989) Determining economic feasibility: four cost/benefit analysis methods. *Journal of Information Systems Management*, Fall.

Eccles, R.G. (1991) The performance measurement manifesto. *Harvard Business Review*, **69** (1).

Faull, N. (1994) Strategies for the successful implementation of the benchmarking process, Unpublished paper presented at AIC Conference in Johannesburg, 7 August.

Hall, G., Rosenthal, J. and Wade, J. (1993) How to make reengineering really work. *Harvard Business Review*, **71** (6).

Hammer, M. and Champy, J. (1993) *Reengineering the Corporation*, HarperCollins, New York.

Harrington, H.J. (1991) *Business Process Improvement*, McGraw Hill, New York

Johansson, H. McHugh, P., Pendlebury, A. and Wheeler, W. (1993) *Business Process Reengineering*, John Wiley, Chichester.

Kaplan, R.S. and Norton, D.P. (1992) The balanced scorecard: measures that drive performance. *Harvard Business Review*, **70** (1).

Kokuryo, J. and Konsynski, B. (1992) *Note on Information Technology and Quick Response Logistics*. Harvard Business School Notes, N9-193-018.

Lloyd, T. (1993) Case study: network south east. *Transformation*, Autumn.

McFarlan, W. (1989) *Competing Through IT*, HBS Video Series, Nathan Tyler Productions, Boston, MA.

Menkus, B. (1989) Five facts about 'Change'. *Journal of Systems Management*, April.

Merrills, R. (1989) How Northern Telecomm competes on time. *Harvard Business Review*, **67** (4).

Meyer, J. (1992) Measuring the time advantage. *The PIMSletter on Business Strategy*, 52.

Moad, J. (1993) Does reengineering really work? *Datamation*, 1 August.

Nohria, N. and Berkley, J.D. (1994) Whatever happened to the take-charge manager? *Harvard Business Review*, **72** (1).

Owen, O. (1994) *Benchmarking to Win*, Longmans-Financial Times, Financial Times Business Toolkit, Management Video Series, London.

Plantling, S. (1994) *Benchmarking to Win*, Longmans-Financial Times, Financial Times Business Toolkit, Management Video Series, London.

Reason, P. and Rowan, J. (eds.) (1981) *Human Enquiry: A Sourcebook of New Paradigm Research*, John Wiley, Chichester.

Remenyi, D., Money, A. and Twite, A. (1993) *A Guide to Measuring and Managing IT Benefits*, NCC Blackwell, Oxford.

Richman, L., Theodor, T., Koonz, P. and Charles, D. (1993) How Benchmarking can improve process reengineering. *Planning Review*, **21** (6).

Rockard, J. (1994) *Towards the Twenty-first Century IT Organisation*, Opening Address, CISR, MIT, Boston, 13 June.

Schaffer, R.H. and Thomson, H.A. (1992) Successful change programs begin with results. *Harvard Business Review*, **70** (1).

Stalk, G. and Hout, T.M. (1990) *Competing Against Time*, The Free Press, New York.

Strassmann, P.A. (1990) *The Value of Business Computers*, The Information Economics Press, New Canaan, CT.

Strassmann, P.A. (1993) Reengineering: an emetic in a perfume bottle. *Computerworld*, 16 August.

Sutherland, F. (1994) Some current practices in the evaluation of IT benefits in South African organizations. Proceedings of the first European Conference on IT Evaluation, Henley, UK, 13–14 September.

Thackray, J. (1993) Fads, fixes and fiction. *Management Today*, June

Valentino, D. (1993) The four R's of business transformation. *Transformation*, Autumn.

Part Three

Implementation: assessing and managing benefits

8

Does IT-enabled business process re-engineering pay off? Recent findings on economics and impacts

Leslie Willcocks

Introduction

Business process re-engineering or re-engineering (BPR) is being widely adopted by organizations in the 1990s. In the United States a 1993 Deloitte and Touche survey found the average chief information officer involved in 4.4 re-engineering projects (Moad, 1993). In the United Kingdom a 1992 survey of *Times* top 100 companies found nearly two-thirds claiming to have adopted process innovation (Haughton, 1992). Price Waterhouse found that during 1993 around 69% of the several hundred client companies surveyed undertook some form of BPR (Price Waterhouse, 1994). Such figures probably reflect survey weighting towards big corporations. For example, a more random-based British survey found that only 27% of all respondents were undergoing or had completed BPR programmes, but that almost all with BPR activity

Investing in Information Systems: Evaluation and Management. Edited by
Leslie Willcocks. Published in 1996 by Chapman & Hall. ISBN 0 412 72670 X.

were large companies (Preece and Edwards, 1993). However, all surveys showed increasing BPR activity throughout 1993–94. This is underlined by the current survey which found 59% of organizations surveyed planning or doing BPR in early 1995. The real take-off point for BPR in the United Kingdom would seem to have been 1993–94 when 65% of BPR programmes in the sample began.

A major issue that arises from previous surveys, case study research, and also more anecdotal evidence is what exactly the pay-off is from all this activity labelled BPR. The more popular management literature contains many startling claims (for examples only see Buday, 1992; Hammer and Champy, 1993; Johansson *et al.*, 1993; Ligus, 1993). However, reports of more detailed research bring in several notes of caution. For example Harvey (1994) found dramatic improvements in some companies. Thus Pilkington Optronics cut manufacturing lead times from fifteen to seven months, raised delivery-to-schedule accuracy from 10 to 97%, cut work-in-progress orders from 9000 to 900, raised purchasing on time from 60 to 90%, and cut design changes from 3500 to 2000. In Western Provident profitability was four times higher following re-engineering than at any time in its history. Reuters brought the delivery of new information services down from weeks to days, and even to minutes for existing customers. However, the research found such examples few and far between. Preece and Edwards (1993) found 53% of BPR respondents in a position to identify types of benefits arising from BPR. Most companies claimed the benefits to be reasonably large, particularly for cost reduction reduced firefighting and higher productivity, although quality of product as perceived by customers did not rate particularly high. However, the survey sample was small and the economics and impact of BPR not the major focus of attention.

Another strand of reportage and research suggests that BPR often fails to live up to expectations. Hammer and Champy (1993) estimated that 70% of the re-engineering efforts they had observed had not ended successfully, though they themselves admit the figure was not rigorously arrived at. Subsequently Hammer and Stanton (1994) suggested that the 70% figure 'implied nothing about the expected rate of success or failure of subsequent reengineering efforts . . . reengineering has no natural failure rate'. The figure probably reflects their own focus on radical 'breakthrough', and therefore high risk projects. However, other surveys have shown re-engineering projects consistently falling short of their expected benefits. As just one example, a 1993 North American survey showed significant corporate disappointment on BPR projects whether objectives related to improvements in customer service, process timeliness, quality, reduced cost, competitiveness, new/improved technology, or sales/revenue impacts (Moad, 1993). In another example Hall, Rosenthal and Wade (1993) studied twenty BPR programmes in detail and found only six achieving an average 19% reduction in business unit costs. Performance improvement in eleven of the cases measured less than 5%, whether evaluated in terms of change in earnings before interest and taxes or in terms of reduction in total business unit costs.

In the face of this bewildering set of claims and findings, derived from research or experiences conducted and analysed by various interest groups with varying degrees of rigour, there would seem to be a pressing need for academic research that looks in detail at whether BPR represents yet another false dawn in the history of management fads and fixes. In particular the present survey was designed to enable investigation into the extent and scope of BPR, the role of IT and the anticipated and actual cost and performance outcomes that typified the United Kingdom experience up to early 1995. The findings reported below usefully complement the detailed suggestions made in Chapter 7 for improving BPR evaluation practice.

The research base

The survey was carried out between July and September 1994, with an additional set of follow-up questions sent out to respondents in the December 1994–January 1995 period. A questionnaire was prepared based on a review of the literature and previous studies including detailed case study research by Bartram (1992), Harvey (1994) and Willcocks and Smith (1994). The initial questionnaire was piloted among fifteen practitioners and academics in the BPR field. The revised questionnaire consisted of a mixture of 34 closed and open questions covering details of the respondent's personal and organizational background, re-engineering strategy, extent of re-engineering programmes, costs and benefits, design and implementation issues and key lessons. A sample of 1200 organizations was selected from the contact database of Business Intelligence, an independent research firm. The database contains over 20000 names and addresses of managers in private and public sector organizations and adequately represents the major sectors of the UK economy. It was accepted that the sample selected would reflect biases in the database in favour of middle and senior management and medium to large organizations. The database is also European based but with a heavy bias towards UK-located (though often foreign-owned) organizations. The sample was selected randomly, initially, but two criteria were observed in the subsequent sample selection process: the proposed respondents, by their titles, could be expected to have detailed knowledge of BPR activities in their organizations, or would know someone who did. Second, given that our preference in the survey was to gain a cross-section of experiences, and also to avoid double counting, the sample would attempt to avoid duplication of responses from the same organization. The questionnaires were sent out with covering letters, definitions of key terms used in the questionnaire, and prepaid, reply-addressed envelopes.

The first mailing attracted 226 replies before the cut-off date of the end of September 1994. This represents a response rate of 18.8% and compares favourably with other mailings carried out under similar circumstances (for example, Preece and Edwards, 1993, attracted a 5.1% response rate). Of these responses, 58 were discounted as containing insufficient information, or information insufficiently reliable for the purposes of the research. This left a final, usable response of 14%, representing 168 organizations. Aware of the dangers of self-selection bias in the sample we investigated reasons for non-response. We took a random sample of 110 non-respondents for purposes of telephone interview. We gained 102 responses. The overwhelming reason cited for non-response to the survey was lack of time (87 cases). The second reason given was lack of interest in/not doing business process re-engineering (20 cases). The other reasons cited were: never received the questionnaire (three cases) and addressee no longer has a BPR role (two cases). Given that the sample adequately provided coverage of the main sectors of the economy, we were satisfied that the sample was not compromised by the non-response rate.

A second mailing of follow-up questions to respondents of the original survey was focused on those 100 organizations planning or doing BPR, and attracted a response rate of 55%. These respondents included all organizations in our sample that had completed BPR projects, thus giving us highly useful detailed information on success rates, costs, and types and levels of improvement experienced.

The respondents occupied senior or upper middle management positions – 25% were IT managers/directors, 21% were directors or managing directors in their organizations, 33% can be described as general/senior managers from various line functions, while 13% had a specific title related to BPR, for example process change manager, BPR or quality manager. The remaining 8% of respondents were managers in advisory or consultancy positions within their organizations. A limitation of the research findings is of course that a wider sampling within each organization could well reveal divergencies of opinion arising from different interests, perspectives and information available to respondents at different work levels. At the same time we found that the sampling of informed practitioner responses, based on BPR experiences, producing a great many pertinent findings and lessons. Furthermore, much of the information sought was factual, and respondents tended to indicate where reliable information was not available, or through internal evidence or assessing against previous findings in our case study research, we could make a judgement on the information's plausibility and usefulness.

The survey findings derive from organizations in manufacturing ranging from heavy industrial, through electronics/computing to light consumer goods; from most major sections of central government, and with some representatives from nationalized industry/services and local government; and from a large range of service industries. Therefore most major areas of economic activity are represented in the sample, though small businesses are under-represented.

The type of organization in the sample also represents a broad spectrum. Independent firms are 33% of the total; subsidiaries are 30%; groups 18%, public sector bodies 10%; and holding companies 5% (other types 4%). When measured by turnover/budget, most of the organizations in the sample are medium or large, with 62% having revenues of £100 million or more per year. This reflects several factors: first the bias in the sample selection process, and second the probability that small businesses were less inclined to respond because, as several other surveys found, they were less likely to be undertaking BPR. This is supported by our own finding that small businesses that did respond were much less likely to be planning or doing BPR than medium or large organizations in the sample (see below). Given the response rate, size of sample and the spread of organizations and economic activities represented, it can be seen that the research base is a potentially rich source of information on the extent and nature of business process re-engineering activity in the United Kingdom.

The scope of BPR activity

We found no particular sectors disproportionately taking to BPR relative to other sectors. Financial services, manufacturing and IT/telecommunications account for some 58% of BPR programmes in the UK, reflecting the size of those sectors. The BPR programmes in utilities (10% of sample) were frequently triggered by recent privatization. Given the large size of the public sector, it seems to be undertaking fewer BPR programmes (6% of sample) proportionately than other sectors. This may be related to the uncertainties surrounding possible privatization in certain areas, for example rail and the post office, to the large number of other changes and restructuring taking place, for example in the health service, and in central government, and also to less clear applicability or perceived need in certain operations. We also found that medium-sized organizations were less likely to be doing BPR than large organizations. As one example independent firms formed 33% of our total sample, but only 21% of organizations with BPR programmes. Groups and subsidiaries formed 65% of the organizations planning or undertaking BPR.

The size of expenditure on BPR programmes is revealed in Figure 8.1. Given that our sample covers medium and large organizations, it is surprising to see that some 43% of organizations undertaking BPR are each incurring related expenditures of under £1 million. Of course, the smaller organizations in the sample are concentrated in this group, but at the same time about a third of the organizations spending up to £2 million on BPR can be classified as large organizations. This would suggest that in many such cases the radical forms of re-engineering are not being undertaken. At the same time it can be seen that in 32% of cases – all very large organizations – organizations are spending in excess of £6 million on BPR. The highest spenders we found were a utility at £60 million, a retail organization at £40 million, and two financial service organizations at £50 million and £20 million respectively.

What are re-engineering programmes attempting to do? To add to the discussion in Chapter 7, a distinction can be made between process improvement – an incremental, bottom-up, narrow change to an existing process achieved within a function over a short time period, and re-engineering or BPR, defined to survey respondents as involving the radical redesign of all, or some, of an organization's business processes to achieve step-change improvements in performance. In the survey we developed this further for respondents into a typology that represents increasing radicalism, moving from single process redesign, through multiple process redesign, single major business model change to multiple integrated business model changes, including developing business network processes extending into customers, suppliers and strategic allies. We found 12% of organizations concerned with single process redesign, 46% with multiple process redesign, 36% with total internal process redesign and 36% with redesigning processes linking the organization with customers/suppliers. Clearly, most organizations are doing much more than single process redesign, but what degree of redesign is being undertaken, which processes are being re-engineered, and can we conclude whether radical redesign or process improvement is the norm?

We provided for respondents a classification (based on work by Earl and Khan, 1994) of types of process to be re-engineered. The type of process being re-engineered can be classified into core (central to business functioning and relating directly to external customers); support (the 'back office' of core processes); management (those

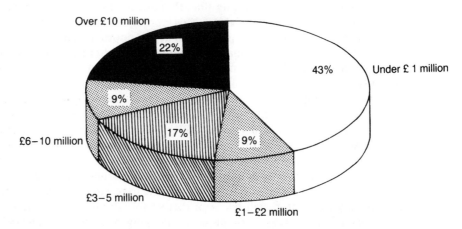

Figure 8.1 The size of spend on BPR.

by which firms plan, organize and control resources); and cross-boundary (those extending beyond organizational boundaries).

Respondents suggest that 83% of them are re-engineering core processes, 59% support processes, 73% management processes and 51% cross-boundary processes (treated by respondents on a wider definition than processes linked with customers and suppliers). Again these figures would suggest a high degree of business re-engineering activity. However, how radical is this activity?

The dominant motif running through the respondents' re-engineering objectives is that of cost reduction combined with improved customer service: 61% of respondents explicitly stated these as their prime objectives, with figures of 20–50% cost reductions often stated, though there was little quantification of the degree of customer service improvement. Some organizations (11%) espoused a 'transformation' agenda, for example to become 'best in class', 'make step change improvements – the quantum leap', while 15% stated that their objectives were predominantly to do with cost reduction and improved efficiency. A further 8% sought what could be called a 'balance or integration' objective, that is achieving a balance of control, service and efficiency, or as one respondent put it, 'an integration of people, culture, technology and processes to achieve a business strategy'. Others had a mix of objectives that embraced cost reduction and/or customer service but included items such as reduction in supply lead times, culture change, management information enhancement, and achieving control and consistency in the credit process. One organization was using BPR to facilitate the recent merger of two separate businesses. Thus, in terms of objectives few respondents seem to be aiming for transformation of their businesses; most were aiming for improvements, albeit often labelled 'radical' or 'dramatic' in costs and levels in customer service, and/or in some other area of the business.

A particularly revealing set of findings on the radicalism or breakthrough nature of the BPR activity we surveyed concerns core processes. The majority (70%) of organizations undertaking re-engineering are dealing with between one and five core processes. However, a detailed analysis of respondents' listings of core processes raises doubts whether many of these processes could be considered 'core' in the sense in which most commentators use the term, that is having high business impact and relating directly to external customers. Our own analysis would suggest that just under half of the processes are not core in this sense, and that in many cases respondents may in fact be rejigging existing functions and process to achieve incremental improvements, rather than thinking organizationally in process analysis terms as a basis for radical redesign. This finding is supported by later evidence on the relatively low levels of expected and actual improvements experienced through BPR activity. On this basis it may well be that the respondents looking to re-engineer five or more 'core' processes may not be at all overly ambitious; indeed our evidence is that, with the exception of some very large programmes, most are simply carrying out a process improvement rather than a radical 'breakthrough' strategy.

A lack of radicalism is also noticeable in the re-engineering of support processes. In fact 41% of organizations with BPR programmes are not dealing with support processes at all, and a further 44% are re-engineering only between one and three support processes. Management processes seem to be gaining higher attention. A third of organizations planning or doing BPR are re-engineering more than five management processes. Only 27% are not looking to re-engineer management processes; the other organizations fall between these two extremes. The relative popularity of re-engineering management processes possibly relates to managerial familiarity with problems with such processes, and the degree to which improvements will have a fairly direct impact on managers' own ability to do their jobs. Another reason for the relative popularity of management processes as targets for re-engineering would also seem to be the type of improvements sought – again the vast majority of the management processes described seemed to be existing ones to which improvements were sought, rather than management processes identified as a result of a radical rethink of how the organizations needed to be reconfigured and managed.

As at the beginning of 1995 the re-engineering of cross-boundary processes was the least popular BPR activity, with only 19% of organizations re-engineering three or more, and 32% one or two such processes. Thus nearly half the organizations planning or undertaking BPR were uninterested in re-engineering processes that cross organizational boundaries. It may well be that such re-engineering lies in the future for many organizations, which prefer to get internal processes improved first, have not thought through the possibilities, or have either not identified appropriate technology to underpin the process or doubt their ability to implement the technology.

This section, then, reveals an ostensibly large amount of BPR either planned or being undertaken, but produces findings that question whether most organizations are undertaking radical redesign as opposed to a process improvement route. Cost reduction together with improved customer service – albeit often declared as needing to be radical, dramatic or significant – dominate the declared objectives for BPR. Business re-engineering for radical breakthrough as portrayed by Hammer and Champy (1993) emerges in aspiration and practice as a distinctly minority pursuit, as far as our evidence is concerned. These conclusions receive further endorsement below when the expected and actual improvements gained from BPR activity are considered.

Is IT critical?

Most commentators point to IT being a critical enabler of BPR (see for example Bartram, 1992; Davenport, 1993a; Hammer and Champy, 1993; Heygate, 1993). But is this really the case, and is there a relationship between the utilization of IT and the BPR pay-off? IT emerges as an important enabler of BPR activity and support for redesigned processes: 58% of respondents rated the IT role in enabling radical process redesign as 'critical', 32% rated the IT role as 'marginal' while 10% said IT had no role to play in their BPR projects. For even more organizations IT plays an important role in supporting redesigned processes: 68% of respondents rated IT process support for BPR as 'critical' in their organizations.

IT, or rather its management, also figures as one of the top ten critical success factors for BPR programmes, while technical deficiencies together with poor IT management are also experienced as seventh out of the ten most significant barriers to BPR. Many respondents saw it as mistake to think of IT as a driver of BPR. Rather, these respondents saw IT as critical enabler. The following comments are typical of this view:

> The IT is essential but often tends to take the lead in the project (senior manager, European bank).
> The way that the IT systems are lagging behind is quite positive . . . This way we are becoming much more clear about the systems and information we really need (nursing manager, major UK hospital).

We checked to see if IT was regarded as a critical element in the success of the top 'best performers' that had completed BPR programmes. This group consists of the 'breakthrough' organizations and the organizations gaining significant profitability, revenue and cost reduction improvements as a result of BPR (see below). These came mainly from manufacturing sectors, including packaging, electricity and gas manufacture, aerospace but also business to business services, financial services and IT consulting. In practice over 75% of the top 30% 'best performers' in BPR did see IT as critical in both enabling radical process redesign and supporting redesigned processes. Only one organization recorded IT as not at all useful but commented that 'it should have been but the area most resistant to BPR is IS (information systems)'. Over half the top best performers were incurring over 40% of their total BPR spend on IT, but for the others IT spend was average or below for the type of process being re-engineered. This finding is based on a small sample but supports research findings elsewhere that there tends to be little or no correlation between size of IT spend and organizational performance (Willcocks, 1994). In BPR as elsewhere, it is the management of IT rather than the size of IT spend that counts.

Finally, what types of technology are being used? Some organizations planning or doing BPR mentioned specific, usually several, types of IT (38%). Of these nearly a third mentioned groupware, a quarter cited EDI, and a fifth workflow. Several technologies were specific to a sector, for example EPOS scanning on store tills, computer-aided engineering. Other technologies mentioned as important in BPR activity were client–server, integrated packages, enterprise modelling, the 'virtual office', e-mail, expert systems, EIS, open distributed applications, pen-based systems, imaging and databases. Among the BPR 'top performers' the most cited technology was groupware followed by databases then e-mail. The data are not strong enough to establish correlations, if there are any, between type of technology used and performance improvements experienced as a result of BPR.

The costs of BPR programmes

In this section we analyse the anticipated costs for all organizations planning or undertaking BPR. The results provide some pattern to the types of costs being aimed for by UK organizations across sectors. To apply some yardstick of actual against expected costs, we also identified 38 organizations in our sample that had completed BPR programmes. These organizations had undertaken 67 BPR projects (there may be more than one project per BPR programme) covering 287 processes in total. In Figures 8.2 to 8.5 we compare the anticipated costs in all organizations planning/doing BPR against the actual costs experienced across our sample of 67 completed projects. This comparison procedure has some obvious limitations that need to be borne in mind throughout, but can provide some useful pointers.

The main cost elements

We first focus on anticipated and actual costs incurred in BPR programmes. An indication of size of spend on BPR was given above. The limitations of these estimates should be recognized – they represent a mixture of anticipated and actual

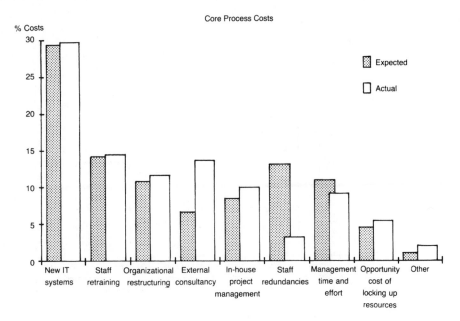

Figure 8.2 Core process costs.

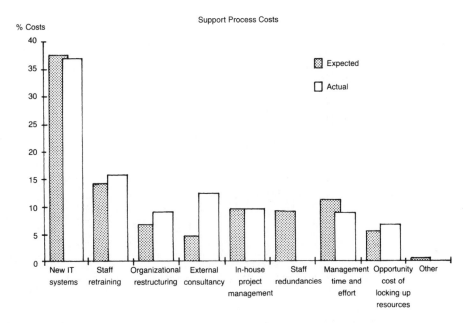

Figure 8.3 Support process costs.

expenditures by organizations at different stages in their BPR activity. To get some sense of whether organizations were incurring higher or lower BPR costs than originally anticipated, 30 of the 38 organizations that had completed BPR programmes were contacted subsequent to the survey. In 18 cases the actual costs were higher by

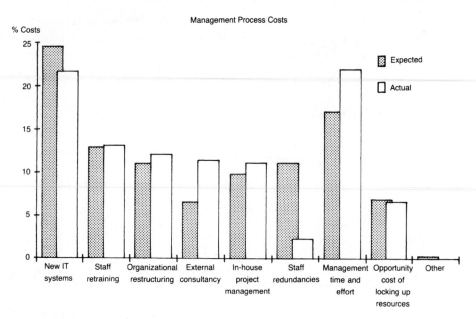

Figure 8.4 Management process costs.

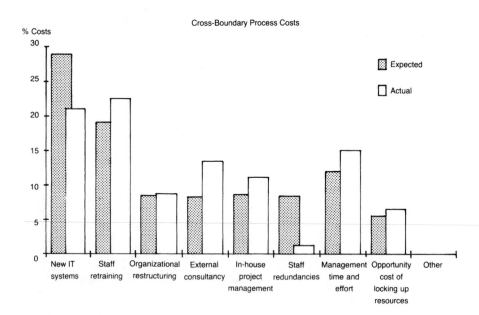

Figure 8.5 Cross-boundary process costs.

between 20 and 60%, in 7 cases the costs were said to be much as anticipated, while in 5 cases respondents found they were unable to separate accurately the total BPR cost from other costs being incurred in the organization.

In the remainder of this section we look at the main costs anticipated and actually incurred, and the percentage they represent of total costs for each type of process. The findings are shown in Figures 8.2–8.5. It should be noted that for simplicity in presentation these figures show average percentages. We indicate extremes in certain categories wherever the average figure conceals a noteworthy finding.

The figures demonstrate that BPR costs are concentrated in eight main areas – new IT systems, staff retraining, organizational restructuring, external consultancy, in-house project management, staff redundancies, management time and effort and opportunity costs of locking up resources. Across all types of process four summary points stand out:

1. **Staff redundancies** – the single issue most often identified with BPR, particularly among employees, are in practice 10–20% lower as a percentage of total costs than being anticipated in organizations still undertaking BPR. For all completed BPR projects and all types of process staff, redundancies average less than 5% of total costs. This raises questions about whether BPR is achieving the job losses it is often portrayed as being introduced to effect. Certainly staff redundancies are an insignificant cost in those BPR projects completed so far. This could mean that radical forms of BPR are not in fact being adopted, or at least, their radicalism is being lost – on the job front at least – along the long path to implementation. There is internal evidence in the survey findings to suggest several additional explanations in practice, though these cannot be quantified. It may well be that organizations are relocating staff rather than making them redundant, or that organizations are looking to improve business performance, partly through lower costs, with much the same staff numbers rather than achieve more or the same performance with less staff. The figures could also indicate that organizations are separating off BPR from redundancy programmes. Several respondents who had completed or were some way through BPR remarked that in retrospect they would not have introduced BPR and redundancy programmes at the same time. Other organizations may be taking account of political concerns and achieving redundancies before or after BPR, though using BPR as the real means of enabling the organization to achieve work with less job numbers.

2. Actual **external consultancy costs** are between 7 and 15% higher as a percentage of total costs than being anticipated by organizations still undertaking BPR projects. It would appear that external consultants are being widely used. On completed BPR projects consultancy fees represent an average of 12–15% of total costs. The figures, of course, may indicate just higher consultancy fees rather than higher use of consultants than anticipated, but, more probably, it is a mixture of both.

3. **New IT systems** represent the biggest anticipated cost across all process re-engineering efforts. On completed BPR projects IT costs typically fall between 22 and 36% of actual total costs, the largest single cost factor for all except cross-boundary process re-engineering, where it is only superseded by staff retraining. Additionally it should be noted that IT would seem to be treated as a major enabler to most BPR activity, a point that will receive further confirmatory evidence below. However, the relatively high expenditure levels do not necessarily translate into effective IT implementation, and indeed, later findings show that IT can be a major trip-wire. IT difficulties, in fact, can have the consequence of raising its relative cost, as a number of our respondents explicitly mention, and this needs to be borne in mind when examining the IT spend on re-engineering.

4. **Staff retraining** emerges as the second largest single BPR cost, representing on average between 13 and 26% of total anticipated and actual costs across all types of process. Later findings will suggest that even high levels of expenditure on

retraining are an insufficient indicator of the effectiveness of retraining efforts. In particular, many respondents who have completed BPR projects suggested that the timing of retraining and education is vital. Early attention to retraining, that is well before implementation phases, in tandem with more open communication activity, would have eased BPR implementation considerably.

The most noticeable feature for core process costs is that, for each type of cost, actual are higher than anticipated as a proportion of total costs in every case, except that of staff redundancies, which are significantly lower than anticipated. This would suggest regular underestimation of the real costs of core process re-engineering, and some overestimation of either the costs of staff redundancies, or at least the number that will be achieved. There have been some very IT-intensive core process re-engineering (CPR) projects. Just over one quarter (26%) of organizations with completed CPR projects registered IT as costing between 50 and 90% of their total CPR bill. Only 8% of organizations planning or still undertaking BPR projects estimate that their IT costs will be between 50 and 90% of total IT costs. A final noteworthy point is that 18% of respondents who have completed CPR projects have been relatively heavy users of external consultancy. In these cases consultancy costs represent between 30 and 50% of total CPR costs incurred.

IT costs as a proportion of total costs are highest (37%) where support processes are being re-engineered (SPR). One third of organizations that have completed SPR projects have IT representing between 50 and 90% of the total SPR cost. This suggests that support process re-engineering tends to be the most IT intensive. SPR also seems to have generated very low levels of redundancies, averaging, in completed projects, under 1% of total re-engineering costs.

Management process re-engineering (MPR) seems to incur higher actual management time and effort and project management costs than being anticipated. In the completed MPR projects we looked at such costs represented on average some 35% of total re-engineering costs, probably reflecting the role of managers as end-users as well as implementors of management process changes. Some 13% of organizations that had completed MPR incurred expenditure on management time and effort representing between 40 and 60% of costs. A different 13% that had completed MPR incurred expenditure on in-house project management that also represented between 40 and 60% of total costs.

The highest single cost incurred in cross-boundary process re-engineering (CBPR) is that of retraining staff and management. Here retraining represents an average of 23% of actual total costs. Higher outlays on retraining are needed for re-engineering cross-boundary processes than for all other types of process. The probability is that this type of process re-engineering inherently requires much more new learning for management and staff because it involves linking up with external organizations. Actual IT and staff redundancy costs are lower as a percentage of total costs than those being anticipated for cross-boundary process change where CBPR is planned or as yet incomplete. A qualifier to this picture is that 23% of organizations that have completed CBPR record IT as between 40 and 70% of total CBPR costs. This would suggest that the rest are not investing anything like the average figure shown in Figure 8.5. In fact the average IT costs for three-quarters of the organizations with completed CPBR comes down to just under 9% of total CBPR costs.

It is not clear that this overall picture indicates a lack of expenditure or lack of ambition on IT and staff redundancies. More likely the finding reflects changes in the overall composition of costs. There are higher than anticipated outlays on staff retraining, external consultancy, in-house project management and management time and effort necessitated by cross-boundary process (CBP) re-engineering. This suggests that cross-boundary processes may be marginally more difficult to re-engineer than core, support and management processes.

The benefits arising from BPR

In this section we first highlight the types and levels of benefits arising from completed BPR activity in 38 organizations. Benefits here cover the reduced cost of doing business; overall figures for whether or not organizations are achieving anticipated benefits; and percentage improvements achieved in the eleven major areas highlighted in our pilot work and by respondents. The section then looks at anticipated benefits from core, support, management and cross-boundary process re-engineering among those organizations planning or still undertaking BPR activity. Finally, these anticipated benefits are then compared directly against actual benefits attained by the 38 organizations in the sample that had completed BPR programmes by early 1995.

Overview of benefits from completed BPR programmes

This section provides insight into the impact of BPR on the costs of doing business. It also shows the type and levels of benefit being gained from BPR programmes in the sample completed between 1990 and early 1995. The findings are based on a limited sample of 38 organizations. The results indicate that the vast majority of organizations completing BPR programmes are experiencing beneficial effects. This somewhat contradicts one impression left from the literature of high failure rates. However, the findings here also question whether most organizations are aiming for or achieving the high levels of benefits registered by the high profile examples of success often found in the literature.

Does BPR result in lower costs in doing business?

Of the organizations with completed BPR programmes 79% are experiencing lower costs of doing business as a direct consequence of BPR. However, some 5% are experiencing an increase in the cost of doing business, though they cannot always quantify the size of this increase. Another 16% are not clear on the effect of BPR, suggesting that BPR has not really had a significant effect on the size of business costs. The figures for the size of decrease in the costs of doing business are shown in Figure 8.6.

Clearly, 59% of organizations with completed BPR programmes are experiencing between 1 and 20% reductions in the costs of doing business, while another 20% are experiencing between 21 and 50% reductions in the costs of doing business. All cost reductions are welcome in every sector of the economy, but we would expect to see more organizations getting sizeable cost decreases give the radical claims often

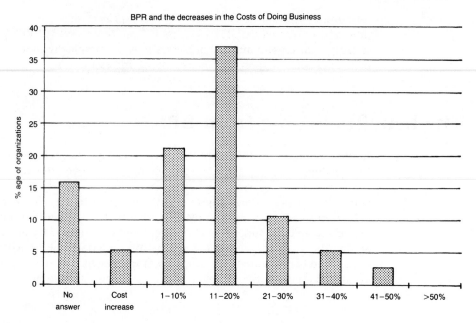

Figure 8.6 BPR and the decreases in the costs of doing business.

espoused for BPR. There is no discernible pattern in the type and size of organizations getting large increases or decreases in the costs of doing business, possibly as a result of the small sample.

Are organizations getting anticipated benefits?

It is clear from Figure 8.8 that 46% of organizations are achieving anticipated or above anticipated benefits from their completed BPR programmes. The level of benefits achieved are not necessarily high, however (see Figure 8.7). About half of organizations with completed BPR programmes are getting less than anticipated benefits, of which only 5% were expecting what could be described as 'breakthrough' improvements. Against this only one organization described its BPR programme as a failure with adverse financial and business impacts. Subsequently this organization was taken over.

What sort of benefits are organizations getting?

The type and level of benefits being achieved from BPR are shown in Figure 8.7. The most typical pattern (for 90% of organizations) is of benefits being achieved of up to 50% improvements on between four and seven of the eleven gains listed, with sometimes marginal improvements on others. In fact the graph overstates the case. It is important to note that two-thirds of these 'typical' organizations, where they are making gains, are getting between 1 and 25% improvements. For these organizations

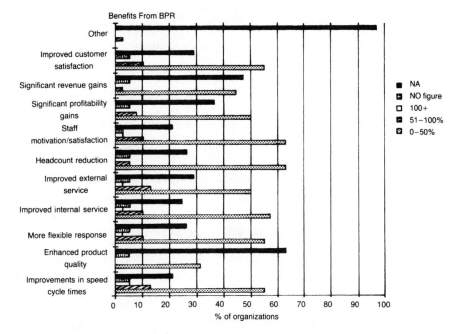

Figure 8.7 BPR benefits from completed programmes: types and levels.

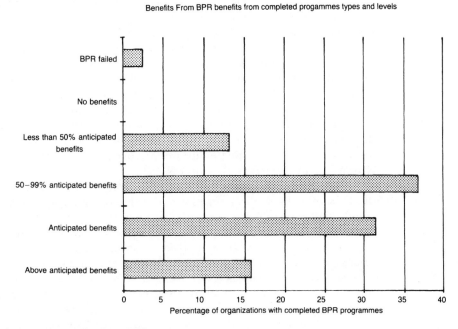

Figure 8.8 Benefits from BPR.

this adds up to process improvement rather than radical or 'step' changes in performance.

As Figure 8.7 shows, some organizations are obtaining over 50% improvements, but for each category of benefit, it is never more than 13% of the organizations in the sample that are getting these 50% plus gains. The organizations experiencing 100% improvements in each benefit category never exceed 6% of the total sample. Where 100% or more improvements are recorded amongst the organizations with completed BPR programmes, these tend to cluster in improvements in speed/cycle times, more flexible response, improved internal service, improved external service and/or staff motivation/job satisfaction. In practice only 11% of the organizations that had completed BPR programmes could claim 'breakthrough' results, here conservatively defined as achieving at least 100% improvements on three of the benefit categories, and above 30% improvements on at least three others. These 'breakthrough' organizations are all achieving 50% or more profitability gains. Among these organizations revenue gains through BPR range from 'not sought' to 10%, while decreases in the cost of doing business range from 1.8% (for the business overall) to 50% (for the processes re-engineered).

Some additional commentary is needed to help interpret Figure 8.7. Some 16% of organizations are achieving profitability gains of 50% or more. An important figure to look at is that half the organizations that have completed BPR programmes are achieving up to 50% profitability gains. This in fact overstates the size of gains being made, with four-fifths of this group actually attaining 25% or less profitability gains – still showing, however, that BPR in these cases is filtering through into important financial improvements.

On headcount reductions 22% of organizations record job numbers declining by 25% or more. On the other hand 55% of organizations are either not experiencing job reductions as a result of BPR, or these job reductions are 10% or less of the original workforce. On job satisfaction/motivation as a result of BPR, this is of course a difficult area to assign quantified measures to: 58% of organizations record either no increases in job motivation/satisfaction or improvements of up to 10% only. On significant revenue gains 85% of organizations record these as either nil or under 10%. Only one company registered revenue gains as high as 60%. On the face of it 67% of organizations are getting improvements in customer satisfaction as a result of BPR. In fact the graph again overstates the case somewhat. A balancing figure is that 55% of organizations are obtaining either no improvements, or improvements in customer satisfaction quantified as 10% or less.

In Figure 8.7, 'not applicable' refers to gains being neither anticipated nor achieved. It can be seen that 62% of organizations were not aiming to enhance product quality, another 48% were not looking to achieve significant revenue gains, while another 38% were not aiming to achieve significant profitability gains through BPR. For each benefit category at least 20% of organizations that had completed BPR had not been trying to achieve, and did not achieve, that particular benefit.

A final way of looking at the results is in terms of those organizations experiencing substantial gains on the main financial measures of success. Did any organizations experience significant improvements in profitability, revenue, and decreases in the costs of doing business? Of the organizations that had completed BPR programmes 26% reported gains on all three measures. However, if a benchmark of significance of 20% profitability gain, 20% revenue gain and 10% decrease in costs of doing business in used, only 18% of organizations have achieved significant financial benefits from BPR on all three measures. These were concentrated in manufacturing, with an IT consultancy and two service companies also represented. Obviously this result partly depends on whether organizations intended to achieve all such gains. The only feature here is that, taking the top 45% financial performers on BPR in the sample, some 16% were not aiming for revenue gains. Using an adjusted benchmark, a total of 40% of organizations with completed BPR programmes are achieving two of at least 20% profitability gain, 20% revenue gain or 10% decrease in costs in doing business. All the 'breakthrough' organizations (described above) are in this group. The manufacturing sector is overrepresented in this group and represents a majority (60%) of the top 45% financial performers on BPR.

Different processes, different benefits

In this section we take the anticipated benefits of organizations planning or still undertaking BPR. These anticipated benefits are then compared against actual benefits gained by the 38 organizations in our sample that had completed BPR programmes by early 1995. It should be noted that the figures in Figures 8.9–8.12 represent averages throughout, and need to be read in the light of the findings on benefits detailed in the previous section. Some general findings are worthy of note:

1. Looking across the findings for all four types of process, it is core process re-engineering that consistently gets the higher than anticipated gains. This occurs across all benefit categories except staff motivation/job satisfaction.
2. Though the figures shown are averages, further detailed analysis of the survey data supports the picture portrayed in the figures: generally speaking, whatever the process being re-engineered, organizations do not seem to be aiming high when

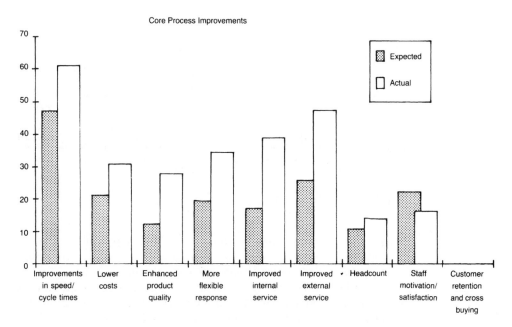

Figure 8.9 Core process improvements.

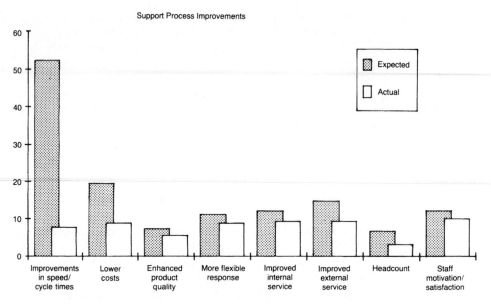

Figure 8.10 Support process improvements.

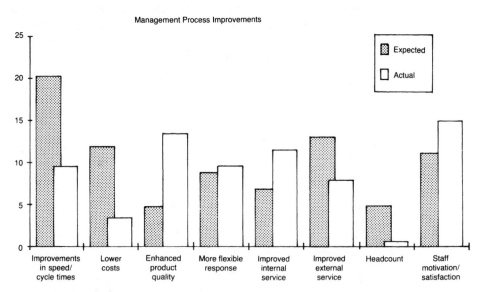

Figure 8.11 Management process improvements.

they look for improvements from BPR. There may well be a cause and effect here, with organizations aiming low and hitting low because the actual improvements being achieved are also relatively low. As indicated above, few organizations are obtaining more than 50% improvements on any of the criteria, whatever process is being re-engineered. The findings in Figures 8.9–8.12 on the whole do not appear to be the results of successful radical redesign.

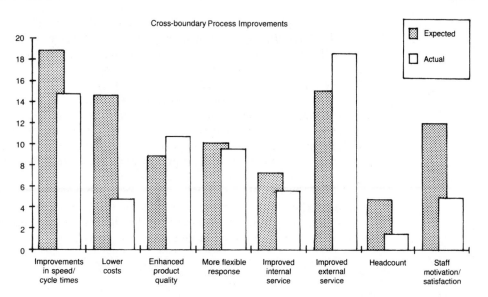

Figure 8.12 Cross-boundary process improvements.

3. For support, management and CB processes actual gains are being made, on average, across all types of benefit, but for improvements in speed/sycle times, lower costs and headcount reductions these gains are consistently below those anticipated. The discrepancy is particularly noticeable on lower costs and headcount reductions. Actual gains in these two areas never average above 8% across the three types of process. (For core process re-engineering, where aimed for, actual gains average 30% for lower costs and 15% for headcount reductions.)

The good news for core process re-engineering is that actual benefits tend to be higher than being anticipated. For each of speed/cycle time, cost reductions, enhanced product quality, more flexible response, improved internal/external service and headcount reductions, the gains are higher than anticipated by at least a 10% improvement on pre-BPR organizational performance. It is consistently the picture that the larger gains across eight major types of benefit are being achieved for core process re-engineering rather than support, management and CB process re-engineering.

Actual improvements as a result of support process re-engineering average under 10% across all major types of benefit. On the whole support process re-engineering does not seem to be delivering significantly large benefits to organizations, and the benefits that are achieved for completed BPR projects are invariably at a lower level than being anticipated for BPR projects still underway.

Management process improvements show a number of higher than anticipated gains, notably in enhanced product quality, improved internal service and improved motivation/job satisfaction. CB process re-engineering would seem to have very little impact on headcount in organizations, however, and achieves cost reductions of 4% on average.

The most noticeable gain arising from CB process re-engineering is, not surprisingly, improved external service, though as an improvement on previous performance this averages only 20%. The next best improvement is in speed/cycle times (15% gain) followed by enhanced product quality (11% gain) and more flexible response (10%

gain). Again while improvements are being achieved across all eight major benefits listed, and though the figures shown are averages, there is little evidence here, or in the detailed data we have analysed, to suggest that radical improvements are forthcoming from cross-boundary process re-engineering.

The overall picture suggests that BPR is very likely to achieve a number of benefits for organizations. However, it is core process re-engineering that is consistently gaining the major benefits, while support, management and cross-boundary process re-engineering tend to be achieving results much more in line with incremental process improvement rather than radical process redesign. Core process re-engineering is achieving particularly high improvements, on average, for improvements in speed/cycle times (60% gains), improved external service (50% gains) and improved internal service (40%). However, the gains from core process re-engineering recorded for different types of benefit were never less than 12%, though it should be remembered that few organizations are aiming for, let alone achieving improvements across all types of benefit represented in Figure 8.7.

Conclusions

The research shows a great deal of activity being conducted, with considerable sums being spent under the banner name of business process re-engineering. However, there were many indicators that little of the activity could be classified as radical redesign. Few respondents seemed to be aiming for transformation of their businesses. In terms of activities, nearly half of the core processes being re-engineered were probably not core in the sense that commentators such as Davenport (1993a) and Hammer and Champy (1993) use the term. Whatever type of process being re-engineered, with a few exceptions, most respondents were carrying out process improvement rather than a radical 'breakthrough' strategy. There is widespread recognition, including among a majority of the 'best performers' of BPR, of the critical role that IT can and does play in BPR programmes. However, we could find no clear relationship between size of spend on IT and 'best performance' on BPR. New IT systems still represent the biggest anticipated and actual cost across the vast majority of re-engineering efforts, typically falling between 22 and 36% of actual costs on completed BPR projects.

The survey produced some discrepancies between anticipated and actual costs of BPR. In particular, staff redundancies incurred in completed BPR programmes were in practice 10–20% lower as a percentage of total costs than being anticipated in organizations still undertaking BPR, while actual external consultancy costs were between 7 and 15% higher than anticipated as a percentage of total costs. On benefits, BPR activities were found to be producing anticipated or above anticipated benefits in nearly half of the completed BPR projects surveyed. However, there was strong evidence that few organizations were achieving 'breakthrough' results. Aiming low and hitting low seemed to be a typical pattern. Of the organizations with completed programmes, only 18% had achieved significant financial benefits on three measures, that is better than 20% profitability gain, 20% revenue gain combined with 10% or more decrease in cost of doing business. The findings of Hall, Rosenthal and Wade (1993) are endorsed here: in most cases business process improvements would not seem to be finding their way to the bottom line for the business unit as a whole.

What needs further analysis is why radical re-engineering is not the typical organizational response to the declared crises and clamour for 'breakthrough' results as found in the management literature. The analysis is not attempted here. However, Grint and Willcocks (1995) have sought explanations in the politics inherent both in BPR rhetoric and practice and in everday organizational operations. And indeed, in the survey there was strong internal evidence that the major barriers to BPR were human, political and cultural, not least at senior and middle management levels of organizations. Pragmatism may well dictate less risky strategies than those frequently espoused by commentators and consultants. Hammer and Champy (1993) declared: 'It is about beginning again with a clean sheet of paper . . . marginal improvement is no improvement at all but a detriment'. However, the evidence is that the majority of organizations undertaking BPR seem more likely to pursue a path either more *ad hoc* or more pragmatic, and certainly less risky. Davenport (1993b) has pointed to 'a revisionist alternative that allows re-engineering and quality to exist in tandem, applying the radical approach only where it is absolutely necessary, and being happy with 10% improvements elsewhere'. This may be an overrationalized version of the actual, more messy practices we are uncovering in organizations. However, our evidence is that something like it represents the more travelled BPR route to delivering the goods, though a small number of organizations are making real the more heady promises inherent in BPR.

References

Bartram, P. (1992) *Business Reengineering: The Use of Process Redesign and IT To Transform Corporate Performance*, Business Intelligence, London.

Buday, R. (1992) Forging a new culture at Capital Holding's direct response group. *Insights Quarterly*, **4**, 38–49.

Davenport, H. (1993a) *Process Innovation: Reengineering Work Through Information Technology*, Harvard Business Press, Boston, MA.

Davenport, H. (1993b) Book review of *Reengineering The Corporation*. *Sloan Management Review*, 103–4.

Earl, M. and Khan, B. (1994, Spring) How new is business process redesign? *European Management Journal*, **12** (1), 20–30.

Grint, K. and Willcocks, L. (1995) Business process reengineering in theory and practice: business paradise regained? *New Technology Work and Employment*, Autumn (forthcoming).

Hall, G., Rosenthal, J. and Wade, J. (1993) How to make reengineering really work. *Harvard Business Review*, November–December, 119–31.

Hammer, M. and Champy, J. (1993) *Reengineering the Corporation: A Manifesto for Business Revolution*, Nicholas Brearley, London.

Hammer, M. and Stanton, S. (1994) No need for excuses. *Financial Times*, 5 October, 20.

Harvey, D. (1994) *Reengineering: The Critical Success Factors*. Business Intelligence, London.

Haughton, E. (1992) Business process reengineering: moving the corporate goalposts. *Computer Weekly*, 30 July, 20–3.

Heygate, R. (1993, Spring) Immoderate redesign. *The McKinsey Quarterly*, **1,** 73–87.

Johannson, H., McHugh, P., Pendlebury, A. and Wheeler, W. (1993) *Business Process Reengineering: Breakpoint Strategies for Market Dominance*, John Wiley, Chichester.

Ligus, R. (1993) Methods to help reengineer your company for improved agility. *Industrial Engineering*, January.

Moad, J. (1993) Does reengineering really work? *Datamation*, 1 August, 22–8.

Preece, I. and Edwards, C. (1993) A survey of BPR activity in the United Kingdom, unpublished Research Paper, Cranfield University Business School, Cranfield.

Price Waterhouse (1994) *Price Waterhouse Review 1994/5*, Price Waterhouse, London.

Willcocks, L. (ed.) (1994) *Information Management: Evaluation of Information Systems Investments*, Chapman & Hall, London.

Willcocks, L. and Smith, G. (1994) *IT-enabled Business Process Reengineering: From Theory To Practice*. Oxford Institute of Information Management Working Paper RDP 94/7, Templeton College, Oxford.

9

Post-investment appraisal

Graeme D. Norris

> *Business procedures, like other great facts of life, are largely governed by tradition, prejudice, and habit . . . and can only be brought under a rule of reason based on careful analysis of concrete facts.*
>
> (Hotchkiss, 1923)

Introduction

Many companies have made, and are making, a considerable investment in IS. It is important to ensure full value is being received from this expenditure. IS must be run both efficiently and effectively. It is relatively straightforward to monitor the systems department's efficiency in running the hardware and writing new applications. Assessing the effective delivery of useful benefits from these services to the business is more difficult. Post-investment appraisals can help the senior managers in a company to review the results of their decisions on IS and IT. The appraisal process includes both checks on the amount of spending and the efficiency of the operation, and an evaluation of how well the initial estimates of cost and benefits turned out. Valuable lessons can be gleaned from hard evidence on the results of the decision-making process.

In practice, however, there must be some concern whether these lessons are being learnt. The results of a detailed survey by Taylor and Norris (1989), on how companies in the UK evaluate IT investments, are summarized in Table 9.1.

Investing in Information Systems: Evaluation and Management. Edited by Leslie Willcocks. Published in 1996 by Chapman & Hall. ISBN 0 412 72670 X.

Table 9.1 Survey of how companies evaluate investments in IT

Process	Sector			Size: (£ million)		
	Finance	Retailing	Manufacturing	<50	50 – 249	250+
Formal	25	18	30	27	20	30
Informal	34	40	30	19	48	35
No system	41	42	40	54	32	35

One hundred companies were chosen at random from *The Times* top 1000. The respondents were asked whether their company had any regular management process for assessing the return on the expenditure on IT. In nearly all cases (93%), respondents said decisions regarding the annual budget for IT, and major investments proposals, were made at the board level. A little under a half, however, could not point to any kind of process for evaluating contribution or following up promises of benefits. Research in the 1990s, reviewed in Chapters 1 and 2 in particular, has also demonstrated continuing weaknesses in evaluation practice across the lifetimes of systems.

Earlier chapters have made clear that the link between an investment in IT, and subsequent business performance, is not straightforward. For example, the systems manager may well believe that a new system played a vital part in improving a company's results. The sales manager, however, gives the credit to the acumen of his staff in spotting business opportunities. The production manager believes it is the customer service initiative associated with the new product range. As Carlson and McNurlin (1989) state, 'It is the application of a system rather than the system itself that delivers benefits . . . a computer is worth only what it can fetch in an auction.'

According to a survey published in the *Computer Economics Report* (1989), as responsibility for IT becomes increasingly decentralized, more and more IT investment decisions are being shared by systems and business managers, or are being entirely devolved to the business units (see also McKenney, 1995; Moad, 1989). When investment cases are submitted, the most common practice is for users to take responsibility for the benefits, and for the IT department to take responsibility for the costs. Subsequently, system development costs are rigorously monitored and controlled. The achievements of the benefits, however, are rarely monitored so closely (see Berger, Kobelius and Sutherland, 1988; Hogbin and Thomas, 1994; also Chapter 1). A study of the 450 companies in the Butler Cox Foundation (1990) claimed that although instructions to conduct post-implementation audits were often included in the system development standards, they are not, in general, carried out.

Reasons put forward for this failure to monitor whether the projected benefits of IT were being achieved, were as follows:

1. 'It is too difficult' – indeed, benefits can be hard to assess after a project has been implemented, because many systems are used by several business or functional areas. Once a project is completed the costs of the system can be assessed fairly accurately, but the benefits that accrue, over the different areas, over a period of time, are often tangled in the general business results of those areas and are not easily identifiable.

2. 'It is not necessary' – some companies appear to adopt the view that if the investment appraisal has been undertaken correctly in the first place and the

project implemented according to plan, there can be no need to check for benefits. By definition they must accrue.

3. 'It is too costly' – undertaking proper post-implementation reviews can be costly and consume resources that may be better deployed on more pressing management problems. A balance must be struck between the need to monitor the achievement of benefits and the costs of undertaking the review.

4. 'It is against our culture' – many systems departments have worked hard at promoting their role with the rest of the firm, as a function providing a service. Acting as a watchdog to check on the delivery of business benefits is appropriate for user management, or an internal audit function, but not for a provider of professional services.

These views need to be seen in the light of subsequent research studies. As just one example, Willcocks and Lester (1994) estimated that at least 20% of UK IT expenditure was not related to business priorities and that, depending on the application and organizational capability, between 18 and 40% of IT investment realized no net benefits whatsoever, however measured. The study found that only 8% of the IT directors surveyed fully analysed their project's return on investment.

Post-investment reviews should be regarded as essential. They may not be easy to do, they will exercise business judgement, they will challenge the prevailing management culture, but they are necessary. They provide valuable feedback on the value being achieved by expenditure on information systems. Many of the normal financial and management controls on major investments apply equally to IT because this is a resource just like any other business resource. Investment in IT does not require unusual analytical methods and does not deserve special treatment. The objectives of this chapter, therefore, are to remind managers of well-established techniques, and to help develop an effective post-investment process, by:

- giving advice on who should do the appraisal;
- outlining three essential concepts which must be in place;
- emphasizing the need to understand the assumptions underlying the base case;
- describing a seven-step approach to conducting an audit;
- providing insights from experience of using the approach.

Who does the appraisal?

Many firms have an internal audit group which undertakes this work; in other cases it is the IT manager or a user group. Consultants and external auditors are also pleased (of course) to offer advice. It is perhaps interesting to note that a study by Kumar (1990), summarized in Table 9.2, suggested that:

- The internal audit department rarely plays a leading role in post-investment reviews of IT expenditure.
- The systems development team often play a more significant role than user groups in determining the evaluation criteria, and method for conducting post-investment appraisals.

The problem that companies fear when assigning user and IT staff to review projects is bias. Indeed, even internal auditors must be responsive to some degree to the desires of top management. For any player in the management game, it is difficult to be, and

Table 9.2 Roles in undertaking post-implementation reviews[a]

Percentage of firms in which each group is involved.	0	10	20	30	40	50	60

Determine evaluation criteria

s ———————————→ (≈30)
u ——————————→ (≈22)
a ——————→ (≈14)

Determine evaluation methodology

s ———————————→ (≈30)
u ———→ (≈7)
a ————→ (≈11)

Review evaluation results

s ———————————————————→ (≈52)
u ———————————————————————→ (≈60)
a ———————————————→ (≈40)

Approve follow-up action

s ——————————→ (≈22)
u ———————————————→ (≈33)
a ————→ (≈9)

No involvement in the process

s ————→ (≈8)
u ———→ (≈6)
a ———————————————→ (≈33)

[a] Where s = systems development team, u = user department management, a = internal audit function.

to be seen to be, impartial. The use of external staff also has its drawbacks. For example, the close link between the management consultancy, systems division and audit practice of the large accounting firms can also create intriguing definitions of professional ethics. Too many companies have experienced problems with applications built or procured by the systems division of their external auditor – on their consultant's recommendation – not to feel there is at least a suspicion of a conflict of interest somewhere.

Genuinely independent external advisers, however, can bring fresh insights. They can focus attention on issues and decisions which have been avoided for various reasons by the management team. Naturally, advisers will wish to be hired again, and considerable skill will be employed in encoding the delivery of 'bad news'. It must be remembered that consultants have a natural aptitude for analysing problems with the 20/20 vision of hindsight. This advantage in suggesting how to make decisions can distance them, and their conclusions, from the practical orientation of busy business managers – people whose careers lie with the company, and who had to take decisions with the scant information available at the time.

The task force approach

A well-established solution to these problems, described in Norris and Wallace (1987), is to establish a task force of IT and user managers, plus a catalyst. Members of the task force are selected on the basis of their individual skills, and tend to be 'fast track' managers who will benefit from gaining a real insight on the costs, benefits and risks. For example, the IT professional may be about to lead a similar major project, and the users may be responsible for delivering the benefits claimed for the system. (An insight into the organization of IT awareness education is given in Norris, 1991.)

Although the role of catalyst can be met by a manager from the internal audit function, the team can often benefit more from the perspective provided by an independent consultant. According to Argyris (1991), this consultant should not only have many years of experience, but also the right blend of technical expertise and management education skill. To be truly effective, however, it is essential that the task force should have:

1. **Authority vested from the top** – senior managers need to see the company is committed to the process and role of the task force, and to work closely with it. For certain types of investment, approval will have been sought from the board or parent company, and the task force must be a recognized arm of top management in ensuring value for money.
2. **Board-level access** – the advice of at least one member of the board helps to ensure that overall business strategy and concerns at the time, and now, are recognized and considered.
3. **Company-wide emphasis** – the task force should identify itself with the business interests of the company as a whole, and should not see itself as representative of the business areas and support functions to which its personnel belong.
4. **Business management insight** – the task force must review the assumptions underlying the investment and any changes in circumstances. It is essential to display a real insight into the business value of the application, and any problems encountered. It is not sufficient to quote generalized benefits or just replay the claims that were made. Quantitative and qualitative evidence is needed to demonstrate that the expected benefits are being achieved.

At the conclusion of their work the task force must provide a clear statement of how to conduct this kind of project in the future, and action to ensure the lessons are absorbed.

Three essential considerations

The author's experience in working in the information economics area suggests that, for the task force to succeed, three essential concepts must be in place. The senior managers in the company must be familiar with:

- **categorizing** the nature of each investment according to the extent that business judgement rather than financial arguments are relevant;
- **the importance of analysing** cost-of-ownership details over the complete lifecycle of a system; and
- **linking benefits** to business goals, and cascading them down, from vague statements of good intent, to specific benefits that can be achieved by specific user communities.

Types of investment

As Silk (1990, 1991) has described, there are clearly definable types of project (see also earlier chapters). Only by categorizing the investment can the task force decide what type of appraisal exercise is appropriate. For example:

1. **Mandatory projects** – these were applications that had to be done, for example, systems to meet statutory requirements. When the Midland Bank launched First Direct, the nature of the banking meant some applications were essential. Rigorous cost–benefit assessments are unlikely to have been conducted. There tends to be a decision between two choices: do what you must at least cost and in the least time, or lever the investment in some way – spend 10% more than the minimum but deliver twice the benefit.
2. **Performance projects** – here a cost–benefit analysis of the proposed efficiency gains should have been carried out. These calculations can then be contrasted with the actual outcome. Documentation should also be available to show how the system was related to the business strategy, what competitive advantage was offered, and how it would increase profitability of market share. It is not unusual to discover, however, that the tangible benefits are much less than the costs – and business judgement on non-financial factors has presumably been brought into play.
3. **Infrastructure projects** – these are difficult to assess. By definition, these investments have no direct application, and the benefits accrue over a relatively long period of time by enabling other investments to proceed. Many companies duck any post-investment appraisal with claims of 'strategic importance'. While it is desirable not to indulge in too much heroic arithmetic, the appraisal team must look at the total cost. With the help of the user population, an attempt should then be made to gauge the business-related benefits delivered by the applications that are being supported by the infrastructure. These figures should then be compared with the consequences of doing nothing.

It is important not to ignore the technical benefits arising from the investment, for example, the cost savings and business advantages from reducing technical complexity, increasing technical choice, improved communication between sites, the ability to operate common or even global systems, easier inter-operability, and the ability to incorporate new technologies. An important question is, if the company reorganizes, makes an acquisition or divestment, or relocates, will the core operations and information systems be able to adapt to the changes quickly and simply?

The first essential, therefore, is to distinguish between the different kinds of investment in IT. Earlier chapters have suggested different categorizations of types of investment. The six categories used by Way and Norris (1991), in a series of practical reviews, were:

- **mandatory** – investments which were done to comply with the law or industry norms;
- **efficiency** – investments which were primarily aimed at cutting the costs of current activities;
- **effectiveness** – investments which were designed to increase revenues or market share by providing better or new services;
- **infrastructure** – expenditure on enabling services, which produce no direct returns, but are viewed as essential to the delivery of benefits from other, more applications related investments;

- **research** – where again the results generate no direct benefits, but the company should be better informed on the potential of new ideas, and so better prepared for the future; and
- **re-engineering** – where the system represented a business opportunity to redesign working practices and transform the way the company operates.

Many disagreements can arise in assessing past IT investments if managers are applying inappropriate criteria – seeking a direct return from an infrastructure project for example. A summary of the benefits, aids to evaluation and main issues for each category is given in Table 9.3. Although different assessment criteria apply to each category, they all have one thing in common. They must be business and not technical criteria. Even a research project should have as its aim not achieving familiarity with object-oriented programming, but perhaps setting the basis for a new billing system in the next two years.

Cost of ownership

The second essential is to examine the fixed and variable costs to the company of the service provided by the system over the entire lifecycle – from initial procurement to replacement. This means going beyond the traditional consideration of hardware, software and basic operational costs shown in the bold section of Table 9.4. Taken over the life of the system:

1. Personnel costs can become a more significant factor than hardware. Salaries have increased by about 25% over the last five years, where as hardware costs have declined.
2. Maintenance and enhancement costs can become a significant charge on resources, particularly if special skills are required to support systems which are not part of the company's preferred IT architecture.

Looking across the life of an information system shown in Table 9.4, there are three main phases of expenditure. First, there was the cost of acquisition and installation. This includes initial hardware and system software, and the cost of new applications development. Second, there was the cost of running the operations and basic system maintenance. The third phase covers the incremental charges that arose to expand the system and update applications to meet new business needs – money that is often allocated without the same scrutiny as the initial acquisition of the system. Experience indicates that one of the major reasons why so much can be spent at the end of an investment programme is that consideration of expansion and incremental costs was not included in the original evaluation. This is particularly true of systems bought by user departments without consideration of company standards, and the potential of linking the system to other databases.

Linking benefits and goals

Cost reductions are important benefits to achieve from the introduction of computer systems. The third essential, however, is to extend this traditional benefit to include a wider definition of the business value that IT can generate. An approach used by

Table 9.3 Six types of IT investment

Type	Purpose	Benefits	Aids to evaluation	Importance of business judgement	Main issues
Mandatory	For commercial or statutory reasons	Satisfy minimum legal requirements	Analysis of costs	Low	Fitness of system to purpose and capability of ITD to maintain
		Keep up with the competition	Analysis of costs to achieve parity, and marginal cost to differentiate service from rivals	Medium	Competitive need Effect on market and rivals Ability to sustain advantage
Efficiency	To do the same job better	Cost savings	Cost–benefit analysis Customer service survey Staff motivation analysis	Low/medium	Validity of assumptions behind the case Morale and service-level effect
Effectiveness	To do a better job	Increase revenue	Cost–benefit analysis	Medium	Validity of assumptions
			Assessment of hard-to-quantify benefits		Business value of claimed benefits
			Prototypes and pilot systems to demonstrate value		Risks involved
Infrastructure	To support present and future systems	Enable the benefits of other applications to be realized	Analysis of costs Performance standards Aggregate of benefits	Medium/high	Corporate need Benefits in both short and long term
Research	To be prepared for the future	To know applicability of new ideas to the company	Setting objectives within cost limits	Medium	Long-term corporate benefit Amount of money allocated
Business Redesign	To change the business	Achieve a competitive edge	Full analysis of all types of costs, benefits and risks	High	Business scenarios and aim of the system Impact on the market and company Risks

Table 9.4 Total cost of ownership[a]

	Acquisition		Operation		Change		Total %
Hardware	Equipment purchase Installation costs	16%	Maintenance warranty Annual lease/rental charges	5%	Hardware replacement or upgrades De-acquisition costs	13%	34
Software	Software purchase Initial licence charge	1%	Annual licence fees Software maintenance fees Warranty	8%	Software upgrades or replacement fees	1%	10
Personnel	Recruiting Planning design and selection Equipment and software installations Programming Contract programming Education	1%	Routine monitoring and operations Problem determination and correction User liaison and administration Programming maintenance Contract programming	37%	User changes Software changes and upgrades Training/education Programming Contract programming	0.2%	38.2
Communications	Initial hook-up charges	0.5%	Monthly tariff charges	1.2%	Additional lines Hook charges Tariff Charges	0.5%	2.2
Facilities	Facilities development Wiring Plumbing	0.5%	Space expense Power Air cooling	15%	Incremental wiring costs Incremental space expense	0.1%	15.6
Total %		19		66.2		14.8	100

[a] Results from CIE survey for clients in the manufacturing sector using DEC equipment.

Parker and Benson (1989) is illustrated in Figure 9.1 where the business benefits from a given system are systematically identified from cost reduction, added value, and revenue acceleration to increased revenue.

Despite the current popularity of the approach, it must be recognized that it is only a highly formalized group estimating method, which can experience as much bias as any other rating technique. Although a useful framework, the claims must be then verified by inspecting empirical evidence. Willcocks and Lester (1994) have also provided a critique of the information economics approach used by Parker and her colleagues.

An alternative approach is illustrated with an example in Figure 9.2. The objectives of a business unit are examined to determine what has to be 'done well' to achieve each objective, and where. This process leads to a definition of the benefits to be assessed, responsibilities for delivering them, and possible metrics. The extent these benefits have been achieved by each party can then be examined (see Norris, 1991).

According to Hammer and Mangurian (1987), the impact of a system can be measured in terms of time, space and relationships. The benefits can be classified as either efficiency gains, effectiveness increases or innovation advantages. These two

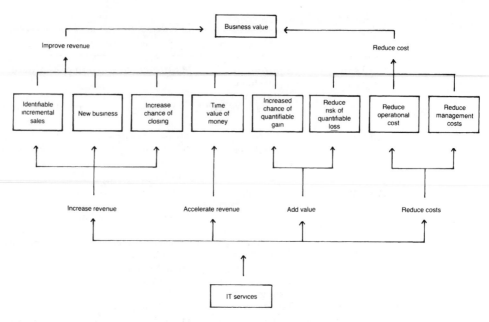

Figure 9.1 A systematic approach to identifying business benefits.

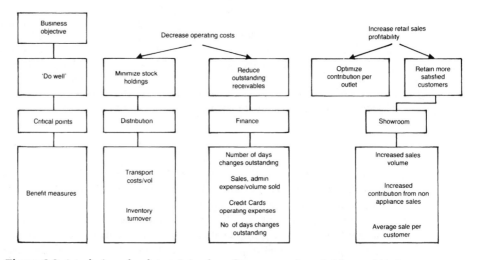

Figure 9.2 A technique for determining benefit measures from business objectives.

dimensions combine to generate a framework of questions, shown in Table 9.5, to guide post-investment appraisals. In practice, however, both efficiency and effectiveness factors coexist and overlap. Indeed, although frameworks stimulate the imagination and help to structure the issues, they do not provide definitive answers. As King, Grover and Hufnagel concluded (1989) in an important study of the various conceptual frameworks: 'most of the literature in the area continues to be anecdotal . . . there is little evidence of an accepted or validated theoretical framework, although a myriad of conceptual and analytical frameworks have been suggested.'

Table 9.5 Strategy impact–benefit questionnaire

Impact	Benefit category		
	Efficiency	*Effectiveness*	*Transformation*
Time	Where was time saved in avoiding the correction of somebody else's errors?	What important decisions have been assisted by more complete information?	Where have clients gained from more timely data from the firm?
	Where was unproductive intermediary information-handling eliminated?	Where has time been saved by more focused management information?	What has happened to save the customers' money?
Geography	Where has the system enabled the firm to gain economies of scale?	What activities have gained by consistency across dispersed operations?	Where has the system enabled the firm to enter a new market place?
	What dispersed activities have benefited from centrally held knowledge?	Where have parochial actions been improved by a consolidated service?	Has the system extended business hours by shifting work across time zones?
Relations	Where has the system eliminated unproductive middle management?	Have business units been strengthened by sharing scarce knowledge known to few?	Has an electronic presence been created on the customers' desk?
	Has the system bypassed intermediaries who are primarily information brokers?	Have up-to-date customer transaction histories been used by staff in the field?	Have customers' access to company knowledge which adds value to products and services?

Strassmann (1990) argues that the real merit of the various frameworks is that they will ultimately lead frustrated executives to the awareness that real systems problems do not have solutions in the form of simple tables containing terse recommendations. There is no substitute for real thinking based on real evidence gained from professionally conducted post-investment reviews.

What to look for

The ideal answer would be a simple, all-embracing formula that measured both the total cost of the technology and changes to working practice, and then the added value to the company. The truth, however, is that the worth of an information system is highly dependent on the judgement of the different categories of user in different parts of the company, and their perception of the costs, risks and benefits. There will be no easy answers, and the process of confirming the contribution is as important as demonstrating that value is being achieved. Indeed, top management must not press for facile reassurances from performance indicators based on oversimplified statistics. For examples of such indicators see Norris (1976).

Further, experience suggests that investments in IT rarely fail to achieve management's expectations of benefits because of faults in the technology. This view is supported by the results of a survey, originally conducted for the Institute of Chartered Accountants, on the most common cause of project failure according to senior business managers. A summary of the findings, by the Center for Information Economics (1990), are shown in Table 9.6.

A detailed analysis of the findings reveals that the main reasons underlying these failures concern:

1. Unacknowledged divisions between users on mandatory and desirable requirements, and the scale of the benefit expected from them.
2. Gung-ho attitudes to managing the risks to the operations of the business, and a failure to produce any contingency plans.
3. An assumption that a short training course at the launch of the system would be sufficient to change well-established working practices, and encourage users to adopt the system enthusiastically.

In essence, post-investment appraisal will be looking at failures of user management rather than technology. This could be the reason why they are so rarely conducted, and IT managers are so often thwarted in their attempts to review the results of their efforts.

Table 9.6 Senior managers' view on the 'top ten' most common causes of project failure (CIE Survey, 1990)

Rank	Factor (% occurrence)
1.	Vague statement of benefits, leading to an uncertain allocation responsibility for managing their delivery (95%)
2.	Underestimate of the extent and scale of organizational change costs (95%)
3.	Risks not thought through, and poorly managed (80%)
4.	Projects ignored the '80–20 rule' and took too long before delivering main benefits (75%)
5.	Too little understanding of the role of user management in directing and exploiting IT (60%)
6.	User management overstretched with other tasks (50%)
7.	Poor match between requirement definition, and user need and capability to deploy (45%)
8.	Interfaces with existing applications and systems too complex relative to the development team's experience (30%)
9.	Database software based on old concepts and inadequate for the task (20%)
10.	Hardware undersized to cope with the actual demand on the system, and code generated from prototyping (10%)

Return on management

For about ten years, Strassmann has promoted the idea that post-investment appraisals should look at the return on management effort as a way to gauge the efficient use of information systems. The notion is that if management is what a company is trying to improve with its investment in IT, it is important to measure the productivity of managers. At this point, Strassmann introduces the concept of value-added productivity as the numerator of a ratio that he divides by management costs to obtain his registered trademark measure of 'Return on Management'. An earlier discussion of this concept appeared in Chapter 2. While the present author endorses the concept, there is no way to compute this numerator from any accounting system currently in use. It can be inferred by eliminating various other costs, until a residue is left which can be thought to represent management's contribution. According to the report produced for IBM by Carlson and McNurlin (1989), this rarely convinces senior management. A commentary by Strassmann (1990) on the deficiencies in the ISIS methodology advocated by IBM salesmen has provided a lively riposte.

Assumptions, costs and benefits – claimed and actual

At a more prosaic but practical level, the obvious starting-point for any appraisal is to review the original documents recommending the investment, and the minutes of relevant discussions, to establish:

- the business and technical assumptions, and the options considered by the company;
- the costs and benefits of the chosen option to the different parties involved in the implementation and use of the system;
- the extent of the business judgement that was required, and by whom, and the degree of risk to different parties.

Enquiries can then be made to determine the actual costs and benefits, and the perception of relevant managers of the success of the investment. The key is to focus the debate on the assumptions rather than the way any numbers have been calculated. A lively discussion on disentangling the relationship between IT investments and the performance of the firm can be found in Weill (1989). Two common difficulties that are likely to be encountered concern:

- The lack of any extant documentation on the reasons for the investment, and little subsequent consideration of the value being delivered when the annual budgets have been submitted.
- Changed circumstances since the original proposal was authorized, which invalidate comparisons of actual performance and the investment case; for example the acquisition or disposal of entire business units which were to use the system.
- Political sensitivities at the time, which are not readily appreciated some years later, when the outcome is known; for example, the outsourcing of computing operations to a third party facilities management bureau.

Base-case scenarios

It is vital to evaluate the IT investment against a base case, that is, a well-formulated view on what would have happened if the investment had not been carried out. As it is difficult to be precise on what might have been, many companies describe two or three possible scenarios that might have occurred. This approach to describing the assumptions can help to:

- reduce concern that the appraisal will uncover management failure, as decisions are placed in the context of the uncertainty at the time, and the relative merits of the choices available;
- describe the different viewpoints at the time on the need for the system, and the implications of the risks to different parties (see Killman and Mitroff, 1979).

Indeed, as Checkland (1984), has described in his work over the last twenty years, different people interpret assumptions about the purpose of a system in different ways. The appraisal process, therefore, must look for both agreement on the validity of these different perspectives, and acceptance of who had the authority, and responsibility, for the final decision.

In summary, scenarios must be realistic, or the incremental cash flows between the do nothing option and the project will be misleading. It is vital to remember that it is incremental worth that the appraisal is trying to determine. There must be a suspicion that some of the claims that IT investments have not delivered the return expected can be explained by looking at the assumptions hidden in the undocumented base-case scenarios. It is rare that the base case is simply a continuation of the status quo. At the very least, therefore, the task force must seek answers to three questions:

1. To what extent did the system achieve agreed expectations on time?
2. Were the expectations appropriate to the problem the business faced, and now faces?
3. Did any of the foreseen or other risks occur, and how were they managed?

How to audit

Proven and systematic approaches to answering these questions, and the supplementary questions, can be found in the publications of the Institute of Internal Auditors – see for example Mair, Wood and Davis (1978). A detailed review of the issues and challenges of assessing information systems, and the evolving criteria for success, can be found in Ginzberg and Zmud (1988). In essence, the main steps are shown in Figure 9.3. The keys to the success of the approach, of course, lie not only in collecting both hard and soft information, but also in gaining (and not betraying) the confidence of those who can supply it.

Step one: define objectives

The first step is always to gain a clear statement of the specific objectives of the review. This does not mean that the objectives need to be limited or narrow. It means that

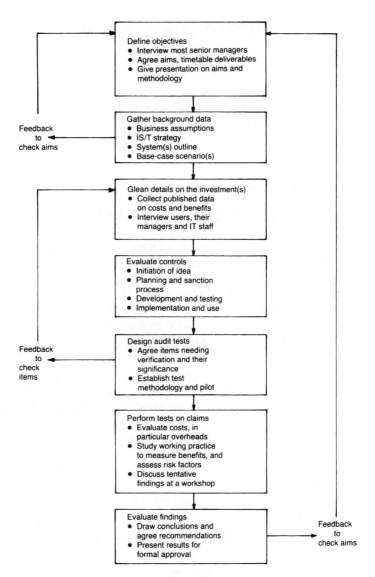

Figure 9.3 Basic seven-step approach to conducting an appraisal.

explicit goals and tangible deliverables need to be stated, so that the task force or auditor, as well as their superiors, will be able to determine later whether the objectives were accomplished. It is important not to be naive about the possible hidden objectives of the different parties interested in the outcome of the study.

Step two: gather basic information

With the objectives firmly in mind, the second step is to obtain a general understanding of:

- the business situation, organization, and IT strategy (both now and at the time the investment was sanctioned);
- the aims and history of the investment, the technical constraints, and the degree working practices were expected to change;
- the logical description and physical components of the system, and the various suppliers and users of the information.

This step is simply an effort to acquire a general comprehension of the system in question, so that subsequent steps are set in the appropriate business and environmental context.

Step three: glean detailed information

Once the general characteristics have been digested, a more precise understanding can be developed. An interesting description of the process of seeking user views and 'wringing value out of systems' had been documented by Bohlin and Hoenig (1989). A well-established, and thorough, approach for collecting performance data on a system had been described in detail by Carlson and McNurlin (1989). The approach was originally devised for IBM by Gold and Albrecht (Figure 9.4), and consists of five sets of questionnaires which cover:

- the amount and rate of expenditure in providing different processing resources (an improvement on this basic data would be to examine the cost of the services as they are seen by the user, rather than the cost of hardware etc.);
- processing performance, for example metrics on CPU uptime, function points delivered and so on;
- contribution to improving the results of current business functions in a tangible way;
- preparedness with respect to the ability to meet new business challenges and technical developments;
- strategic impact on the competitiveness of major operating units in the future.

A simpler methodology, aimed more at the assessment of business results, has been devised by Meyer and Boone (1987) to see if a system has led to tasks:

- taking less resources;
- being completed in less time;
- being done with greater quality;
- offering greater job satisfaction.

A major problem with their methodology is that it tends to over-attribute benefits to IT, and neglects the impact of other management efforts. For example, they cite the market valuation of a start-up venture of US $85 million some years later, as the result of an entrepreneur's original expenditure of US $5000 for an on-line search for potential opportunities. Such phenomenal calculations are based on a simple flaw. The appropriate value of the on-line search was not some arbitrary percentage of US $85 million, but the least expensive amount needed to obtain the identical information without the on-line computer search.

A questionnaire can be drawn up and used as part of the methodology. A sequence of open-ended questions, which can be piloted, and then used by the task force to interview key users and their managers, is as follows:

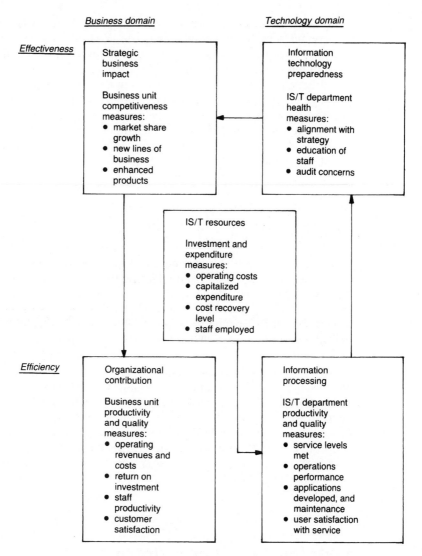

Figure 9.4 IBM's IT value measurement framework.

1. **Productivity** – what is the time they saved being used for? Doing more work? Does this mean that you (or your boss) have been able to reduce or reassign staff, or plan to hire fewer in the future?
2. **If not, check** to see if work not done before is now being done. Doing work not done before? Doing a better job, so there are fewer errors or queries later?
3. **Timeliness** – what is the hurry? Are business processes being finished more quickly, and therefore delivering benefits sooner?
4. **Tasks not previously done** – why bother? Why is this worth doing? What would happen if you stopped doing it?
5. **Improved quality** – so what? In what way is it better? How much better? How is it reducing the possibility of additional costs or increasing the chance of more revenue?

6. **Increased revenue** – what is the credibility? Odds of winning sales multiplied by average sales revenue and number of sales per year effected (the sum must be done with the system and then with the alternative to the system, as it is the difference that is required). Odds of identifying market opportunity multiplied by forecast present value of revenue from the new business activity (again the sum must be calculated for the system, minus the base-case alternative to the system).
7. **Reduced costs** – how much? Estimate cost savings to different categories of user.
8. **Accelerated benefits** – how much quicker? Take the time value of money, that is, the difference between the present values of the cost–benefit stream at the time of the actual start and at the time it otherwise would have started.
9. **Reduced risks** – impact and likelihood? What were the risks to the business before the system? What are the risks now? How much money is at stake?
10. **Job satisfaction** – so what? Why is job satisfaction worth paying for? What would happen if there was no system, or the company had to revert to the old system?

Care must be taken in using the above questionnaire not to double count benefits, or only take success stories. To understand the trap that must be avoided in using this type of questionnaire, the 'case of the missing US $10 million' is instructive. Meyer and Boone (1987) describe the value of an office automation system in preparing the budget on military spending for approval by a congressional committee. In the consolidation process, a line item worth US $10 million was accidentally left out. A subsequent check of totals using a spreadsheet program found the error before it was too late. Meyer and Boone estimated that there was a 60% greater chance of detecting the mistake by using a personal computer which cost less than US $10 000. By dividing the huge gains from catching the error by the small cost of the computer they came up with the amazing one-year return on investment of 59 900%! The answer of course, is that the value of the computer is the relative cost advantage of the office system over having another accountant check the budget proposal. Indeed, it might have been cheaper to pay an accountant to check the figures than buy a computer – or better, employ a clerk who can put a budget together without making such a large mistake.

Step four: evaluate controls

Once the task force understands the system, and the shades of opinion on its worth, thoroughly, the next step is to identify and evaluate the controls that were, and are being, exercised. First this involves differentiating between the activities in the development or use of the system which are subject to control and those which provide control. Once this differentiation has been made, the team:

- identifies those controls on the development, maintenance and running costs, and delivery of the benefits, whose absence allow, or would allow, significant exposures to different parts of the company;
- searches for exposures which might exist in the current version and use of the system, but which could be eliminated by management action.

A frequent issue that must be faced is the evolution of the business requirement, and the acceptability of the change control process. Often system features are added

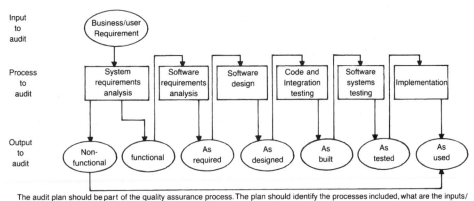

The audit plan should be part of the quality assurance process. The plan should identify the processes included, what are the inputs/outputs, what will be measured, how will they be measured and what constitutes an adequate outcome.

Figure 9.5 The system requirement specification to implementation process.

or postponed without consideration of their impact on the relative costs and benefits. The traditional steps in implementing a system are shown in Figure 9.5 (see Keen, 1987). The documentation and progress reports from each step should be examined to track the evolution of the development.

A comprehensive discussion of reviewing techniques can be found in Freedman and Weinberg (1982). Three important points to bear in mind are:

1. The need to link the (usually forgotten) non-functional requirements like user-friendliness, with the actual usage. Typically the audit just looks at the IT design and builds metrics because hard data exist in this area. Almost the only book that discusses auditing the maintenance of a software project is by Vallabhaneni (1987).
2. The need to understand the whole judgemental process in gauging costs, benefits and risks from the genesis of the idea, through gaining formal approval to spend money, to allocating credit and blame once the system is working (see Marsh *et al.*, 1988).
3. The genuine lack of hard evidence on benefits, and the need for business judgement, and accountability for that judgement. A thorough description of the problems and solutions associated with different perspectives on information systems has been documented by Lyytinen (1987).

Step five: design tests

To verify the statements on the costs, benefits and controls, the task force must next design its auditing procedures, using the most appropriate techniques. Sometimes the data can be gleaned from the management accounts and reports. In other cases it is necessary to establish specific studies to investigate working practices and how IT is affecting them. The skills of the old time and motion departments will come in use again. Further, as Noble (1989) has pointed out, it is important to consider the whole chain of activities affected by the new system. For example, when reviewing a system to improve customer service, it is important to examine not only the costs and benefits to the users and suppliers of data in the company, but also the cost and value of the benefits to the customer!

Step six: perform tests

The next step is then to perform the audit tests. Available data on the actual costs – in particular organizational change costs – should be scrutinized. Evidence to support the benefits claimed (or denied) by different users should be examined. It is not unusual to find a detailed and glowing description of the benefits expected, but no timetable for their delivery by specific groups of user.

Step seven: evaluate findings

The final step is to agree the conclusions that can be drawn from the detailed findings. Like all good projects these have (naturally?) been documented in the interview notes, working papers and progress reports, of the task force. Recommendations should be prepared on any corrective action that should be taken on the system to increase its value to the company. Lessons for similar investments should also be accompanied by constructive suggestions as to what actions could be taken.

Post-investment appraisal, like any other form of sophisticated analysis requiring professional skill, depends on collecting valid data, analysing them carefully, and constantly testing the inferences drawn from the data. The toughest tests are reserved for the conclusions. Good auditors make sure their conclusions can stand all kinds of critical questioning. An approach which can be used to help draw out the conclusions, in a workshop with the relevant managers, had been described by Way and Norris (1991). It assumes that the overall value of an application can be viewed along three main dimensions:

- business effectiveness;
- technical cost-efficiency; and
- financial worth.

Business effectiveness can be gauged according to how well the system is seen to support the achievement of the company's objectives, or critical success factors. Similarly, the users are asked to rate the efficiency of the process which delivered the system at each stage of its lifecycle. The results of these two subjective measurements are illustrated by the example shown in Figure 9.6. The two ratings by each user, are used to plot the x-y coordinates of the pie chart showing the incremental net benefit of the system to them. The area of each pie indicates the percentage of the total financial benefit to the company. The segments of each pie can be used to illustrate the magnitude of the different benefits that made up the total. Colour can be used to show positive and negative sums. There are a number of variations to the construction of these CIE charts according to the unique features of each appraisal (see Norris, 1986).

The aim of the approach is to take a portfolio view of investing in systems. The focus of post-investment appraisals then moves from just looking at the returns on an individual system to the total return from all the systems funded by the company. This is the same approach that investors take when they create an investment portfolio of shares and bonds. Overall, the portfolio can show a good return even though some of its component items are losers. The aim is to seek to maximize the return while keeping risk at an acceptable level to the stakeholders. General guidelines are to:

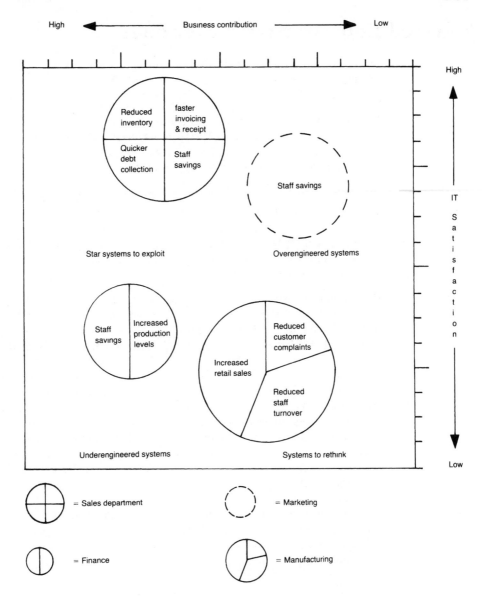

Figure 9.6 CIE charts on business impact, IT satisfaction and benefits.

- Keep investments with high but uncertain paybacks as small as possible until benefits are more clearly understood.
- Include projects in the portfolio that are likely to succeed, even if their payback does not appear to be large.
- Stop projects when their payback appears to fall below their level of risk.

It must be remembered, however, that these charts are only visual aids to overcome the problems of seeing a number of complex factors at the same time. The CIE charts only illustrate the business impact, technical satisfaction and incremental worth to focus debate. They do not provide a definitive view.

Selected findings from experience

After examining the results from a range of post-investment reviews, Norton (1985) considered there were several problems with the way companies handle their expenditure on IT. In summary, Norton claimed that too many organizations were:

1. **Taking too short a view** – firms have a tendency to focus on yearly budgets for IT, and annual expectations of return. As many systems last ten years, or more, and their data longer, IS should be seen as long-term assets, where it can be several years before there is a measurable impact.
2. **Seeing application software as an expense** – few companies treat applications as if they were strategic assets, and capitalize their development costs. (This claim is rather a red herring, as it muddles an accounting convention with the cash figures which should be used in financial appraisal.)
3. **Viewing people as an expense** – staff are a vital asset, and in order to increase profit, a firm should be aiming at leveraging people with IT, in order to make them more productive.

Similar work by Marsh *et al.* (1988), suggested that a fundamental problem was the overestimation of the competitive advantages to be gained – all investments in a competitive environment have a zero net present value in the long term. Further, the optimism behind the projections of costs and benefits are often more a function of the sponsors' enthusiasm for the project than any tangible evidence at the time. The experience of the Centre for Information Economics reveals that another problem is a bias towards incremental investment. While it is good practice to phase expenditure according to the achievement of performance targets, it is important to assess the value of the total investment being contemplated. Arbitrary authorization levels can set artificial ceilings on investment, and so lead to suboptimal investment. While each incremental investment may apparently be adequately justified, together they add up to a poorer return than total innovation. Or worse, the existence of ongoing incremental investment precludes any consideration of more revolutionary investment proposals.

A number of general, but vital, lessons emerge from an analysis of the recommendations from post-investment reviews. The messages which regularly crop up from the reviews conducted by the Centre for Information Economics can be divided into the following areas:

- pre-sanction analysis;
- the approval process;
- the project manager;
- project definition;
- monitoring and control;
- design and build; and
- implementation and use.

Within each area the findings have been ranked according to frequency. A sweeping conclusion that could be drawn is that rather basic management disciplines are lacking more frequently than would be openly admitted . . . but of course, part of the purpose of post-investment appraisals is to alert managers to fundamentals that have been overlooked.

Pre-sanction analysis

1. Every investment should have a clearly defined client who is identified with the overall requirements of the system, and is accountable for its progress within time and budget.
2. In view of his or her responsibility to the client to complete the project to specification, it is desirable that the project manager is appointed well before sanction to allow input into the definition documents.
3. It is essential to have in-depth feasibility studies for major projects, and for their conclusions to be discussed by those concerned with examining the investment proposal.
4. The importance of the assessment of hardware, storage, development, and organizational change costs cannot be overstressed. A contrived low figure could encourage an unsatisfactory investment while an unnecessarily high valuation could endanger a potentially profitable investment.
5. Where investment is contemplated which involves new technology, new techniques, or a very large-scale development, great caution should be exercised to ensure that it is either the only practical route to the attainment of the business objective of the system – or that the expected rewards are very high! An interesting review of approaches for managing investment in innovative applications of IT was presented by Davies and Norris (1990).
6. The importance of involving the proposed users of the system, their managers, and the IT professionals to build commitment must be generally recognized.
7. The value of an installed system is the replacement cost. When acquiring a company, where the sale price includes software that has been developed as an asset, it must be remembered that previously incurred costs, no matter how large, are irrelevant and should be stripped out.

The approval process

1. Investments which have been thoroughly researched by the managers in the business, who will have to deliver the benefit, the IT management, who have to build and run the system, and the directors who have to allocate funds, are more likely to prove good investments. Rushed cases with deficiencies or ambiguities will result in poor decisions, and could lead to the unnecessary rejection or deferral of otherwise sound investments. A useful survey of cost–benefit methodologies for justifying IT expenditure can be found in Sassone (1988).
2. It is essential that the fit with an approved business and IT strategy is clearly established. For example, see a description of a portfolio approach to evaluating IT investments by Ward (1994).
3. It is important that if there are any reservations about any technical, commercial or other aspect of the project put forward for sanction, these should be tested and resolved even if this means delaying approval – or ultimately not approving. Phased approval according to demonstrable progress could be the way to proceed.
4. The predicted DCF rate of return or NPV should never be used as the sole criterion for project appraisal. It should be used to support the business judgement on the

value of the investment and the relative risks to the company (see also Chapters 2 and 7).

5. Circumstances may arise where there is a significant change of scope in the application of the system. In all such cases the project should submit a revised case for approval, whether additional funds are required or not.

6. Sensitivity analysis should cover all foreseeable risks in addition to variations on the critical assumptions used to forecast the cash flows. In particular, the impact of more than one factor at a time should be examined together with an indication of the probability that this might occur.

The project manager

1. The selection, training and track record of the project manager and his or her team are crucial to a successful outcome. Where possible, the team should be chosen with regard to their recent direct involvement in a successful, related type of project.

2. Wherever possible the project manager should be appointed for the duration of the assignment. Efforts must also be made to ensure the continuity of other staff engaged on, or in support of, the project. If it becomes necessary to replace a project manager when a project is well advanced, but behind schedule, it is unlikely that his or her successor will be able to recover lost ground.

Project definition

1. Although often difficult to achieve, a precise, unambiguous definition of require-ments is essential for all investments regardless of type, size, or complexity. Failure can result in unrealistic forecasts of costs and completion dates, with consequent erosion of benefits; inadequate project staffing levels, scheduling of scarce re-sources (usually experts in the business), resulting in inefficiency and delay; poor control over project progress; and unreliable information for contract tendering and consequent exposure to delays and claims.

2. Project costs can be seriously underestimated if the effort in moving from a prototype to the production version is not well understood by the users.

3. The capability of users to employ the system in practice is usually too optimistic. Training and education budgets need to reflect the changes in working practice expected.

4. There is a general need for much greater resistance to incremental changes in requirements, which build up over time, to have a major impact on the design. Significant amendments to the scope of an investment must always be agreed by all parties to the original idea. The full implication of any change must be clarified and the economics revisited.

Monitoring and control

1. The course of a project is set in its very early stages. Senior management must place great emphasis, from the start, on ensuring adequate planning and provision of resources, and early identification of potential problems.

2. Effort must be made to establish realistic rather than overoptimistic targets. An excess of optimism will inevitably prove self-defeating as morale declines when goals are significantly or continuously missed.
3. If a project has become seriously delayed, and there is no immediate prospect of returning to schedule, consideration should be given to halting the investment until the problems have been resolved, since to continue undeterred often compounds the problem further.
4. Critical reviews are necessary of the viability of projects which are subject to business changes and rapid technical advances. Cancellation can be a better option than the eventual underutilization or shut-down.
5. The project management philosophy can be too user driven, rather than business led. A tripartite management style, where business management must take responsibility for the tradeoffs between: the wish list of desirable system facilities and price expectations, expressed by the user community; and the professional view on the technical constraints, and full lifecycle costs expressed by the IT department.

Design and build

1. Contractors should only be invited to tender for major contracts after a full investigation of their track record, resources for this assignment, and planning and control procedures. This will include visits to reference sites, and their offices.
2. The quality of key personnel in the contractor's team is critical to the success of the project. Nominations of specially screened individuals to such positions should be a normal requirement, and named individuals contractually committed.
3. In order to minimize delays in approving progress reports and recommendations at each milestone in the project, it is essential to review carefully the classification for approval and the time allowed for turn round.
4. Vigilant inspection of the specification and system design should not be sacrificed for speed even if this does result in delayed approval. A little extra effort at this stage, to ensure that the user agrees that the design meets the mandatory requirements in the specification, always saves much time and additional cost later in the project.
5. Measures taken to accelerate system development without detailed planning may be counterproductive. For example, to increase programming staff without a clear definition of the interfaces can reduce overall productivity without a worthwhile improvement in the rate of progress.
6. Responsibilities for full system testing and handover frequently cause confusion, and effective coordination between contractors, the system department and the users must be agreed in advance.

Implementation and use

1. The virtues of intangible benefits usually remain unsubstantiated, and cause scepticism about future requests for investment. A view on how to measure intangible benefits can be found in Smith (1983).

2. Non-functional requirements, like 'easy to update', are not fully met because they have been inadequately described from the outset.

3. The management effort on the part of user management to test the system, and ensure it worked as required and specified, is underestimated by the users.

4. The benefits are smaller and later in arriving than promised. The concepts of project management – named responsibility for each subproject, explicit milestones and demonstrable deliverables – are not always continued from system development into the process of delivering benefits on implementation. By themselves, information systems cannot deliver benefits. Once a system is implemented the achievement of the promised benefits are usually left to the line-management process. As responsibilities for inputting, processing and using information tend to cross divisional boundaries, this approach can delay the drive to bring in the benefits on time.

5. Management of change costs are higher than estimated. Indeed, a company's staff development and management education programme is often not sufficiently primed to have established a sufficiently informed user community who can balance the opportunities, and more importantly, limitations of information technology, or developed the all-round depth of consulting and organizational change skills needed by IT staff, and the business knowledge to be able to contribute to the redesign of business processes to take full advantage of IT.

6. In a rapidly changing would, the system builder can be perceived as moving with bureaucratic precision towards distant targets that may no longer be relevant when reached. Taking an evolutionary approach to delivering very large systems not only gives more control over costs and the phased delivery of benefits, but also allows people to evolve simultaneously. Further, business priorities and technical options need to be checked. For example, the US post office spent four years and millions of dollars changing to a new nine-digit zip code format. In the meantime, optical scanners arrived which could read the original hand-written five-figure code.

7. The system strategy on the merits of 'open systems' and prototyping etc. was more a statement of good intent than a guide to what was practically achievable at the time.

8. There is no base case to compare actual performance and the possible alternatives.

9. Projected benefits are not incorporated into the budgets, or performance targets for the business areas affected.

A pre-investment checklist

Based on this post-investment experience, which could be fairly widespread, a number of checklists to aid pre-investment decisions can be developed (see Cox and Norris, 1990, and Jacobson and Norris, 1991, for further examples). It can be argued that general management has three distinct roles in directing and exploiting information systems and technology: setting the appropriate framework, making decisions on investment and ensuring the delivery of results.

Setting the framework

Senior management in manufacturing, marketing and sales etc. do not have to become embroiled in the technical details of information systems. As Clemens and

Weber (1990) argue, no one else can set the necessary framework for the full and successful exploitation of the systems by the company. In setting this framework, senior management in the business has to ensure that:

- there is a systems strategy and a process to keep it in tune with the evolution of business priorities;
- the strategy provides guidance on the portfolio of applications, the provision of facilities, the acquisition of systems (make of build), the choice of hardware and software, system interfaces, and data management;
- the strategy is reflected in the budget for the delivery of services, and performance against budget is monitored;
- the IT division is structured to reflect the needs and capability of its customers;
- business priorities are communicated;
- potential developments in technology are assessed for their relevance to the company;
- business processes are questioned;
- there is a consistent approach to IT investment decisions;
- there is the 'right' degree of management understanding, control, and participation at the next management level.

Without such a framework, IT-related decisions must necessarily be *ad hoc*. Each manager and each IT specialist does what he or she thinks is right, but there is no touchstone for their decisions, no overall sense of direction, and no coherent relationship between systems. It is quite an easy test for any manager to turn the above list of requirements into a series of questions, along the lines of 'Do we have ...?' If the answer to any item is no, then the organization does not have the right framework in place to exploit IT. Further, senior management is either failing to recognize its role or simply abdicating part of this to the technicians.

Making investment decisions

Given the right framework, decisions on the value of individual projects or opportunities become clearer – but that does not necessarily make them easier. The problem is that even where there is a willingness to take the decision, the necessary information is seldom laid out in a way that enables management judgement to be properly exercised. The following checklist gives the questions to which decision-makers need answers if they are to do their job properly:

1. **Objectives** – does everyone understand precisely why the company wants this system? (Correcting a weakness, exploiting a strength, minimizing a threat, meeting an opportunity?) Why now? Is there sufficient commitment? Will it satisfy the expectations of the shareholder?
2. **Requirements** – Have the underlying business processes been questioned? What is the effect of tackling only part of the requirement?
3. **Solution** – Is the system appropriate relative to the competition and the usage our staff will be able to make of the application? What are the alternatives? How big or complex is the system? Where do the risks to the project, the users of the system and the company lie? How proven are the approach, hardware, software, suppliers, delivery team? What are the organizational change implications? What are the long-term implications? What is the fit with the preferred system architecture?

What does the user management have to do to ensure success? Is it consistent with our competence and resources?

4. **Timescale** – What assumptions and constraints? What degree of confidence?
5. **Costs** – What is the effect of shortening or relaxing the time schedule? What degree of confidence? What is the balance of development and running costs? What costs are excluded? How much (scarce) management time will it require?
6. **Benefits** – Are they the real benefits as far as the business is concerned? Who is giving this evaluation? Who is going to be responsible for achieving them?
7. **Evaluation** – Whose decision is it? What is the basis for the decision? What are the most important criteria?
8. **Keys of success** – Do we have a sponsor and a champion? How good is the project manager? Will it lead to a concentration of effort?

At the next decision on a new project, or on further investment in systems, it is worth running through the above questions to see whether the answers are available. Having the answers, however, does not necessarily mean that the right decision is easy or obvious. But without the answers how can a meaningful decision be made?

Ensuring the delivery of results

Circumstances change, projects go off course and managers move on. Even if the original decision was right, development projects and their implementation have to be steered and directed through to their conclusion. Regrettably, using today's missile terminology, there is no such thing as a 'fire and forget' development project. Moreover, benefits never accrue automatically when the system is installed, they have to be squeezed out. Senior management's responsibilities endure throughout development and implementation of any new system. Monitoring and keeping a project on course is not difficult provided it is done regularly and systematically. There must be:

- regular reaffirmation (or review) of business objectives and priorities;
- an explicit and agreed plan of campaign, divided into a distinct sequence of steps, with agreed responsibilities, and demonstrable deliverables from each step;
- clear accountability for specifying, building, accepting and using the system;
- change, control and update procedures;
- reliable reporting procedures on areas of concern/potential problems, spend to date/accomplishment, and effort to complete;
- continuous accountability for the overall investment;
- the active involvement of the project sponsor and the user management;
- the management ability and will to intervene decisively.

Conclusion

Establishing value for money depends on the business judgement of the managers involved – it is no more amenable to numerical analysis than any other value judgement. Regular post-investment audits, however, can provide valuable feedback on the evidence and perceptions on the value being achieved by IT projects. When combined with quality approaches such as that detailed in Chapter 5 post-investment audits can yield powerful results. The audit can measure the internal efficiency of the IT department in developing systems, and relate expenditure on systems to key performance measures used to monitor the health of the user department employing the system. One main benefit is that future estimates can be made more realistic. It may become apparent that the costs of implementing new applications are being consistently underestimated. The errors may be 'honest' ones or may come from the sponsors of these projects putting a bias into the figures to give their projects a better chance of acceptance. In either case it is important that forecasts are checked against subsequent events.

A second benefit is that corrective action can be taken to ensure the timely delivery of benefits, and to target controls on similar investments. In an extreme case, further expenditure on the system may need to be abandoned because the benefits fall far short of expectations. In other cases, less drastic action to reorient the investment may ensure a successful outcome. A final benefit is that confidence can be built in the professionalism and business orientation of the IT department. The business contribution of IT investments can be verified, and the scale of the return gauged relative to other (competing) claims on the company's purse. It is important, of course, that post-investment audits do not degenerate into a hunt for scapegoats. Few projects go so smoothly that there are no lessons for the future.

Interestingly, research by Argyris (1991) shows that senior managers in large companies tend to be successful at what they do, and rarely experience failure. And, according to Argyris, because they have rarely failed, they have never learnt how to learn from failure. So when things go wrong, and audits always discover something, they become defensive, screen out criticism, and put the blame on anyone and everyone but themselves. Indeed, the most difficult companies to help with post-investment appraisals are those where the middle management believe it is a sign of their management skill and loyalty to the firm, to bypass and cover up difficult issues. In short, their ability to learn shuts down at precisely the moment they need it most. For the lessons of post-investment appraisal to be genuinely absorbed, the appraisal must be linked to a wider objective of organizational growth and staff development. The use of recent post-investment appraisals as case studies in a firm's management education programme offers both relevant lessons and lively discussion. In the last resort, however, good working relationships and mutual trust within the company are the best defence against unrealistic forecasts and late corrective action.

In the end, systems themselves have no value. Their only worth is in the information they generate, and information is an intangible product that only its recipient can value. In many ways the real purpose behind post-investment appraisal is in the way it helps users to see the business value, relative to the cost. As Silk (1990) concludes: 'IT/IS has no special claim on scarce investment resources. Justification of such investment, in business terms, will be an increasing priority for IT professionals in the 1990s.'

References

Argyris, C. (1991) Teaching smart people how to learn. *Harvard Business Review*, **69** (3).
Berger, P., Kobelius, J. and Sutherland, D. (1988) *Measuring Business Value of Information*. Technologies, International Centre for Information Technologies Press, Washington, DC.

Bohlin, R. and Hoenig, C. (1989) Wringing value from old systems. *Datamation*, **35** (15), 57–60.

Butler Cox Foundation (1990) *Getting Value from Information Technology*. Research Report 75, Butler Cox Foundation, London.

Carlson, W. and McNurlin, B. (1989) *Measuring the Value of Information Systems*. I/S Analyzer Special Report, United Communications Group, Bethesda.

Centre for Information Economics (1990) *Value for Money: How to Direct and Exploit Investments in Information Systems*. CIE Report for ICAEW CHARTAC Seminar, March, Centre For Information Economics, London.

Checkland, P. (1984) *System Thinking, System Practice*, John Wiley, New York.

Clemens, E, and Weber, B. (1990) Strategic information technology investments: guidelines for decision making. *Journal of Management Information Systems*, **7** (2), 9–28.

Computer Economics Report (1989) Trends in IT decision making. *Computer Economics*, **11** (12).

Cox, G. (1990) *Directing and Exploiting Systems*, Cranfield IT Institute Seminar, Cranfield University, Milton Keynes.

Davies, C. and Norris, G. (1990) Managing investment in innovative applications of IT. *Proceedings of the ICI IT Conference*, CMS, Harrogate.

Freedman, D. and Weinberg, G. (1982) *Handbook of Walkthroughs, Inspections, and Technical Reviews*, Little, Brown, New York.

Ginzberg, M. and Zmud, R. (1988) Evolving criteria for IS assessment. In *Information Systems Assessment: Issues and Challenges* (eds. N. Bjorn-Anderson and G. Davies), Elsevier, Amsterdam.

Hammer, M. and Mangurian, G. (1987) The changing value of communications technology. *Sloan Management Review*, Winter, 65–71.

Hogbin, G. and Thomas, D. (1994) *Investing In Information Technology: Managing The Decision-Making Process*, McGraw Hill, London.

Hotchkiss, W. (1923) *Harvard Business Review*, **1**.

Jacobson, V, and Norris, G. (1991) *General Management's Role in Directing IT Investments*. Glaxo Group Research IT Planning Division, Glaxo Pharmeceuticals, Greenford.

Keen, P. (1987) *Managing System Development*. Wiley, New York.

Killman, R. and Mitroff, I. (1979) Problem defining and the consulting intervention process. *California Management Review*, **21**, 26–33.

King, W., Grover, V. and Hufnagel, E. (1989) Using information and information technology for sustainable competitive advantage. *Information and Management*, **17**.

Kumar, K. (1990) Post-implementation evaluation of computer based information systems: current practice. *Communications of the ACM*, **33** (2), 203–12.

Lyytinen (1987) Different perspectives of information systems. *ACM Computing*, March.

Mair, W., Wood, D. and Davis, K. (1978) *Computer Control and Audit*, Institute of Internal Auditors, Touche Ross, FL.

Marsh, P., Barwise, P., Thomas, K. and Wensley, R. (1988) *Managing Strategic Investment Decisions in Large Diversified Companies*, London Business School, London.

McKenney, J. (1995) *Waves of Change: Business Evolution through Information Technology*, Harvard Business School Press, Boston, MA.

Meyer, N. and Boone, M. (1987) *The Information Edge*, McGraw Hill, New York.

Moad, J. (1989) Asking users to judge IS. *Datamation*, **35** (21), 93–100.

Noble, J. (1989) Techniques for cost justifying CIM. *The Journal of Business Strategy*, January/February, 44–51.

Norris, G. (1976) Identification of performance indices for central computer services. OECD Conference 20–22 January, Paris.

Norris, G. (1986) A knowledge-based system for investment appraisal. *Proceedings of the International Conference on KBS*, On-line Advanced Computing Series 2, London.

Norris, G. (1989) *Assessing Innovative IT investment*, BBITS Conference Proceedings, Southcourt Publications, Partridge Green.

Norris, G. (1991) IT education: what are the objectives? *Mortgage Finance*, March, 46–8.

Norris, G. and Wallace, E. (1987) *Choosing and Managing Information Systems*, Saxon House, Gower Press, Farnborough.

Norton, D. (1985) Information technology, the investment enigma. *The Consultant Forum*, January/February, 9–12.

Parker, M. and Benson, R. (1988) *Information Economics: Linking Business Performance to Information Technology*, Prentice Hall, London.

Robson, W. (1994) *Strategic Management and Information Systems*, Pitman, London.

Sassone, P. (1988) Cost justification: a survey of cost benefit methodologies for information systems. *Project Appraisal*, June 73–83.

Silk, D. (1990) Managing IS benefits for the 1990s. *Journal of Information Technology*, **5** (4), 185–93.

Silk, D. (1991). *Planning IT*, Butterworth Heinemann, London.

Smith, R. (1983) Measuring the intangible benefits of computer based information systems. *Journal of Systems Management*, **34** (9), 22–7.

Strassmann, P. (1990) *The Business Value of Computers*, The Information Economics Press, New Canaan, CT.

Taylor, I. and Norris, G. (1989) *Myth and Reality: The Strategic Impact of IT on Britain's Leading Businesses*, The Datasolve Report, Sunbury-on-Thames.

Vallabhaneni, R. (1987) *Auditing the Maintenance of Software*, Prentice Hall, London.

Ward, J. (1994) A portfolio approach to evaluating information systems investments and setting priorities. In *Information Management: Evaluation of Information Systems Investments* (ed. L. Willcocks), Chapman & Hall, London.

Way, R. and Norris, G. (1991) *Value from Investment in Information Technology: A Framework for Assessments*, Electricity Audit Group, South Wales.

Weill, P. (1989) *The Relationship between Investment in Information Technology and Firm Performance*, Doctoral Thesis, School of Business, New York University.

Willcocks, L. (ed.) (1994) *Information Management: Evaluation of Information Systems Investments*, Chapman & Hall, London.

Willcocks, L. and Lester, S. (1994) Evaluating the feasibility of information systems investments: recent UK evidence and new approaches. In *Information Management: Evaluation of Information Systems Investments* (ed. L. Willcocks), Chapman & Hall, London.

10

From strategy to implementation: identifying and managing benefits of IT investments

Glen Peters

Introduction

Much effort has been concentrated in the last few years on designing IT strategy and most large organizations in the developed economies by the mid-1990s will have complex IT investment portfolios (Galliers and Baker, 1994; McKenney, 1995). Managing the benefits of the investment portfolio continues to present challenges. I have previously published the first stage of a method for linking investment strategy to benefits. Peters (1994) discussed the classification of benefits and the evaluation of an overall IT investment strategy. This chapter develops the evaluation methodology by adding a second stage of the process enabling identification of benefits for specific investments to ensure their realization. The process ensures that sponsors not only

Investing in Information Systems: Evaluation and Management. Edited by
Leslie Willcocks. Published in 1996 by Chapman & Hall. ISBN 0 412 72670 X.

understand the impact of the investment on key operating variables but also take responsibility for ensuring the improved performance.

Figure 10.1 shows the stage discussed in this chapter. Whereas the evaluation of an overall investment strategy allows a company to assess the appropriateness of its IT strategy to its business strategy and culture, individual investments need to be assessed in terms of their impact on company objectives and other key success variables. The first part of this chapter deals with the development of a cost–benefit hierarchy for project evaluation, while the second half deals with worked examples. In developing this part of the methodology, it was necessary to examine some of the attitudes of managers in evaluating specific investments. These attitudes were gathered from research I conducted in the late 1980s. Thirty projects were reviewed at different stages in their lifecycles and both sponsors and implementers were interviewed. The resultant method suggested in this chapter has been piloted on three major projects in the petrochemical, process and retail sectors, and has been found to be robust in continuing work with companies in this area.

Findings on the evaluation process

The following findings are relevant to the evaluation of this methodology. Managers questioned, commented on the following:

1. Although companies had short- and long-term objectives such as 'increase marketshare', 'to be the preeminent supplier' or 'to improve customer service', the final irreducible objective was to improve or, at worst, maintain profitability. Profitability was the common currency of success in the eyes of stakeholders and, inevitably, any form of investment must, in the longer term, be judged on its impact on profitability. Clearly, this would not apply to non-profit-making organizations.
2. Once an investment appraisal had been performed on a project and approval given for implementation, few organizations (less than 10%) carried out subsequent

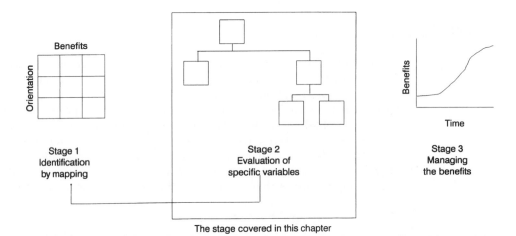

Figure 10.1 The three-stage methodology.

follow-up reviews to measure the actual performance of an investment against its original assumptions. This was because the original appraisal was couched in far too general terms and it would be difficult to appropriate an increase in market share, say, to a specific investment. Another reason given was that frequently the justification for an investment was in intangible terms such as 'improving customer service' and, consequently, it was difficult to measure the real impact on such broad variables without incurring substantial cost. Some companies never bothered with regular post-investment appraisals because it did not suit their culture.

3. The eventual users of a system were frequently so far removed from the process of investment appraisal that there was little bridging of the identifiers of the investment and the eventual users who were actually responsible for their success. Project managers appointed to projects may have been good managers but concentrated on meeting their objectives of keeping to time and cost. There appeared to be no individual or group of individuals managing the benefits of an investment.

The successful management of projects was outside the scope of this research, and some guidelines and comment have already been provided in Chapters 7 and 9. However, as part of the research it was necessary to review projects where the benefits had been managed well. The companies that appeared to have positive attitudes, in part, regarding the management of the benefits of projects had the following qualities:

1. They set up project boards or steering committees, led by a senior user group member, at an early stage of the project (at the evaluation stage). The project board followed the project to a late stage of implementation and frequently members of the board took actual responsibility for delivering benefits for subcomponents of the investment.
2. A number of variables affected by the investment were identified. All of these were measurable but not all were measurable in cost terms. Variables such as sales calls per day, delivery schedules met and customer throughput per hour were such examples.
3. Project boards reviewed the benefits gained at regular intervals up to three months in duration and seemed more concerned with obtaining benefits that may have been missed in the original investment.
4. Projects which had clearly defined responsibilities with key variables overperformed their original appraisal.

The following attributes were therefore considered essential in a methodology for evaluating individual investments.

1. Measurable variables (not all necessarily of a financial nature) should be identified to allow users and developers to understand the full scope of the investment and its impact on performance.
2. A method of decomposing cost and benefit components should be developed to give greater clarity to the various benefits and cost areas and reduce the investment to a common objective or goal.
3. A framework should be established for clearly identifying responsibilities for benefits.

The cost–benefit hierarchy

A framework was developed and is subsequently referred to as the cost–benefit hierarchy of an investment. This is shown in Figure 10.2. The cost–benefit hierarchy has the attributes discussed below.

At the lowest level, key variables are identified. These key variables are measurable indicators that may have physical or cost performance characteristics. The important nature of these key variables is that they are measurable. Examples such as sales calls per day, cost per invoice, stock turnover and average customer queuing time are measurable key variables that can, in many instances, be reviewed as a direct result of a report from a well-constructed management information system. The existence of measurable variables dispels the concern expressed that unquantifiable benefits are often stated in support of an investment and that it is neither practical nor desirable to attempt to measure such non-quantifiable benefits. 'Improvements in customer service', for example, the frequently quoted benefit, are impossible to measure other than by perception. Conversely, defining 'customer service' by a number of key variables such as waiting time, average lead times and time to fix defects, begins to give managers more tangible measures with which to question the validity of intangible claims. This approach assumes, however, that all intangible or 'gut feel' invest-

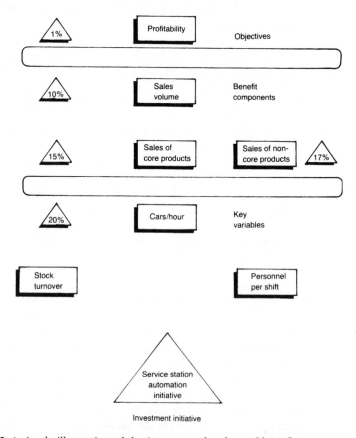

Figure 10.2 A simple illustration of the impact on the chart of benefits.

ments can be reduced to measurable physical or financial variables. This can be the subject of some debate but, during the trials of this method, no impossible barriers were encountered to this supposition.

Cost–benefit components divide into two separate streams similar to a balance sheet. They form a hierarchy like a chart of accounts in an accounting system and enable a step-by-step analysis of the costs and benefits arising from an investment. Figure 10.2 illustrates the use of the benefits hierarchy. A worked example has been drawn from an oil company that was involved in the business of marketing and distributing oil to the retail, commercial and industrial trades. This example has been developed after the company elected to trial this methodology in early 1988. Seven major IT projects were identified by users as follows:

- Retail site automation involving the provision of electronic point of sale terminals at service stations, automated payment systems and the provision of management information to run each site.
- An accounting systems project including a new general ledger, accounts payable and accounts receivable module. The existing general ledger was 15 years old and ill equipped to deal with the fast changing business environment. Accounts receivable and payable activities were handled largely manually and provided poor information on credit offered to curstomers.
- Order processing systems to centralize distributed order taking in regional depots, thereby making substantial savings in manpower. Functions to enable automatic order taking were also to be added.
- The provision of a new database (DB2) and software development language (PL1) to improve integration of management information, the quality of existing software and reduce development times.
- Electronic data interchange to automate ordering of goods for retail stores with suppliers and to allow customers to place orders.
- The provision of office systems to automate many office functions and to improve the efficiency of office staff across all management levels.
- Value-added software for customers to manage their own business. There were a number of initiatives in this area from fuel management to administration of accounts. All these initiatives were aimed at offering additional service to customers thereby aiding product differentiation.

IT investment mapping

The planned initiatives were subjected to stage 1 of the methodology, mapping the investments. Each investment was scored for its 'benefits' and orientation areas. The results of this score are shown in Table 10.1. The investments were plotted to give a map of the planned projects, as illustrated in Figure 10.3.

The maps were used as a discussion document in a 'workshop' session with senior business managers. The following points were discussed:

1. How did the map reflect their current business strategy?
2. How did the map compare with known investments by competitors?
3. Should some of the investments be reconsidered if there was incompatibility with business strategy?

Table 10.1 Scores for investments

Project	Orientation	Benefit
Office systems	(−3, −10)	(+7, +1)
Retail site automation	(−4, −13)	(+13, −11)
EDI	(+3, −6)	(+7, +4)
Order processing	(2, −6)	(+1, −6)
Programme environment	(+12, +7)	(+6, −6)
Accounting	(6,0)	(2, −7)
Value-added software	(−5, −14)	(+14, +10)

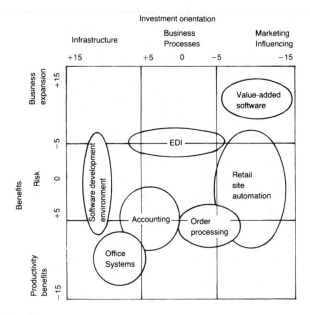

Figure 10.3 Example map.

The discussion of (1) revealed that business managers were firmly of the view that the retail gasoline market was moving quickly into an area of fierce price competition and that price rather than added value would be the prime motivation for consumers. In a price-led market it would be crucial to focus on cost reducing investments to reduce the company's cost structure. This is illustrated in Figure 10.4. Two of the investments of major competitors were assessed on the basis of information available from sales staff and third party distributors. It appeared that their investments in IT focused on market influencing rather than cost reduction. This was consistent with the view that both competitors aggressively passed a strategy of downplaying price as a buying issue. This is illustrated below in Figure 10.5.

The illustration of competitors' maps further reinforced management thinking that the best way forward was clearly a differentiation strategy of price. Cost reduction therefore had to be the major focus of their IT strategy. As a result, two investments were amended in scope and a third was dropped completely. Value-added software was thought to be misplaced in this strategy, while retail automation and EDI were changed in scope to remove the market influencing characteristics of their

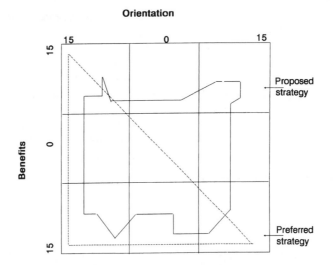

Figure 10.4 Comparing the proposed and preferred strategy.

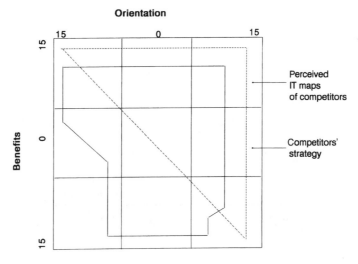

Figure 10.5 Comparing competitors' maps.

functionality. The electronic point of sale investment was, however, retained within the initiative as reducing queues at pumps helped increase sales volume and thereby reduce the fixed cost contribution per gallon of fuel. The map of the agreed strategy therefore looked as illustrated in Figure 10.6.

Stage 2 evaluation

The first step in the stage 2 evaluation was to identify the key variables associated with each investment. The key variables were identified by the used departments who acted as lead sponsors for the investments. A table of the sponsoring departments, the relevant investments and their key variables is shown in Table 10.2. In order to construct the benefit hierarchy described earlier, benefit components were associated with each key variable (see Figure 10.7). The increase or decrease of each key variable and associated component was also assessed.

The order processing project had five key variables identified. Four of these affected cost-creating components while one (lead times) affected income. Lead times would be reduced by half by being able to compress the order/scheduling and distribution chain. The elimination of manual intervention, data entry and paper-based communication between multi-sites facilitated this. Managers perceived that these signifi-

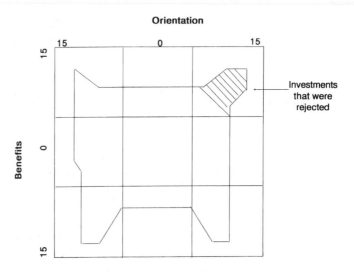

Figure 10.6 Map of agreed IT investments.

Table 10.2 Some of the key variables identified with each investment

IT investment	Sponsor (user)	Key variables
Retail automation	Marketing	Cars per hour
		Leakage
		Stock losses
		Stock turnover
		Personnel per shift
		Repeat sales frequency
Order processing	Sales	Salesmen per 100 customers
		Cost per order
		Credit days
		Lead times
		Average stock holding
Accounting proj.	Finance	Cost per invoice
		Credit days
		Site profitability
Software environments	IT	Development lead times
		Defects listing
		Test and acceptance
		Maintenance costs

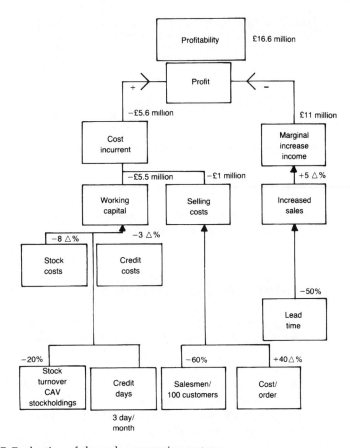

Figure 10.7 Evaluation of the order processing system.

Table 10.3 Rate of return calculations

	Year 1	Year 2	Year 3	Year 4	Totals
Cost of investment (£million)	6	10	2	1	19
Income (£million)	—	—	16	10	32
					IRR 37%

cantly shorter lead times could capture an additional market share amounting to an estimated 5% increase in sales. This was equivalent to an increase in £11 million on net margins.

All four key variables which affected cost-creating components caused a reduction in working capital and selling costs of £5.5 million and £0.1 million respectively. The overall improvement on profitability was assessed as £16.6 million. A summary rate of return calculation was made to allow for the cost of the investment (Table 10.3). It is interesting to note that, in evaluating the investment, the emphasis has been put on the analysis of benefits rather than rate of return.

The results of similar evaluations for the other investments yielded the summary shown in Table 10.4. It should be noted that, although the accounting project and the

Table 10.4 The results of similar evaluation for the other three investments yielded the following summary

Investment	Profit impact	5-year net (£million)
Retail automation	15	28
Order processing	16.6	13
Accounting project	1.4	−2
Software environment	0.2	−5
Overall	33.2	34

software environment yielded negative IRR values, they were still retained because of their close associations with the overall investment strategy. This strategy was evaluated in stage 1 when investment maps were drawn.

Involvement of managers

The stage 1 of the methodology was executed in a four-hour workshop with managers representing the various key functions of the company, marketing, finance, logistics and IT. These managers were empowered to sign off on a three month IT strategy which had been previously developed. Stage 1 was being used as a technique to encapsulate the overall strategy and to carry out a final check. The technique was successful in achieving these goals.

The stage 2 methodology was then carried out following a board presentation of the strategy and involved separate groups of a representative manager and the author (on each session) to agree key variables and the profitability impact. The combined submissions as shown in Table 10.4 were then made to the board.

A further example of applying the methodology

In another application of the method, an international consumer products company in the tobacco manufacturing, marketing and distribution businesses employed the technique. In this case the technique was applied jointly by a company representative and a consultant working for the author. The results of stage 1 and 2 of the evaluation are reported below.

Investment identified

Nine IT investments were identified for evaluation:

1. A worldwide database for monitoring the stocks and harvests of tobacco leaf. At the time there was an impending world shortage of tobacco leaf as many farmers in Third World countries had switched to more lucrative crops during a period of price

destabilization. It was important to the company to have information fed by its buyers around the world on future sources of leaf and to make buying decisions on the basis of leaf already in stock and the need to secure future supplies. The benefit of the application was seen to be one of risk minimization. Without the basic raw material the product could not be bought to the marketplace. The leaf database led to secured supplies.

2. Materials procurement using EDI ordering of materials for wrapping and packaging was performed partly on demand and partly to replenish inventories. The initiative planned to link a bill of materials schedule generated by an MRP system with orders directly to suppliers. The benefits perceived were lower inventories and some clerical and administrative reductions. The administrative reduction would be achieved by cutting out manual ordering, and implementing self-billing by suppliers.

3. A shipping information system to monitor consolidate companies import and export requirements. At the time one department handled all the shipping of tobacco leaf imports from around the world for processing in the UK, while another department (distribution) was responsible for export shipping of all finished goods. Both departments frequently used the same shipping company but had been unable to take advantage of discounts for volume. By being able to put together the import and export requirements, the company would be able to jointly negotiate better discounts. (Most shipping companies price on the basis of a one-way cargo, i.e. the ship will return empty.) The primary benefit of this initative was reducing third party costs.

4. The factory had expensive high speed machinery which operated at 65% of its total available time. Industry averages for this type of manufacturing operation were above 90%. The company sought to implement a plant scheduling system to increase machine utilization. The system would attempt where possible to schedule the largest possible production runs depending on plant operating constraints, order sizes and special requirements for customization. The plant scheduler would be an expert system. The benefits were therefore seen to be increasing asset utilization thereby making processing economic.

4. A computer-aided design and manufacturing system was sought to improve the lead times for new product developments. The company had to react frequently to new products launched by competitors. The package design was a crucial component of new products and the company had been unable to react quickly enough to new products. Investment in CAD/CAM was seen as a means of cutting new product lead times in half. Packaging could be designed on a screen in 3D and prototypes prepared in minutes for test marketing. What used to be a three to four week process could be completed in less than a day. The company was therefore trying to enhance its business in new product areas.

5. A database and fourth generation language environment was selected for all future development. This was to ensure that future systems were more reliable, data was more accessible and applications could be developed quicker. Benefits therefore lay in both risk minimization and enhancing productivity categories.

6. Value-added software for tobacconists. The investment was an attempt to influence customers (tobacconists) to give the company's products preference in shelf space and display. In return the tobacconist would get a software package specifically geared to solve administrative needs such as book-keeping, VAT etc. This would be given free to customers with linking software to factory reordering.

Analysis

The analysis in Figures 10.8 and 10.9 showed that the company has a heavily cost-reduction-orientated strategy, with five out of seven investments in this area. A presentation to the director of corporate planning revealed his concern as to the IT strategy. The corporate plan had called for an ambitious strategy of business expansion into new markets and new areas to compete vigorously with competitors in a tightening market. The director wished to see a rethink of the strategy. A reinvestigation gave

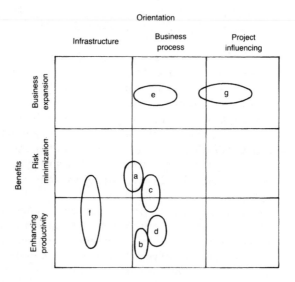

Figure 10.8 Evaluating a tobacco company's IT investment strategy.

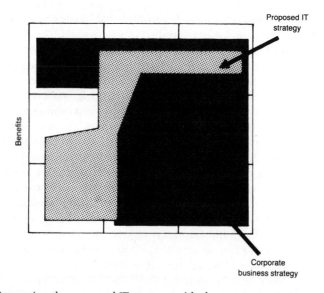

Figure 10.9 Comparing the proposed IT strategy with the corporate strategy.

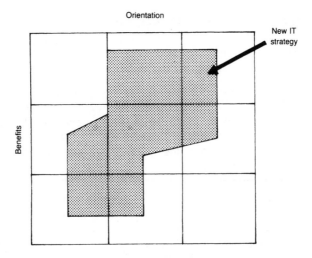

Figure 10.10 The new IT strategy.

Table 10.5 Profit impact on investments

Investment	Profit impact (£million)
1. Leaf database	1.75
2. Materials procurement	0.25[a]
3. Shipping database	0.65
4. Plant scheduling	0.10[a]
5. CAE	1.20
6. 4GL/database	0.10
7. Value-added software	2.10
8. Price promotion	1.40

[a] Investments which were dropped.

rise to a new IT investment – a price/promotion system. The benefit of the system was seen to be reducing the variability in the business profile by using promotion and price offers to stimulate demand in sectors which appeared sluggish. The system monitored customer orders and compared them with previous periods. These 'sales intervention reports' would alert marketing to the need to promote special offers of discounts in sectors where growth was appearing to tail off. The new system would therefore minimize risk and influence the market. The new investment worked more in line with the corporate business strategy. This was thought to be acceptable to the business planners. Figure 10.10 shows the new IT strategy.

The methodology was considered by the director of planning as not only useful in matching the two strategies, but also in identifying where the gaps were and creating the opportunity for further discussion on new initatives. In the second stage of the methodology, two investments were dropped on the basis that they did not offer enough return and that they were not essential to supporting the overall IT strategy. Interestingly '(f)', the 4GL/database investment, was approved despite its direct cash benefit unattractiveness. It was seen as necessary to supporting the overall strategy (see Table 10.5).

Discussion and conclusions

Some of the features of the two stages of this method make it a robust approach to evaluating IT investments:

1. The method covers the complete range of evaluation stages from the initial identification of investments to the management of benefits identified.
2. It combines an early evaluation process with the formulation of an IT investment strategy and produces output which is visually simple and easily communicable to management not closely associated with IT.
3. It contains two of the most sought after parameters in its evaluation model: benefits and orientation in the supply.
4. It permits projects, which have traditionally been marked down for lacking hard benefits, to be awarded equal ranking for the contribution they make to the success of an overall strategy.
5. Its approach to identifying the key variables which affect business performance focuses on both physical and cost aspects.
6. The specific evaluation process (stage 2) forces the project to examine the inter-relationship of the investment with other IT projects and of their impact on the performance of every part of the business.
7. It gives relatively little importance to the internal rate of return as a means of investment appraisal and pays greater attention to the contribution of a family of investments to the company's overall business strategy. This meets many of the criticisms in earlier chapters on overreliance on financial measures.
8. It provides a framework to manage the benefits of the investments, thereby ensuring that the impact of the investment is maximized.

Several other characteristics of the method address fundamental problems in evaluation practice as identified by other authors (see for example Banker, Kauffman and Mahmood, 1993; Hogbin and Thomas, 1994; Weill, 1993; Willcocks, 1992).

A cradle to grave methodology

The method embraces all three crucial stages in the evolution of IT projects: the initial identification of investments, the evaluation of specific investments and the eventual management of the benefits. In this way it responds to the call in Chapter 1 for an evaluation across systems' lifetimes. In the past, methods have specialized in at least either identification or evaluation. Users have described one of its major benefits as being the provision of a framework by which to analyse in detail the impact of the investment on their business. The emphasis on key variables identification for every investment, for example, forces managers to think about the measurable indicators that are affected by changes in customer, supplier or company practice. This provides the opportunity to maximize the gains from the investment during implementation. It emphasizes the findings of earlier studies, for example, those of the Department of Trade and Industry report (1988) that concluded 'nothing sought, nothing gained'. Generally, strategy formulation techniques do not incorporate a robust evaluation method, a weakness recognized by most practitioners (Galliers and Baker, 1994; Ward, 1994). This method attempts to retain a continuity of the evaluation process throughout the life of the investment, i.e. from 'cradle to grave'.

A useful supplement to the strategic planning process

The output from an IT strategic plan must be communicable to a wide range of staff and management and should form the blueprint for all future investment in IT (Silk, 1991). Past methods have fallen short of this ideal and managers who have used this method have commented on the simple way in which a complex strategy can be represented by the use of IT investment maps. In addition, the use of maps helps in a further evaluation of the overall strategy, in comparing it to the company's business strategy, its competitors' strategies and its overall business ethos. This has proved to be a valuable 'back stop' before signing off the strategy and was demonstrated in the example shown in the previous chapter.

Combines benefits and orientation

In interviews with managers, the importance of identifying the benefits of investments was repeatedly quoted as being of the utmost importance. The orientation of the investment towards the various business activities was the next most requested attribute. Investment maps in the stage 1 evaluation process address both these requirements and combines them into a single evaluation model. We saw how, in the examples illustrated earlier, one investment was dropped and the other modified because they did not fit in with the overall business thrust to the organization. This was despite the fact that these initiatives had been identified by users as contributing to their business.

Consideration for infrastructure projects

Infrastructure projects have not been awarded the same priority as market-led investments and this has frequently led to non-integrated developments as each division has promoted projects which contribute to their activities (Weill, 1993). This has meant that the development of corporate networks, databases, company data management and computer security reinforcement type of projects has been postponed to the detriment of the company's overall computing strategy. IT investment maps allow all investments to be evaluated alongside each other and the interdependence of, say, infrastructure projects and 'market influencing' projects is instantly recognized.

Later, stage 2 of the specific evaluation focuses more on organization and business performance criteria (key variables) rather than on traditional rate of return criteria which have historically undervalued technically orientated infrastructure projects.

Attention to generic performance

Many managers and commentators have argued for some time that traditional cost management methods reduce monitoring and decision-making to a common basis of financial criteria (see also Chapters 2 and 3). In fact, most businesses are better run by controlling physical indicators and financial indicators. The closer these indicators can be related to each company activity, the better they reflect generic performance. Hence, frequency of 'repeat sales' is a better way of monitoring the success of customer service campaigns than, say, sales revenue.

The benefit hierarchy in stage 2, by setting up 'key variables', addresses this need to monitor the benefit to the businesses at the lowest level of unit performance.

Encourages a thorough understanding of business impact

The process of evaluation in stage 2 encourages the project sponsors and those who eventually take on responsibility for managing the benefits to understand clearly the interrelationship of benefit components and key variables. For example, in the investment discussed above concerning service station automation, managers had to clearly understand the impact of EPOS tills and automated payment methods on the throughput of cars through a forecourt. This involved some market research combined with work measurement studies. The assessment was made following this work on the potential increase in throughput (cars per hour).

Managers then had to enable an assessment of the impact this was likely to have on sales volumes. The resulting assumption was that sales of non-fuel products would rise in greater proportion than fuel sales. This demonstrated how useful the technique was, understanding how the investment should be expected to perform and how it ought to be monitored after testing and handover.

References

Banker, R., Kauffman, R. and Mahmood, M. (1993) *Strategic information Technology Management: Perspectives On Organizational Growth and Competitive Advantage*. Idea Group Publishing, Harrisburg.

Department of Trade and Industry (1988) *Profiting from Automation*, Volume B, Department of Trade and Industry, London.

Galliers, R. and Baker, B. (eds.) (1994) *Strategic Information Management*, Butterworth Heinemann, London.

Hogbin, G. and Thomas, D. (1994) *Investing in Information Technology: Managing the Decision-making Process*, McGraw Hill, London.

McKenney, J. (1995) *Waves of Change: Business Evolution through Information Technology*, Harvard Business School Press, Boston, MA.

Peters, G. (1994) Evaluating your computer investment strategy. In *Information Management: Evaluation of Information Systems Investments* (ed. L. Willcocks), Chapman & Hall, London.

Silk, D. (1991) *Planning IT*, Butterworth Heinemann, London.

Ward, J. (1994) A portfolio aproach to evaluating information systems investments and setting priorities. In *Information Management: Evaluation of Information Systems Investments* (ed. L. Willcocks), Chapman & Hall, London.

Weill, P. (1993) The role and value of Information Technology infrastructure. In *Strategic Information Technology Management: Perspectives on Organizational Growth and Competitive Advantage* (ed. R. Banker, R. Kauffman and M. Mahmood), Idea Group Publishing, Harrisburg.

Willcocks, L. (1992) Evaluating information technology investments: research findings and reappraisal. *Journal of Information Systems*, **2** (3), 243–68.

Part Four

Routine operations and IT sourcing issues

11

Assessing the existing systems investment

C. James Bacon

Introduction

Investing in information systems generally implies a focus on new development, new equipment or new projects. There is often little recognition of the investment in existing systems, and little recognition of systems maintenance and support as a key activity in protecting that investment. As for systems developers, maintenance tends to be something you do when you get the time, or delegate to trainees. It might also be outsourced; anything so that you do not have to do the 'dirty work' yourself. And software tools, notably CASE tools, tend to focus on new development. The same is true in the academic environment, where the implicit paradigm is new development. For example, in the waterfall model of systems development, maintenance is a virtual afterthought (Boehm, 1981).

And yet various estimates indicate that between 50% and 80% of all systems work is taken up with systems maintenance (Gibson and Senn, 1989; Vail, 1991). Systems maintenance therefore represents the majority of systems work. As time goes on, systems are getting bigger, more graphical, more telecommunications based, more user-friendly and more complex. Thus, notwithstanding the promises of object oriented code, high level languages and various software tools, it is unlikely that the proportional effort devoted to existing systems, as opposed to new systems, will diminish. Consequently, it is likely that effective support of the existing systems investment will remain a critical requirement in many organizations. This implies that

Investing in Information Systems: Evaluation and Management. Edited by
Leslie Willcocks. Published in 1996 by Chapman & Hall. ISBN 0 412 72670 X.

evaluation of the existing systems is also critical, though, as Chapter 1 showed, adequate practice is not always forthcoming.

Perhaps a more fundamental reason for the critical nature of systems maintenance/support is that, even though they are not shown as such in most statements of financial position, existing information systems usually represent a significant corporate asset. For many organizations, day-to-day survival depends upon the organization's information systems. So does excellent customer service, and other critical success areas. It is not just a case of an organization grinding to a halt if its information systems fail; it is a case of the organization losing competitive effectiveness, little by little, if its existing information systems investment is not effectively maintained. Assessment of the effectiveness of that maintenance and its management therefore becomes an imperative.

But what is systems maintenance? Systems maintenance is the process of modifying existing, operational systems. It is also referred to as software maintenance. However, systems maintenance incorporates not only software but documentation and procedures, overall design, and the hardware platform as well, i.e. the whole system. The term maintenance is also being replaced, in leading-edge organizations, by the term support, which better reflects the importance of existing systems. Systems support may therefore be a more appropriate term, rather than systems or software maintenance, in referring to the process and function of modifying existing systems.

Assessing the strategic significance

For any given organization, how significant or important is its existing systems investment, versus new or prospective systems, in terms of customer service, efficient production, effective marketing, and so on? And, therefore, how significant is the maintenance and support of existing systems, compared to new systems development? A conceptual model for making this assessment is shown in Figure 11.1, the systems service–product grid. This model builds on others, particularly the strategic grid, which distinguishes between the importance of existing systems versus new systems (Cash, McFarlan and McKenney, 1992). The strategic service–product grid aims to show that where the strategic significance of systems maintenance and

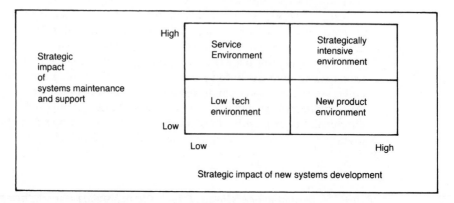

Figure 11.1 The systems service–product grid.

support is high, there is a service environment. That is, the organization is not just dependent on the existing installed systems for its day-to-day operations and survival. It is also dependent on its clients/users receiving effective service, in responding to their changing needs with those systems. This dependency is a characteristic of the situation where excellent service to the organization's external customers is a critical success factor. Thus, continuous improvement in and effective support of existing systems is essential, because it is a component of excellent customer service.

In contrast, where there is a continual and strategic need for new systems development, and therefore new systems products, there is a new product environment. This may be the case where the business must engage in a continuous process of bringing out new or differentiated products and/or services, to meet changing market needs and opportunities. It may also occur where 'orders of magnitude' improvement in business functions are the focus, as in business process re-engineering. A third case is where the organization needs to be at the 'leading edge', and continually brings in new information systems to implement new information technology.

If systems maintenance/support and new systems development are both strategically important, then the organization is operating in a strategically intensive environment. However, where maintenance/support and new development both have a low strategic impact, it is evident that the organization is not utilizing information systems and technology (IST) as a strategic resource, and is operating in a 'low-tech' environment, as far as the use of information technology is concerned.

In many cases, therefore, the focus in information systems investments needs to be not only new development or new products, but also existing systems. This implies that when efforts are directed at reducing the size and expense of the maintenance task, the motivation may be wrong, if it is to free up resources for new development. Instead, there needs to be a complementary focus, on existing as well as new systems investments. This appears to be the focus in leading edge organizations (Layzell and Macauley, 1990; McKenney, 1995). In such organizations, the role of systems maintenance and support is recognized as being of key importance in the overall IS/IT strategy. In such organizations, a systems support function has a key responsibility in maintaining and protecting the current systems portfolio in good order (Swanson and Beath, 1990; Hayes, 1991).

A taxonomy of systems maintenance/ support types

A fundamental reason for the commonly negative view of systems maintenance is its traditional orientation to corrective work, and this is at the coding level rather that the design level. But this is only one kind of maintenance need and, from a strategic perspective, it is not the most important.

Three kinds of maintenance have traditionally been defined: corrective, adaptive, and perfective (Lientz and Swanson, 1978). These three kinds have had wide acceptance, in representing the totality of systems maintenance work. Corrective maintenance is defined as that carried out to repair or correct processing performance. It is made necessary by design failures, and is characterized by emergency changes and problem fixes. Adaptive maintenance responds to required changes in the data and processing environments. It is made necessary by modifications to other application systems, changes in systems software, and related changes in the production environment. Perfective maintenance eliminates processing inefficiencies and enhances performance. It is undertaken to improve efficiency and is sometimes referred to as enhancement, since it may include improvements in system functionality (Swanson and Beath, 1989).

But other types of maintenance have also been defined. For example, there is functional maintenance, which specifically refers to minor enhancements of system functions (Hall, 1987). Two further kinds of maintenance that have been proposed are: preventive maintenance, to improve future maintainability and reliability, and deletion maintenance, to delete capabilities that are no longer needed (Computer Science and Technology Board, 1990). Thus, there have been at least three others added to the three kinds of maintenance traditionally seen as constituting systems maintenance work. In addition, two further kinds or types of maintenance are herein proposed, namely mandated maintenance and post-implementation maintenance. The different kinds are indicated in Table 11.1, which represents a taxonomy of systems maintenance and support types. The taxonomy relabels deletion maintenance as rationalization maintenance, and includes definitional enhancement of the other types. It also distinguishes between nondiscretionary systems maintenance and discretionary systems support. Thus, maintenance is something that you are more or less forced to do. Support is something that you choose to do.

The different kinds of maintenance and support in the taxonomy are not mutually exclusive. For example, perfective support could include some functional support.

If systems maintenance and support of the existing systems investment is to be effectively managed, the specific types need to be identified. This is the aim of the taxonomy. The essential reason for this is 'granularity', in which respect there is a parallel with project management. If a systems development project is not divided into discrete phases, activities and tasks, then planning, evaluation and control cannot be effective. Metrics maintained on such projects are of limited value, since there can be no meaningful validation (Jones, 1991). In a similar way, the taxonomy facilitates assessment of the existing systems investment through meaningful metrics on the different types of systems maintenance and support. For example, it may be used to

Table 11.1 A taxonomy of systems maintenance and support types

---

Non-discretionary systems maintenance

1. Corrective maintenance: the repair or correction of design errors, including emergency changes and fixing of stoppages/failures
2. Adaptive maintenance: modification made necessary by changes in the systems software, machine/processing, data base or network environments
3. Mandated maintenance: modification made imperative by changes in the organization's external environment, as in legislative and tax changes

Discretionary systems support

4. Perfective support: the improvement of processing, data base, or network efficiency
5. Rationalization support: the deletion of superfluous output, input, programs, data, or redundant processing
6. Preventive support: development and documentation of changes to improve maintainability and/or reliability
7. Functional support: minor additions to or enhancements of system functions, in response to evolving user/client needs
8. Post-implementation support: the addition or enhancement of functions following system implementation, as agreed during the process of new development

---

show the proportion of resources consumed by discretionary support as opposed to non-discretionary maintenance.

In managing the existing information systems investment, efforts to reduce or minimize the amount of work need to focus on non-discretionary maintenance, since this is the form of work that the organization is forced to do. In the case of mandated maintenance, for example, this could be combined with types of discretionary support, so that the time and effort expended obtains some value. Rationalization support reduces system size and complexity, by getting rid of 'petrified code' (Carlyle, 1989). Consequently, it helps to reduce corrective maintenance, and makes other kinds of maintenance and support work easier. Preventive support can have a similar effect on non-discretionary maintenance.

Discretionary support, being the form of work which the organization chooses to do, needs to be planned. For example, if project target dates are to be met, it is necessary to plan for post-implementation support, as defined. Otherwise, inclusion of functions that users/clients request after project schedules have been agreed can have a negative impact in meeting target dates. In addition, there needs to be planning for functional support, particularly on those application systems which leverage critical business processes, or support the critical success factors of the organization.

Assessing the organization

If an organization is undertaking its own systems development and support (i.e. 'insourcing' the work), how should the work be organized? In some organizations the work is organized along the traditional lines of separating programming work from analytical work. Since it is specialization by type of work, this has been called the type W organization (Swanson and Beath, 1990). It may be used where programming expertise in assembly or complex languages is important. In other organizations, systems work is organized by business domain or application. This is where systems or software engineers specialize by application or business area. This is the type A organization, since it is organized by application area. In a third form of organization, the work is organized, first, according to business application area, and second, by type of work. Systems staff specialize in specific business domains and, within these domains, there are analysts and programmers. This is an application–work or a type AW systems organization. A fourth form of organization is the lifecycle or type L organization. In this case, analyst/programmers or software engineers specialize by new development or systems maintenance and support.

There are advantages and disadvantages with each of these organizational forms. For example, type A, a common form of organization, suffers from an inherent lack of flexibility. There are always 'peaks and valleys' in the need for new development in each business application area; systems development needs are 'lumpy'. This means that systems staff may be overworked in one period while waiting for work in another, or staff may be overworked in one application area while those in another are waiting for work.

On the other hand, combining the programmer and analyst roles, as in the type A organization, does address a number of key motivators that are important in systems work. These include: task identity – doing a complete job with an identifiable outcome; task variety – using a variety skills in a variety of tasks; task significance – having an identifiable impact on the organization; accomplishment – achieving and accomplishing objectives and tasks; responsibility – accountability for results; and autonomy – freedom in making decisions relative to the job (Couger, 1988). Assessing the organization of systems maintenance and support therefore needs to include a consideration of the degree to which these motivators are present.

The type W, type A, and type AW forms of organization are distinct from the type L organization in that they combine the maintenance/support of existing systems with the development of new systems. In comparison, the L type or lifecycle organization separates the two areas of work.

Owing to the traditionally negative view attached to systems maintenance, there may be resistance to the idea of separating it from new development, as in the L type organization. No one wants to be assigned to a separate maintenance function, if it is perceived as having to clean up 'other people's mess'. The advantages of combining both areas are shown in Table 11.2.

In comparison, the advantages of separating maintenance/support from new development work is shown in Table 11.3.

Table 11.2 The advantages of combining new development work with maintenance/support work

1. When the same people are responsible for new development and maintenance/support, there may be a better understanding of requested changes to those systems
2. When people doing new development know that they will have to correct their own mistakes (in maintenance changes), there may be a better motivation to get things right in the first place
3. Response to users/clients may be quicker, since systems staff may be so familiar with the specific business area concerned that they do not need to spend singnificant time in studying systems documentation, before making maintenance/support changes
4. Human communication costs may be minimized since there is no need, in making modifications to existing systems, to refer to a separate group (new development versus maintenance/support), or for two groups to interface with the client/user

Table 11.3 The advantages of separating maintenance/support form new development work

1. There can be reduced risk exposure for the organization, in terms of: (a) loss of knowledge when a person leaves, and (b) lack of availability in the event of absence due to various reasons, when at least two people (a new development person and a systems support person), have knowledge about a given application area
2. System documentation tends to improve (because it is forced to), when people other than those who originally developed a system are maintaining/supporting it
3. There may be reduced interference and less distraction from new development when new development people do not have to stop and devote time to changes in existing systems, thus enhancing the prospect of meeting scheduled targets on new projects
4. Since effective maintenance\support is the focus in separate systems maintenance/support work, rather than new development, 'quick-and-dirty' fixes or 'patches' tend to be avoided, and the design integrity and maintainability of installed systems may be enhanced
5. In a separate maintenance/support group, ongoing response to and support of users/clients becomes a primary focus, with positive implications for user/client satisfaction, since change requests are not seen as a distraction and 'nuisance' interfering with new development
6. Specific responsibility can be assigned for 'custodianship' of the organization's existing systems investment, within a systems support group, in accordance with the strategic asset/portfolio view of existing systems

In some organizations a separate maintenance/support group is used as a training ground for developers. This may exacerbate the negative perception of this type of work, if it is associated with junior level work. In other organizations a separate maintenance/support group is used as the jumping point to a senior-level position. In this case, it is not for training of junior people, but rather is used to give people already experienced in a particular area a wider understanding of the whole business, so as to reduce the problem of inflexibility in the various organizational forms. In this case, people may advance to senior responsibility through a tour of duty in systems maintenance/support work.

An assessment of the organization's position on the systems service–product grid may show it to be in the top half, because the maintenance and support of existing systems is seen as being as important or more important than new development. In such a case, it may be that the advantages of separating systems maintenance and support work outweigh the advantages of combining it with new development.

Assessment factors for existing systems

Under the portfolio view of the existing information systems investment, it is necessary to periodically assess each installed system, with respect to its strategic, functional and technical value (Hayes, 1991). This portfolio view essentially sees the various information systems of an organization as an integrated set of assets requiring appropriate upkeep, periodical assessment, and effective management. The assessment includes factors such as those listed in Table 11.4.

These assessment factors need to part of a maintenance and support methodology, and be included as a framework for evaluating the existing systems investment at the 'front end' of such a methodology.

Table 11.4 Assessment factors for existing systems

Strategic factors
1. Pertinence to and/or role in organizational plans
2. Effectiveness in supporting the organization's critical success factors
3. Effectiveness in leveraging critical business processes
4. User/client satisfaction
5. Importance and value of the business function(s) or process(es) concerned

Functional factors
6. Dependence of the business function(s) or process(es) on the system
7. Effectiveness in supporting the business function(s)/processes; or performance under service-level agreements
8. Costs of operation and maintenance
9. Backlog of change requests
10. Utility and actual use made of respective screen, printed or other output
11. Integration of data with other systems

Technical factors
12. Maintainability (modularity, simplicity, consistency and self-descriptiveness)
13. Reliability (as per operations records/logs)
14. Viability and vendor support
15. Interconnectivity with other systems

Assessing maintenance and support methodology

Under the traditional view of systems maintenance, the methodology or approach is to: study the source code to understand the problem; make the needed changes to the code; and test the changes. This approach is unlikely to be associated with the portfolio view of existing systems, which takes a more strategic view of systems maintenance and support. When the portfolio view is adopted, maintenance and support begins early in new development, rather than at its 'back end' (Pfleeger and Boehner, 1990). That is, maintenance/support and the inevitability of future change become a consideration throughout new systems development.

If, however, the traditional view and approach to maintenance changes is followed, a system will tend to lose its architectural integrity. This is because evaluation and change is at the code level only, and consideration of overall design tends to be excluded. The result is entropological deterioration. Fourth generation languages (4GLs), and object orientation may help to reduce this. But to the degree that they encourage a 'lazy' development methodology, and prototyping as a substitute for (instead of a complement to) formalized methodology, they may exacerbate the phenomenon. With entropic deterioration, the system becomes more difficult to understand, for the purpose of making needed changes to it. In the latter respect, it has been estimated that this traditional first step of understanding and evaluating existing code and documentation can consume up to 60% of a developer's time, in making changes to an information system (Hayes, 1991). The implication in all this is that there needs to be some form of architectural impact analysis, prior to coding work, to include an analysis of the effects of prospective changes on overall system design.

What sometimes happens with installed systems is that *ad hoc* maintenance changes continue to be made until a total rewrite becomes necessary. But there is a middle course between these two extremes that aims to preserve architectural integrity. This is the transformation approach, which is based on the idea of recovering design abstractions, in reusing design and code components from the existing system (Arango *et al.*, 1986). Thus, instead of starting with and focusing on source code, the approach starts with the design of the existing system, starting at the highest or overall level then working down, reusing existing design and code as much as possible. The transformation approach is not a rewrite of the existing system, but it is more than the quick fix approach. The benefit is that it promotes continuous evolution of the system design, thus avoiding entropic deterioration, and making future maintenance and support easier.

Assessment through metrics

It is difficult to evaluate how well you are doing in a given area of activity without meaningful measurement. Basically, it is difficult to manage what you do not measure. The organization and management of systems maintenance and support can only, therefore, be objectively evaluated as effective and successful to the extent that it is measured and validated as such.

The need for measurement in the area of IST, is directly related to its economic impact (Jones, 1991). The surging interest in software quality measures, project productivity, and information systems value-for-money indicators is therefore an indication, if any were needed, that IST has become a strategic economic resource, and a vital area of activity for today's organization. Consequently, it is likely that such measures will become increasingly important.

However, there are a number of imperatives in any maintenance and support measurement programme. First, it needs to be fully supported by senior management, because it involves cultural change and therefore needs authoritative endorsement; and it requires resources, in a similar way to which cost and management accounting require resources. Second, maintenance/support measurement requires learning and training. Third, it needs to be positive rather than punitive. In the latter respect, people need to be rewarded for finding errors, rather than being faulted for making them (Robinson, 1993). The fourth imperative is, therefore, that effective measurement and targets need to be built into the reward system for individual members of management and staff.

There are four general areas where metrics can be applied to maintenance and support. These are shown in Table 11.5. The taxonomy for the different types of non-discretionary maintenance and discretionary support work provides a means of comparing the proportional effort being taken up by each type, and facilitates metrics specific to each.

A second area for metrics is quality and maintainability. The four attributes of systems software and documentation that optimize maintainability/support are consistency, simplicity, modularity and self-descriptiveness. Consistency refers to the uniformity and standardization of design, notation and techniques. Simplicity refers to ease of understanding and avoidance of complexity. Modularity refers to a design structure of independent modules, achievable through structured methodology or the object oriented paradigm. Self-descriptiveness refers to the degree to which the software and documentation provide explanation of functions.

A third area for metrics is that of 'soft' factors, which involves measurement of such things as: the morale of systems support staff; the level of service perceived by clients/users; the cooperation and assistance received from clients/users; the skill, experience and training needs of systems support staff and/or users/clients; and environmental assistance/constraints, as in the provision of technical tools and/or physical resources.

A fourth area is that of productivity. However, although metrics have been developed for measuring new development, there has been very little research in applying productivity metrics to the maintenance and support of existing systems. Function point analysis (FPA), was developed for new systems development (Albrecht, 1984). With the increasingly strategic importance of IST, and the need for optimizing systems development productivity in supporting business needs, FPA is enjoying increased usage. Thee is even an active international function point users group (IFPUG). FPA appears to hold the greatest promise for benchmarking and assessing maintenance and support productivity. It has had some application, specifically to three kinds of support work defined in the taxonomy, namely perfective, functional, and post-implementation support (Cote and St-Pierre, 1990). However, using FPA for main-

Table 11.5 Areas of assessment in maintenance/support metrics

1. Taxonomic: measure and compare the different kinds of maintenance
2. Quality and maintainability: measure ease or difficulty of maintenance
3. Soft factors: measure human and environmental factors
4. Productivity: measure performance

tenance and support work is more complex than it is for new development work. This is because it must take into account other factors, such as the quality of existing documentation and familiarity of support personnel with the system concerned, and the need to change or suppress some functions, while adding others.

Conclusion

Management and assessment of the existing systems investment is potentially a large subject area. However, it is often treated as a Cinderella subject, neglected and taken for granted. But the installed base of existing information systems is growing, becoming more complex, and represents a key asset area for most organizations. Poorly maintained and supported systems may even represent a 'time bomb' for some of them. Thus, systems maintenance and support needs to receive a higher profile, and considered complementary rather than secondary to new systems development. More than anything else, this requires a cultural change, perhaps a 'paradigm shift', in organizations. This leads to the conclusion that the general need, in effective systems maintenance and support of the existing information systems investment, is more a question of management than technology.

References

Albrecht, A.J. (1984) *Productivity Measurement and Estimate Validation*, IBM Corporate Systems & Administration, Purchase, NY.

Arango, G., Baxter, I., Freeman, P. and Pidgeon, C. (1986) TMM: software maintenance by transformation, *IEEE Software*, **3** (3), 27–39.

Boehm, B.W. (1981) *Software Engineering Economics*, Prentice-Hall, Englewood Cliffs NJ.

Carlyle, R.E. (1989) Fighting corporate amnesia. *Datamation*, 1 February, **35**, 41–4.

Cash, J.I., McFarlan, F.W. and McKenney, J.L. (1992) *Corporate Information Systems Management: The Issues Facing Senior Management*, Dow Jones-Irwin, Homewood, IL.

Computer Science and Technology Board (1990) Scaling up: a research agenda for software engineering. *Communications of the ACM*, **33** (3), 281–93.

Corbi, T. (1989) Program understanding: challenge for the 1990s. *IBM Systems Journal*, **28** (2), 294–306.

Cote, V. and St-Pierre, D. (1990) A model for estimating perfective software maintenance. *Conference on Software Maintenance 1990*, IEEE Computer Society Press, Los Alamitos, CA.

Couger, D.T. (1988) Motivating IS personnel. *Datamation*, 15 September, 59–64.

Gibson, V.R. and Senn, J.A. (1989) Systems structure and software maintenance. *Communications of the ACM*, **32** (3), 347–58.

Hall, R.P. (1987) Seven ways to cut software maintenance costs. *Datamation*, 15 July, 81–4.

Hayes, I. (1991) Software as assets increases returns. *Computerworld*, 23 September, 13–15.

Jones, C. (1991) *Applied Software Measurement*, McGraw-Hill, New York.

Layzell, P.J. and Macaulay, L. (1990) An investigation into software maintenance: perceptions and practices. *Conference on Software Maintenance 1990*, IEEE Computer Society Press, Los Alamitos, CA.

Lientz, B.P. and Swanson, E.B. (1978) Characteristics of software maintenance. *Communications of the ACM*, **6** (21).

Mankin, D., Bikson, T., Gutek, B. and Stasz, C. (1988) Managing technological change: the process is key. *Datamation*, 15 September, 69–75.

McKenney, J. (1995) *Waves of Change: Business Evolution Through Information Technology.* Harvard Business School Press, Boston, MA.

Pfleeger, S. and Boehner, S. (1990) A framework for software maintenance metrics. *Conference on Software Maintenance 1990,* IEEE Computer Society Press, Los Alamitos, CA.

Robinson, J.A. (1993) The dark side of software metrics. *Information Strategy: the Executives Journal,* Winter, 44–7.

Schaffer, R.H. (1992) Successful change programs begin with results. *Harvard Business Review,* Jan–Feb, 80–9.

Swanson, E. Burton and Beath, C. (1989) *Maintaining Systems in Organisations,* John Wiley, New York.

Swanson, E. Burton and Beath, C. (1990) Departmentalisation in software development and maintenance. *Communications of the ACM,* **33** (6), 658–67.

Vail, S. (1991) Happiness is a fault-free system. *Management Today,* November, 115–16.

12

Risk analysis for information systems

David G.W. Birch and Neil A. McEvoy

Introduction

As pointed out in Chapter 1, in the particular case of IS, there has been a reluctance to tackle the subject of risk – due to perceived complexity and inexactness – and therefore handle risk analysis and risk management effectively. This has led to a situation where many IS do not retain even the simplest risk management techniques which were present in the paper systems that they are replacing (Dunn, 1990). Clearly, with the growing importance of IS in all aspects of corporate operation, IS must be made subject to appropriate risk analysis and risk management disciplines. Some of the techniques for project appraisal and development are discussed in earlier chapters (see also Willcocks and Margetts, 1994).

The purpose of risk analysis should be to assist managers in making informed decisions about investment and developing risk management policies. In the case of computers and communications, the countermeasures that can be employed to reduce risk are well known and an array of techniques have been available for some time (Seberry and Preprzyk, 1989). High countermeasures expenditure on every aspect of an IS is out of the question in a commercial organization. Therefore, this expenditure must be directed to reduce corporate exposure to IS risks in the context of overall business risks. In particular, risk analysis must be able to answer the following questions:

- How much is it appropriate to spend on countermeasures?
- Where should this spending be directed?

Investing in Information Systems: Evaluation and Management. Edited by Leslie Willcocks. Published in 1996 by Chapman & Hall. ISBN 0 412 72670 X.

There are many insecure systems in operation which may cost businesses millions of pounds (or have equally deleterious effects on non-business organizations) if the insecurities are exploited. There are also many systems with inappropriate and over-expensive security countermeasures, which are just as responsible for losing money. By way of illustration, suppose a risk loses a business £10000 per year. It is clearly inappropriate to spend £200000 to close this risk, since the same investment would yield more than enough to cover the losses if placed in a bank.

Historically, the security side of IS has been driven by the development of counter-measures. The types of countermeasure and their use in different situations is a subject which has been well developed and will not be the focus of this chapter (see, for example, Reed and Watt, 1989).

Investment decisions are complicated – it is important that an organization has the best possible information on risks in order to decide whether or not to invest (scarce) resources in countermeasures, and if so, how much. It should be remembered that risk is an inescapable part of being in business. IS risks are no different in this respect from any other business risk and may well be less in magnitude. In all cases, it is essential that risks are adequately managed and for this purpose, risks must be quantified.

Business risks

Context

Being in business is a risk. However strategic an IS may be to a business, the threats to that IS – whether fire, flood or hackers – are only part of the spectrum of threats that surround the business. For most commercial organizations, the value of the information associated with an IS greatly exceeds the value of the technology associated with it (unless the IT strategy of the organization is inappropriate). It can be the case that whereas the value of the technology assets is known to seven significant figures (because they appear on balance sheets), the value of the information assets is not known to the nearest order of magnitude (Keen, 1991). Proper business invest-ment decisions cannot be made in such an environment.

The object of risk management is to reduce business exposure by balancing counter-measure investment against risk. It may be that the countermeasure expenditure would be better directed to other parts of the organization. If this is the case, then risk management should confirm it. It is important to remember that the purpose of risk analysis and risk management procedures is not simply the definition of countermeasures.

Risk analysis and risk management must be part of the ongoing operations of an organization but within that organization should be no more or less important than any of the other disciplines associated with IS.

Risk analysis requirements

A great deal of work has already been undertaken in the general field of risk analy-sis and methodologies such as CRAMM have been developed (Moses, 1990). In reviewing these existing methodologies and techniques, a number of problems were uncovered which made them unsuitable for current business needs. One of the major problems was that much of the work on the subject was rooted in the technology of the 1970s, assuming a large central hub accessed through terminals, and did not assist in the analysis of decentralized and workstation–server IS (Davies, 1990).

While many methodologies have recognized that risk analysis is now fundamental to the development and operation of IS (see, for example, Reed and Watt, 1989), none has been able to deliver the prescriptive and specific information that managers require to make real business decisions. The approach to the risk analysis itself has largely been based on the use of checklists for managers to try to think of all possible risks and take appropriate action. It is possible to make very long lists that are reasonably comprehensive for a particular type of system, but this approach does not give any confidence that all risks have been identified (Jamieson and Low, 1990). Hence the need for an approach that is complete, consistent and correct.

The primary requirements for a risk analysis methodology were therefore determined to be that the methodology should:

- integrate fully with the structured methodologies that have been developed for IS analysis and for which CASE tool support exists;
- not require specialized software or complicated training;
- be sufficiently flexible to cope with all IS models: centralized, decentralized and distributed;
- be both prescriptive and specific, so as to furnish managers with real decision-support information.

These requirements were the starting point for the development of SRA.

Business analysis

Structured analysis

One of the primary requirements for a cost-effective risk analysis methodology is that proper examination of IS risk should be founded on the same structured techniques as other IS analysis activities. Over the past few years, the use of structured analysis techniques to handle IS has become widespread and many methodologies are in use. Methodologies such as structured systems analysis and design methodology (SSADM) are in use in many organizations and are well supported by CASE tools, training courses and other materials (Nicholls, 1987; McEvoy and Harris, 1990). All of these methodologies share the use of structured models, easy to understand in diagram form, as the basis for collecting, verifying and disseminating information. They also share the same fundamental view of an IS, which separates the data structure, data processing and events in a system as shown in Figure 12.1. We are very much in favour of the use of such structured techniques for business analysis because:

- Any policies developed will have a proper audit trail, allowing decisions to be traced and modified in the event of the structured models being updated (because of changes in the business or systems).
- Standard structured analysis techniques allow the use of off-the-shelf CASE tools and other support, making the analysis process more efficient.
- Analysis techniques such as SSADM are widely used and therefore staff within the target organization will understand the model and be able to contribute to them.

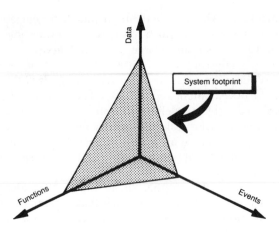

Figure 12.1 Structured analysis concepts.

- They ensure the capture of all relevant information and therefore do not require guesswork.

There are a number of suitable structured techniques and whether information modelling, enterprise modelling or structured modelling is used, the benefits are the same. It is worth noting that a set of IBM case studies on the subject showed that every single organization which adopted the technique found that it improved their business decision-making (Katz, 1990).

Three structured analysis models are required to capture all of the information necessary to support risk analysis These are the business model (often called the logical model or the service model), the information model (often called the logical data model or entity relationship model) and the technology model (often called the physical model or system model). The business model shows the organization and the services delivered to users, clients or whoever. The information model shows the corporate information entities and the relationship between them. The technology model shows the computer, communication and other systems used to support the provision of services.

Business model

The business model shows the information flows in an organization, the sources and sinks of information and the information processing or retention centres. Business analysis begins by creating the level 0 business model (L0BM) which treats the business (or the part of a business that is under examination) as a single information processing centre and identifies all of the sources/sinks of information. Analysis then proceeds to level 1, which identifies major information processing centres (see Figure 12.2).

The business model can be expanded to the necessary level of detail. We can assume in this case that one level of expansion is adequate, so the L1BM is all that needs to be created. Note that once the business model is in place, a unique labelling scheme now exists for all information flows.

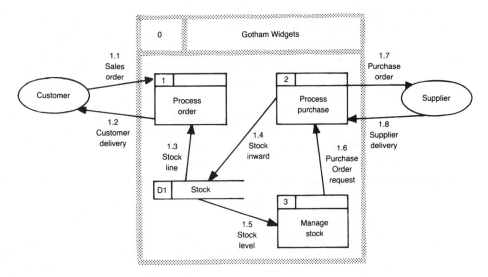

Figure 12.2 Example business model.

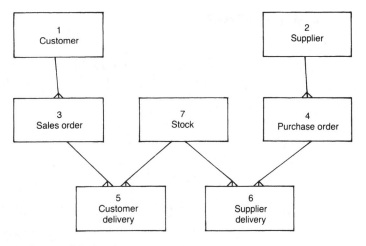

Figure 12.3 Example information model.

Information model

The information model shows the elements of information (not data) in the business and the relationships between those elements. In essence, the elements of information are business entities and the relationships between them are business rules.

Figure 12.3 shows the level-1 information model (L1IM) which corresponds to the business model in Figure 12.2. Each element on the L1IM (i.e. each business entity) is an information asset. This L1IM is very small because of the highly simplified business model used in this example. In any case, in order to carry out high-level analysis to highlight the main areas of exposure, a high-level information model is sufficient to identify the primary corporate information assets. Once the information model exists, we have a unique labelling scheme for all information assets.

Technology model

The technology model shows the actual computer and communications systems that are in place in an organization, with no reference as to their actual purpose or use. This separation of concerns is fundamental to the structured business analysis procedures.

Each entity in the technology model is a physical asset of the IS. These physical assets may be hardware, software, communications links and so on. Given our assumption that the value of information assets greatly exceeds the value of the physical assets, it is not necessary to determine the value of these physical assets: in fact, we can assume that these physical assets are covered by insurance and so it is not necessary to include them in calculations.

Figure 12.4 shows the level 1 technology model (L1TM) for our example which corresponds to the business model in Figure 12.2 and information model in Figure 12.3. Note that any one of a number of technology models could support any given business model, a property which becomes very useful when evaluating potential implementation of an IS that is still at the feasibility or specification stage.

Construction

The construction of the business and technology models, using a structured method-ology, can be achieved using any one of the myriad of computer-assisted software engineering (CASE) tools on the market. In many organizations, these structured

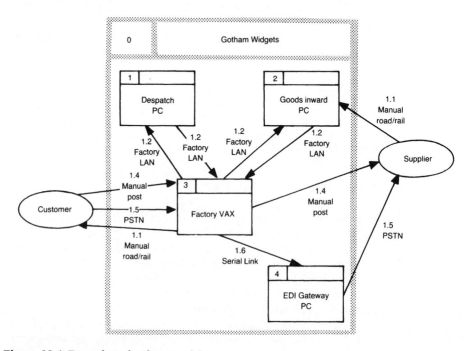

Figure 12.4 Example technology model.

models should already exist anyway and are not put into place solely for the purposes of risk analysis.

Risk analysis

Concepts

Risk analysis is based on the principal concepts of threat, vulnerability, countermeasure, risk and attack. These basic concepts, as shown in Figure 12.5, exist in one form or another in all risk analysis techniques. It is the precision of their specification in SRA which makes the results of SRA prescriptive (and therefore of value to business). A **threat** is something which will have an adverse effect on an organization. A threat exists whether or not there are any practical or apparent ways in which it might ever be manifested. The threats to an IS are independent from the physical implementation of the IS.

A **vulnerability** is a characteristic of a physical system which, while being independent from any specific threat, allows (in principle) a threat to be exploited. Vulnerabilities are a property of the physical implementation of the IS and are independent from any threats to the IS.

A **risk** is something which exists when a threat and a vulnerability overlap. That is, there is a threat to the business and a vulnerability which may be exploited to realize this threat. An attempt to exploit a risk – that is, to realize a threat – is called an **attack** and the person, agency or organization attempting to exploit that risk is the **attacker**. Note that the same attack may be attempted by different attackers: in each case, this constitutes a separate risk. In the exposition of SRA-IS in the chapter, we have made the simplification that there is only one attacker for each attack. This reduces the complexity of the analysis.

A **countermeasure** is something which reduces exposure, either by reducing the probability of attack (reducing vulnerability), the business losses associated with a threat (reducing impact) or the losses resulting from a successful attack (reducing exposure).

There is **threat** that a competitor might undercut us and take our business

There is a **vulnerability** that our customer records are copied and left in various offices

There is **a risk** that a competitor will see our customer and discount list and undercut us

There is an **attack** when a competitor tries to see the customer records to obtain the customer and discount list

There is a **countermeasure** that we lock away customer records when we're not using them

Figure 12.5 Structured risk analysis concepts.

Threat analysis

Threat analysis consists in cataloguing each and every threat to a business. In the case of IS, this means cataloguing the threats to the information assets on the information model. Given the structured approach, this is straightforward. Thus, for every information asset on the information model, three threats are catalogued: the integrity threat (TI), the confidentiality threat (TC) and the availability threat (TA). Each information flow is already uniquely labelled (because of the structured analysis) and so each individual threat is similarly labelled for cataloguing. So, information assets 3 (say) would have three entries in the threat catalogue: TI3, TC3 and TA3.

This approach may seem broad, but it works very well. There is no point in analysing the system down to the nth level at the beginning. Instead, the broad analysis of level 1 is used to identify 'problem' areas (i.e. areas of high exposure) of the system. Then, it is only necessary to analyse those particular areas down to level 2 (and so on, as necessary, through the levels).

The next step is to assign impacts to the threats in the threat catalogue. In this simplified case, only one impact is assigned to each threat because we have made the assumption that there is only one attacker for each attack. It is not possible to define a generalized impact metric because the nature of business impact varies from business to business. In the case of commercial information systems, a money-based metric is obviously useful. To avoid the difficulty of working with large numbers, a logarithmic metric can be used. As an example, a suitable impact metric (based on the FIPS metrics) might be as shown in Table 12.1.

Assigning an impact to each of the threats determined from the information flows on the information model leads to the creation of the threat catalogue. A section from an example threat catalogue is shown in Table 12.2. This shows an excerpt from the threat catalogue for the example system.

Vulnerability analysis

As in the case of threat analysis, vulnerability analysis proceeds by cataloguing all vulnerabilities of a system (this time using the technology model) and then assigning a probability of the vulnerability being exploited in a given time. The number and diversity of vulnerabilities that need to be covered is the factor which causes the most problems. To assist in dealing with vulnerabilities, it is worth developing a broad classification. The use of some recent examples will illustrate these basic categories:

Table 12.1 Example impact metric

Maximum potential loss	Assigned impact metric
£0	0
£10	1
£100	2
£1 000	3
£10 000	4
£100 000	5
£1 000 000	6
etc	etc

Table 12.2 Excerpt from threat catalogue

Item	Name	Threat	Description	Impact
1	Customer	I1	Customer lost/corrupt	3
	Customer	C1	Customer disclosed	2
	Customer	A1	Customer not available	2
2	Supplier	I2	Supplier lost/corrupt	2
	Supplier	C2	Supplier disclosed	2
	Supplier	A2	Supplier not available	2
3	Sales order	I3	Sales order lost/corrupt	2
	Sales order	C3	Sales order disclosed	2
	Sales order	A3	Sales order not available	2
4	Purchase order	I4	Purchase order lost/corrupt	3
	Purchase order	C4	Purchase order disclosed	1
	Purchase order	A4	Purchase order not available	2
5	Customer delivery	I5	Customer delivery lost/corrupt	3
	Customer delivery	C5	Customer delivery disclosed	2
	Customer delivery	A5	Customer delivery not available	2
6	Supplier delivery	I6	Supplier delivery lost/corrupt	4
	Supplier delivery	C6	Supplier delivery disclosed	2
	Supplier delivery	A6	Supplier delivery not available	3
7	Stock	I7	Stock lost/corrupt	4
	Stock	C7	Stock disclosed	2
	Stock	A7	Stock not available	2

- The recent theft of automobile blueprints from BAe through unauthorized access to a satellite communications link is an example of the malicious exploitation of an IT vulnerability of an IS – this is a class A vulnerability (malicious, IT).
- The collapse of the AT&T long distance telephone network because of a software fault is an example of the non-malicious attack on an IT vulnerability (the telephone switch software) of an IS – this is a class B vulnerability (non-malicious, IT).
- The disruption of the ICAO AFTN network (a worldwide message switching network used by airlines) because of the failure of the Kuwait switching centre following war in the area in the early 1990s is an example of malicious attack on a non-IT vulnerability of an IS – this is a class C vulnerability (malicious, non-IT).
- The recent failure of our office file server because someone spilt coffee in the power supply is an example of a non-malicious attack on a non-IT vulnerability of an IS – this is a class D vulnerability (non-malicious, non-IT).

The vulnerabilities are catalogued against the physical assets in the technology model. Again, each vulnerability must be uniquely labelled for cataloguing. Each data flow on the technology model is already uniquely labelled, so each of the four vulnerabilities will be similarly labelled. Data flow 2.2 of the technology model has the vulnerabilities VA2.2, VB2.2, VC2.2 and VD2.2 associated with it.

Next, a probability of occurrence must be assigned to each vulnerability. As in the case of threat impacts, we will in this case use a general purpose logarithmic occurrence metric as shown in Table 12.3. This metric shown is sufficient for a wide spectrum of commercial systems.

The frequency of occurrence of the exploitation of any particular vulnerability is actually a very complex function. This function depends on such elements as the gain to the attackers, the cost of the attack, the chance of detection and so forth. More complex models can be, and have been, developed (see, for example, McEvoy and

Table 12.3 Example frequency metric

Likely frequency of exploitation	Assigned frequency metric
more than daily	3
more than weekly	2
more than monthly	1
more than yearly	0
every decade	−1
every 100 years	−2
less frequently	−3

Table 12.4 Excerpt from vulnerability catalogue

Item	Name	Vulnerability	Description	Frequency
1	Despatch PC	A1	Despatch PC unauthorized access	−1
1	Despatch PC	B1	Despatch PC equipment/sware failure	−1
1	Despatch PC	C1	Despatch PC vandalized/destroyed	0
1	Despatch PC	D1	Despatch PC fire/flood/strike/power	0
2	Goods in PC	A2	Goods In PC unauthorized access	−1
2	Goods in PC	B2	Goods In PC equipment/sware failure	−1
2	Goods in PC	C2	Goods In PC vandalized/destroyed	0
2	Goods in PC	D2	Goods In PC fire/flood/strike/power	0
3	Factory VAX	A3	Factory VAX unauthorized access	−1
3	Factory VAX	B3	Factory VAX equipment/sware failure	−1
3·	Factory VAX	C3	Factory VAX vandalized/destroyed	1
3	Factory VAX	D3	Factory VAX fire/flood/strike/ power	0
4	EDI Gateway PC	A4	EDI Gateway PC unauthorized access	−1
4	EDI Gateway PC	B4	EDI Gateway PC equipment/sware failure	−1
4	EDI Gateway PC	C4	EDI Gateway PC vandalized/destroyed	1
4	EDI Gateway PC	D4	EDI Gateway PC fire/flood/strike/power	0

Harris, 1990) and may be used where more detailed or specialized analysis is required. In our simplified case, the assumption that there is only one attacker means that we need assign only one frequency of occurrence value to each vulnerability.

Although there may be a great many physical assets (depending on the level to which the technology model has been developed, of course) it is usually straightforward to assign the vunerabilities and probabilities because they are generic – it takes the same effort to tap a PSTN connection whether the PSTN line is being used for credit card verification or playing games over a network.

The catalogue of vulnerabilities derived from the technology model, together with the assigned frequency of occurrence metric, forms the vulnerability catalogue. An excerpt from an example vulnerability catalogue is shown in Table 12.4.

Risk catalogue

Now that threats and vulnerabilities have been catalogued, a risk becomes something very precise and specific. In the general case, a risk can be said to exist where there is a correspondence between a threat and a vulnerability which share an attacker.

In our simplified case, a risk exists where there is a threat and a vulnerability that coincide. In order to find risks, then, each threat in the threat catalogue is examined and matched against the vulnerability catalogue. The best way to do this is in two stages. First, a cross-reference between the business model and the technology model is created (this may already be present in system architecture documentation). Then a further cross-reference between the information model and the business model is created. Thus, we can match threats and vulnerabilities in the following way:

- For each threat, select the underlying information asset.
- Cross-reference the information asset to the business model to determine which information flows involve that asset.
- Cross-reference the information flows from the business model to physical assets in the technology model.
- For each physical asset, select the associated vulnerabilities.

If no vulnerabilities corresponding to the threat are found, then there is no risk. Where one or more vulnerabilities are found, the risks must be (as always) uniquely labelled. For example, if threat T17 can be exploited through two vulnerabilities, say VA2.2 and VA2.4, then two risks must be entered in to the catalogue: R17–A2.2 and R17–A2.4.

Since, for each of the risks in the catalogue, we know the frequency of occurrence (from the vulnerability catalogue) and the impact (from the threat catalogue), we can define the exposure, as shown in Figure 12.6. Once again, the metric varies depending on the system but will we continue with the general case and measure exposure using a logarithmic money per time period metric. The simple metrics set out in Table 12.1 and Table 12.3 mean that we can define the annual exposure to a risk as the sum of the impact (of the associated threat) and the frequency (of the associated vulnerability). An excerpt from such a risk catalogue is shown in Table 12.5.

The various catalogues can be stored in any PC-based spreadsheet or database package, so the exposure calculations are trivial to automate. Furthermore, since the catalogues are automated, the risk analysis model can be used to extract a wide variety of types of information.

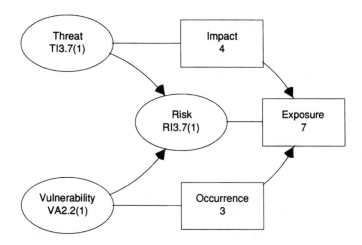

Figure 12.6 Risk catalogue creation.

Table 12.5 Excerpt from risk catalogue

Tht	TA	Vul	No.	Ex	Attack
I5	1.1	A1.1	257	2	Customer delivery lost/corrupt because unauthorized access
I5	1.1	B1.1	258	2	Customer delivery lost/corrupt because equipment/sware failure
I5	1.1	C1.1	259	4	Customer delivery lost/corrupt because vandalized/destroyed
I5	1.1	D1.1	260	3	Customer delivery lost/corrupt because fire/flood/strike/power
I5	3	A3	261	2	Customer delivery lost/corrupt because unauthorized access
I5	3	B3	262	2	Customer delivery lost/corrupt because equipment/sware failure
I5	3	C3	263	4	Customer delivery lost/corrupt because vandalized/destroyed
I5	3	D3	264	3	Customer delivery lost/corrupt because fire/flood/strike/power
C5	1.1	A1.1	265	1	Customer delivery disclosed because unauthorized access
C5	1.1	B1.1	266	1	Customer delivery disclosed because equipment/sware failure
C5	1.1	C1.1	267	3	Customer delivery disclosed because vandalized/destroyed
C5	1.1	D1.1	268	2	Customer delivery disclosed because fire/flood/strike/power
C5	3	A3	269	1	Customer delivery disclosed because unauthorized access
C5	3	B3	270	1	Customer delivery disclosed because equipment/sware failure
C5	3	C3	271	3	Customer delivery disclosed because vandalized/destroyed
C5	3	D3	272	2	Customer delivery disclosed because fire/flood/strike/power
A5	1.1	A1.1	273	1	Customer delivery not available because unauthorized access
A5	1.1	B1.1	274	1	Customer delivery not available because equipment/sware failure
A5	1.1	C1.1	275	3	Customer delivery not available because vandalized/destroyed
A5	1.1	D1.1	276	2	Customer delivery not available because fire/flood/strike/power
A5	3	A3	277	1	Customer delivery not available because unauthorized access
A5	3	B3	278	1	Customer delivery not available because equipment/sware failure
A5	3	C3	279	3	Customer delivery not available because vandalized/destroyed
A5	3	D3	280	2	Customer delivery not available because fire/flood/strike/power

At the end of this step, the exposures for each risk in the risk catalogue can be totalled (remembering they are logarithmic) and converted back to money to obtain a good approximation to the total financial exposure of the business for the system under consideration.

Countermeasure identification

Countermeasures are applied to reduce exposure. Depending on the nature of the risk, an organization may choose from a range of countermeasures. For the purposes of SRA, we can categorize these as:

- **Risk shifting**, where the risk is shifted by applying a countermeasure (such as insurance or subcontracting) to the risk itself which moves all or part of the exposure to a third party – such countermeasures involve no change to the business or technology models.
- **Risk reduction**, where the annual exposure is reduced because a countermeasure is applied to the vulnerability which, in essence, reduces the frequency of occurrence – such countermeasures involve a change to the technology model but no change to the business model or information model.
- **Risk avoidance**, where the exposure is reduced because a countermeasure is applied to the threat which reduces the impact of the threat – such countermeasures involve a change to the business model but no change to the technology model.

Countermeasure identification tends to be an interactive process. Some vulnerabilities, for example, lead to more risks than others and therefore overall exposure can be minimized by applying countermeasures to these vulnerabilities. A simple way to determine these hot spots is by sorting the risk catalogue twice, first by vulnerability and then by exposure. A pattern will generally emerge which will direct effort in the most productive way by helping to close vulnerabilities which have the major effect on high exposures.

The catalogues created by SRA-IS therefore give a simple and straightforward means of evaluating the effect of various countermeasures on organizational exposure. Once again, assuming that the catalogues have been implemented using standard database or spreadsheet technology, it is an interactive process to insert different countermeasures and let the model recalculate the new exposures.

The models give results that have confidence attached. If the effect of a countermeasure is to reduce exposure by more than the cost of the countermeasure, then the countermeasure is worth implementing. In this case, the cost of the countermeasure and the resulting reduction in exposure can be factored into business planning.

Conclusions

SRA has been developed by Hyperion over the last six years. SRA-IS is a subset of SRA specific to IS. It has been simplified by taking into account certain characteristics of IS – in particular, the fact that the value of information assets is substantially greater than the value of physical assets – so that it provides a simple but powerful means of dealing with risk in commercial organizations.

SRA has been applied, very successfully, to a number of systems. These include an information gathering and dissemination network for the International Stock Exchange and IT for the European Space Agency manned space mission Colombus.

The SRA-IS methodology outlined in this chapter represents a step forward in the handling of risk analysis and management. It provides a structured method of dealing with the broad class of IS in such a way as to give specific and prescriptive results. It is:

- complete and consistent, fully integrated with structured analysis methodologies – it uses standard structured models which already exist in many organizations and so does not require a large initial investment;
- straightforward, as it does not require special software or overcomplex training – it is hierarchical in the same way that the structured models are, so that high-level analysis can be used to identify areas requiring further attention and then more detailed analysis can be applied to these specific areas;
- able to cope with all implementations of information systems, whether centralized or fully distributed – it makes no assumptions as to the characteristics of the technology model (or models) that will be supporting the business model.

As the procedures can be automated using readily available spreadsheet or database programs, risk management becomes a cost-effective and interactive process. This means that the cost of countermeasures and resulting reduction in exposures can be evaluated in their proper business context. This further means that decisions on countermeasure expenditure can be taken in confidence.

The use of the methodology to maintain a management picture of risk and to assess the effect of changes in the business, information or technology models on organizational exposure provides a structured basis for effective risk management during routine operations, and complements other risk analysis techniques that can be used during the appraisal and development phases of making IS investments.

References

Davies, A. (1990) Computer risk management. *Computer Law and Security Report*, **5** (6).

Dunn, J. (1990) Data integrity and executive systems. *Computer Control Quarterly*, **8** (3), 23–5.

Jamieson, R. and Low, G. (1990) Local area network operations: a security, control and audit perspective. *Journal of Information Technology*, **5** (2).

Katz, J. (1990) Business /enterprise modelling. *IBM Systems Journal*, **28**, (4).

Keen, P. (1991) *Shaping The Future: Business Design Through Information Technology*, Harvard Business School Press, Boston, MA.

Moses, R. (1990) The current status of CRAMM: the CCTA risk methodology. *Proceedings of the Unicom Conference Information Security: Confidentiality, Integrity and Availability*, Unicom, London.

McEvoy, N. and Harris, R. (1990) Structured security analysis using SSADM. *Proceedings of the SSADM User Group Conference*, SSADM User Group, Keele.

Nicholls, C. (1987) *Introducing SSADM: The NCC Guide*, NCC Publications, Oxford.

Reed and Watt (1989) *Computer Risk Manager: A Manual, For EDP Contingency Planning*. Elsevier, Amsterdam.

Seberry, L. and Preprzyk, R. (1989) *Cryptography: An Introduction To Computer Security*, Prentice Hall, Hemel Hempstead.

Willcocks, L. and Margetts, H. (1994) Risk and information systems: developing the analysis. In *Information Management: Evaluation of Information Systems Investments* (ed. L. Willcocks), Chapman & Hall, London.

13

A holistic approach to IT function evaluation

Dan Remenyi

Introduction

This chapter addresses a holistic approach to the evaluation of the performance of the IT function. The approach used in this chapter is based on the service quality work originated by Parasuraman, Zeithaml and Berry (1985) and developed by others including Miller and Doyle (1987), and Remenyi and Money (1991).

The IT function of an organization is involved in the development, implementation and maintenance of numerous IT systems. These systems aim to meet needs of users at all levels within the organization. In evaluating the success or effectiveness of the IT department it is sometimes necessary to evaluate the performance of the individual systems, and then use the aggregate of the performances on the individual systems as an overall measure of the success or effectiveness of the IT department. On other occasions it is possible to assess the effectiveness of the IT department as a whole. One of the keys in deciding which approach to take is the degree of centralization. In organizations where there is a high degree of decentralization of the IT function, the evaluation is not focused so much on the IT department but rather on the users of the IS. The approach described in this chapter may be used to evaluate single systems, departmental computing as well as the whole IT function.

Having an instrument to measure IT effectiveness is becoming more and more critical to many firms. The surveys reviewed in earlier chapters reveal that general management consider measurement of IT effectiveness a key issue (see

Investing in Information Systems: Evaluation and Management. Edited by
Leslie Willcocks. Published in 1996 by Chapman & Hall. ISBN 0 412 72670 X.

Chapters 1 and 2). Unfortunately, there is little agreement on how to measure effectiveness.

The measurement problem is exacerbated by the many ways in which effectiveness can be viewed (King, 1984). For example, an IT department can be considered effective when it:

- is meeting its objectives;
- operates within its budgets;
- delivers on time;
- is a major catalyst in directing the firm's use of IT;
- ensures that the firm is using IT competitively;
- its role in the organization is clearly understood;
- it is generally perceived to be an ally;
- its internal efficiency is at least equivalent to the industry average, whatever that might be;
- it can deliver systems for no greater cost than they can be purchased in the open market;
- it is perceived by top management to be value for money and users believe that IT is being deployed in a way which supports their pursuit of excellence (Remenyi *et al.*, 1993).

There is, however, one thing on which there is agreement, which is that success is not necessarily reflected in the level of investment in IT (Strassmann, 1985, 1990).

Despite the obvious difficulty in defining, let alone measuring, the effectiveness of the IT function, the fact that IT is competing for resources with other functions, such as marketing, finance, production and so on, means it is essential that there are available credible ways of measuring its effectiveness.

User satisfaction (US) is recognized as an important indicator (surrogate) of MIS effectiveness (Raghunathan and King, 1988; Baroudi and Orlikowski, 1988; Rands and Cumberbatch, 1993). It is on this approach to the measurement problem that this chapter focuses, and in particular on perceptual measures of US. This involves incorporating user feelings, beliefs, opinions and attitudes towards IT into the evaluation procedure.

In the context of IS effectiveness, it is generally believed that if users declare themselves to be satisfied with the system then the system may be said at least to some extent to be effective. Clearly if users are not satisfied with the system/s then it is unlikely that it/they are capable of being effective. Such a satisfaction measurement is at best an indirect and relative measure which must be used with considerable care. In some organizations users could be happy with inadequate or inappropriate systems. The approach used here does not take these situations directly into account, although the final question in the questionnaire is an open one in which respondents may make any comment they chose, and it is hoped this would highlight any such situations. However, trends over time in user satisfaction are perhaps the most revealing aspect of this type of study.

User satisfaction (US)

User satisfaction is generally considered to result from a comparison of user expectations of the IS with the perceived performance of the IS on a number of different facets of the IS. This is considered to be a holistic approach to systems effectiveness as it addresses either a whole system, a department or the complete IS function.

More specifically, overall attitude to the IS function can be considered to be influenced by the size and direction of the discrepancies (or gaps) between expectations and performance. A negative gap results when perceived performance is below expectation. A 'large' gap implies considerable dissatisfaction with the IS capabilities. A 'large' positive gap can be interpreted as indicating more attention to a particular function than necessary, i.e. that IS resources are being wasted, whereas a 'large' negative gap indicates a need for more resources to improve performance.

A variant to the above approach is to use the correlation between expectations and performance scores as a measure of 10 'fit'. The correlations also provide a means for assessing the overall effectiveness of the IS function, where high positive correlations can be taken to imply 10 'consensus' of views. In addition to gap analysis and correlation analysis, this approach to IT effectiveness lends itself to exploration by a number of other statistical tools. Thus factor analysis, which would allow us to summarize the variables (Kerlinger, 1969) and correspondence analysis, which would allow us to perform perceptual mapping (Greenacre, 1984) may also be used. These techniques, however, demand a non-trivial knowledge of statistics. For the purposes of this chapter the author has decided to use only gap analysis which requires an elementary knowledge of statistics.

The above describes one gap between users' expectations and their perception of the systems performance. There are, however, several other gaps which may be measured using the same approach. In the original paper by Parasuraman, Zeithaml and Berry (1985) five gaps are discussed. This work has been developed directly by Kim (1990) who has produced a three-gap model to describe IT effectiveness. This approach is conceptually very sound but it has a number of difficulties in its operationalization.

Three-gap approach to measurement

The Kim model

A feature of the conceptual model developed by Kim is that US is considered to be influenced not only by post implementation experience with the IS but also by pre-implementation expectations of the IS. The latter is captured through the user's initial expectations of the IS.

In this approach, US is measured by the discrepancy between the user's perception score of the IS performance and the user's initial expectation score of the IS. Further, the model describes how US is influenced by the discrepancies that arise during the developmental and service delivery processes. The developmental stage comprises two substages, namely, the determination of the users' requirements of the system and the design and installation of the system. These various stages give rise to three gaps which influence the US. These gaps may in turn be influenced by various organizational factors. Examples include user participation in defining the IS requirements; top management support which may take the form of increased investment in IS, thereby influencing the gap between the design specifications and the quality of the system installed; and the extent of user training which is likely to have an effect on the

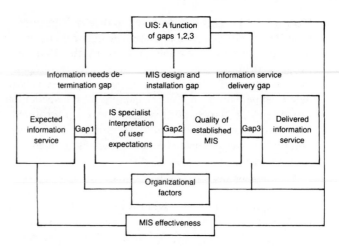

Figure 13.1 A UIS model.

gap between the actual quality of the system installed and what the user perceives the quality to be through use of the system. There may also be other organizational factors which directly affect the system. The Kim model is represented diagrammatically in Figure 13.1.

Interpreting the model

Interpretation of the gaps

- **Gap 1** – this is the discrepancy between the users' original expectations of the system and the systems designers' interpretations of these expectations. This gap is due to a lack of understanding of the business procedures required. This has been the source of much trouble and many problems over the years.
- **Gap 2** – this is the discrepancy between the systems specialist's interpretation of the users' needs and the quality of what is actually installed for the user. This gap arises from internal operational problems within the ISD itself.
- **Gap 3** – this is the discrepancy between the quality of what is actually installed and what the user experiences when interacting with the system. This gap is due *inter alia* to inadequate training, manuals etc.

Incorporation of organization factors

The model postulates that the three gaps can be affected by organizational factors. For example, gap 1 could be influenced in a positive way by encouraging user participation in the design stage. This involves determining the information require- ments desired from the system. On the other hand, top management support for MIS, exhibited through, say, the provision of enough resources, should be positively correlated with gap 2. Finally the provision of proper training should be positively correlated with gap 3.

Formulating and fitting the model

US is measured as the discrepancy between user expectations and the perceptions of the system. Furthermore, the model assumes that overall US can be explained by gaps 1 to 3 and also organizational factors. More formally:

$$US = f(\text{gap1, gap2, gap3 organizational factors})$$

To operationalize the model, it will be necessary in the first instance to develop instruments to measure the three gaps. Although this has not yet been done, it should be possible by applying the methodologies used by researchers when modelling consumer satisfaction with quality of service, where consumer satisfaction is expressed as a function of a number of gaps (Parasuraman *et al.*, 1985, 1988, and Brown and Swartz, 1989). However, this multi-gap analysis is a difficult and time-consuming process and is not discussed further in this chapter.

Attention is rather focused on a single-gap model as discussed above which provided extensive information for the management of the effectiveness of the ISD.

A gap model applied to an office automation/network system

To demonstrate the use of a single-gap model the effectiveness of a computer network system of a leading business school is investigated. The focus is on users of the system which include academics, secretarial and administration staff, and MBA students.

The approach was to distribute self-completion questionnaires to users of the system in an attempt to measure user satisfaction with the network system, the information systems staff and the other information systems arrangements offered by the business school.

A total of 74 questionnaires were returned of which 9 were completed by academics, 10 by secretarial/administration staff and 55 by students.

The questionnaire required respondents first to give their views concerning their expectations from the network and the information system staff supporting it with regard to 25 main attributes. The questionnaire then asked the respondents to report on the performance of the network system and the staff in respect of the same 25 main attributes. In addition respondents were asked to give their view of the overall level of service offered by the IS function. Data concerning the number of years at the business school and the length of experience using personal computers and networks were also collected. Finally respondents were asked to make general comments about the effectiveness of the IS function, and these were summarized.

(A full copy of the questionnaire is supplied in the appendix.)

In the following pages the data obtained from the respondents have been analysed and a number of graphs have been drawn.

Results of the survey on IT effectiveness

General information about the respondents

Most of the respondents were students who had only been at the business school for a short period. This is reflected in the results of the question 'How many years have you been at the business school?', which were as shown in Table 13.1.

The number of years experience using a personal computer varied considerably and is reflected in the results of the question 'How many years' experience have you had working with a PC?', which are shown in Table 13.2.

The number of years experience using a network did not vary so much and is reflected in the results of question 'How many years' experience have you had working with a PC network?', which are given in Table 13.3.

A summary of the results of the performance ratings on an attribute by attribute basis indicates the results shown in Table 13.4. Although these results do not appear to include items which have a good rating, if an upper confidence limit is calculated using the standard error then they appear as shown in Table 13.5.

In order to see more clearly which attributes are regarded as performing better they were next sorted by the average score. The results are given in Table 13.6. Thus 10 out of the 25 attributes may be considered with 97.5% confidence to have been rated good.

Table 13.1 Number of years at the business school

No. of years	No. of respondents
1	53
2	10
3	4
4	1
5	0

Table 13.2 Number of years' experience with a PC

No. of years' PC experience	No. of respondents
1	21
2	9
3	9
4	7

Table 13.3 Number of years working with a PC network

No. of years' network experience	No. of respondents
1	41
2	14
3	10
4	4

Table 13.4 Mean performance score by attribute

A1	2.93
A2	2.72
A3	2.92
A4	2.35
A5	2.69
A6	2.95
A7	2.65
A8	2.49
A9	2.61
A10	2.89
A11	2.31

Table 13.5 Performance score with standard error

	Mean	SE-2	upper limit	
A1	2.93	0.27	3.21	Good
A2	2.72	0.26	2.98	Poor
A3	2.92	0.18	3.10	Good
A4	2.35	0.30	2.66	Poor
A5	2.69	0.29	2.98	Poor
A6	2.95	0.30	3.25	Good
A7	2.65	0.27	2.92	Poor
A8	2.49	0.27	2.76	Poor
A9	2.61	0.27	2.88	Poor
A10	2.89	0.21	3.10	Good
A11	2.31	0.29	2.60	Poor

Table 13.6 Performance scores sorted

		Mean	SE-2	Upper limit	
1.	A16	2.99	0.21	3.20	Good
2.	A18	2.97	0.26	3.23	Good
3.	A21	2.96	0.22	3.18	Good
4.	A6	2.95	0.30	3.25	Good
5.	A1	2.93	0.27	3.21	Good
6.	A3	2.92	0.18	3.10	Good
7.	A10	2.89	0.21	3.10	Good
8.	A20	2.88	0.28	3.16	Good
9.	A19	2.84	0.24	3.08	Good
10.	A13	2.74	0.31	3.05	Good
11.	A2	2.72	0.26	2.98	Poor

The next step in the analysis was to calculate the gap between the expectation and the performance ratings. This is one of the key figures in the report. The result of these gap calculations is shown in the snake and gap diagram in Figure 13.2. Two attributes have positive gaps and one attribute has a zero gap. This indicates that only with respect to three attributes is the ISD performing to the level expected by the users.

The ISD's performance with respect to attribute A10 – data security and privacy – which has a zero gap, which some would regard as a happy coincidence, appears to perfectly match users' expectations. This is regarded as the ideal.

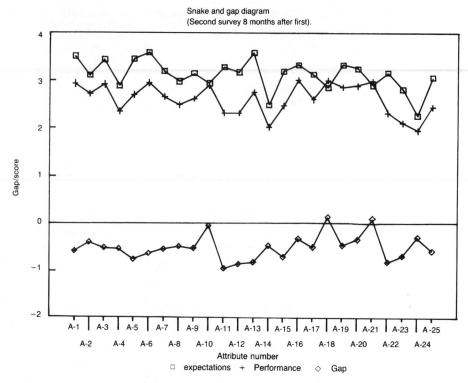

Figure 13.2 Snake and gap diagram (second survey eight months after first).

Attributes A18 and A21, which are overall cost-effectiveness of information systems and standardization of hardware respectively, exhibit positive gaps. This suggests that in the view of the users too much attention is being paid to these issues. With regard to attribute A18 the interpretation of this result could be that the users feel that the ISD is too strict with funds. With regard to attribute A21 the interpretation of this result could be that the users feel that the ISD is too concerned about standards, i.e. perhaps users want more freedom to choose their own systems. However, in general, the positive gaps do not offer as much concern to management as do the negative gaps.

Unfortunately all the other attributes in this study have negative gaps which suggest that performance does not meet expectation. This means that the ISD will need to employ more effort and perhaps more funds to raise the level of service to rectify this situation.

Moving on from the overall gap analysis Figure 13.3 shows the average performance scores on an attribute by attribute basis as well as the overall evaluation score and the all data average. Eight attributes score particularly well. One of these is the positive attitude of the IS staff towards the users. This is a particicularly encouraging indication as it shows a very healthy relationship between the user community and the ISD. Another interesting feature of this figure is the fact that the overall evaluation score is higher than the all data average of the performance scores. This suggests that the user community believes that the IS function in the business school is better than the sum of its parts. This is a very positive feature of the work of the ISD in this organization and contrasts with other work done by the author where the ISD was not held in such high regard.

In Figure 13.4 the performance scores were plotted for each group as well as for the average of all groups. Although this figure is rather crowded it does shows that in general the opinions of the different groups, with few exceptions, concur.

In order to attempt to find differences in the opinions of each group, and thus highlight where the system is more and less acceptable, the average of all groups was plotted against the score of each different group. Figure 13.5 shows the academic and the average scores while Figure 13.6 shows the secretarial and the average scores; Figure 13.7 shows the average and the student scores.

From these figures it may be seen that there are some differences between the view of the academics and the whole sample as well as between the secretarial/administration and the whole sample. The academics have quite a positive attitude towards the network as do the secretarial/administration staff. Figure 13.7 first shows how the large number of student responses have dominated the average scores. In addition this figure clearly indicates that the student population has a significantly lower opinion of the network. For nearly all attributes students rated the network lower than average.

This result suggests that there is an important difference between the views of those who are in a position of authority and power, i.e. the staff, and those who have to accept the service which is offered.

Finally Figure 13.8 shows the academic staff's expectation from the system compared with the students' expectations. It is worth noting that on 21 attributes aca-

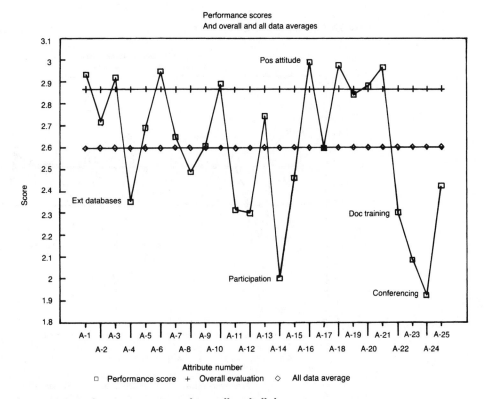

Figure 13.3 Performance scores and overall and all data averages.

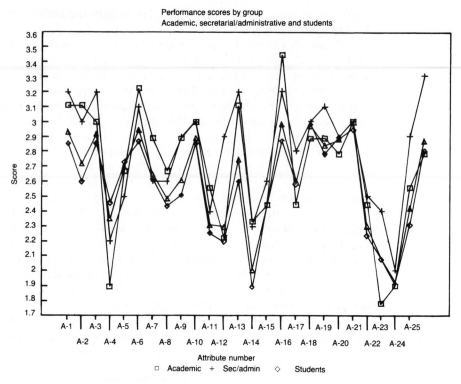

Figure 13.4 Performance scores by group: academic, secretarial/administrative and students.

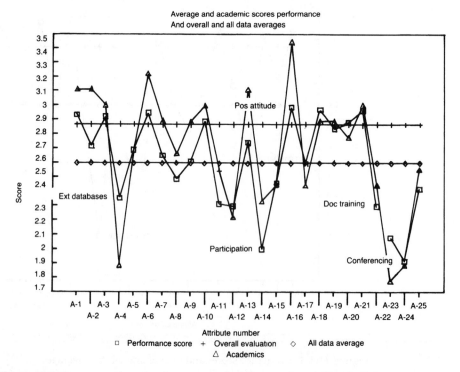

Figure 13.5 Average and academic scores performance and overall and all data averages.

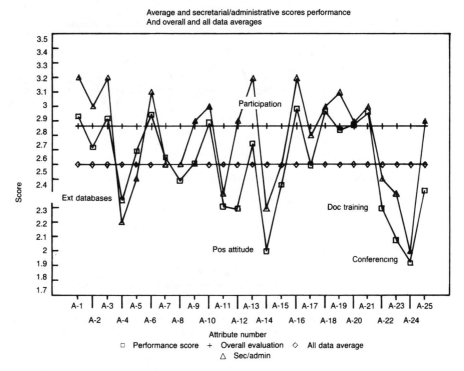

Figure 13.6 Average and secretarial/administrative scores performance and overall and all data averages.

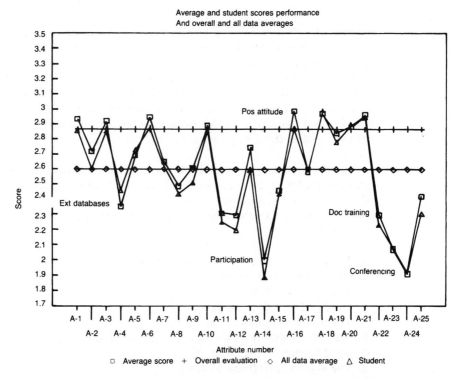

Figure 13.7 Average and student scores performance and overall and all data averages.

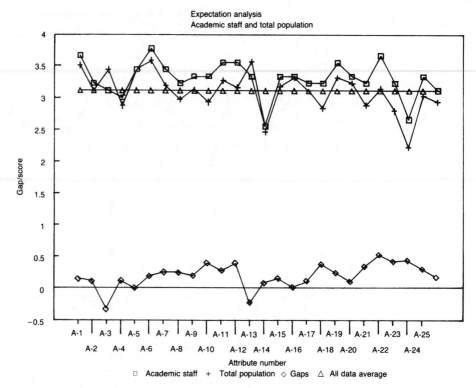

Figure 13.8 Expectation analysis: academic staff and total population.

demic staff have a higher degree of expectation than the students. This is an interesting result which shows just how much more work is required from the ISD if it is to meet users' expectations.

The last section of the questionnaire asked for general comments about any aspect of the system. This was included in order to be able to obtain specific information about areas which concerned the users which were not covered by the attributes. Also it was hoped that users would mention personal problems which they were having with the system. In all 34 respondents used Part D of the questionnaire to raise specific issues.

The technique of content analysis was used to summarize the issued raised by the respondents. In all 23 issues were raised. Some issues occurred a number of times, while others were raised only once.

The following is a summary of the content analysis, giving frequency of individual responses.

1. Printers are difficult, slow and inadequate — 15
2. Slow response of system — 8
3. Software out of date — 7
4. Outdated and slow hardware — 5
5. The new computers are much more efficient — 4
6. No added value from the network for established PC users — 2
7. Hard to find support staff — 2
8. The system is well run by Lucy — 2

The remaining comments were made only once:

9. Poor initial training
10. Equipment often malfunctions
11. Part-time students denied access after 10.00 p.m.
12. Poor Lucy has a huge work load
13. No DTP training
14. Accommodation for the systems unsuitable
15. Only sufficient for a business school
16. The fact that the system closes down over the exams is disgraceful
17. Not easy access to the system
18. Not user friendly
19. Extensive problems with Ventura on the system
20. Plenty of frustration from the system
21. The system is not poor but it could be much better
22. The network was real good
23. The ISD has not seen fit to establish any sort of continual feedback communication between themselves and the users

Conclusion of the study

The ISD reviewed in the above study was not without its problems.

Although it performed positively in some aspects largely it was not really well regarded by the majority of its users. Its effectiveness is highly questionable as it appears that with regard to the majority of the attributes it is substantially underperforming.

It may be concluded from this study that a considerable amount of attention and funds need to allocated to this network if it is to meet the expectations of its users. In fact as a result of this study funds were found to upgrade a number of the network's services which led to a considerably improved level of service.

Discussion

Most organizations actually know whether their IS departments are functioning effectively without using this technique. However, this knowledge is frequently based on informal feedback in the form of complaints and very occasionally praise (see Chapter 1). This knowledge is clearly subjective with the loudest and most senior voices being heard the clearest. Although this knowledge is useful it does not really allow the information systems department to have a balanced view of their strengths, weaknesses and their general level of effectiveness. The approach described here is also subjective in that it relies on the opinions of the users. However, the data are egalitarian as each questionnaire is given equal weight. If a reasonably large sample is used, say over 30, then the views of those with special axes to grind will largely be averaged out. Thus one of the most important attributes of this holistic method is that it offers a formal approach to the presentation of problem aspects as well as areas which are performing well.

The issues raised in the questionnaire are standard for most organizations. Having used this measuring instrument in more than a dozen situations, it is now clear that users easily relate to the questions. It is not a burdensome task to complete the questionnaire and thus a reasonably high response may be achieved. The data collected with this questionnaire is amenable to a considerable amount of analysis.

In this paper only the Parasuruman gap analysis and rudimentary content analysis has been discussed. However, readers with some knowledge of quantitative methods may wish to further explore the data using multivariate techniques such as factor analysis and correspondence analysis. These techniques can provide an even more thorough understanding of the functioning of the ISD as well as assisting with the communication of the results of the survey.

From a practical point of view an important feature of this holistic approach is its low cost and its ease of use. A survey may be conducted using a standard questionnaire such as the one described in this chapter. Respondents may be given a week to reply. Data entry for a hundred respondents will require only a few hours. All the analysis described in this chapter required only two hours' work.

However, most value will be derived by those organizations who regularly conduct this type of holistic evaluation. If a survey is conducted every six to twelve months then it will be possible to identify trends in the scores of various attributes. It would be possible to observe the effect of corporate action on the attribute scores and thereby fine-tune the way the IS department is managed.

Finally, such an evaluation may be done on its own or it may be conducted as part of a greater scope review such as a value for money study. In either event, it is probably better if the study is not conducted by the ISD itself but by the TQM or management services department or by internal or external auditors. This technique should not only be used where there are problems but on a routine basis in order to ensure that the IS department is remaining on track.

Conclusion

There is a growing trend in the utilization of user satisfaction measurements as a surrogate for IS effectiveness. This is a holistic approach which enables the organization to obtain an overview of the effectiveness of the IS function as seen by their users or clients. Gap analysis together with content analysis is the most popular way of conducting these studies. It is not difficult to construct an appropriate questionnaire, in fact a standard, off the shelf questionnaire may be used. The statistics required for the technique described above are quite elementary and do not require the use of a sophisticated statistical package or assistance of a statistician to interpret the results. This approach is inexpensive and can be concluded in quite a short period of time. It is likely that more and more organizations will make use of this technique and as this approach really comes into its own when used on a longitudinal basis, those organizations which are already using this approach will continue to use it to monitor their IS department's progress towards improving their effectiveness.

References

Baroudi, J.J. and Orlikowski, W.J. (1988) A short measure of user information satisfaction. *Journal of Management Information Systems*, **4** (4), 44–59.

Brown, S.W. and Swartz, T.A. (1989) A gap analysis of professional service quality. *Journal of Marketing*, April.

Greenacre, M.J. (1984) *The Theory and Application of Correspondence Analysis*, Academic Press, New York.

Kerlinger, F.N. (1969) *Foundation of Behavioural Science*, Holt, Reinhart and Winston, New York.

Kim, K.K. (1990) User information satisfaction: towards conceptual clarity. *Proceedings of ICIS*, Copenhagen, December.

King, W.R. (1991) *Evaluating an Information Systems Planning Process*, Working Paper, University of Pittsburgh, PA. Cited by Raghunathan, B. and Raghunathan, T.S. in information systems planning and effectiveness: an empirical analysis, *OMEGA International Journal of Management Science*, **9**.

King, W. (1994) *Evaluating an Information Systems Planning Process*. Working paper 592, University of Pittsburgh, Pittsburgh, PA.

Parasuraman, A., Zeithaml, V. and Berry, L. (1985) A conceptual model of service quality and its implications for future research. *Journal of Marketing*, Fall.

Parasuraman, A., Zeithaml, V. and Berry, L. (1988) SERVQUAL: a multiple item scale for measuring consumer perceptions of service quality. *Journal of Retailing*, **64** (1), 12–40.

Raghunathan, T.S. and King, W.R. (1988) The impact of information systems planning on the organization, *OMEGA International Journal of Management Science*, **16** (2), 85–94.

Rands, T. and Cumberbatch, D. (1993) Service Quality As a Measure of IT Effectiveness. Oxford working paper 93/2 Oxford: Templeton College.

Remenyi, D. and Money, A. (1991) A user-satisfaction approach to IS effectiveness measurement. *Journal of Information Technology*, November.

Remenyi, D. *et al.* (1993) *A Guide to Measuring and Managing IT Benefits*, NCC-Blackwell, Oxford.

Silk, D.J. (1990) Managing IS benefits in the 90s. *Journal of Information Technology*, **5** (4),185–93.

Strassmann, P.A. (1985) *Information Payoff, The Transformation of Work in the Electronic Age*, Free Press, New York.

Strassmann, P.A. (1990) *The Business Value of Computers*, The Information Economics Press, New Canaan.

Appendix: the measurement of IS effectiveness in a business school environment

The following questionnaire has been designed to help assess the effectiveness of the computer network system used by academics, and secretarial and administration staff as well as students in your business school. This is part of an academic initiative at the UK business school, Henley – The Management College, where a number of the staff have worked in the area of measuring and managing IT benefits.

The questionnaire has been divided into three parts. Parts A and B use the same set of 25 questions. Part C is one open ended question.

Your answers to the questions in Part A refer to the system's attributes which you believe are important to the effectiveness of the system. Your answers to the second set of 25 questions in Part B refer to how the Information Systems Department of the business school performs in terms of these systems attributes.

Finally in part C we would welcome any comments that you would like to make concerning your own experience with the computer network and/or with the Information Systems Department in respect of its effectiveness.

The questionnaire uses a four point scale.

First set of 25 questions:	Second set of 25 questions:
Critical	Excellent
Important	Good
Not important	Poor
Irrelevant	Very poor

For example, you might think that ease of access to computer facilities is critical, and therefore your rating in the first set of questions will be:

Irrelevant	Not Important	Important	Critical

If you feel that the performance of the Information Systems Department in providing these facilities is good, this will mean your rating in the second set of questions will be:

Very poor	Poor	Good	Excellent

The Questionnaire should not take more than 15 minutes to complete. All information supplied by respondents will be treated with the utmost confidence.

Please supply the following information about you position in the Business School:

Are you Academic, Secretarial/Administration or Student:

Academic	Sec/Admin	Student

How many years have you been working and/or studying at the Business School: [ ]

How many years' experience have you had working with a PC: [ ]

How many years' experience have you had working with a PC network: [ ]

Thank you very much for your assistance in this research. Please return your completed questionnaire to Miss Lucy Vieira.

Dr. Dan Remenyi
Information Management Department

PART A

Answer the first set of questions by ticking the box which corresponds to your opinion of the importance of the following 25 attributes in ensuring the effectiveness of your system.

1.   Ease of access for users to computing facilities.

Irrelevant	Not Important	Important	Critical

2.   Up-to-dateness of hardware.

Irrelevant	Not Important	Important	Critical

3.   Up-to-dateness of software.

Irrelevant	Not Important	Important	Critical

4.   Access to external databases through the system.

Irrelevant	Not Important	Important	Critical

5.   A low percentage of hardware and software down time.

Irrelevant	Not Important	Important	Critical

6.   A high degree of technical competence of systems support staff.

Irrelevant	Not Important	Important	Critical

7.   User confidence in systems.

Irrelevant	Not Important	Important	Critical

8.   The degree of personal control users have over their systems.

Irrelevant	Not Important	Important	Critical

9.   Systems responsiveness to changing user needs.

Irrelevant	Not Important	Important	Critical

10.   Data security and privacy.

Irrelevant	Not Important	Important	Critical

11.   System's response time.

Irrelevant	Not Important	Important	Critical

12.   Extent of user training.

Irrelevant	Not Important	Important	Critical

13.   Fast response time from systems support staff to remedy problems.

Irrelevant	Not Important	Important	Critical

14.   Participation in planning of the systems requirements.

Irrelevant	Not Important	Important	Critical

15.   Flexibility of the system to produce professional reports, e.g. graphics and desktop publishing.

Irrelevant	Not Important	Important	Critical

16.   Positive attitude of information systems staff to users.

Irrelevant	Not Important	Important	Critical

17.   User's understanding of the system.

Irrelevant	Not Important	Important	Critical

18.   Overall cost-effectiveness of information systems.

Irrelevant	Not Important	Important	Critical

19.   Ability of the system to improve personal productivity.

Irrelevant	Not Important	Important	Critical

20.   Ability of the system to enhance the learning experience of students.

Irrelevant	Not Important	Important	Critical

21.   Standardisation of hardware.

Irrelevant	Not Important	Important	Critical

22.   Documentation to support training.

Irrelevant	Not Important	Important	Critical

23.   Help with database or model development.

Irrelevant	Not Important	Important	Critical

24.   Ability to conduct computer conferencing with colleagues.

Irrelevant	Not Important	Important	Critical

25.   User's willingness to find time to learn the system.

Irrelevant	Not Important	Important	Critical

PART B

Answer this set of questions by ticking the box which corresponds to your opinion of the performance of the Information Systems Department in terms of the following 25 attributes.

1.   Ease of access for users to computing facilities.

Very poor	Poor	Good	Excellent

2.   Up-to-dateness of hardware.

Very poor	Poor	Good	Excellent

3.   Up-to-dateness of software.

Very poor	Poor	Good	Excellent

4.   Access to external databases through the system.

Very poor	Poor	Good	Excellent

5.   A low percentage of hardware and software down time.

Very poor	Poor	Good	Excellent

6.   A high degree of technical competence of systems support staff.

Very poor	Poor	Good	Excellent

7.   User confidence in systems.

Very poor	Poor	Good	Excellent

8.   The degree of personal control users have over their systems.

Very poor	Poor	Good	Excellent

9.   Systems responsiveness to changing user needs.

Very poor	Poor	Good	Excellent

10.   Data security and privacy.

Very poor	Poor	Good	Excellent

11.   System's response time.

Very poor	Poor	Good	Excellent

12.   Extent of user training.

Very poor	Poor	Good	Excellent

13.   Fast response time from systems support staff to remedy problems.

Very poor	Poor	Good	Excellent

14.   Participation in planning of the systems requirements.

Very poor	Poor	Good	Excellent

15.   Flexibility of the system to produce professional reports, e.g. graphics and desktop publishing.

Very poor	Poor	Good	Excellent

16.   Positive attitude of information systems staff to users.

Very poor	Poor	Good	Excellent

17.   User's understanding of the system.

Very poor	Poor	Good	Excellent

18.   Overall cost-effectiveness of information systems.

Very poor	Poor	Good	Excellent

19.   Ability of the system to improve personal productivity.

Very poor	Poor	Good	Excellent

20.   Ability of the system to enhance the learning experience of students.

Very poor	Poor	Good	Excellent

21.   Standardisation of hardware.

Very poor	Poor	Good	Excellent

22.   Documentation to support training.

Very poor	Poor	Good	Excellent

23.   Help with database or model development.

Very poor	Poor	Good	Excellent

24.   Ability to conduct computer conferencing with colleagues.

Very poor	Poor	Good	Excellent

25.   User's willingness to find time to learn the system.

Very poor	Poor	Good	Excellent

PART C

Please rate your overall opinion of the computer network system.

Very Poor	Poor	Good	Excellent

Please supply any further comments you wish concerning the effectiveness of your computer network system.

_____
_____
_____
_____
_____
_____
_____
_____
_____
_____
_____

Optional

If you are prepared to discuss your comments with the researchers, please write your name below.

_____
_____
_____
_____

14

Using service-level agreements in maintenance and support functions

Jenny Dugmore

Introduction

This chapter describes the author's experience in implementing a range of service-level agreements (SLAs), and discusses those aspects that have contributed to or detracted from the success of the agreements. The author has been involved in implementing agreements to describe the development of environment service, help desks and the process of software maintenance, as well as the more common agreements on the production processing service. The chapter includes a description of a range of SLAs and functions, processes and tools necessary for the delivery of service to agreed target levels. It also includes a discussion of the cultural changes associated with successful agreements.

Service-level agreements have been in use for many years. Despite this, they have received little academic attention in the evaluation literature. In the early to mid-1980s many data centre managers adopted the use of SLAs to help solve particular management problems, such as the need for management to not only understand

Investing in Information Systems: Evaluation and Management. Edited by
Leslie Willcocks. Published in 1996 by Chapman & Hall. ISBN 0 412 72670 X.

the customer's service requirements, but to be able to prove that the agreed service levels are being delivered. The decision to implement SLAs was often taken in an atmosphere of customer dissatisfaction with the IT department's service and a tendency for individual user communities to 'go it alone' and set up a small IT department under their direct control.

The use of SLAs to describe data centre services has encouraged the extension of SLAs to describe other IT services, such as applications support, help desks etc. Several IT service agreements are described below. The external, customer oriented SLAs have also been combined with internal (back to back) SLAs, each internal agreement covering a component of the whole service delivered to the customer. These have the benefit of cascading targets through the entire support organization, so that there is comprehensive support for the external service commitments. In practice, formal internal SLAs are much less common than external agreements. Many organizations recognize the need for them, but seem to have greater difficulty reaching agreement within their own departments than between themselves and their customers. The rise of outsourcing IT assets and services to external vendors in the 1990s has seen a renewed interest and emphasis on the importance of SLAs in monitoring and managing IS/IT services to the business (see for example Lacity and Hirschheim, 1993).

Whether SLAs are drawn up for internal purposes or to monitor an external vendor, experience has shown that in practice successful implementation of SLAs occurs when there is clear understanding of why the agreements are being introduced. This is not just awareness of the general benefits quoted for service-level agreements, but the reasons specific to that organization. It is important that the objectives of introducing the agreements are understood during the development and implementation.

What is an SLA?

Most effective SLAs have the following characteristics:

- They describe issues critical to the customer.
- They are short.
- They are worded in the customer's terminology.
- They include only targets that can be objectively measured against.
- They define both the supplier and customer's responsibilities.

SLAs represent the managed approach to service delivery. An SLA can be likened to the detailed functional specification developed, agreed and used as the basis of a systems development project. The SLA defines what the customer wants and what it is paying for. By doing this it removes the ambiguity that can mar what would otherwise be a good supplier–customer relationship.

In some cases the SLA will be a schedule attached to the main body of a contract, i.e. part of the actual contract. More commonly it is formally agreed with the customer, without being contractual or without penalties being applicable, both parties being part of the same organization.

A number of alternatives exist to SLAs. These include declarations of good intent, charters backed by a complaints procedure, and partnership agreements. Many of these bring to the customer–supplier relationship the benefits brought by formal SLAs. However, any such agreement, including an SLA, is open to abuse. If developed and adopted for cynical reasons any such document can be counterproductive and represent a major lost opportunity. The less formal the document, the more easily any commitments can be avoided. This can effectively mean that both the supplier and customer skirt around major issues, never really understanding each other's concerns. Conversely, a very formal, legally binding document is not normally realistic for customers and suppliers who are both in the same or closely linked organizations. In situations of outsourcing to external suppliers, there is some case study evidence supporting a more formal, comprehensive approach, however, including penalties for non-performance (see Willcocks, Lacity and Fitzgerald, 1995).

In the mid-1990s many high profile documents, similar to service-level agreements, have been drawn up to describe many non-IT activities. The Citizen's Charter produced by the UK government has been just one example.

Why SLAs?

An SLA can bring rewards to both the supplier and the customer. Ensuring that the SLA implemented is effective can take a long time and a great deal of effort, particularly where service has been traditionally delivered in a relatively informal way. However, it is normally worth the time and effort required for even the most protracted negotiations. For example, for the customer and supplier to agree jointly both priorities and service targets results in much greater realism and understanding by both parties. The customer is also required to forecast growth (or decline) in computing facilities, perhaps for the first time, providing essential planning information for the supplier. In addition, the customer comes to terms with the trade-off between costs and service levels and, in the process, can become more realistic in the demands made of the supplier. In turn, the supplier is focused on improving the effectiveness of the service delivery organization and procedures.

The inclusion of targets provides an objective basis for judging the service – is the service good enough and is it getting better or worse? The objectivity of the service targets and service reports minimizes or eliminates the misunderstandings that can easily lead to acrimonious and unproductive discussions.

Targets in SLAs also lend themselves readily to use as both personal and organizational goals. Provision of tangible goals for staff can bring about improvements in motivation, even if initially the targets are seen as a threat. The benefits of targets for staff motivation can be explained by the position of support activities in the project–process spectrum. At one extreme of the spectrum a large project (such as installing a new mainframe) has a distinct beginning and end. The project has clearly identified output and time scales that are agreed before the project begins. The agreed output and time scales readily provide team goals. The team is also aware of whether the goals have been met or missed. Staff feel a sense of achievement and can be rewarded when the goals are reached (see Figure 14.1).

In contrast, support activities such as problem management and help desks and many aspects of change management, are at the other end of the project–process spectrum, and provide few natural goals. This is because each task is essentially short term and may be repetitive. The only milestones may be solving a particularly serious problem, and working hard may only result in being given more work to do. Staff can be demotivated by a role in support, however important the delivery of the support service may be to both the supplier and the customer. Demotivated staff do poor quality work.

Consistent reporting of the actual service levels achieved against each target in a service-level agreement is essential to the effective use of SLAs. The need for reports on actual service levels for comparison with targets may force the recording and reporting of management information for the first time – or at least ensure that that which is already in existence is used more effectively and has a much higher profile in the supplier and customer areas. However, targets are not always met and action following missed targets needs to be planned for.

Missing a target may not seem the most obvious benefit of an SLA. However, planning in advance for how missed targets will be dealt with can drive the development of more effective support management, such as better change and problem management. For example, improved change management reduces the incidence of problems, and also encourages more rigorous problem management which means problems that do occur will be resolved faster (reducing the total lost service) and with a lower risk of problem recurrence. The time taken to solve problems will be reduced if problem reporting is fast and simple, usually via a help desk. The use of SLAs may actually trigger the establishment of service management functions. Normally the effect is to make existing functions more effective.

Changing an organization into a service-oriented culture is neither easily nor quickly achieved. SLAs assist in a change to a service culture by being tangible; it is relatively easy to know if the customers' needs have been met (or not). Staff motivation, led by service-level targets as goals, changes the day-to-day behaviour of support staff. Even if the changes are small, they are an essential precursor to a change in culture. The small changes in behaviour, added together, may be more substantial than the often short-lived effects of customer care campaigns in the form of group sessions and enthusiastic speeches about the need for being service and customer oriented.

Many support staff have no actual contact with customers, and some have a role that means they only receive complaints or problem reports. For example, it is rare for a help desk to be telephoned to be told the service is fine and they are doing a good job. Under these circumstances it is difficult for support staff to care about at best, an unknown entity and at worst a source of nothing but complaints. SLAs, by describing the customer's concerns, can go some way towards bridging the gap between the supplier's support staff and the customers. Inclusion of the customer's responsibilities can help the supplier's support staff feel they are part of a partnership. This is particularly effective if there is feedback about the customer's views on the overall service, rather than just reports of problems. Service reports should be produced on service levels achieved as well as those missed, even if they are used only internally.

A factor that is difficult to quantify but which can be important is the sense of purpose engendered when reports show that the effort directed towards service has resulted in improved service levels and a satisfied customer.

The risks

All changes carry some risks. A risk of introducing SLAs arises from the common underestimation of the skills needed to develop, implement and support them. An SLA is, in principle a simple document, and many example are available as models. However, writing the first draft is probably the easiest part of the process. This stage can be followed by refusal of both colleagues and customer representatives to even discuss the document, through to protracted and hostile negotiations, or agreement to unrealistic targets by an inexperienced negotiator.

This risk is closely linked to the usual need to change attitudes, and even the organizational structure, in the support service areas. The risks are increased if the people involved have failed to consider their own organization's objectives in implementing the agreements. A management dictat such as 'Implement SLAs this year', is all too common but also carries a particularly high risk for the subsequent SLA programme. Unless the objectives of the programme are defined and understood, there is little likelihood that they can be met.

In addition, unless an SLA provides demonstrable benefits it will be seen, quite rightly, as an administrative overhead, be rejected, and soon fall into disrepute and disuse.

Finally, agreeing to service-level targets, then subsequently either consistently failing to meet the targets, or ignoring them shortly after agreement, is counterproductive. It may worsen the supplier–customer relationship, even though the commitments are not normally contractually binding.

Contents

The detailed contents of an effective SLA obviously differ from service to service and customer to customer as recent case study work has shown (Willcocks and Fitzgerald, 1994). The targets should be set for those aspects of the service that are critical to the customer, and are also measurable in objective and meaningful terms.

An agreement is easier to negotiate and formalize if it is short and easily understood (Malitoris, 1990). Keeping it short means that only those issues that are important (to either one or both of the service supplier and customer) are included. Attention is focused on important issues.

It is advisable to restrict targets to those aspects of service for which it is possible to measure and report actuals on the same basis as the targets. Statements of good intentions' are not enough and can be counterproductive. It is also advisable to include only details of *what* will be delivered, and *what level* it will be delivered at, i.e. excluding the details of *how* it will be delivered. Including the how of service means the customer is forced to become involved in the service supplier's internal management issues of 'who does what'. This type of issue should be dealt with by internal targets and be invisible to the customer. Internal targets are very useful in their own right, but are normally counterproductive in a customer's SLA.

A range of SLAs are described below. These include agreements for mainframe production processing by a data centre, an applications software support contract and a desktop support service. If these SLAs are used as models, it would be inadvisable to include all the targets listed, even in a draft agreement for discussion. Only the most critical services should be targeted, even if other services are listed in the scope of the service. A large number of targets distracts attention from issues that matter and can be counterproductive.

An agreement should normally emphasize a particular aspect of service. For example, support of a point of sale device could set exacting targets for availability, incident frequency and maximum incident duration, with targets at single output level, and not include batch processing targets at all. Conversely, a support service where timely delivery of printed output is critical (e.g. a legally required document) could emphasize the importance of this by setting exacting targets for both input and output deadlines and including details of remedial action to be taken should any critical output be late or lost.

The commitment of the customers to the agreement will also be improved by tailoring the agreement to individual requirements, rather than forcing a standard agreement on all customers, some of whom may consider themselves to have unique requirements.

Data centre SLA

On-line service targets

1. **Availability** – this is the term used to define the percentage of hours that an on-line service is usable, compared to the total possible or scheduled. It is very commonly used, but the definition of availability varies from organization to organization, and even from agreement to agreement. This is not always clear from the agreement, although the differences can have a significant effect on the calculation of the actual service level and the ability of the supplier to meet the target.
2. **Incident frequency** – this would be set as an upper limit for the number of incidents in the agreed target period. A common variation is 'mean time between failures'.
3. **Maximum incident duration** – this is less common than either availability or incident frequency, partly because it presents information similar to that given by the two previous targets.
4. **Terminal response times** – this is normally represented by an average response time and/or the time for percentage of transactions to be completed. Response times should be as seen by the 'end user'. This is often difficult or impossible, or there may be an unacceptable overhead in providing this information.
5. **On-line workload limits** – the workload limits are those on-line workloads above which response time targets cease to be achievable. The limit would not normally be applied as a guillotine, above which processing is prohibited. Instead it is used as a reminder to the customer that some aspects of the service can be affected by customer activities. The SLA should refer to the control of the work-loads as being the customer's responsibility. One of the difficulties in including workloads in an agreement is how to accurately convert the customer's units of work (e.g. processing of a cheque) into IT transactions.

Batch service targets

1. **Input deadlines** – normally this defines the customer's responsibility for ensuring that the batch process can start at the scheduled time.
2. **Output deadlines** – this defines when output will be available to the customer or the customer's representative and where it will be delivered to. It distinguishes between critical and non-critical output. Output may be in any form, i.e. printed or magnetic media.

3. **Workload limits** – the workload limits are included to show the limits to processing capacity beyond which the targets for batch output are at risk.

Documentary items

1. **Signatures** – both the service supplier and customer representative *must* authorize the agreement. Without this level of commitment the agreement will be ineffective.
2. **Validity period** – a start and end date for the agreement should be included. An agreement that has an indefinite term is unlikely to be a true representation of the customer's needs for very long. The actual validity period should match the expected changes within both the IT area and the customer's business activities. A period of six months or a year are chosen commonly.
3. **Change control** – this text describes the conditions that will result in a change to the agreement and how this process work. This is particularly important when large changes in the services required or the services delivered mean the agreement is renegotiated before the end of the validity period.
4. **Scope and objectives of the agreement** – this is a description of what is and what is not included in the agreement, and why the agreement has been produced. For support of production applications this is typically a single application, perhaps uniquely defined by charge or cost codes. Alternatively the scope of the agreement may be determined by location of the user communities.
5. **Normal service hours** – used in calculations of availability etc. but also defining periods of guaranteed support.
6. **Critical periods** – each group of customers may have times when the service is particularly important to their business activities. This is not stated elsewhere surprisingly often. Many individual business groups have critical service periods that do not match the overall peak periods for machine usage.

Application support agreement

Application support can be divided into:

- error fixes;
- small enhancements;
- large enhancements.

Process–project spectrum

Error fixes are at one extreme of a process–project spectrum, with large enhancements towards the other end. This is illustrated in Figure 14.1. Processes can be translated relatively easily into targets, for use in a service-level agreement. As shown in Figure 14.2, the stages of software error fixing/small enhancements can be divided into:

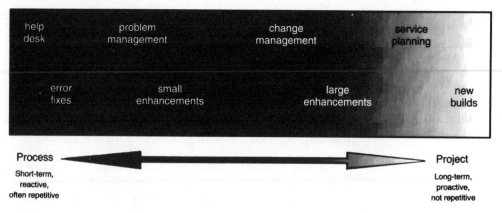

Figure 14.1 Process–project spectrum.

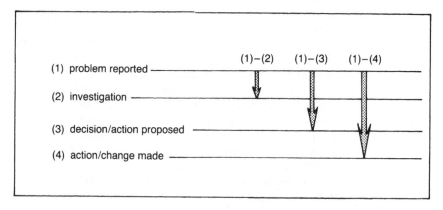

Figure 14.2 Stages of error fixing/small enhancements.

1. problem report/change request received;
2. start of investigation;
3. decision (action proposed);
4. action (change made).

Targeting time from (1) to (2)

The time between problem reception and the start of investigation is suitable for targeting, as the start and end times are usually unambiguous. A target of:

X % of calls/requests will be responded to within Y minutes

has worked well for a number of organizations.

Targeting (1) to (4), total time to fix/implement the change

The total time to fix an error or make a change is given by the time taken between (1) and (4). It is an aspect of service of interest to the customer, as it usually represents the time taken before the service is performing as required. This may therefore be requested for inclusion in an SLA. However, for software errors it can be relatively difficult to measure unambiguously. For example, when an error is fixed by a change that has to be handed over for user acceptance testing before implementation, and in particular if the user acceptance is partial.

The time between (1) and (4) is not always under the control of the supplier. The SLA needs to reflect the role and responsibilities of the customers

Targeting (4) to (3) and (3) to (4)

These stages are more suitable for internal target and effective change and problem management; procedures need to include progress of user acceptance testing as well as supplier staff activities if targets are at risk.

Desktop and help desk SLAs

Over the last decade the role of PCs and LANs has become much more important. PCs are being increasingly used for handling business critical data and an estimated 35–40% of processing is done using PCs. Providing effective desktop services is therefore of much greater importance for the IT supplier who wishes to keep their user community satisfied with the IT support service.

Although much of the desktop support is provided centrally, in many organizations PCs are connected to a LAN set up with little or no IT department involvement, and without any central control.

A particularly key element of the desktop support service is the help desk, and the contents of the SLA should reflect this situation. This is largely because the help desk is a prime point of contact for the desktop customer, who increasingly expects 'instant' solutions to problems, normally during a short telephone call. The importance of the help desk in determining the image of the IT supplier is illustrated in Figure 14.3. The help desk can be seen to be the most visible part of the IT supplier's organization, and

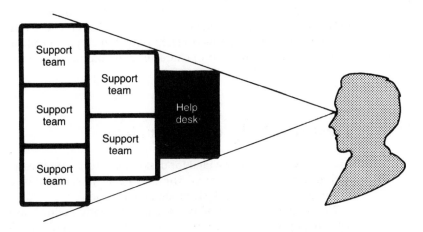

Figure 14.3 Role of the help desk in forming the image of the IT supplier.

as such very influential. SLAs need to reflect the high visibility of the help desk services.

Scope

Help desk is a loosely defined term used to describe a wide range of functions and responsibilities. Help desks may also be described as service desks, service centres, support desks, by a relatively meaningless departmental name or even remain unnamed.

The type of help desk is usually expressed as a skill level (unskilled through to expert). Occasionally reference is made to intelligence rather than skill. The descriptions 'unskilled', 'expert', 'intelligent', are a reference to the level of technical IT skill of the help desk staff, and are normally used to indirectly reflect the proportion of problems reported that are resolved by the help desk.

A highly skilled 'expert' help desk may actually be staffed by individuals with poor communications and interpersonal skills. This desk may be labelled as 'expert' despite being unsatisfactory, from the customer's viewpoint, as a result of this lack of interpersonal skill. Customers ringing a help desk are normally anxious about a problem and resent anything but diplomatic treatment.

In the interest of staff motivation, use of the terms 'skill' or 'intelligence', is considered inadvisable. Not only are technical skills an incomplete description, such terminology is likely to be demotivating (for example, when an area is described as 'unskilled' or 'unintelligent').

Quantifying a help desk

The proportion of calls resolved by the help desk and the proportion referred elsewhere for resolution are good measures for both help desks and desktop support service-level agreements. Unlike skill level, which is anyway a qualitative measure, calls resolved/referred is a quantitative measure.

Call resolved/referred rates have the added advantage of representing an aspect of the help desk service that is visible to, and has a direct influence on the customer. Conversely, skill level reflects how the service will be delivered.

Call referral rate remains constant only if the types of call and callers contacting the help desk remain constant in character and volume, over a period of time; this has to be monitored and managed.

Desktop/help desk services

Many of the services provided for desktop user communities are often not understood and may not be documented. The SLA needs to clarify this. Examples from desktop agreements are given below, in alphabetic order.

The supplier's responsibilities should be clearly defined, as should the customer's. This requires more than the workload limits listed for data centre mainframe processing service-level agreements. It is advisable to include, under the customer's responsibilities, issues such as virus checking, illegal software, back up procedures and the data protection act.

This additional information is recommended because many PC systems have insecure A drives, customers have often used mainframe systems where they had little or no responsibility for back up of their systems or data, and at the same time may have access to business critical or other confidential data with the more controlled and structured software, without having been trained in the need for different practices.

Services commonly provided for desktop users or responsibilities of the desktop customers include those listed below.

- configuration management;
- contingency/back up (occasionally done centrally, normally at individual level);
- consumables (purchase, control and use);
- help desk and problem management services: call reception/logging; call resolution/ referral; call progression/escalation.
- local support (potentially a wide range, but printer management as minimum);
- PC/LAN installation/move services;
- problem reporting (how and to whom);
- procurement;
- security (virus checking, data protection, illegal software etc.);
- testing;
- third party supplier management: contract negotiation; contract management; support call management.
- training.

Suitable service targets

Typical targets for desktop services are given below.

- service/support hours;
- help desk call ring times: this term describes the number of times a phone rings before being answered by the help desk. The target is normally phrased as $XX\%$ of calls answered before Y rings;
- help desk call referral rates;
- call response times;
- call resolution times (incident duration);
- call volumes/types.

This is the workload element of the help desk, above which the help desk and desktop service as a whole, may not be achievable. Help desks are also susceptible to changes in workload due to implementation of new software or other changes, so that types of call are necessary to reflect the true nature of the workload.

Urgency of calls

All calls must be classed according to importance. Targets such as response time or resolution time should also be dependent on the classification. This is necessary so that the priorities are understood and resources of the support areas are allocated so that they match the customer's business needs. Proposals for classification of calls should be included in the discussion and agreed with the targets. Similarly escalation procedures can usefully be included, as an extension of the prioritization of calls.

Implementation of SLAs

Laying foundations

If it is possible to do so, monitoring and reporting of actual service levels should be started before implementing SLAs (Lacity and Hirschheim, 1993). This step has been common to most successful implementations with which the anthor has been involved, although the agreements have covered a very wide range of services and organizations. Reporting is discussed below.

Agreeing targets

The actual values of targets in SLAs are almost inevitably a compromise between the wishes of the service supplier and the customer. Service suppliers naturally feel some caution about committing to targets that they may not be able to meet every time. The customer is equally cautious about agreeing to service levels that may be inadequate for support of the business.

It is not unknown for the customer to demand service levels that are not achievable within the restrictions that arise from hardware, software or third party suppliers. The staff involved may make the unrealistic demands on the assumption that this is a suitable way of bargaining, i.e. ask for twice as much as you need, on the assumption that you will get half what you ask for.

Piloting SLAs

Experience has shown that a pilot SLA can take up to six months to design, implement and agree achievable targets. It is not an easy task and requires commitment. SLAs, piloted for only a short time, can be a useful introduction to 'what SLAs are all about'.

The pilot period also presents an opportunity to fine tune the service support functions, processes and tools. It also provides a period where the benefits of SLAs can be illustrated and mutual trust developed. In order to achieve a successful pilot the time scales of the pilot must be chosen carefully. Too short a time and too little will be achieved. Too long and the pilot will be seen as the 'real thing'.

SLAs in context

An SLA cannot and must not exist in isolation. It should not only be the heart of service management, and more particularly service-level management, but be part of a group of documents which cascade objectives, targets and goals through the whole of the support team. These can take the form of internal SLAs, or of key accountabilities at team or even individual level.

SLAs need to from part of both day-to-day activities and longer-term planning. This will require at least some changes to functions, processes and tools; in reality SLAs implemented without changes in the service support area are extremely unlikely to be successful.

A number of functions have been identified as being necessary. In a very large organization these functions may be small departments; for smaller organizations one person may perform one or more of the functions. It is also common for the functions to be split over several departments. The functions described are not intended to represent ideal departmental structures.

Liaison/service coordination

Customers prefer to deal with people, and not impersonal organizations. Providing continuity of contact over a period of time is an asset for service delivery and service-level agreements. Initial tailoring of SLAs, negotiation of targets and formal authorization is much easier if there is already mutual trust arising from this continuity of contact.

This is also a planning function that is aware of projected changes to customers' business activities. For example, extensive advertising of an existing product can be expected to result in rapid growth in workloads handled by the production processing service and without advance warning this can take the service supplier by surprise.

Change management

The change management function assesses each change for risk to service, then ensures that the risks are minimized and acceptable. This applies irrespective of whether the change is a direct result of a service problem impacting the service (i.e. a problem fix) or the result of a change in a customer's business activities. In practice the management of low risk changes such as a terminal move requires minimal effort, and only major changes are reviewed by specialists.

Incident/problem management

However carefully the service is coordinated and changes managed, there are inevitably some problems. Periods of rapid business and technological change are also periods when service levels are most at risk. Problem management is therefore essential.

Help desk

The help desk is highly visible to the customer and is important in establishing the image of the IT supplier (see Figure 14.3). The help desk should also have a direct influence on service levels; problems solved at the help desk are solved with the minimum of delay, and therefore the minimum of disruption to the service.

Measuring and reporting service levels

Service management is based on the premise that:

- Service can only be managed if it is being measured (Rands and Cumberbatch, 1993).
- Service levels become SLAs when the service levels are targeted, reported, discussed and authorized.
- Service management becomes service-level management when missed targets prompt special action.

Service-level reports therefore provide the following benefits:

- improving service levels by taking informed management decisions;
- service information, when used as a management tool, allows direction of scarce and expensive resources into activities which are of greatest benefit to the customer;
- quantifying service-level achievements means that individual incidents are put into the context of service trends;
- an objective measure and record of the service provided to support the customer's business;
- a focus for any service supplier–customer discussions.

The intention of the service supplier is obviously to 'get it right first time'. However, there are inevitably some problems and less than perfect service can be the result. Under these circumstances it is necessary to identify weaknesses and stop weaknesses becoming poor service levels. A weakness in the service provided can be identified by examining service reports. These could, for example, show an underlying weakness affecting all or some customers. Alternatively, trend information can show a problem is periodic, for example, associated with end of month processing. An important part of improving service is knowing what matters, why it matters and how much it matters. Formally agreed service targets are ideal for this. Targeting service means that critical service components will be distinguished from the non-critical.

Managing the customer interface

The reports issued to the customers (or customer representative) need to reflect the interests of the customer, not the interests of the service supplier. For example service at business function/application level is normally a suitable basis for customer reports. The reports will be most effective if used as part of a regular service supplier–customer liaison process. The frequency of report production should be linked to a regular service review, forming part of the liaison process.

Internal service provider management

The service delivered to the customer is the composite of the service provided by each of several different internal service supplier areas:

Impact on overall service level

In order to ensure that the overall customer service is satisfactory it is important to be aware of what individual contributions to service are needed, as well as what service is actually provided. Comparison of actual service levels to internal targets is of benefit even if the internal targets are less formal than the external/customer service targets. By using the service information the cause or causes of any significant service loss or deficiency can then be tracked and identified. This process relies on regular reporting of normal service levels to assist the identification of abnormal service levels. The agreement of internal service targets can improve motivation by providing clearly defined goals. However, there is always the possibility that the monitoring and reporting of actual levels of service components will be seen as Big Brother monitoring of individuals.

Improvements in efficiency of service delivery

Service reports can also be used to manage improvements in the efficiency of support activities (e.g. the number of people needed to support a gigabyte of storage, or for production of printed output etc.). The benefits of service-level reports as a management tool are not restricted to service components directly impacting or interfacing with the customer. They can be used for a much wider range of activities. Examples include improvements in ancillary service, such as turnround times for typing pools.

Service costs

In general the attention given to service reports, and therefore their effectiveness, will be improved if service costs are reported and discussed at the same time as service levels, even if there is no direct link between actual service levels and the charges levied.

This applies to the management of the supplier–customer interface in particular. For example, it can be used to present the customer with service options. This leaves some of the control for decisions with the customer. It can also make costs more acceptable to the customer, who of course ultimately pays.

Size of reports

Experience has shown that the impact of sending a large volume of reports to an individual or single group can actually detract attention from the significant information. The reports can easily reach a volume at which the recipient is daunted by the prospect of reading them. The result can be that none of the reports gets read.

Similarly reports should only be issued if they fulfil a specific need and have a clearly defined objective. Each report should be tailored to individual (or group) needs. By implication the same set of reports should not be issued to everyone.

Selective or exception reporting is generally a bigger administrative overhead, but is normally worth the additional effort. Regular checks on the currency of the circulation lists, and relevance of the report contents to the audience are strongly advised.

Visibility of the service reports

The effectiveness of a service-level agreement is increased if the targets (and actuals) have high visibility within the IT organization, and perhaps within the customer's organization.

It is often productive to select some reports for production as posters, at least A3 in size. These can be displayed in and around the help desks and in management offices. Updating and adding new reports keeps up interest in service. It is also effective if posters are occasionally produced to mark a special event. Surveys of customers' attitude to the help desk and the support areas are useful for this. Alternatively, major changes to workloads due to the implementation of a new system or automation of a process can be marked. Posters can be used to disseminate information to a wide audience, without the need for large numbers of copies or circulation so slow that information is out of date when received.

Format of reports

Information for most service reports is presented by analysis/reanalysis of the same basic data. Reports are primarily intended to represent the impact of the following factors:

- time;
- service provider/components;
- service customer/business grouping.

Geography may be important when applications are extensively networked or distributed, and the customers are relatively autonomous business functions. However, this is normally a subset of the second and third items.

Lists/tables versus graphs

Conventional wisdom is that graphs are better than lists or tables for representing information. Under most circumstances this applies to service supplier information, particularly because graphs can show information (e.g. how two factors interrelate) in an easily assimilated form. This is ideal for the busy manager in the service provider areas.

The choice of format of the reports should be influenced by the need to use the simplest and therefore most effective method of displaying of data, but the preferences of the target audience need to be considered. Most audiences prefer a mixture of graphs and text; occasionally audiences have a strong preference for all information to be presented as table or lists, because they are used to receiving their business information in this format and have learned to assimilate it rapidly. Some customers associate pictorial reports with unnecessary expense, and may not be aware of the readily available, and relatively cheap, facilities for production of graphs. Under these circumstances it may be advisable to increase the proportion of graphs gradually, as the graphs become acceptable to the customer.

Types of graphs

Despite caution about the need to be aware of the preferences of the recipients, graphs are normally the most suitable format for service supplier reports. However, there is a difference in the acceptability of different styles of graphs. Simple bar charts are universally popular, being simple to understand. This is followed closely by simple line graphs and pie charts. The next level of acceptability is a group of charts that combine bars and lines, as long as a strict limit is put on the number of variables displayed. Too many variables usually make the chart too complex. Stacked bars, surface charts and tower charts, although they have an interesting appearance, are normally considered too difficult and therefore time wasting to read. Finally, the least acceptable charts are polar or vector charts, for all but very specialist audiences. Experience has also shown that normally the 'entertainment' value in developing the graphs is inversely proportional to the acceptability of the product to the target audience.

Colour versus monochrome

Colour can be used to distinguish separate items of information very effectively. However, an important, but easily forgotten issue is that reports are often photocopied either by the reporter or by the recipient. Normally the photocopier available is monochrome, and valuable detail may be lost in the process. This effectively restricts the level of complexity that any one graph can have before it becomes difficult to understand. If colour is used, the graphs should be developed so that when photocopied they still present the reader with easily assimilated information, albeit perhaps less attractive. The producer of the reports should also bear in mind that photocopiers are not all sensitive to the same colours, and a coloured chart that is acceptable when copied on one type of machine, may not be when copied on another type. The frequency of colour blindness (approximately 10% of males, 1% of females) should also be considered before developing complicated graphs that rely on colour differences for legibility and impact.

Networked/online reports

Many of the restrictions on the use of coloured charts arise when they are made available as hard copies. However, experience in providing service reports online has been disappointing. Not only has some reluctance to use online facilities been encountered, even when online reports are supported by the target audience, the hard copy version has always been required as well. A common comment by busy managers is that they need hard copy versions to read on the train going home from work. Graphics are also network intensive and can be a significant load on the network if widely accessed.

Supplementary text

Text, normally giving details of why something went wrong and what was done about it, has been found to be an inevitable requirement, whatever the format and level of detail of the rest of the reports. The manpower needed to provide even a small amount of supplementary text can easily become as great as the remainder of the reports. *Ad hoc* text reporting is also relatively error prone, due to the human element of its production. This will increase the effort spent on quality assurance. The text, far more than the statistics, can provoke contention and discussion, particularly if the text is directed at identifying what went wrong, as this is so easily translated into 'who made a mistake?'

Targets are likely to vary with time, so they are also a variable. Including both a target and actual in a graph means that only one service can be reported in each graph, before the information starts to become confusing to read. A simple but effective method of representing targets and actual on a chart is to report the ratio of the actual: target. This is illustrated in Figure 14.4. Experience has also shown that the ratio is most effective if always calculated so that 'more is better', i.e. a ratio of over 1.0 is better than target, a ratio of 1.0 is on target, a ratio of less than 1.0 is a missed target.

This is normally achieved by dividing actual by target, as in availability and applies to Figure 14.4. However, for some service elements 'more is better' is achieved by the ratio of target divided by actual, i.e. the reverse of the availability ratio. An example of needing to reverse the ratio is the time a help desk takes to answer calls, shown in Figure 14.5. In this example a value of greater than target is clearly a worse service.

The alternative is to use the same ratio for all values. However, experience has shown that this is normally less acceptable to the reader than the simpler logic of

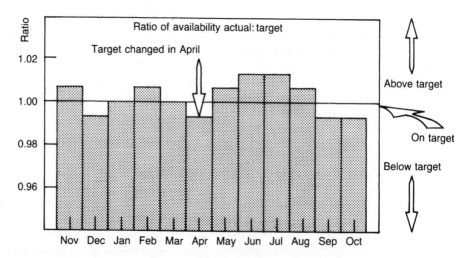

Figure 14.4 Use of a ratio of two variables to simplify a bar chart.

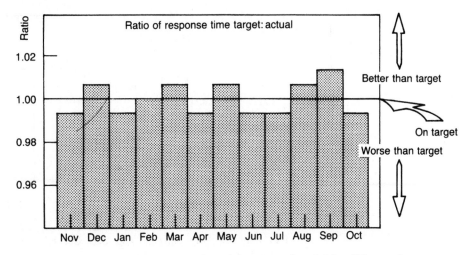

Figure 14.5 Use of a ratio target: actual, so that greater than 1.0 is still better than target.

'bigger is better'. This is because the reader has to slow down and consider each report to establish the merits of a ratio of over 1.0 or under 1.0.

Time series data/*Y*-axis position

An extremely common service report shows changes over time. Time series or trend information is valuable for putting recent events into the context of a trend. This readily identifies whether a recent result is normal or abnormal. With time series data it is possible to identify periodic fluctuations or continuous trends. Whatever the objective in providing time series information experience has shown that the reader usually wishes to know the actual value of the most recent result. A convenient method of assisting this is to put the *Y* (vertical) axis numbering on the right of the report, as in Figure 14.6, rather than on the left, which is more conventional (as in Figure 14.4). Many graphics packages support this.

Accuracy versus precision

Much service-level information, such as workloads, is machine measured and under most circumstances can be assumed to be accurate. Conversely, it is relatively difficult to ensure accuracy of any information, where measurements are partly or completely manual. Experience has also shown that data are often unintentionally represented to unrealistic levels of precision. It can be relatively difficult to assess the actual precision that is justified by the accuracy of the measurement process. Admitting data are not accurate to better than +/−1%, by use of appropriate precision in reports, is often received as a statement that the data are 'wrong'. Conversely, reporting values to high levels of precision, such as availability given to two decimal places, is interpreted as meaning that the data are highly accurate, and therefore believed to be better. This

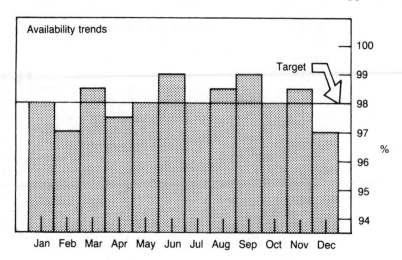

Figure 14.6 Sample service level report, illustrating use of values on the right hand *Y*-axis.

practice can lead to differences in service actual being incorrectly attributed to a trend in service levels, when the difference is simply the cumulative effects of many small random errors. For example, availability, reported to two decimal places, is often derived from incident start and end times that are each logged rounded to the nearest five minutes. It is also possible for the start of down time to be unknown and therefore based on a guess or instead using the time the problem was reported. Unjustified precision will not normally be visible to the reader when graphs are used for reports.

Conclusions

SLAs, which have moved in and out, and now back into popularity as a service management tool in the IT industry, can have considerable benefits to both the supplier and customer, including in situations of outsourcing (see Chapter 16). Many SLA programmes have failed due to lack of understanding about why the agreements were being implemented, lack of commitment and resistance to any changes, particularly where being set targets was seen as a threat to individuals. The greatest benefits have been seen where the SLA was used to catalyse changes to attitude, procedures and the organization, as well as the customer–supplier interface. Willcocks and Fitzgerald (1994) report several cases with these outcomes. SLAs have been applied successfully to a wide range of processes, including software support, desktop services and help desks. A key component of a SLA programme is the production and active use of service level reports. The most successful reports are those that compare actuals to targets. The least successful reports are those that are so voluminous that important issues are lost in a wealth of irrelevant detail. Managing the service without measuring and reporting actual service levels can be likened to driving a car with your eyes shut. It can be done but is not recommended. Managing the service by looking only at actual service levels and not targets can be likened to driving a car with your eyes open, but without any idea of the destination, or how much time you have for the journey.

References

Lacity, M. and Hirschheim, R. (1993) *Information Systems Outsourcing: Myths, Metaphors and Realities*, John Wiley, Chichester.

Malitoris, J. (1990) IT Measurement: delivering the goods, Paper at *The Technology And People Conference*, EI Unit and Baddeley Associates, London, 15 June.

Rands, T. and Cumberbatch, D. (1993) *Service Quality as a measure of IT Effectiveness*, Oxford Institute of information management Working paper, RDP93/2, Templeton College, Oxford.

Willcocks, L. and Fitzgerald, G. (1994) *A Business Guide To Outsourcing IT*, Business Intelligence, London.

Willcocks, L., Lacity, M. and Fitzgerald, G. (1995) IT outsourcing in Europe and the USA: assessment issues, in *Proceedings of the Third European Conference in Information Systems*, Athens, 1–3 June.

15

The role of benchmarking in demonstrating IS performance

Mary C. Lacity and Rudy Hirschheim

Introduction

Two of the greatest challenges that information systems (IS) managers face are to deliver cost effective IS products and services, and to convince senior executives that the IS function is cost effective (Rockhart, 1982; Moad, 1994). The first challenge is rational, and the second challenge is political. One increasingly fashionable tactic for addressing both these challenges is benchmarking, i.e. measuring internal IS performance against other companies' IS performance (Ambrosio, 1992; Betts, 1992; Carlson and McNurlin, 1992; Cusak, 1990; Davis, 1992; Eckerson, 1991a and 1991b; Linsenmeyer, 1991; Molloy, 1990; Prairie, 1993). From a rational perspective, IS managers can use benchmarks to identify improvements to performance. From a political perspective, IS managers can present benchmarks to senior management as 'objective' evidence that IS is cost effective. In particular, the political use of benchmarks seems to be increasing: 'Threatened by outsourcing and admonished by senior executives to reduce costs and improve quality, many managers are using

Investing in Information Systems: Evaluation and Management. Edited by
Leslie Willcocks. Published in 1996 by Chapman & Hall. ISBN 0 412 72670 X.

benchmarking as a tool to illustrate their strengths and diminish their weaknesses' (Eckerson, 1991, p. 27).

The question remains, however, whether benchmarking is an effective strategy for selling IS to senior management. Do senior managers view benchmarking as appropriate evidence of IS effectiveness? Based on in-depth case studies with 19 US companies the answer depends on the source, type, purpose, and quality of the benchmarks.

The chapter proceeds as follows. The next section describes the case sites and research methodology. We then describe the four sources of benchmarks – informal peer comparisons, informal outsourcing queries, formal outsourcing evaluations, and benchmarking services. The four types of benchmarks are then described – data centre operations, telecommunications and networks, application development and support, and IS effectiveness/customer satisfaction. The purpose and quality of benchmarks and how they affect senior management's perceptions of IS are then discussed. We conclude with a prescription for buying benchmarks that sell.

Research method

The research project commenced in 1991 as an in-depth study on outsourcing evaluations. In the first phase of the project, 37 senior executives, IS managers, and IS staff from 14 companies were interviewed about the process and consequences of their outsourcing decisions. One lesson learned from the first phase is that large companies should have reduced their own costs because economies of scale are achieved with shops as small as 150 MIPs. Why, then, did these companies select outsourcing? Among the myriad of political and rational reasons, IS managers claim they failed to demonstrate IS effectiveness to senior management. After the first phase of the study (see Lacity and Hirschheim, 1993), 25 additional participants were interviewed in 1993 – one site was revisited and five new case studies were conducted – to specifically address the issue of senior management's perceptions of IS. In addition, the president and vice-president of an international benchmarking service were interviewed because many of the participating firms had either considered use or actually used this firm.

The duration of the interviews spanned from thirty minutes to five hours with an average interview lasting one and a half hours. All interviews were conducted in person at the company site. Regardless of the length, interviews followed the same protocol which proceeded from an unstructured to a structured format. Senior executives were merely asked to characterize their perceptions of IS while IS managers were asked to characterize their perceptions of how their senior executives viewed IS. They were then asked how these perceptions were formulated. The unstructured format allowed the participants free rein to convey their interpretations. After participants had completed their stories, they were asked to provide specific evidence to support their viewpoint. The evidence consisted of anecdotes as well as documentation such as benchmarking reports, IS budgets, and outsourcing bids. Participants were also asked specific questions about their company and IS department. In connection with their companies, participants described the organizational structure, the major products and services produced, competition in their industry, financial situation, corporate goals, business successes and failures. In connection with IS, participants described the number of MIPs, headcount, budget, chargeback system, user satisfaction, challenges, goals and reputation.

The semi-structured interviews were tape recorded and transcribed into a 590 single-spaced document. The transcribed text was analysed using interpretive analysis, which borrows from the hermeneutic tradition. Intentional analysis prescribes four steps for helping researchers make sense of text data (Sanders, 1982). Thus our research methodology is qualitative and interpretive. The 19 companies represent a wide variety of industries. Using *Fortune* magazine's taxonomy, participants are employed in the following industries: aerospace, chemicals, commercial bank, diversified services, food products, mining, petroleum refining, retail, transport and utility. Of the 19 companies 15 are characterized as large (as designated by their existence in the *Fortune* 500), while four of the companies are characterized as small. The 19 companies are geographically dispersed among California (one), Colorado (two), Louisiana (one), Missouri (two), New York (one), Oklahoma (one), Pennsylvania (one), Texas (nine), and Washington DC (one). Taken as a whole, the companies represent a variety of industries, venues and sizes.

Benchmarking sources

The participants in the study consulted a variety of sources to compare their performance with external companies. Companies benchmark in four ways: (1) IS managers informally compare cost and service data from a network of peers, typically in the same city or same industry; (2) IS managers informally compare current costs to an outsourcer's costs; (3) IS managers – but more typically senior executives – initiate formal outsourcing evaluations to compare internal costs with a vendor costs; (4) IS managers hire benchmarking services to compare their IS departments against a database of previous clients. These four methods are further explained below.

Informal peer comparisons

IS managers in 18 of the 19 companies use a network of peers to informally compare IS performance. IS managers place great validity on informal peer comparisons because they know and trust their peers. A corporate manager of technology development for a petroleum company adds that peer comparison provides information on why costs may differ: 'So-and-so has some unearned residual that was rolled into a lease and that's why their technology costs are high.' He believes that formal benchmarking services do not explain differences in the data because the benchmarks are created against a blind reference group.

An IS manager of a utility company uses informal peer comparisons because he feels that the US $50 000 cost of benchmarking services is too high. Instead, he takes 'a poor man's approach' to benchmarking by exchanging cost information with IS peers from other companies that operate in the area. Whether the issue is trust or cost, most IS managers rely on peers to evaluate IS performance. Typically, IS managers continually monitor peers to provide constant feedback on IS effectiveness.

Informal outsourcing queries

IS managers from nine of the companies periodically (on average once a year) call outsourcing vendors to test the market. Unfortunately, most outsourcing vendors do not seriously attend to such calls. For example, a new IS manager at a food company tried to understand the IS department's costs by soliciting informal outsourcing bids. As his data centre manager explained:

> Early on, he [the new IS manager] came over and called some outsourcers. He said, 'We have X amount of computer, X amount of disk, my budget is X, can you do it cheaper?' He had no idea what he was doing, but he made some early calls. The vendors get a lot of these calls and it's people trying to justify their existence. They say, 'We're not interested.' They hang up.

According to participants, senior executives tend to discount informal outsourcing queries. Instead, they place more faith in formal outsourcing evaluations.

Outsourcing evaluations

Of the 19 companies 16 conducted formal outsourcing evaluations to assess/improve IS cost-effectiveness. Outsourcing evaluations, by far the most rigorous way to benchmark, entail creating a request for proposal (RFP), soliciting vendor bids and comparing bids against internal costs. Senior executives tend to view this method as the most reliable because it compares apples to apples and requires bidders to commit to their costs. Outsourcing evaluations, however, are extremely disruptive to the organization and are typically only conducted once or twice per decade. Outsourcing evaluations, which cover a myriad of political implications, are treated elsewhere (Lacity and Hirschheim, 1993; see also Chapter 16).

Benchmarking services

IS managers from seven of the companies hire benchmarking services every year because they provide more formal comparisons than peer review or informal outsourcing queries. Benchmarking services collect data, normalize them, and create reports which plot the cilent's performance against a selected reference group extracted from the service's client database. Although the reports do not identify the companies in the reference group, participants theorize that senior executives view benchmarking services as a more objective way to assess IS performance than informal comparisons.

Of the four sources of benchmarks, this chapter focuses on benchmarking services for four reasons. First, benchmarking services provide a wealth of comparative data in which to compare performance – some benchmarking services have as many as 400 companies in their client database which provides ample opportunities for comparisons. Second, external benchmarking firms are perceived as more rigorous than informal peer evaluations or informal outsourcing inquires. Third, external benchmarking services are perceived as less disruptive than formal outsourcing

Table 15.1 Case studies classified by type of benchmark services

Company pseudonym	Type of benchmark(s)
Diverse	Data centre operations
	Applications development and support
Food	Data centre operations
	Network and telecommunications
Petro1	Data centre operations
Petro2	Data centre operations
Retail1	Data centre operations
	Customer satisfaction/IS effectiveness
Retail2	Data centre operations
Utility	Customer satisfaction/IS effectiveness

evaluations. Fourth, as the benchmarking industry continues to grow, practitioners will need to understand how to differentiate among services to avoid jumping from service to service (as some case participants experienced).

The chapter proceeds with an examination of benchmarking services. In order to facilitate the discussion, the seven companies that use benchmarking services are assigned pseudonyms (see Table 15.1). It is important to note that these seven participants repeat benchmarks annually or biannually. In addition, Food, Petro2 and Retail1 have changed their benchmarking service, i.e. selected another firm because they were dissatisfied with their previous service.

Benchmarking types

According to Walter Carlson, a marketing consultant, benchmarking services can be categorized into five areas: information technology resources, IS efficiency, IS effectiveness, business efficiency and business effectiveness (Carlson and McNurlin, 1992). Within each category, benchmarking services range from broadly focused benchmarks on the total IS organization to narrowly defined processes such as a help desk.

In this study, participants from the seven companies that employ benchmarking services categorize their benchmarks primarily by IS function: data centre operations, networks and telecommunications, and applications development and support. In addition to these functional benchmarks, two participants purchase user-oriented benchmarks for IS effectiveness/customer satisfaction (see Table 15.1). All participants feel their benchmarks includes both quality and efficiency measures, although benchmarking services seem to favour one aspect over the other. Table 15.2 contains a sample of measures the benchmarking firms use in developing the participants' benchmarks.

Data centre operations

Participants from the six companies that use benchmarking services to assess effectiveness feel that data centre benchmarks are the most mature. Many benchmarking services provide comparisons with hundreds of clients on cost and service measures

Table 15.2 Benchmarks for various IS functions

Customer satisfaction/IS effectiveness	Data cent operations	Networks/ telecommunications	Applications development and support
Headcount	Allocated DASD storage	Availability	Analyst/programmer turnover rates
IS costs as a percentage of revenue	Availability	Average connect time	Average age of systems
IS leadership style	Batch turnaround time	Average bytes per call	Average development cycle time
IS involvement in strategic planning	Costs per MIP	Cost per kilobytes per mile	Average size of applications
Management to worker ratio	Hardware costs per MIP	Cost per person	CASE tool productivity
Organizational structure	Management to worker ratios	Cost per device	Cost productivity based on function points
Perceived system quality	Overall utilization	Cost per call	Defect per 1000 function points
Perceived system functionality	Personnel costs per MIP	Cost per minute	Length of the backlog
Perceived quality of IS staff	Prime shift utilization	Management to worker ratios	Management to analyst ratios
Perceived analyst knowledge of user needs	Response time	Number of failures	Number of programming languages supported
Perceived IS management knowledge of user needs	Software costs per MIP	Utilization/capacity ratios	Number of customer complaints
Perceived information content	Total data centre costs		Percentage of new development versus enhancements
Perceived contribution of IS to user goals			Percentage of time spent in each SDLC phase
Policy flexibility			Percentage of custom-made software versus packaged
Standards enforcement			Personal productivity based on function points
Total IS costs			Total estimated number of function points

related to data centre hardware, software, and staff. Measures are either geared towards service excellence or cost efficiency, depending on the benchmarking service.

Network and telecommunications

Although many participants have an interest in network and telecommunication benchmarks, they feel that the benchmarking market for telecommunications is immature. IS managers from Food were the only participants to hire a benchmarking service to assess this area. Food participants were generally pleased that the benchmarking service identified enough cost-saving tactics to cover the benchmark fee and noted that the market was maturing; several reputable benchmarking services have a growing database of network clients to compare cost and service of voice and data communications over wide and local area networks.

Applications development and support

Only one participant – Diverse – hires a benchmarking service to assess applications development and support effectiveness. The reticence to benchmark this area may be that of all benchmarking services, applications is the most difficult area in which to find a comparable base. Many benchmarking services use function points, which participants consider controversial at best. Dennis Farley, president of the Development Center, complains that the problem with application benchmarks is: 'Getting bogged down in arcane statistics, such as measuring "function points delivered", may be a mistake anyway because it fails the "so what test" of business managers'. (Betts, 1992, p. 20)

IS effectiveness/customer satisfaction

Two companies – Retail1 and Utility – employ a broad-based IS effectiveness/customer satisfaction survey. Although the benchmarking services claim to measure IS effectiveness on business variables such as rate of return on equity, the majority of the measures are based on users' perceptions of IS effectiveness. As an applications manager for Retail1 notes, 'Perceptions are ninety percent of the game when it comes to IS.' Participants at Retail1 believe the survey was valuable in understanding users' perceptions of IS. In some departments, IS thought they were performing well but users rated them poor. In other departments, IS thought they were performing poorly, but users rated them good.

Regardless of the type of benchmark used by participants, their main concern was whether senior executives attend to the results.

The effectiveness of benchmarking services in shaping senior management's perceptions

Do benchmarks affect senior management's perceptions of the IS function? The answer depends on the purpose and the quality of the benchmarks. IS managers may benchmark for the purpose of obtaining a good report card or to identify improvements. When benchmarks are used for soliciting a good report card, senior executives often fail to be impressed by the results because they are not viewed as objective. Instead, senior executives seem most impressed when the benchmarks are coupled with concrete, feasible recommendations for improvement. IS managers who use benchmarks for improvements, however, contend that successful benchmarking projects only temporarily appease senior management. Once the benchmarking project is complete, little glory remains. Instead, IS managers return to the firing line to face the next challenges, such as client–server technology, downsizing or layoffs.

The quality of the benchmarks greatly affects whether senior executives view them favourably. Senior executives complain that benchmarks do not measure what is important to them and that the benchmarks are not valid for many reasons, including the belief that the reference group competition is too weak.

The purpose and quality of the benchmarks – and how they relate to senior managers' perceptions – are further discussed below.

The purpose of benchmarks

If you want a bunch of graphs that say you are pretty good, you can buy those. If you want improvement ideas, you can buy those. You can buy a

> combination. So many people don't know what they want to buy. I think
> benchmarking hurts because it gives a false sense of security, or a false sense
> of insecurity. (Data centre manager at Food)

According to participants, IS managers benchmark for one of two reasons: to solicit a
good report card or identify improvements.

Benchmarking for a report card

Although benchmarking for a report card appears politically motivated, participants
feel this is a valid reason to benchmark. As the president of a benchmarking service
indicates, 'The climate is so defensive that a lot of people are willing to pay money
to benchmarking companies only to get an alibi that they are doing at least as good
a job as somebody else.' This is not to suggest that IS managers are poor managers.
They may be convinced that their IS department is cost-effective based on their years
of experience, network of peers with other IS managers, trade reports and the like.
The problem is trying to convince senior management. Some IS managers use benchmarks to sway senior management's perceptions because they believe 'objective'
measures are more effective than informal anecdotes. Unfortunately, many participants report that senior executives do not view the benchmarks as objective because
IS managers typically hire the benchmarking service. As several participants noted,
almost anyone can find a consultant to corroborate IS managers' effectiveness or
efficiency claims.

The best way to convince senior executives that benchmarks are objective is to
involve them in the selection of the benchmarking service. At Food, for example, the
IS manager hired a benchmarking service without asking for senior management's
input. When the benchmarks indicated that IS costs were half of the average reference
group, a subsidiary president claimed that IS costs were still too high. He hired his own
consultant to assess IS costs. The food company's data centre manager explains the
process as follows:

> The president hired [a consulting firm] and said, 'Hey guys, I'm in a pissing
> contest with the VP of IS, would you go and tell the guy I can get it cheaper
> outside?' Well they poked and prodded and examined and I couldn't talk to
> them because of the politics. So they got through and told the president, 'You
> guys are getting a good deal. You can't get it cheaper on the outside.' So this
> was an unbiased consultant. Well actually he was biased because the guy that
> was paying wanted to outsource.'

The president was finally convinced by his own consultant's report and ceased to
harass the IS manager. The IS manager still feels, however, that benchmarks – even
benchmarks he solicits – truly help senior management to evaluate IS. Although
benchmarks alone are not enough to sway senior management opinion, they help
mount a case for IS: 'I've learned a lot about marketing [to senior management]. I've
learned to position us. I've used various benchmarking services and those tidbits
effectively.'

Thus, one way to convince senior executives of the validity of the benchmarking
results is to involve them in the selection of a benchmarking firm. Even without senior
executive input, participants feel that benchmarks provide at least some external

validation of the IS function. Even if benchmarks alone can not convince management, they help mount a case.

Benchmarking for improvement

While many participants claim benchmarks identify improvements, others debate the usefulness of mimicry. An applications manager at Retail1 notes that benchmarks merely describe the characteristics of good IS departments. This does not imply that cost or service improvements will follow if an IS manager imitates these characteristics:

> [The benchmarking service] doesn't recommend mimicry. They are just saying, if they model high performers, that is what they look like. It's going to be different [for each company].

Participants' disagreements reflect sentiments debated by benchmarking experts. Dissenters argue:

> How can benchmarks yield a competitive advantage if you are only learning what your competitor already knows? Aren't we just bringing companies up to the same level of mediocrity? (Linsenmeyer, 1991, p. 35)

> A practice that works for one company may harm another. (Richard Swanborg of Ernst & Young in Sullivan-Trainor, 1993, p. 72)

In contrast proponents argue:

> If all the companies in the US pursued best practices function by function, we might have some major gains. (Bob Camp of Xerox, in Linsenmeyer, 1991, p. 35)

> Welcome to the world of quality benchmarking in which stealing great ideas is an honorable profession. (Betts, 1992, p. 1)

> We steal shamelessly from anyone who has an idea that we perceive to be world class. (John Rudasill in Betts, 1992, p. 20)

Thus, many participants – as well as benchmarking experts – disagree whether benchmarks can be used to identify and adopt the best practices. The best argument in favour of benchmarking for improvements is from case participants who actually used the benchmarking service to identify and improve performance:

- An IS manager from Food used his benchmarks to cut data centre costs by 45% over a three-year period.
- An IS manager from Petrol used his benchmarks to consolidate data centres and reduce headcount from 143 people to 67 people in one year.
- An IS manager from Retail2 used his benchmarks to reduce data centre headcount by 37% over a three-year period.

How did the benchmarking services accomplish these improvements? They first determined the participant's performance *vis-à-vis* a reference group. Then, the benchmarking services identified areas of strengths and weakness and recommend improvements. For example, one benchmarking service noted that Retail2 had more console operators for a given size shop than the reference group. The benchmarking service consultant believed the additional headcount was attributable to a lack of console automation. The benchmarking service then estimated the cost of automation and the associated decrease in headcount. Thus, the participant was given this and other specific recommendations for improvement.

In addition to identifying specific improvements, a benchmarking service may encourage clients to swap success stories. The president of a benchmarking service explains:

> What we encourage as a second step is for clients to talk to each other and we will do the matchmaking, saying, 'You need to talk to this guy, talk to this company about this aspect of what you are doing here because they have mastered that. They have taken that to perfection.'

Thus, many participants believe that benchmarks can be used to identify and adopt the best practices.

The quality of benchmarks

Some senior executives view benchmark results with scepticism because the benchmarks do not measure what is important to them or because they view the measures as invalid.

Benchmarks may fail to impress senior executives because the benchmarks do not measure what is important to them. Senior managers claim that benchmarks are too technical, fail to indicate whether IS uses the best architecture, or focus on the wrong IS values. An example of each complaint follows.

Benchmarks are too technical

A data centre manager for Food claims his VP of manufacturing was unimpressed by the benchmarks because they focused on technical issues:

> My new boss was disappointed because what the [benchmarking service] did, given an MVS data centre, your costs are good. He doesn't care. He wants to know given you have a consumer products business of two billion dollars, how are your costs? He was really disappointed with the benchmark because it was a narrow technical benchmark. He wants something that monitors for a company of your size in this business – is your inventory variance about right? Things like that.

Benchmarks do not indicate whether IS has adopted the right architecture

In another case, an IS manager at Retail2 used a benchmarking service to assess the cost efficiency for his data centre. To his surprise, his data centre scored much lower than anticipated, probably because the benchmarking service compared his IS shop to a best of breed. The benchmarking service identified specific remedies to reduce costs. After three years of working closely with the benchmarking firm, the IS manager reduced the headcount by 37%. The third year, his IS shop was placed among the best of breed. He proudly presented the benchmarking results to senior management. However, senior management dismissed the results. The IS manager explains:

> After this last report, I walked out of the policy meeting and thought, 'Alright, we've done something real good.' Well after we left, some of the finance guys said, 'Yeah, that's fine and dandy, you look good against MVS shops, but how does that stack up against some other platform? How does that compare to an AS400 shop of the same size?' So they took a lot of self esteem we accumulated on the report and blew it away.

Benchmarks focus on the wrong IS values

The experiences of one IS manager at Food underscores the importance of selecting benchmarks that are important to senior management. The IS manager prided himself on excellent service. He bought extra equipment to reduce response time and purchased redundant systems to protect availability. To demonstrate his effectiveness, he hired a benchmarking service that also values service excellence. Not surprisingly, the benchmarks indicated an above-average service performance. Business unit leaders, however, were unimpressed by the benchmarks because their agenda for IS was cost containment, not service excellence. The IS manager was fired. The new IS manager, who listened to the business unit leaders, reduced costs by eliminating the hardware and software his predecessor installed to protect service. His users responded:

> You cut my bill by a couple of million dollars. My response time is a little more erratic. If you made response time slower, could you save me a couple of million more?

Ironically, the new IS manager eventually hired the same benchmarking service his predecessor used a few years later. He received a terrible report card. The data centre manager explains:

> [Benchmarking Service A] is one hundred percent correct within their value set. So, what happens, they value response times; if a company aligns with their values, the benchmark is good. They look at us as we are not running a big modern CPU; their value set is different. My costs are about half of their average but they felt I was incompetent because response times are only average.

In this instance, the bad report card confirms that the IS manager responded to the senior management's main concern: costs.

Benchmarks may not be viewed as valid

Some senior executives view benchmarks with scepticism because the reference group selection, normalization process, measurement period, data integrity, and report design quality influences the results. By controlling these five variance factors, IS managers can obtain benchmarks that senior executives believe. The general rule seems to be, the stiffer the competition, the more senior executives heed the results.

Reference group selection

The firms with which an IS organization is compared obviously affect the outcome of the benchmark. As the president of a benchmarking service notes:

> I can make you appear as the best ski jumper; it's just a question of who I choose as a comparative base. I can always make you appear as the best ski jumper. If you tell me you know nothing about ski jumping, we just have to find a comparative base where people know even less.

Benchmarking services either compare a current client with the best of breed or with a larger pool from their client database. If IS managers are primarily concerned with a good report card, they will fare better against a larger reference group. Senior executives, however, are more impressed by favourable reports when a best of breed reference group is selected; falling in the fiftieth percentile of a huge, unknown client database is less impressive than scoring in the fiftieth percentile among the best of breed.

An example from one of the cases will highlight the importance of selecting a best of breed reference group. When the previous IS manager at Food received a favourable report from one benchmarking service, he naively assumed that the benchmarks indicated that an outsourcer could not undercut his current costs. The data centre manager explains:

> [The benchmarking service] said, 'You guys are a pretty good data centre. Your costs are pretty good.' So we said, 'Fine.' Well [one of the business unit managers] found an outsourcer who could do it cheaper.

The IS manager questioned how such a discrepancy could exist between his benchmarking results and the outsourcing bid. The data centre manager responded that since they failed to benchmark against best of breed, their benchmarking results merely confirmed that they were adequate compared to the benchmarking service's entire database:

> The [benchmarking service] compares you to data centres of your size. I guarantee you that other data centres of your size are not the outsourcing competition. You need to benchmark against the toughest in town.

In addition to deciding whether to benchmark against a best of breed or a larger pool, IS managers must understand the criteria each benchmarking service uses to select a reference group. The criteria may be based on size of the IS shop, geographic region, or industry. The size of the IS shop is the most common selection criterion. The economies of scale associated with size greatly affect unit costs and efficiency measures. Most experts agree it is unfair to compare a small AS400 shop with an IBM 3090 shop, for example. Some clients prefer comparison to firms in the same geographic region because rents and salaries may be more comparable, although most benchmarking firms will normalize data for geographic differences. Some clients prefer comparison to other companies in the same industry. Airlines, for example, have very different computing environments from petroleum companies. Some benchmarking firms, however, have too few clients in their database from the same industry to make such comparisons. Benchmarking services may compensate by selecting other industries with similar on-line and batch processing requirements, such as using banks as airlines in the same reference group.

To highlight the importance of the reference group selection criteria, consider one IS manager's experience from Petro2. He hired a benchmarking service to assess costs at each of his three data centres. Figure 15.1 contains a report which plots total data centre costs against computing capacity for each data centre (Site A, Site B, Site C). The benchmarking report indicates a clean bill of health – all three data centres have average or below average costs compared to the reference group. The IS manager, however, did not consider the cost of running three separate data centres. If total costs are plotted against total capacity, the client's costs are above average (see Figure 15.2). In this case, a vendor convinced senior management that outsourcing could save money and senior management responded with an outsourcing evaluation. Thus, the benchmarks failed to convince senior management that IS was efficient because the reference group was other small data centres rather than one large data centre. Fortunately, the IS manager hired another benchmarking seivice to help him prepare an internal bid that eventually beat external bids.

Normalization process

Effective benchmarks are normalized to attempt to ensure that IS shops are fairly compared to one another. All normalization algorithms are limited, however, and so many IS managers feel that organizations should repeat benchmarks in subsequent years. Senior executives seem more impressed when IS improves over time rather than relying on a one-time snapshot of IS performance.

Although no normalization process is perfect, IS managers feel that it is important to understand how a benchmarking service normalizes data. Each benchmarking

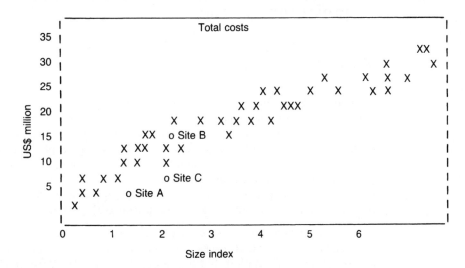

Figure 15.1 A petroleum company's costs for three separate data centres.

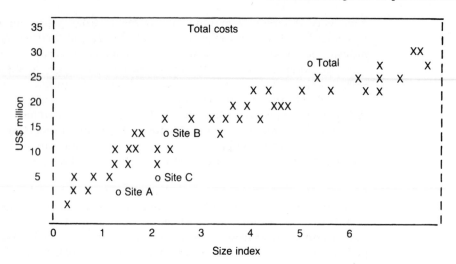

Figure 15.2 A petroleum company's total costs of running three data centres.

service has its own normalization formula, typically based on items such as the cost of floor space or personnel per geographic region. Some benchmarking services share their algorithms with their clients, while others merely give a description of the normalization process.

One IS manager at Petro2 claims that dissatisfaction with the normalization process will prevent him from benchmarking again.

> They normalize for floor space. Someone in New York City versus someone in Oklahoma, I have a much lower cost of doing business. He's just normalized away all my benefits. I think I am doing a good job at managing technology costs – we decided to build the data centre in Oklahoma and not New York. All of these things that we have successfully done. I think he's just averaged me into oblivion.

Measurement period

Benchmarking services either monitor operations for an average period or peak period. If they monitor average periods, the peaks and valleys are smoothed. The benchmarking results will reflect better service levels in terms of response time, availability and turnaround time, but benchmarking results may suggest that the client has excess capacity. Benchmarking services that monitor peak capacity counter that their measures provide a better test of service level measures and resource requirements. A president of a benchmarking service describes why he feels benchmarking data should be gathered during peak periods:

> Customers are interested in what capacity they need on board to handle peaks. What is it that drives the capacity requirements up? It's typically not the average utilization. It's the peaks. For the New York Stock Exchange, they estimate ten times as much load during a rally.

Data integrity

The adage 'garbage in, garbage out' certainly applies to benchmarking. The data gathered for benchmarks are either gathered manually or automatically. Manually collected data include customer satisfaction surveys, headcount, salary, and types of equipment. Automatic data collection is typically limited to software monitors that gather information such as response time, tape mounts and batch turnaround time. Manual data collection, in particular, provides opportunities for skewed data through discriminate selection of survey respondents or by having the IS personnel being evaluated provide the data. Examples of each are discussed below.

With a customer satisfaction benchmark, for example, the internal IS department often selects the pool of users to be surveyed. This pool can obviously be selected in such a way as to overlook notoriously unsatisfied users. After hearing that user confidence was very low, an IS manager at Retaill blamed the user sample. He asked the benchmarking service to recalculate the numbers: 'If we took these four [users] out, what would confidence be?'

One assurance of data integrity is to request senior management or business unit leaders to select survey respondents. An applications manager at Retaill explains how this ensures data integrity:

> Our first [Benchmarking Service A] study was an attempt to demonstrate to management that the DP operations area of the company was effective, as effective as any company out on the market. We came out of that looking pretty good. The problem with [Benchmarking Service A], I can fix the survey with my answers. The [Benchmarking Service B] one I couldn't fix, I had no control over what users said. With [Benchmarking Service A], the people being surveyed are the ones supplying the answers. I can manipulate the answers, I can control the answers through my responses. This survey is unique in that it depends on the users' perspective of IS, which is important.

Another way to prevent invalid data is for the benchmarking service to conduct a data validation seminar. The vice-president of a benchmarking service explains how to correct fallacious data:

> The answer is twofold. One is the people who collect the data are usually at a higher level. And two, there are many checks and balances. Occasionally you do see things that are jaded and then it's found at the correction meeting because people see that and say, 'You don't have three people, you have five people.' And so those things come out.

Report design

Some managers reject benchmarks because the reports look suspicious to them. Participants shared reports that included percentages that summed to over 100%, an average response far from the fiftieth percentile, and a report in which all the data points clustered around zero. These errors are obvious, but one benchmarking service used by Retaill had a subtler problem with its reports: the scales kept changing. When scales are altered from report to report, interpretation of the results becomes difficult. An example will illustrate.

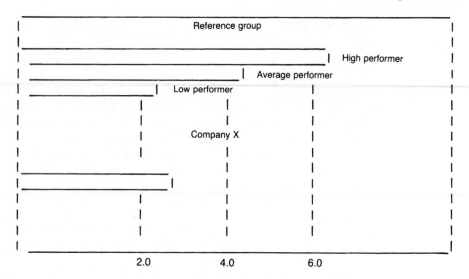

Figure 15.3 Benchmark report with significant variance.

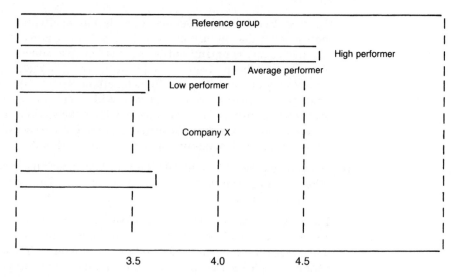

Figure 15.4 Benchmark report with little variance.

Figures 15.3 and 15.4 contain two typical reports that a benchmarking service provides to a client. The reports are based on a survey that rates different aspects of user satisfaction on a seven-item Likert scale, with seven representing the highest level of satisfaction. The client's average response is plotted for each measure as well as the high, average and low performers from the reference group. The client is advised to attend only to measures that fall below the average in the reference group. Thus, if the client meets or exceeds the fiftieth percentile, he or she is given a clean bill of health for that measure. In Figures 15.3 and 15.4, the client appears below average on both measures. The variability in the reference group in Figure 15.4, however, is significantly less than the variability in Figure 15.3. The benchmarking service claims Figure 15.4 indicates an area of weakness even though the variance is very small.

Conclusion: buying benchmarks that sell

IS managers are challenged to demonstrate IS effectiveness to senior management. Because most IS departments are accounted for as an overhead function, IS managers cannot use profitability as evidence of effectiveness. IS managers try to influence management perceptions with softer evience such as successful application projects, user endorsements, and other IS anecdotes. However, senior executives seek more objective proof of IS's effectiveness. As the president of a large food manufacturer explains: 'You can tell me you are good, and you probably are, but I don't have any other data points that I can compare it to. You may or you may not be, I don't know how to judge.'

Many IS managers turn to benchmarking services for some external validation of IS. As identified by participants, senior executives are most impressed by benchmarks that are used for the purpose of improvement and by quality benchmarks against the stiffest competition. Specific guidelines for selecting benchmarks effective in demonstrating IS performance to senior management include:

Benchmark what is important to management

In some organizations, senior management and IS managers possess different views on the primary concern for IS. IS managers, for example, may incorrectly perceive the relative importance of service excellence verses cost containment. Benchmarking results may be discounted or ignored if IS managers hire benchmarking firms to validate performance on measures that are unimportant to senior management.

Have senior management select the benchmarking service

Participants claim that senior managers may not attend to benchmarking results because the benchmarks are not viewed as objective. As Peter Drucker once noted, anyone over the age of 21 can find data to support his or her position. Senior managers think, 'big deal, you hired a guy to prove you are good.' To counteract these claims, IS managers should involve senior managers in the selection of the benchmarking service.

Select the reference group which represents the stiffest competition possible

Senior managers do not seem to care if performance is adequate against the multitudes represented in a client database. Who cares if you are average among the run of the mill? Senior managers are most impressed by benchmarks against the stiffest competition, such as best of breed within an industry.

Select the reference group based on criteria important to management

Benchmarking services can select reference groups based on size, geographic area, industry or other criteria. Participants note that reference group selections should be based on senior management's preferences. For example, senior executives most concerned with salary levels may prefer comparisons with other local companies. Senior managers primarily concerned with direct competitors may wish comparisons with other companies within the same industry. Senior managers most concerned with overall efficiency may prefer comparisons to the best of breed operating similar sized shops.

Gather data during a peak period

As a corollary to the toughest comparison using best of breed, participants note that senior managers are most impressed by measures taken at the busiest time. After all, who cares what response time and availability are at 2.00 a.m.? Measures taken during peak load are viewed as a fairer test of IS effectiveness.

Validate data before benchmark calculations

The adage 'garbage in, garbage out' applies to benchmarking. Participants claim senior managers have more confidence in the validity of the benchmarks if (1) senior level people (those not threatened by the benchmarks) gather the data or at least select survey respondents, (2) the benchmarking service conducts a data validation meeting, and (3) the benchmarking service uses automated data collection software.

Repeat benchmarks

Participants claim that senior executives place more validity in benchmark results if measures are repeated periodically. While senior executives favourably view positive benchmarks, they are more concerned that IS managers improve performance over time. As Xerox's guru of benchmarking, Robert Camp notes: 'The fact is you can't rest on your laurels. You've got to be continuously looking for better ways to do things' (Linsenmeyer, 1991, p. 34).

References

Ambrosio, J. (1992) Management by Comparison. *Computerworld*, **26** (38), 67, 70.

Anon. (1993) New COMPASS: services, *Capacity Management Review*, **21** (1), 9–10.

Betts, M. (1992) Benchmarking helps IS improve competitiveness. *Computerworld*, **26** (48), 1, 20.

Carlson, W. and McNurlin, B. (1992) Do you measure up? *Computerworld*, **26** (49), 95–8.

Cusak, S. (1990) What, exactly, is the value of MIPS? *Computerworld*, **24** (48), 18.

Davis, D. (1992) Does your IS shop measure up?. *Datamation*, **38** (18), 26–32.

Eckerson, W. (1991a) Benchmarking aids IS in tough times. *Network World*, **8** (36), 27, 29.

Eckerson, W. (1991b) Firms measure value of IS/net investment. *Network World*, **8** (14), 23, 24.

Lacity, M. and Hirschheim, R. (1993) *Information Systems Outsourcing: Myths, Metaphors and Realities*, John Wiley, Chichester.

Linsenmeyer, A. (1991) Fad or fundamental: a chat with Bob Camp of Xerox, the man who wrote the book on benchmarking. *FW*, **160** (19), 34–5.

Moad, J. (1994) 1994 information technology outlook: IS rises to the competitiveness challenge. *Datamation*, **40** (1), 16–24.

Molloy, M. (1990) Benchmarkers help users keep IS expenses in line. *Network World*, **7** (39), 31–2.

Prairie, P. (1993) An American Express/IBM consortium benchmarks on information technology. *Planning Review*, **21** (1), 22–7.

Rockhart, J. (1982) The changing role of the information systems executive: a critical success factors perspective. *Sloan Management Review*, **24** (1), 3–13.

Sanders, P. (1982) Phenomenology: a new way of viewing organizational research. *Academy of Management Review*, **7** (3), 353–60.

Stephens, C., Ledbetter, W., Mitra, A. and Ford, F. (1992) Executive or functional manager? The nature of the CIO's job. *MIS Quarterly*, **16** (4), 449–67.

Sullivan-Trainor, M. (1993) Study: users key to system development. *Computerworld*, **27** (17), 72.

16

Sourcing decisions: developing an IT outsourcing strategy

Leslie Willcocks, Guy Fitzgerald and David Feeny

Introduction

In this chapter IT outsourcing means handing over the management of some or all of an organization's IT, systems and related services to a third party. The Yankee Group estimated global revenues for all types of IT outsourcing as US $33 billion in 1992, and projected a rise to over US $49.5 billion by 1996 (Loh and Venkatraman, 1992). Recent research uncovered a range of factors helping to explain the general rise of IT outsourcing across developed economies in the 1990s (Willcocks and Fitzgerald, 1994). Financial reasons figure highly. Thus IT outsourcing has been a response to cost pressures in a recession, an attempt to reduce the cost of future IT capital investment, and/or seen as an opportunity to improve the balance sheet and cash flow (see also Huber, 1993). IT outsourcing has also been undertaken for technical reasons, such as to improve the IT service, give access to more or different expertise and technologies and/or assist moves to distributed systems, downsizing or systems replacement. Organizations have also used IT outsourcing to enable refocusing on the core business and/or on IT/IS strategy rather than service and operations. IT outsourcing has also often been occasioned by wider business and organizational changes, such as merger

Investing in Information Systems: Evaluation and Management. Edited by
Leslie Willcocks. Published in 1996 by Chapman & Hall. ISBN 0 412 72670 X.

or acquisition, business start up, restructuring and/or privatization. The bandwagon effect also cannot be ignored (Lacity and Hirschheim, 1993).

This paper is based on reviewing the evidence from 30 detailed case histories in the United Kingdom, and from a 1993 survey of IT sourcing practice in 162 medium and large European organizations. Here we found some 80% of organizations surveyed had considered outsourcing, while 47% actually did outsource some or all of their IT activities. However, we found 70% of all organizations surveyed did not have a formal IT outsourcing policy in place, while only 43% of organizations that outsourced IT had a formal IT outsourcing policy. In the main the survey found only a few organizations approaching IT outsourcing in a strategic manner, despite the fact that, where practised, IT outsourcing averaged some 24% of total IT expenditure.

The chapter complements Chapter 4 where the focus was on software make/buy decisions. Here we argue for and detail the basis of a decision-making framework and a more strategic approach towards sourcing all forms of IS/IT activity within the organization. Throughout the book the focus has been on assessing performance with IT with a view to enhancing its business performance. Increasingly the IT/IS services market offers opportunities for alternative sourcing arrangements. Here we draw mainly on detailed analysis of the 30 case histories and the levels of success achieved with different IT sourcing decisions in various sets of circumstances. Additionally we have compared our findings and frameworks against other published research and case histories concerned with the outsourcing phenomenon. The evidence suggests that a strategic approach toward IT sourcing decisions can pay long-term dividends. We detail the major factors that need to be considered when determining how, if at all, the external IT and services market should be used. These are then utilized to develop a framework for assessing the business and technical imperatives that should govern IT sourcing decisions. We then show how any strategic IT outsourcing decision needs to be checked against a final set of considerations that emerge strongly from the research as potential tripwires to success.

IT outsourcing: the need for strategy

In our case studies we found organizations following one of three main paths into outsourcing. The first path was one of **incremental** outsourcing. This involved starting small on an obvious discrete area usually to achieve clear cost savings, and/or because of lack of internal expertise or inability to retain the IT staff required. A second approach was to drift, or be pressured into some quite large-scale outsourcing with little experience of how it should be managed, and make many mistakes over several years and contracts. This could be called the **hard learning** approach. In a period that could stretch from four to eight years these organizations learnt how to draw up and manage contracts, but also identified the necessity for developing an outsourcing strategy which (to varying degrees in different organizations) fitted with what the business was requiring in terms of service from information systems. The third approach has seen a much greater emphasis on developing a **strategic** approach to outsourcing, both on how it fits with what the rest of the business is doing, and on how IT outsourcing can be managed. In the latter case it was not always large-scale outsourcing that prompted moves toward being more strategic in approach. In some cases IT outsourcing represented under 20% of the total costs of IT to the organization in any one year. However, in every case the organization tended to take a more strategic approach to its use of IT generally.

An example of incremental outsourcing is at W.H. Smith, the UK-based retail and distribution company. Here the central telecommunications network was outsourced to DEC in 1990. The group IS director, Martin Cutler comments:

> The telecommunications contract was simple because we had it contained into really just providing the lines. For instance the data that goes across between the [company] branches and the centre, we still control that, so the only thing we have outsourced is the basic operational telecommunications. DEC make sure the line is there, working and ready to be used. That can be outsourced easily, there is a clear break.

In 1992 W.H. Smith felt able to outsource the telecommunications network for Our Price Records, a group company, this time to Racal. The learning from the first contract transferred into the drawing up and running of the second. Both contracts represented a small part of the overall group IT budget, and covered discrete parts of the IT infrastructure. Among the 30 cases we researched 5 organizations, in varying degrees, following the hard learning route. In the case of Unilever, Quest International and Civil Aviation Authority the bulk of the learning was at the front end of outsourcing experiences in the mid- or late 1980s. Clearly all outsourcing experiences will involve a degree of learning that will transfer back into future practice. However there are ways of cutting out much of the hard learning. As one IT manager commented on earlier experiences of outsourcing in his organization:

> The key thing is for the business to decide what it wants, to have a strategy. You cannot drift into outsourcing. If you do everyone could suffer, and here everyone did. For example on one contract they [the vendor] lost a lot of money. They did not really know what we wanted. The contract was biased towards us on that occasion, because it was fixed price but it made for a bad relationship. Start with the strategy and once that is set up decide who you want to do it. But throughout you must be, as the customer, in control of your destiny. We learnt from that and have made sure we are now much more in control. (IT director)

An example of a more strategic approach to IT outsourcing has been at Pilkington, the UK-based flat and safety glass manufacturing multinational. Here, head office IT operations and development were outsourced to EDS-Scicon in 1992. The following comment by the head of group information systems at PIlkington reveals the concern for a strategic approach:

> There is a lot of confusion out there about the strategic nature of IS or IT. A lot of it is because people mix up the information management with the provision of services by information systems and IT. I do not think services need to be a strategic element. It is purely providing a delivery of the systems. However it is important that the service provider stays close to the business. You have to retain an informed buyer potential and expertise within the company but it does not need to be deep into the technology. Just deep enough to understand what the potential is of the technology and what the pitfalls are. (Bill Limond, Pilkington)

As a preliminary to making outsourcing decisions, it is useful to have an overview of what to keep in-house and what can be outsourced effectively. This is provided by Figure 16.1. This is based on detailed findings from looking at successful and less successful IT outsourcing decisions and contracts. It shows only the major tendencies among those running contracts largely considered effective. In practice there may be variations from the pure model. Such variations are influenced by different risk assessments and circumstantial factors. As examples, not all organizations cede ownership of assets to a vendor, or transfer all IT staff from the IT area contracted out.

Several different terms used in Figure 16.1 need clarification. It is quite common for the following terms to be used interchangeably but conceptual confusion can lead to mistakes in outsourcing decisions. Here we use definitions developed at Oxford Institute of Information Management (Earl, 1989). IT refers to the technical means available – equipment and attendant techniques – and is essentially activity based, supply oriented and technology and delivery focused. IS are business applications, more or less IT based. The concern for information systems is a concern to be business focused and demand oriented. Information systems are the business ends to which IT supplies the means. Information management is organization based, relationships oriented and management focused. It deals with questions like 'how should we organize', 'what policies should be in place', 'who does what, where should IT be located'.

The overall substance of Figure 16.1 is that it is unwise to outsource control of information management, IS and IT strategies. It is IT supply and service that can be outsourced, including operational management of that service, but strategy, responsibility and control should not be outsourced. The demand side of IS – the definition and management of business requirements – is best done in-house. The supply element of IS – running, maintenance and support of business applications – can be successfully outsourced, as many of our respondent organizations found. However other organizations also chose to retain some or all of these in-house. Among reasons cited for this approach, by way of example, were confidentiality of information, flexibility of running, to retain the advantages of existing strong links between in-house IT group and business users, and user dissatisfaction with vendor cost/service levels.

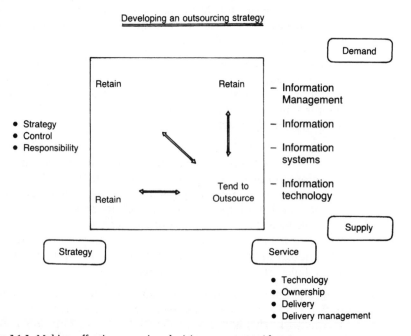

Figure 16.1 Making effective sourcing decisions: recent evidence.

An important issue here is the maturity of the organization about:

- the relationship of IT to strategic business requirements; and
- how this relates to the development of a strategic approach to outsourcing.

This point is made well by one of our respondents:

> Outsourcing is something for a mature company to undertake. If the company is not mature severe problems can occur. In our Group the majority of companies are not mature. They would come to outsourcing from a low understanding of IT and might see the cost benefit but not have the understanding of the relationship between themselves, the IT strategy, the use of information and the use of outsourcing agents. (Senior IT manager)

A further maturity factor that comes into play is the ability of the organization to develop a partnership-type relationship with the vendor company. Our own evidence is that the more an organization moves toward the top left corner of Figure 16.1, the more the risks of doing so need to be offset by developing longer-term partnering relationships with the vendor. As a general rule organizations with little experience of IT outsourcing would be advised to start outsourcing on issues close to the bottom right hand corner of Figure 16.1, unless they have, or plan to put in place before outsourcing, most or all of the items in the checklist illustrated in Table 16.1. Even organizations that consider themselves mature and experienced in their handling of IT can usefully ask themselves whether, when it comes to outsourcing, they have the eight items in place detailed in Table 16.1. This checklist has been built up from detailed analysis of actual outsourcing experiences discussed in our survey returns and case histories, and also from a review of the major available literature on the subject.

The major point of this section is that IT outsourcing must be part of an overall strategic framework that takes into account business, IS and IT objectives and requirements. Outside such a strategic framework outsourcing is likely to remain an incremental, *ad hoc* response to circumstances driven by cost minimization criteria. This

Table 16.1 Towards an IT outsourcing strategy

IT outsourcing strategy

We have an outsourcing strategy that fits with our business and information management and IT strategies. The strategy includes and goes beyond the period of any outsourcing contract we have or are planning

Our outsourcing strategy includes plans for how to manage the IT supply and services market and how to choose, relate to, manage, and retain leverage with, vendors

We are able to make decisions as to what IT services to outsource, and what to source in other ways. These decisions make sense on business and technical grounds

We have in place a process and management capacity to select a suitable vendor

There is a human resource plan in place to deal with the decision, transition and subsequent phases of outsourcing

We have the management and specialist capacity to negotiate and draw up an outsourcing contract

We have retained in-house sufficient management and technical capacity to manage the vendor, monitor contract performance and keep strategic business and technical options under review

We have in place detailed measurement systems enabling us to draw up a detailed contractual agreement and monitor vendor performance

---

may well, and often does, produce tangible cost savings for each contract. However, this approach runs a number of dangers. A piecemeal approach to contracts may not add up to total cost savings across all contracts in the light of what else could have been done with IT. A further potential risk, particularly in an organization that does not identify IT use as strategic to the business, is to allow itself to get locked into seeing IT as a 'commodity' to be outsourced. With IT in the hands of a vendor, future opportunities for identifying IT as a source of strategic advantage and competitive differentiation for the organization can become cut off. A 'hollowing out' or 'baby out with the bathwater' syndrome can occur, where the ability of the organization to compete through IT is increasingly adversely affected over time. This point is reinforced by one of our respondent companies:

> As regards both networks and mainframe services, provided we are competitive, we should visit the outsourcing decision in about 1995/6 when we are clear on our electronic services strategy rather than doing it now and suddenly finding we have given away a core capability to a potential competitor.
> (Jean Irvine, Post Office)

As we have argued elsewhere (see Lacity, Willcocks and Feeny, 1995), taking a strategic approach to outsourcing means recasting the question 'to outsource or not?' into a more useful question, with potentially more powerful answers. That question is: 'how do we use, if at all, the opportunity of what is available on the IT and services market to leverage business advantage?' The issue then becomes not outsourcing, but rightsourcing, with in-house options and a range of options for relating to and utilizing the IT services market always in play. The next section gives insights based on case histories researched by ourselves and others, into the major critical factors that should be taken into consideration before making strategic sourcing decisions.

Making a strategic decision: major factors

There are high costs to getting outsourcing decisions wrong. The costs relate not just to additional management time and effort, unanticipated vendor bills, and the effect on the business during the course of an ineffective outsourcing contract. There may also be high switching costs going to another vendor or rebuilding the in-house technical capability. The costs of buying out of an unsatisfactory contract may also be high. Given the risk of such high potential costs, it is important to think through the issues in a structured manner. Here we first isolate the main contextual factors that direct IT sourcing decisions. Their interrelationships are then developed and explored through a framework that relates the market options to the business and technical imperatives facing an organization.

From our analysis six contextual factors determine how (if at all) the external market should be used.

The potential contribution of the IT activity/ service to business positioning

An IT activity/service can be defined as a differentiator or as a commodity. Activities which are differentiators provide a potential basis for competitive advantage;

executing them particularly well is important to the firm. In P&O European Ferries the central reservation system processes up to 12 000 customer reservations a day. The system is not only integral to most of the company's operations; it also gives it a distinct, and possibly sustainable, competitive advantage over other ferry companies operating on the same routes. In this case the system is run in-house.

An activity is a commodity if its execution does not distinguish the firm from a competitor in business offering and performance terms. This type of activity needs to be done competently, but no more. At BP Exploration and Civil Aviation Authority, for example, the computerized financial accounting systems have been outsourced to Arthur Andersen, the accountancy firm and IT consultancy. In BP Exploration's case the 1991 £55 million four-year contract covers accounting services and transfer of 250 staff, as well as related computer systems.

In practice differentiators can quickly become commodities as competitors catch up or the basis of competition changes. Apart from this time element, the conditions that make a system a differentiator or commodity also vary from sector to sector. The following characteristics will push an IS application into being a differentiator:

- high sensitivity to competitive exposure, e.g. information;
- strong need to retain intellectual property;
- high business knowledge of the IT products/services;
- very competitive business environment.

Some of these characteristics, and how they impact on sourcing decisions, are present in the case of ICI Paints:

> In each of the areas where we have talked internally about outsourcing we have highlighted some system or application there is no way we want to give away control of. This is either because key, sensitive information comes from it or because it gives a competitive advantage, probably temporary, that therefore we really do not want to give away. (Ed Jasnikowski, ICI Paints)

Barclays Bank had over 15 outsourcing contracts as at 1995 but:

> Financial services these days is so competitive that if we have a new idea there is no way we are going to let any outside supplier near it until pretty near the date it comes to fruition. No matter what statements you sign with suppliers, confidentiality or otherwise, there is just no way you can get 100% confidentiality. (Brian Bath, Barclays Bank)

The relationship of the IT activity/service to business strategy

A distinction can be made between strategic and useful activities. Strategic activities are integral to the firm's achievement of goals, and critical to its existing and future business direction. Organizations need to maintain control of these. A strategic IS may, or may not, differentiate an organization from its competitors. The common thread is its criticality, the extent to which it underpins the organization's strategic direction. As one example, Norwich Union Health Care are in the personal health care insurance business. In a start-up situation in 1990 they identified a strategic need for a computerized policy administration system. Though its development was initially outsourced, by 1992 the strategically important system had been placed under the control of an in-house IT department that had built up its expertise in the 1990–92 period.

Useful activities, on the other hand, can make incremental contributions to the bottom line but do not affect the firm's competitive positioning. In fact useful IT/IS can be mandatory or discretionary. For example, in many, perhaps most, industries payroll applications would be considered useful and mandatory but not strategic. In PC environments many software packages may well be seen as useful and 'nice to have', that is discretionary, but not mandatory, let alone strategic. PC maintenance will be seen as mandatory. Some firms decide to outsource such work. For example, as at 1995 and for some eight years previously a major UK retailer had outsourced maintenance of over 3000 head office PCs.

The degree of uncertainty about future business environment and business needs, and hence longer term IT needs

A high degree of business uncertainty seems to be a perennial characteristic of the external and internal environments of the vast majority of UK organizations in the 1990s. While there are variations in business volatility by sector and organization, all our case study respondents saw this as a critical determining factor when it came to outsourcing decisions. As one example Pilkington outsourced head office computing and IT development in 1992. The head of group IS comments:

> We are dealing with a terrific amount of change within the business and within head office itself over a two year period. We did not know what it was going to look like at the end, though we had some ideas on that. Luckily we [the senior IT staff] were very involved in the organization of that change from a business point of view. A long term contract would have been inappropriate here; there is too much change involved. In any case we wanted to retain a certain amount of negotiating independence on the back of that change. (Bill Limond, Pilkington)

The problem lies in the way business uncertainty feeds into the ability to identify information, IS/IT requirements. Again, unlike in the Pilkington case, not all businesses keep IT staff highly involved or able to anticipate fluctuating business requirements. High uncertainty suggests that the 'buying in' of resources or partnership relationships with vendors are preferable unless the contract is very short term. Some of the dilemmas in making such decision in conditions of high business volatility are revealed in the following:

> Businesses are so rapidly changing that predicting requirements even two years on is extremely difficult. In the Post Office for example both Royal Mail and Counters reorganized, resulting in a significant restructuring and shifting in their communications requirements. Recently we [the internal IS department] were asked to quote on a Thursday afternoon for the Monday morning what it would cost to move 50% of the lines. That sort of thing would make an outsourcing vendor laugh all the way to the bank because it would not be in the contract. The problem is the many future changes which are unplanned, but that is what tests the strength of the partnering concept

– the extent to which you get contract flexibility without getting ripped off.
(Jean Irvine, Post Office)

Degree of technology maturity associated with the activity/service in question

Moving on to technical factors, a particularly critical issue is that of technological maturity. Some attention to this area was also given in Chapter 4. The concept of technological maturity derives from research by Feeny, Earl and Edwards (1994). An organization is low on technology maturity when any of the following conditions apply:

- the technology is new and unstable in functions, specification and performance;
- a well-established technology is being used in a radically new application;
- the organization has little in-house experience in implementing this technology in this application.

New technology/low maturity implies high uncertainty about future IT needs. Feeny *et al.* found that in situations of low maturity a user focus was needed. Teamwork was important; business users needed to be highly involved in all aspects of planning, development, support and delivery, development; immediate goals were less clear than the overall aim of business effectiveness. However, as technological maturity increased and the technology became less problematic and immediate goals more clear a specialist focus could be adopted. Tasks could be increasingly delegated to IT specialists who could work to clear targets to produce an efficient result. The process is mapped in Figure 16.2.

Note here that even in situations of high technological maturity activities concerned with direction – that is determining IS and IT strategies – should remain a joint user-focused activity.

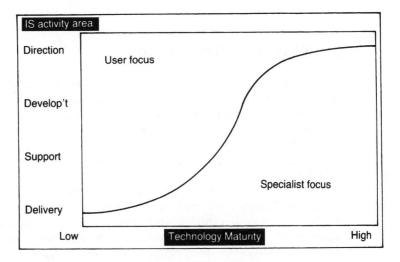

Figure 16.2 User and specialist focus (Feeny *et al.*, 1994).

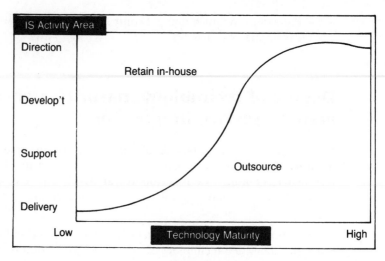

Figure 16.3 Technology maturity and outsourcing (Feeny *et al.*, 1994).

How does this translate into making IT outsourcing decisions? This is shown in Figure 16.3, which suggests that outsourcing should be restricted to situations where IT is well understood and unproblematic to the organization, and where a specialist focus can be suitably applied by the vendor (see also Chapter 4).

In our detailed case studies, as a general rule, the prescription – never outsource a problem – held up well. Where there were variations to this, in each case the successful organizations took a number of explicit actions to reduce the risks incurred. The rule emerged as particularly applicable to the systems development area. As one example, in the late 1980s Quest International outsourced development work on an automated factory project to two vendors. The main reason was lack of in-house expertise. The project was completed but took longer that projected, cost a lot more and did not produce some of the anticipated benefits. In subsequent development projects the company moved to buying in resources and adopted a user focus.

Level of IT integration

Some IT activities may have simple technical interfaces with the rest of the organization's systems, and be easy to isolate and contract out. Additionally these systems may well have simple interfaces with business users, and the effect on business users if something went wrong could be isolated from large parts of normal business activity. In our cases this was found to apply to telecommunications networks at W.H. Smith for example, and to payroll and financial accounting applications in many organizations.

Other systems may be highly integrated, however. This means they will have complex and extensive interactions with a wide range of other systems. These systems may also interface in complex ways with many business users who will be impacted significantly by the levels of service experienced. Such systems tend to be more difficult to outsource successfully. We found organizations more reluctant to outsource such systems, in fact. For example, while Citibank outsourced its London-based data centre in the early 1990s, the bank has been more reluctant to outsource to a third party vendor its network and messaging infrastructure.

In-house IT capability relative to that available on the external market

A final factor relates to in-house technical capability (see also Chapter 4 for a further discussion). This factor is distinguishable from 'technological maturity' on two counts. First, it is the in-house capability relative to that available on the IT service market that is important, not just the level of in-house technical capability itself. Second, the cost of utilizing in-house capability, including opportunity costs, as compared to the price of using equivalent capacity from the external market is also an important factor. High relative in-house capability will suggest keeping IT services in-house. However, one major UK retailer, for example, tends to redeploy in-house expertise on to developmental work and outsource what has been identified as 'low value' IT tasks such as data processing. As at 1994, United Biscuits and ICI ran highly efficient data centres in-house, but constantly evaluated their costs against what was available from third party suppliers.

Making the strategic sourcing decision

In this section we advance the decision-making process further by examining the trade-offs that organizations need to make on the critical variables in order to achieve effective decisions. The decisions arrived at then need to be tested against the 'reality check' outlined in the next section.

As a result of the research we have carried out we have been able to identify what makes effective sourcing decisions in 30 case histories. Our findings have also been compared, and are fairly robust against cases in other research studies on IT/IS outsourcing. The approach we detail brings another dimension to the evaluation issues discussed throughout this book. It enables assessment not just of whether to outsource a specific activity, but also how the market can be used in each case within a portfolio of decisions that can be deemed strategic. Each of our 30 cases has been analysed primarily against the six critical variables identified above in terms of what type of sourcing decisions were made, and whether or not these were successful. The criteria for success, in number and type, varied from organization to organization. However, to generalize, where an external vendor was involved as a result of the sourcing decision, the criteria for success fell within the following range: targeted cost savings achieved or better than anticipated; service levels maintained or better; user management satisfaction; low levels of vendor–client dispute; vendor responsiveness and attention; general favourable comparisons between objectives and outcomes; and decision to renew the contract. Similar criteria, suitably adapted, were applied to where IT services were delivered by in-house IT staff.

In order to organize the results and discussion we have formulated a decision matrix, and this is shown in Figure 16.4. For mapping purposes we have conflated the 'differentiator–commodity' and 'strategic–useful' parameters into a 'core–non-core'

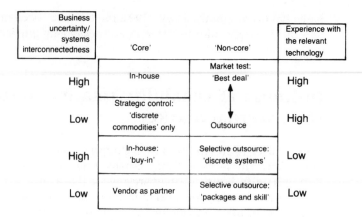

Figure 16.4 Decision matrix for sourcing IT.

continuum. Additionally we have conflated the technology maturity and in-house capability relative to that available on the market into a high–low continuum measuring relevant experience with technology.

When to stay in-house

The most sure case for staying in-house with IT, is in the following set of circumstances:

- business positioning impact – high;
- link to business strategy – high;
- future business uncertainty – high;
- technology maturity – high;
- level of IT integration – high;
- in-house versus market expertise – high.

The P&O European Ferries case and its central reservation system, discussed earlier, provides an obvious example where these circumstances prevailed as at 1995. The IT/IS strategies here have been to continue to build up internal IT expertise and improve IS–business user relationships within the company. The central reservation system represents, in the current competitive situation, a strategic differentiator that will not be outsourced. However within an overall 'core' system there may be parts that can be identified as discrete and not core (see Figure 16.4). In the P&O case, for example the maintenance of shipboard systems was considered as a 'commodity' service and, as such, was contracted out to a third party supplier. The reasons were lower cost, and to allow in-house staff to focus on systems development. In the event outsourcing resulted in a lower quality service and the business users demanded that the service be brought back in-house.

Clearly an organization will have a portfolio of IT/IS applications, activities and services, and not all will fall into this 'must stay in-house' category. Even so, companies like P&O European ferries, having built up an in-house IT capability, may well prefer in-house options even for non-core systems. Indeed, the in-house option may well prove more cost-effective as we found for example with mainframe data processing at United Biscuits and ICI. Alternatively even in situations of 'total' outsourcing, companies will find it necessary to retain certain vital functions in-house. These issues will receive more detailed discussion below.

IT outsourcing: the best case scenario

The surest case for outsourcing is where the following circumstances apply to the IT/ IS in question:

- business positioning impact – low;
- link to business strategy – low;
- future business uncertainty – low;
- technology maturity – high;
- level of IT integration – low;
- in-house versus market expertise – low.

In fact our evidence suggests that outsourcing IT is most safely done on shorter-term (one- to five-year) contracts, for commodity type IT, in situations of high in-house experience of relevant technology, where discrete systems or activities can be identified, and in conditions of some business certainty leading to confidence about technological needs of the organization for at least the life of the contract. In such situations the cost effectiveness of the in-house operation can then be compared to what is available on the market by a market testing process, and the best deal sought (see top right of Figure 16.4).

An obvious case here is the outsourcing (to DEC) of telecommunications networks at W.H. Smith, the UK retail and distribution chain, mentioned earlier. A discrete technology and service identified as non-core was outsourced because a vendor could provide a similar or better service at lower cost. Future business uncertainty was adjudged low in this case as long as the contract was for three years, with an option to renew for a further two. Cost savings of between 20 and 30% per annum have been achieved on this contract. On similar criteria, Civil Aviation Authority outsourced their accounting systems to Arthur Andersen in the early 1990s on a contract to 1995. The difference was that, in the market testing phase, the vendor was chosen primarily for its greater expertise rather than on cost saving criteria alone.

IT outsourcing: dealing with mixed case scenarios

Organizations that are successful in applying an 'incremental' approach to outsourcing invariably are found to have applied the criteria detailed above to their early contracts. However, when looking across the portfolio of IT/IS applications, activities and services that an organization has, it is unlikely that circumstances for many of the items will be so clear cut in their pointers for decision-making as those outlined in our first two scenarios.

In practice we have found most organizations taking a selective approach to outsourcing. North West Thames Regional Health Authority has been a successful practitioner of selective outsourcing. Here mainframes and data centres were outsourced, together with IT staff, to Sema Group in April 1991. The staff had high experience with the relevant technology, a fairly short-term (five-year) contract was signed to minimize risk but also because the systems had limited usefulness beyond 1995, and the outsourced assets, including staff, were considered 'non-core'. Outsourcing also offered prospective cost savings. Essentially NW Thames were not outsourcing a problem here, and this is a typical pattern among the more successful contracts we have studied.

Certain other items were outsourced separately on *ad hoc* contracts. One of these was applications development. Here, though in-house technology maturity was low, it was felt that no great specialist skills or NHS knowledge were required by the vendor because the policy was to move to packages already available rather than commission new development work (see bottom right, Figure 16.4). The development of a wide area network for the RHA, however, was seen as a strategic project involving highly interconnected systems and potentially touching many users within the health authority. It was retained in-house, the aim being to build up in-house skills on this technology. A buy-in (or 'insourcing') strategy was pursued here. To balance the outsourcing, further elements identified as core were retained in-house. These included IT/IS planning, liaison, training and consultancy and ability to manage the outsourcing contracts. Where these were inadequately resourced a strategy of insourcing IT capability, basically recruiting experienced staff, was adopted.

Pilkington, the UK-based glass manufacturer, provide an illustration of selective outsourcing within Pilkington as a whole (manufacturing systems were left largely under in-house IT staff) but almost total outsourcing at Pilkington head office. The situation in 1991–2 was one of considerable business and organizational change, devolution of the business, and the head office being slimmed down. Head office IT was outsourced to EDS. The items outsourced consisted firstly of the ageing data centre mainframes and most of the IT staff, including the IT manager, who became the vendor's account manager. This was seen as a positive move, guaranteeing continuity and minimizing the risk. Pilkington knew who they were dealing with and also had guarantees that transferred staff would stay working on this contract. The circumstances are represented accurately by the top right hand box of Figure 16.4.

More unusually, as part of the deal, Pilkington also outsourced applications development of new office and network systems. Pilkington were low on skills here. We have found that generally the more effective arrangement in these circumstances for development work is to use a buy in approach. This is certainly the case in Quest International, for example, where in several 1990s' contracts vendors were seen as team members who help to build up in-house development capability. Pilkington looked to the vendor to provide additional skill/expertise through training transferred staff, and bringing new staff on to the contract (Figure 16.4, bottom right). This outsourcing approach has proved successful because of action taken to minimize its risks. Pilkington knew the vendor staff and account manager – the relationship side was fairly secure and guaranteed some flexibility. Second, there was a short-term contract. Third, Pilkington made sure it would own the assets being developed. Fourth, Pilkington retained in-house capability to manage the contract. More broadly, Pilkington identified as core, and retained, their ability to manage strategy and contracts, business knowledge, together with a pool of technical skill needed to control the overall architecture of the company (see Willcocks and Fitzgerald, 1995, for more case details).

Generally speaking the effective policy is not to outsource core IT/IS applications, activities and services. However, in less risky situations, vendors can be used provided it is on a true partnership basis. One example is Sterling Security Services in the security guarding industry. In the early 1990s, in a low-tech industry, the firm identified computerization of payroll and manpower systems as a strategic differentiator, producing higher staff quality and retention. However, the company lacked in-house IT know-how (Figure 16.4, bottom left). This led to an arrangement to develop software with a software house on a more or less partnership basis.

The 'total outsourcing' decision

When talking about effective decisions, in several ways the phrase 'total outsourcing' must be a misnomer. Generally speaking in effective 'total' outsourcing contracts 'strategic differentiators' would not be outsourced; 'strategic commodities' might well be. Of course there can be mistakes in definition, but generally speaking companies will recognize most IT/IS as 'non-core' before they decide on the 'total outsourcing' route. However, even where all IT/IS is deemed 'non-core' and outsourced, there always have to be certain IT/IS capabilities left in-house.

This was recognized at NV Philips, the electronics manufacturer. From the mid-1980s the company consolidated and rationalized its IT capability. Business exigencies required shedding of labour and non-core activities. As a prelude to total outsourcing Philips pulled out of its in-house IT department some hundred business systems analysts and put them back into the businesses that made up the company. This meant that each business had it own IT capability on the demand side. Philips then outsourced all its software and systems development, including 180 related staff, through forming a separate partly owned company in a joint venture with a Dutch software house. Philips also outsourced all its communications and processing capability, including some 140 staff, through setting up another partly owned company that could sell its service on the open market. Following Figure 16.1 Philips have outsourced IT supply but have retained in-house capability to define business demand. In addition, there is a central management capability to define strategy, identify and coordinate IT/IS needs across the group, provide internal consultancy and manage contracts. The risks of total outsourcing are also ameliorated by the 'vendors' being partly owned and highly dependent on business from Philips. Strong pre-existing mutual relationships and business knowledge are held by client and vendors.

This section has given only a few examples by way of illustration of the principles we have found guiding effective sourcing decisions. However, a general point can be made here. Many organizations deviate from the principles behind the best-case scenario for outsourcing described above. In many such cases in our research base the outsourcing subsequently proved successful. In each case the managers involved could describe policies, tactics and practices they had consciously adopted to minimize the risks of outsourcing in less favourable circumstances.

Developing the decision: a reality check

The strategic IT outsourcing decision needs to be checked against a number of other factors. The following emerge strongly as likely tripwires to making the decision effective in reality. We would recommend that any IT outsourcing decision be checked against the following issues.

Is there an economic rationale?

Our survey found there to be a primary widespread concern to link IT outsourcing to cost savings, or at least cost control. Some organizations, however, utilize outsourcing for other purposes; even so it is important that the decision makes economic, if not economical sense. Thus Whitbread wanted to refocus management attention against a background of declining and volatile mainframe processing demand:

> Over five years it breaks even. The savings are about efficiencies in development support, support of application systems, and greater productivity in, for example, function points delivered. It takes a long time for them to come through and be measured but it wasn't a cost thing, apart from avoiding a lot of redundancy costs. (Fraser Winterbottom, Whitbread)

However, declaring the objective, and delivering upon it can be in two different worlds as several cases discussed in this study will attest. Before outsourcing it is therefore very useful to examine carefully the implications of proposed actions, and any proposals by potential vendors. In particular four major issues that need to be explored are:

- Are projected in-house costs static, or can we take action to reduce them ourselves?
- Will the vendor motivation to increase profit by reducing its costs affect service quality?
- How fixed is the price? Will there be expensive add-ons? How does and will price compare to what else is available on the market?
- Even if we do not expect to make cost savings, are we still likely to pay too much for what we get from IT outsourcing?

Effective outsourcing involves exploring these questions. Companies that did so in our study invariably came up with discoveries that greatly influenced the way in which they went about outsourcing. One identified the need to renegotiate regularly and have guaranteed cost reductions:

> I pay for inflation, but then I have guaranteed reductions in various areas that build up over the years. It's about 4% per year, but some of it will get renegotiated anyway because of changes in computer usage. There are also regular checks on market prices. (Retail company)

At another, close monitoring of in-house costs found reasons for not outsourcing certain activities:

> What United Biscuits doesn't get through outsourcing is economies of scale. Because it's so big it needs a lot of focus anyway. Nobody puts an outsourcing proposition to me that talks of benefits of scale. (Andy Young, managing director, group services, United Biscuits)

How does the decision fit with the rate of technological change?

An important supply-side issue is uncertainty/volatility in the technologies available. Technologies for business have changed, and will continue to change dramatically, not least as a function of competitiveness in the IT industry. The degree of volatility in this supply side of the business environment, and how future IT could support the business, feed into what sorts of IT/IS outsourcing decisions can be made:

> We have reservations about long-term contracts. You are seeing terrific changes in information technology and IS. For instance if you are going through downsizing, what you start out with will not be necessarily appropriate at the end of ten years. One thing you can be sure of at the end of ten years is that the technology will have changed completely – as will what you need to have in an outsourcing contract. (IS director)

If going down an outsourcing route, the dilemmas and decisions relate to type of contract and type of relationship with the supplier. Are these flexible enough to permit the organization taking business advantage of unanticipated technical developments without prohibitive costs from the vendor? A further important question relates to the vendor's technical capability – can the vendor actually supply/support future technical developments? And even if the answers to these questions are affirmative, the vendor will have its own interests and these may differ from the client's. Something that makes technical sense to your organization may not make technical sense for the outsourcing vendor.

Are there issues around ownership when transferring people and assets?

Respondents to the survey placed a major emphasis on the risk of irreversibility of contract. This raises questions about the wisdom of transferring people and ownership of assets to a vendor. The following salutary experience suggests it might be sensible to prepare for divorce even while negotiating the 'marriage' contract:

> After a costly battle to end the contract, the client company is rebuilding its internal group minus several good people who found other jobs during the chaos. Rebuilding that staff is turning out to be far harder than expected. You can't put Humpty Dumpty together again as easily as they'd thought. (Industry consultant, quoted in Houghton, 1991)

Organizations might feel the need to take action to minimize the likelihood of such costly outcomes. As one example, in its 1990 US $450 million ten-year deal with EDS, First Fidelity Bank kept 250 systems developers on its payroll to protect the bank's ability to develop and maintain new systems in the future.

Turning to assets like hardware and software, many organizations have found it advantageous to sell off equipment to the vendor in order to get it off the balance sheet and also gain a cash influx. This will gain present financial advantage, but could be at the expense of future technical security or flexibilities. However, another reason for transferring asset ownership can be to get rid of old equipment – ageing mainframes for example – and prepare the ground for their replacement. As referred to above, Pilkington did this in their 1992 contract with EDS. Interestingly, though they also contracted out development work, they ensured that they retained ownership of the new systems and software being put in place. The reality check questions here are:

- What advantages do we gain from transferring all/any people and/or assets to the vendor?
- Are there critical skills and assets we should not transfer?
- What are the identifiable risks in making the specific transfers we have planned?
- Can we protect ourselves against the risks of transferring people and/or assets?

Is a suitable vendor available?

It is not enough to make an intellectually appealing decision; is there a vendor that can actually deliver on your identified requirements? Generally speaking, we have found that vendors are better at selling their services than client organizations are at buying them. The first important point to remember is that despite the richness of what is available generally on the market, vendors are also in high competition against one another over clients and contracts. It falls ultimately on the client to identify the strengths of possible vendors against the client's own identified requirements.

The second related point is that what each client needs from a vendor will probably be very specific to that client and its circumstances. In the outsourcing cases we have reviewed this has invariably been the case. Thus Whitbread chose FI Group because as a vendor its core competencies were in the areas required – support and enhancement. The competencies of other bidders seemed to be focused mainly around data centres or development. National Grid needed a vendor with proven experience in the specific hardware and sofware outsourced, that could match the company's geographic requirements and was a large vendor in the market to stay. When BP Exploration chose SAIC it was partly because of its large size and its outsourcing experience, but also because it had a base of scientific and geologist staff. For an oil exploration company this meant that the vendor could be a partner that could add some value.

Beyond this issue of getting the specifics right there may be some general principles that need to be observed. These include the following, based on the experiences of a vendor manager:

> The critical thing is getting the partnership right. When a company looks at outsourcing it had better make sure the vendor has the right skills not just for now, but the future. Only outsource the service not the strategy and control. Make sure the vendor is looking for a long-term business relationship and is not in it for the quick profit and then get out – otherwise you can get left high and dry. (Tony Rickels, EDS-Scicon)

Do we have the management capability to deliver on the decision?

An organization whose strategic decision-making has pointed to outsourcing should ensure that it possesses enough management capability to:

- select a suitable vendor;
- negotiate a contract;
- draw up a contract;
- manage the contract and relationships with the vendor;
- manage relationships with and needs of business users;
- identify and look after existing and future IT/IS needs of the organization.

While this may sound obvious, it is all too clear from our case studies that organizations inexperienced in outsourcing frequently underestimate both the degree to which these capabilities are required, but also the number of staff that might be needed to fulfil these responsibilities. Like every solution, outsourcing brings its own set of problems. For one thing the character of management needs to change. It may well be that the managers involved will need to be replaced or reinforced. Those able to run an in-house IT department may not have the skills required to fulfil the above responsibilities, at least by themselves. On the first three areas mentioned above, we found several inexperienced organizations taking more expert advice, from outside, but also, where applicable, from other companies within the same group. On the fourth point, this will need specific skills and may require a new appointee; it is quite common to underestimate the large time requirement for this role, especially in the first eighteen months of a new contract, even where it is running fairly smoothly. On the last two points it is clear from our case study work that whatever the degree of outsourcing, in addition to the above capabilities, these two issues must be covered by retaining in-house the following:

- ability to track/assess/interpret changing IT capability, and relate this to the needs of the firm;
- ability to work with business management to define the IT requirements successfully over time;
- ability to identify the appropriate ways to use the external market to help specify and manage 'rightsourcing'.

These relate to retaining strategy and control capability within the client organization (see Willcocks and Fitzgerald, 1995b, for a discussion of roles within the 'residual' IS organization).

Will significant human resource issues arise?

This final checklist item does not appear that significant in our survey findings. However, when we turned to examining case histories in detail, all respondents remarked on the need for sensitivity on human resource issues. In particular several respondents from organizations more experienced in outsourcing remarked on how easy it was to get wrong, and gave us case histories from their own organizations to illustrate the point. Two of the largest outsourcing contracts being contemplated during 1993 were at British Aerospace and the Inland Revenue. Both experienced strikes from IT staff during the build up to awarding contracts. They were not alone in experiencing staff problems in this respect in that year in the UK, and strikes are only the more visible versions of potential problems on the human resource front.

Clearly the objective should be to manage sourcing decisions and their communication in such a way that staff do not feel the need to take strike action. The problem may rest as much with how a sourcing decision is implemented, as with the actual content of the decision. Therefore an important reality check on an outsourcing decision is to assess whether or not the content and method of implementation will secure in-house and vendor staff motivation across the contract. As one example, in the North West Thames Regional Health Authority case the first inclination was to go for a total outsourcing approach. However, staff enthusiasm was low for both that option and that of a management buyout. Eventually the decision was to go for a selective outsourcing route, ensuring that the vendor selected was the one offering the best deal to the staff to be transferred.

Conclusions

We have identified the general conditions for effective IT outsourcing decisions – high technology maturity; vendor offers better deal compared with in-house; IT identified as non-core, that is IT is not a strategic differentiator; discrete systems; in situations of reasonable business certainty across the life of a contract. However even where all these favourable conditions apply there still needs to be in-house management action during the contract on a number of fronts which we have identified. Additionally we have found examples of organizations outsourcing IT even where not all, or even only some of these favourable conditions apply. But success seems dependent on taking careful action to minimize the additional risks to which the conduct of the contract then becomes exposed. The following formula may be suggested for IT outsourcing:

- market logic not management despair;
- rationalization not rationing;
- commodities not differentiators;
- targeted not total.

The suggestion here is that if you are outsourcing IT because you despair of your in-house IT, you seek to cut costs, you are outsourcing differentiators and you are going down the total outsourcing route, then you will probably end up in serious trouble (see also Lacity, Willcocks and Feeny, 1995). Sourcing decisions should follow a market logic. From a management perspective the issue is perhaps better cast as not whether or not to outsource IT, but whether or not, and if so how, to use the market for IT and associated services for organizational advantage. In some situations 'insourcing' approaches may well be more appropriate. A sourcing decision should be based on in-house rationalization first and outsourcing should focus essentially on commodities. Furthermore a targeted rather than a total outsourcing route reduces risk. It may be that targeted outsourcing eventually, or quite quickly becomes total outsourcing; however the point is that the targeting stage should be part of the way in which a decision is arrived at.

References

Earl, M. (1989) *Management Strategies for Information Technology*, Prentice Hall, Hemel Hempstead.

Feeny, D., Earl, M. and Edwards, B. (1989) *Organizational Arrangements for IS: Roles of Users and IS Specialists*. Oxford Institute of Information Management RDP 94/6, Templeton College, Oxford.

Houghton, J. (1991) *Outsourcing Information Technology Services*. CIRCIT Policy Research Paper No. 17, CIRCIT, Melbourne.

Huber, R. (1993) How Continental Bank outsourced its crown jewels. *Harvard Business Review*, January/February, 121–9.

Lacity, M. and Hirschheim, R. (1993) The information systems outsourcing bandwagon. *Sloan Management Review*, **35** (1), 73–86.

Lacity, M., Willcocks, L. and Feeny, D. (1995) IT outsourcing: maximizing flexibility and control. *Harvard Business Review*, May/June, 86–93.

Loh, L. and Venkatraman, N. (1992) Diffusion of information technology outsourcing: influence sources and the Kodak effect. *Information Systems Research*, **3** (4), 334–58.

Willcocks, L. and Fitzgerald, G. (1994) *A Business Guide To Outsourcing IT: A Study of European Best Practice in the Selection, Management and Use of External IT Services*, Business Intelligence, London.

Willcocks, L. and Fitzgerald, G. (1995a) Pilkington plc: a major multinational outsources its head office IT function. In *Management Information Systems* (eds. E. Turban, E. McLean and J. Wetherbe), John Wiley, New York.

Willcocks, L. and Fitzgerald, G. (1995b) The changing shape of the information systems function. In *Information Management: The Organizational Dimension* (ed. M. Earl), Oxford University Press, Oxford.

Index